P9-ASN-241

A HANDBOOK OF ENGLISH GRAMMAR

A HANDBOOK OF ENGLISH GRAMMAR

R. W. ZANDVOORT
Professor of English
in the University of Groningen

LONGMANS, GREEN AND CO
LONDON · NEW YORK · TORONTO

LONGMANS, GREEN AND CO LTD
6 & 7 CLIFFORD STREET LONDON W I

BOSTON HOUSE STRAND STREET CAPE TOWN
531 LITTLE COLLINS STREET MELBOURNE

LONGMANS, GREEN AND CO INC
55 FIFTH AVENUE NEW YORK 3

LONGMANS, GREEN AND CO
20 CRANFIELD ROAD TORONTO 16

ORIENT LONGMANS PRIVATE LTD
CALCUTTA BOMBAY MADRAS
DELHI VIJAYAWADA DACCA

First published 1957

PRINTED IN GREAT BRITAIN
BY WESTERN PRINTING SERVICES LTD BRISTOL

PREFACE

THIS book was originally designed as a manual of English grammar for Dutch students. As such it ran into six editions in less than twice as many years, and drew a good deal of attention outside the Netherlands. A French version (*Grammaire Descriptive de l'Anglais Contemporain*) appeared in 1949, and more than one reviewer urged the desirability of a unilingual edition for general use, with the comparisons with and translations into Dutch left out. The author is obliged to Messrs. Longmans, Green & Co. for enabling him to comply with these flattering suggestions, and to Messrs. J. B. Wolters, the publishers of the English-Dutch edition, for their co-operation. He has availed himself of the opportunity to subject the whole work to a thorough revision, and to introduce a number of additions and textual alterations where these seemed to be called for.

As the French title well expresses it, this is a descriptive grammar of contemporary English. It deals with accidence and syntax, leaving aside what belongs rather to idiom and is not amenable to general statement. It likewise eschews historical digressions; contemporary and historical (or, in the terminology of modern linguistics, synchronic and diachronic) grammar are, in the author's opinion, best treated separately. In this, as in other respects, he confesses himself a pupil of Kruisinga, whose *Handbook of Present-day English*, despite certain extravagances in its fifth and final edition, is still the most original and stimulating treatment of English syntax.

While specific comparisons with Dutch usage have been removed, some of them have been replaced by references to other languages. They may help both British and continental students to realize some of the peculiar features of the English language. Identity is sometimes most clearly brought out by contrast. If I have anywhere erred by generalizing, I shall be glad to have instances pointed out to me.

As will be seen, this book contains numerous references to other publications. This is done deliberately, to impress upon the student the fact that a handbook is only a point of departure. If it has not roused his curiosity and encouraged him to further research, it has at least partly failed of its purpose.

Groningen R. W. ZANDVOORT

CONTENTS

[1] Except in the right-hand margin, references, as throughout the book, are to sections.

PART II

Nouns

PART III

Pronouns

PART IV

Adjectives and Adverbs

PART V

Sentence Structure

PART VI

Order of Words

APPENDIX

INDEX

The phonetic transcription is identical with that used in Daniel Jones's *English Pronouncing Dictionary*

PART I

VERBS

INTRODUCTORY

A. Regular Verbs

1. An English verb normally has the following forms:

a. the stem: *play*, *call*, *wait*, *pass*;

b. the stem + *ing*: *playing*, *calling*, *waiting*, *passing*;

c. the stem + sibilant-suffix:[1] *plays* [pleiz], *calls* [kɔ:lz], *waits* [weits], *passes* [ˈpɑ:siz].

As appears from the examples, [iz] is used after stems ending in a sibilant, [z] in other cases, except after breathed consonants, [s] after breathed consonants, except sibilants.

[iz] is spelt *es*; if the stem ends in *e* in the spelling (e.g. *change*), *s* only is added. [z] and [s] are spelt *s*. On spellings like *cries* (stem *cry*), *goes* (stem *go*), see Appendix, p. 338.

d. the stem + dental-suffix:[2] *played* [pleid], *called* [kɔ:ld], *waited* [ˈweitid], *passed* [pɑ:st].

As appears from the examples, [id] is used after stems ending in [d] or [t], [d] in other cases, except after breathed consonants, [t] after breathed consonants, except [t].

The spelling is *ed* in all three cases; if the stem ends in *e* in the spelling (e.g. *fade*), *d* only is added. — On spellings like *cried* (stem *cry*), *admitted* (stem *admit*), see Appendix, p. 338 f.

2. The stem of an English verb is used in the following functions:

a. INFINITIVE, often preceded by *to*[3] (13 ff.);

b. PRESENT TENSE, with the exception of the third person singular (127 ff.);

---

[1] The sibilants (or hissing sounds) are [s], [z], [ʃ] and [ʒ].

[2] 'adj. & n., (phon.) of certain consonantal sounds formed by placing point of tongue against, or near, the upper teeth; such sounds as [t, d, n, θ, ð].' (Wyld, *The Universal English Dictionary* s.v. *dental*.)

[3] When referring to a verb by itself, it is customary to mention the stem preceded by *to*: '*To play* is a regular verb.' Verbs that are not used as infinitives, however, are indicated by the mere stem: 'What is the past tense of *can*?' (See 6.)

c. SUBJUNCTIVE (214 ff.);
d. IMPERATIVE (605 ff.).

3. The stem + *ing* is used in the following functions:
a. GERUND (62 ff.);
b. PRESENT (or IMPERFECT) PARTICIPLE (75 ff.).

4. The stem + sibilant-suffix is used as THIRD PERSON SINGULAR of the present tense (127 ff.; also 215 ff.).

5. The stem + dental-suffix is used in the following functions:
a. PAST (or PERFECT) PARTICIPLE (106 ff.);
b. PAST TENSE (or PRETERITE [ˈpretərit]) (135 ff.).

B. Irregular Verbs

6. The following verbs have only one of the four forms enumerated in 1, viz. the stem: *can*, *may*, *must*, *shall*, *will*.

This stem is used in only one of the functions mentioned in 2, viz. the present tense, including, however, the third person singular, which in other verbs is expressed by the stem + sibilant-suffix (4).

On *must* as a preterite, see 165.

7. The verbs *dare* and *need* occur in all four forms, but usually take no sibilant-suffix in the third person singular present tense when used as auxiliaries.

8. The verbs *be*, *do*, and *have* have irregular forms in the third person singular present tense: *is* [iz], *does* [dʌz], and *has* [hæz], besides being irregular in other respects.

9. Instead of the stem + dental-suffix, a fairly large number of verbs use an irregular form in the function of the past tense or the past participle, or of both.

Verbs with an irregular past tense and a regular past participle are rare: *crow* — *crew* (usually *crowed*) — *crowed*; *dare* — *durst* (usually *dared*) — *dared*.

Verbs with a regular past tense and an irregular past participle are somewhat more numerous (nine in all): *hew* — *hewed* — *hewn* (or *hewed*); *show* — *showed* — *shown*.

Most of these verbs, however, have irregular forms for both functions.

10. Verbs with irregular forms for both the past tense and the past participle may be divided into four groups:

a. Both the past tense and the past participle are identical with the stem: *cut*, *let*, *spread.*

b. Either the past tense or the past participle is identical with the stem: *beat* — *beat* — *beaten*; *run* — *ran* — *run.*

c. The past tense and the past participle are identical, but differ from the stem: *bend* — *bent*; *bleed* — *bled*; *seek* — *sought.*

d. The past tense and the past participle differ from each other as well as from the stem: *begin* — *began* — *begun*; *fall* — *fell* — *fallen.*

11. Special mention should be made of the forms *could*, *might*, *should* and *would*, which serve as past tenses to *can*, *may*, *shall* and *will* (6). They are not used as past participles.

On the isolated form *ought* see 167.

For further details of the irregular verbs, and for the conjugation of *to have* and *to be*, see Appendix.

C. Grouping of Forms and Functions

12. Of the functions of the verb stem enumerated in 2, two, viz. the present tense and the subjunctive, form a group with the third person singular (4) and the preterite (5*b*): (*I*) *play* (*the piano*) — (*I suggest that she*) *play* (*the piano*) — (*She*) *plays* (*the piano*) — (*I* or *She*) *played* (*the piano*). While the subjunctive is invariable (216), the stem as present tense may, in a given context, be replaced by one of the inflected members of the group.

The other two functions of the stem, viz. the imperative — *Play!* — and the infinitive — (*Will you*) *play?* (*It is your turn to*) *play* — are mutually exclusive, nor can either of them in a given context be replaced by an inflected member of the above group.

The infinitive in English may, therefore, be defined as that function of the verb stem which (*a*) cannot by itself express a command, (*b*) does not belong to the group of four described above.

CHAPTER ONE

INFINITIVE

Plain Infinitive

13. The infinitive may occur either with or without a proclitic[1] particle.[2] This particle is written *to*, and pronounced [tu] before a vowel, [tə] before a consonant. The infinitive without *to* is known as the PLAIN INFINITIVE.

14. The plain infinitive is only used in a verbal, never in a nominal function. In cases where other languages use a plain infinitive as the subject, object or nominal predicate of a sentence, English uses either an infinitive with *to* or a gerund.

To know him is to like him.
Do you like swimming? (Cf. 68 ff.)

15. The plain infinitive is used either by itself, or in combination with another verb. The latter use, which is the commonest, will be discussed first.

16. The plain infinitive is used:

a. with *can/could*, *may/might*, *must*, *shall/should*, *will/would* (cf. 6, 11 & 149 ff.).

Tell him he may go home.
She should have been more careful.
Will you open another window?

b. with *to dare* and *to need* (cf. 7 and 203 ff.), chiefly in negative and interrogative sentences:

How dare you come here?
He need not return the letter.

---

[1] 'Proclitic', a. & n., is defined by the *Concise Oxford Dictionary* (abbr. COD) as '(Monosyllable) closely attached in pronunciation to following word & having itself no accent' (the latter with reference to Greek).

[2] A particle, acc. to COD, is a 'minor part of speech, esp. short indeclinable one'. (On the term 'part of speech', see 770.)

c. with *to do* (cf. 8 and 194 ff.) when used as an auxiliary of emphasis or periphrasis.

Oh, *do* tell us what has happened.
She did not seem to notice us.
Don't you think he is awfully clever?

d. with *had better, had rather, had sooner.*

Had not [hædn(t)] we better stop now?
I'd [aid] rather go on, if you don't mind.
I'd sooner stay where I am.

1. *I'd rather* and *I'd sooner* also serve as contracted forms of *I would rather* and *I would sooner*. The phrases with *would* sometimes occur in print, though those with *had* are commoner.

In somewhat archaic English we also find *I would as lief* (or: *I had as lief*, cf. COD) (*lief* = *gladly, willingly*). The phrase is mostly used to repudiate a suggestion:

She cannot abide him, and would as lief marry a seal.[1]

2. In sentences denoting some action taken in preference to another *rather than* is usually followed by a plain infinitive.

He resigned rather than stifle his conscience (COD).
They determined to die rather than surrender (Wyld).

3. Note also the plain inf. after *better*: *Better bend than break* (cf. *Better late than never*). See also 26, last ex. (= *You'd better . . .*).

17. There are a few more combinations of a plain infinitive with another verb; they differ, however, from those mentioned in 16 in being restricted to a number of more or less stereotyped phrases. Thus, to express one's complete indifference to something one may say: *Oh, let it go hang!*[2] The phrase *go hang* is invariable; not only could the plain infinitive *hang* be combined with no other verb (apart, of course, from those mentioned in 16), but *go* (in this combination) occurs only as a plain infinitive. Compare also *go fetch!* (order to dog, COD).

To make believe = *to pretend* is likewise a stereotyped phrase, in so far as the plain infinitive *believe* can only be combined with *to make* (apart, again, from the verbs of 16); it is a little more variable, however, in that the forms *made* and *making* also occur in this combination. The same applies to *make do* (= *manage*).

---

[1] Poutsma, *A Grammar of Late Modern English*, 2nd ed. (henceforward denoted by *Grammar*[2]), I, Ch. II, § 29.
[2] Wyld, *Universal Dictionary*, s.v. *hang* B 2.

He made believe he was rich.
She had to make do with a day-girl.

Similar groups with *to hear* are *to hear say, tell, talk, speak.* (On the noun ˈ*hearsay* see 812.2.)

I hear say that there will be an election soon.[1]
We have all of us heard tell of Robin Hood.

To let may be combined with the plain infinitives *drop, fall, go, pass, slip*:

In the course of the conversation he let fall an obvious hint.
Let go of that rope!
It would be a pity to let slip such an opportunity.

In the examples given, *let fall, let go, let slip*, form inseparable units. But we also find: *he let himself go* ('give way to enthusiasm, impulse, etc.', COD), *he let the reins slip out of his hands.* — Cf. p. 19, n. 1.

Combinations with *to help* are rather freer, as it may be combined with almost any other verb. Except in American English, however, *to help* usually takes an infinitive with *to*; and when it does take a plain infinitive, in the majority of cases the stem without any ending (infinitive or imperative) is used.

He offered to help carry her basket.
Go to the scullery and help wash up at the sink.[2]

In all these cases the first verb is subordinated in stress to the second.

On constructions of the type *I'll go and see*, cf. 663.

18. The plain infinitive is also used in the so-called ACCUSATIVE-WITH-INFINITIVE construction (see 37 ff.), after *to hear, to feel, to see, to watch*, and one or two other verbs denoting physical perception; after *to let, to make* in the sense of 'to cause'; after *to have* in various senses, such as 'to permit', 'to get' (often in combination with *would, would have* being practically equivalent to 'want', 'wants' or 'wanted'), 'to experience'; after *to find, to know* (in the sense of 'to experience'); sometimes after *to help* (cf. 17).

We heard her come downstairs.
She watched the postman cross the street.
He would not let me go.
They made him repeat everything the man had told him.

---

[1] For an alternative construction see 114; also p. 134, n. 2.
[2] Collinson, *Spoken English*, p. 20.

I won't (or: can't) have you say such things.
He would have the Government control all railways.
Vergil has a court minstrel recite the creation of the world.
I had an extraordinary thing happen to me.
In the most trying conditions I have never known him lose his temper.
Please help me translate this.[1]

1. For alternative constructions after some of these verbs, see 77; for the inf. with *to* after *to find*, see 44. *To have* and *to know* sometimes take an acc. with inf. with *to*. *To bid* (= to command, to tell), which is only used in literary English, may take either construction, though the plain inf. is probably commoner (*He bade me stay*).

2. On the analogy of *to hear* and *to see*, *to listen to* and *to look at* are sometimes followed by an accusative with plain infinitive, though mainly in American English.

Her whole life had been spent listening to other people talk.
Look at that horse jump!

19. In combinations with one of the verbs of 16 *a* and *b*, the infinitive is sometimes put first for emphasis. The construction is confined to literary style. Cf. the 3rd ex. of 448.

I have my work to do, and do it I will.
Return I dare not.

20. A superficially similar construction is illustrated by such turns of phrase as *Come what may*; *Try as he would*. Between these and the inversions of 19 there is an essential difference, however. The two verbal forms are connected by a relative pronoun, by *all*, or by *as*; and the meaning of the clause[2] is concessive. The second verb is one of the auxiliaries *can/could*, *may/might*, *will/would*.

Say what you will of him, there is not a better officer in the regiment.

And I must think, do all I can,
That there was pleasure there.
(Wordsworth, *Lines Written in Early Spring*.)

Try as he might, he could not get the window open.

In the first example, with a subject pronoun in the second person, the infinitive seems to merge into the imperative. That it is distinct from the imperative, however, is seen when we substitute a subject pronoun of the first person: *Say what we will of him . . .*

21. The plain infinitive may be used by itself in questions beginning with *why* or *why not*:

Why spend such a lot of money?

---

[1] Collinson, *Spoken English*, p. 20.
[2] Cf. 615.

A suggestion made in such a question (or in some other way) may be rejected as impossible or absurd in a following exclamatory sentence, which may again take the form of a question:[1]

> Why not apologize and ask his pardon? — Ask that man's pardon? Never! (See also 574, last ex.)

An exclamatory infinitive may be preceded by a subject of its own:

> Do you think George could write a novel? — George write a novel? Hardly likely.

In the last two examples we have to do with the repetition of a plain infinitive from the preceding questions.

Infinitive with *to*

22. The INFINITIVE WITH *to* is used with *to be* (cf. 32), *to have* (cf. 166), *ought* (cf. 167), *used* [ju:st] (cf. 210 ff.); sometimes with *to dare* and *to need* (cf. 203 ff.).

> I am [aim] to see him to-morrow.
> You will [juəl] have to wait a moment.
> She ought to have been more careful.
> I used to go there every day.
> He did not dare to speak.

In these constructions the first verb is subordinated in meaning (and usually in stress) to the second.

23. This may also be the case in constructions with *to begin*, *to come*, *to fail*, *to happen*, *to seem*, *to stand*, as in the following examples:

> The barometer began to fall.
> I've come to see the problem in another light.
> His promises failed to materialize (= did not materialize).
> I happened to meet him in town yesterday.
> I seem to be deaf to-day.[2]
> Britain stands to gain by the treaty.

There is no subordination, however, in:

> The mountaineers failed to reach the top.[3]
> He *seems* to be reliable.

---

[1] For examples followed by a note of exclamation, see Kruisinga & Erades, *An English Grammar*, I², 7th ed., p. 331; also Jespersen, *Modern English Grammar* (abbrev. MEG) V, 20.32.

[2] COD s.v. *seem*. The first verb is subordinate to the verbal group *to be deaf*.

[3] Opposite: *succeeded in reaching the top*.

24. When the first verb is not subordinated in meaning to the second, the infinitive with *to* serves as an ADJUNCT[1] to the preceding VERB, which may be intransitive (see the last examples of 23), but is usually transitive.[2]

My uncle decided to sell his business and retire.
We intend to go to Denmark.
She promised to write every day.
He thinks (= intends) to deceive us.[3]
I tried to open a window.[4]
I want to earn my own living.

Note that the first verbs (not the infinitives) in these examples express purpose. On infinitive-adjuncts to other transitive verbs, see 35.

25. An infinitive with *to* may also serve as an ADJUNCT to a preceding NOUN, both to such as are connected with verbs that take an infinitive-adjunct (*a*) and to such as are not (*b*).

a. He made no attempt to deny his guilt.
My uncle announced his decision to retire.
There is no need to worry.
She expressed a wish to be buried very quietly.
b. He is not the man to do it.
It's the right thing to do.
He has a large family to keep.
I have the honour to inform you . . .[5]
It's time to go to bed.

1. Note the various relations between the noun and the infinitive. In the first example of *b* the noun is the subject of the infinitive, in the second and third examples the object. In the fourth example the infinitive stands in apposition (590) to the noun; in the fifth the infinitive adjunct is semi-adverbial (= *for going*).

2. The preceding noun in *a* may be connected with an adjective that takes an infinitive-adjunct (26): *her inability to sleep*; the infinitive in *b* may qualify an indefinitive pronoun in *-thing* or *-body* (or *-one*) as well as a noun: *something to eat, somebody to talk to.*

3. *To come* is used as an adjunct in the sense of 'future', 'forthcoming': *in days to come, Books to Come* (= about to be published); cf. 32.

---

[1] Cf. 588.
[2] On the distinction between transitive and intransitive verbs, see 584.
[3] COD. Similarly: *I did not think* (= expect) *to find you here; I never thought* (= remembered) *to ask.* But *He thinks* (= fancies) *he is very clever.*
[4] On constructions of the type *I'll try and come early*, cf. 663.1.
[5] Cf. 72.

26. An infinitive with *to* may serve as an ADJUNCT to an ADJECTIVE, especially to such as express a feeling. The adjective is either used predicatively or qualifies a predicative noun. (Cf. 581–583.)

He was afraid to seem ungrateful if he refused.
I am very glad to see you.
I shall be pleased to come.
She was unable to sleep.
You were wrong to contradict him.
That's difficult to say.
He is a hard man to please.

Similarly after *the first* (*second*, *next*, etc.) and *the last*, and after the adverb *about*:

She was always the first to get up and the last to go to bed (cf. 25*b*).
The porter was about to lock the door.

The predicative adjective is subordinate in meaning to the following infinitive (cf. 23) in cases like:

Cast iron is apt to break.[1]
The children are not likely to be home before nine.
Better take an umbrella, it's sure to be wet.

1. In *It's too good to be true — You are old enough to know better*, the infinitive is less closely connected with the preceding adjective than in *pleased to come*, etc.

2. On constructions like *It was not easy to get a taxi* cf. 378 f.

27. An infinitive with *to* is frequently used as an ADJUNCT OF PURPOSE. As such it may qualify a verb[2] or a noun, though it often qualifies all the rest of the sentence. In that case it may have front-position.

He got up to ask a question.
I've come here to work.
She bought a small camera to take snapshots with.
A blue shirt with a tie to match.
To obtain good results the treatment must be repeated daily.

In so-called 'free adjuncts' (cf. 611), the idea of purpose may be weakened, and even shade off into that of circumstance or condition.

To speak frankly, I don't quite like the idea.
To hear him talk, you'd think he knew all about the subject.

On the *to*-infinitive in so-called absolute adjuncts, see 87.

---

[1] Fowler. *A Dictionary of Modern English Usage* (abbrev. MEU), p. 29.
[2] On comparison with 24 it will be seen that here it is the infinitive, not the first verb, that expresses purpose.

28. The idea of purpose may be emphasized by *in order* or *so as* placed before the infinitive.

You'd better repeat them every day, in order not to forget them.[1]
I do them very carefully, so[2] as not to spoil them.

So may be separated from *as* by an adjective or adverb; in this case result is expressed:

He was so fortunate as to escape.

In other contexts, too, an inf. with *to* may express result rather than purpose:

He would sometimes force himself to work on till midnight, only *to find* himself unable to do anything the next day.

Sometimes the two verbs are practically co-ordinate (cf. 83 and 659):

He awoke with a start, to find the whole house on fire.

As is pointed out by Mr. P. A. Erades in *English Studies*, Febr. 1954, 'the idea denoted by the verb stem is represented as, in retrospect, unpredictable at the time to which the leading verb refers.'

29. When preceded by an interrogative pronoun or adverb (*a*), or by a conjunction (*b*), an infinitive with *to* is often equivalent to a dependent clause (*what to do* = *what I am to do*).

a. I do not know what to do.
Tell me where to go.
How to learn a foreign language.[3]

b. He looked at the clock, as if to indicate that the interview was over.

30. To express way or manner, an infinitive after *to know* is preceded by *how*.

He knows how to captivate his audience.
I don't know how to do it.
(Similarly: I'll show you how to do it.)

How is similarly used after *to forget*, *to learn* and *to teach*.

We've forgotten how to read.
His brother taught him how to catch butterflies.

When the idea of manner is weak or absent, *to forget*, *to learn* and *to teach* may take an infinitive without a connecting adverb.

She had forgotten to bring her music.
You must learn to be patient.

---

[1] Palmer, *Grammar of Spoken English*, § 327.
[2] As indicated in Palmer, *so* is high-pitched. In the next example the first syllable of *fortunate* would be high-pitched.
[3] Palmer, § 325. *How* is pronounced on a high pitch.

His father taught him to swim.
I'll teach you to cheek me![1]

31. Like the plain infinitive (18), the infinitive with *to* is used in the ACCUSATIVE-WITH-INFINITIVE construction (see 37 ff.), in this case after verbs like *to allow*, *to ask*, *to command*, *to force*, *to order*, *to permit*, *to persuade*, *to request*, etc., all of which express an act of the will.

Allow me to congratulate you.
He asked me to sit down and have[2] a cigarette with him.
We at length persuaded him to withdraw his resignation.

The infinitive with *to* is also used in constructions with verbs like those of 18 and 31 in the passive (see 46 ff.).

a. She was heard to come downstairs.
b. The troops were ordered to cease fire.

32. The infinitive with *to* is often used predicatively (cf. 581–583) with the present or past tense of *to be*, to express an ARRANGEMENT. Such an arrangement may be:

1. personal:	*a.*	mutual	(agreement);
	b.	one-sided	(command);[3]
2. impersonal:	*c.*		(destiny).

a. We are to be married next week.
It was understood that everybody was to pay his own expenses.
[See also 146, last ex. but one.]
b. I suppose I am to be home before ten?
Mother says you are to go to the butcher's at once.
c. The worst is still to come.
John was to perish in a shipwreck at forty, and to leave a wife and two children.

This use of the infinitive is similar to that of the infinitive expressing purpose discussed in 27. Cf. also the use of *to come* illustrated in 25.3 (and the title of Bunyan's famous book: *The Pilgrim's Progress from this world to that which is to come*).

1. We have essentially the same construction with a form of *to be* understood, as in the following headlines from the *Daily Telegraph*, May 2, 1952: 'Bad Farmers to Go—Government Policy.' Cf. 87.

---

[1] Cf. Kruisinga, *A Handbook of Present-day English*, 5th ed. (henceforward denoted by *Handbook*[5]), § 234, where examples of *to learn* + *how* + *to*-inf. may be found.

[2] *to* is not repeated here before the second infinitive; as a result, the two verbs (*sit down* and *have*) form a closer group than if it were.

[3] In the sense of 'the expressed wish of another person'.

2. Sometimes the subject is understood, as in: *To be left* (*kept*) *till called for* (of letters, etc.); '. . . church hymnbooks inscribed, *Not to be taken away.*' (E. A. Armstrong, *Shakespeare's Imagination*, p. 106.)

3. Not every combination of *to be* with a *to*-infinitive is an instance of the construction described above. Thus in the following description of a photograph in *Elephant Bill* by J. H. Williams (Penguin Books 1120) *is* is equivalent to *serves*: 'Elephants being saddled before work. The log floor is to avoid a quagmire of mud under the saddle rack.'

33. The meanings distinguished above may shade off into those of propriety, possibility or contingency.

Such men are to be pitied rather than despised.
How am I to get through all this work to-day?
The porter was nowhere to be found.
If anything is to come of the plan, work should be started at once.

On the use of *were to* + inf. in conditional clauses (*If I were to tell you all I know, . . .*), see 223.

34. *To blame*, *to let* and *to seek* may be used predicatively, meaning resp. *blameworthy*, *for hire*, and *lacking*.

No one was to blame; the accident could not have been prevented.
Is this house to let?
Accuracy is far to seek in his description.

Instead of *to blame, to be blamed* is occasionally used: *He is greatly to be blamed for his negligence* (Wyld). The passive infinitive is indispensable in *to be let or sold*.

35. In some of the examples of 24 the function of the infinitive with *to* borders on that of a direct object. In the last examples of 30 it cannot well be interpreted otherwise; similarly in a case like

She liked to learn, but hated to teach.

An example of the infinitive with *to* as a subject and as a nominal predicate (*To know him is to like him*) was given in 14. As Jespersen (MEG V, 11.24) observes, in such a sentence 'the second act or state is regarded as a necessary or immediate consequence of the first'. See also p. 29, n. 3.

Here are two more examples of the *to*-infinitive as a subject:

To scold the boys would be foolish.
To be obeyed was natural to her.

On the commoner construction *It was natural to her to be obeyed*, see 378 f.

36. Like the plain infinitive, the infinitive with *to* may be used in exclamatory sentences. These, however, express surprise or indignation (*a*), or a wish that is not likely to be fulfilled (*b*).

a. To think that all his efforts to help her had gone for nothing!
My own flesh and blood to rebel![1]
b. Oh, to be in England
Now that April's there![2]

Accusative with Infinitive

37. The term ACCUSATIVE WITH INFINITIVE is applied to groups consisting of a noun or pronoun plus an infinitive (with or without *to*), subordinated to another part of a sentence, usually a preceding verb.

The traditional term 'accusative' stands for the stem of a noun or of a demonstrative or indefinitive pronoun, as well as for the object form of a personal pronoun (*me*, *him*, etc.).

It is probably unnecessary to point out that English has no 'accusative' in the sense that Latin and some other inflected languages have. The term cannot very well be dispensed with in the present instance, however. Some grammarians prefer to speak of an *object* with infinitive; which involves them in the paradox of explaining that the 'object' is not really an object in cases like those described in 41–43. See, for instance, Kruisinga's *Handbook of Present-day English*, § 248.[3]

38. The 'accusative' noun or pronoun stands to the infinitive in the relation of a subject. Its relation to the part of the sentence on which the accusative with infinitive depends (that is, usually, to the preceding verb) may be that of an object, though there are many cases in English in which no such relation can be shown to exist (for examples see 41 ff.).

39. English agrees with some other languages in using an accusative with infinitive, *a.* without *to*, after some of the verbs mentioned in 18; *b.* with *to*, after those mentioned in 31.

The 'accusative' can usually be regarded as the object of the preceding verb, at least after those of *b*.

---

[1] Shakespeare, *The Merchant of Venice*, III. i. 37. [2] Robert Browning.
[3] Kruisinga also rejects the term 'infinitive' in favour of 'verb stem'. See the present writer's article, 'Progress in Syntax', *English Studies*, XIX (1932), 123–136 (also *Collected Papers*, Groningen, 1954).

a. She saw him lift the latch and pause a moment in the doorway.
I felt something crawl up my arm.
b. Of course, if they want to go, we cannot force them to stay.
May I request you to leave the room this instant?

40. The verbs of 31 express an action by which we try to impose our will on another person. The action, therefore, concerns an object as well as a subject.

In this respect they differ from verbs like *to want*, *to wish*, *to like*, *to prefer*, *to hate*, and one or two others, primarily expressing an act of the will that concerns the subject only. Unlike those of 31,[1] the latter may take an infinitive with *to*.

I do not want (wish) to stay here all day.
Would you like to wait till she comes?
I should prefer to meet her to-morrow.
I hate to trouble you.[2]

41. In English, however, these verbs (*to want*, etc.) may also be construed with an acc. with inf. with *to*, when the act of the will concerns another person besides the subject. Other languages use a dependent clause.

I do not want (wish) you to stay here all day.
Would you like me to wait till she comes?
I should prefer Jane to meet her to-morrow.
I hate you to talk like that.

Syntactically, the acc. with inf. after *to want*, etc., differs from that after *to allow*, etc. (31), in that the 'accusative' can hardly be regarded as the object of the preceding verb. From *Allow me to congratulate you*, we may isolate *Allow me*, without altering the meaning of the isolated part; but *I like boys to be quiet* may be said by a master who does not like boys at all, and *I hate you to talk like that* may be said to a friend.

If we are asked to say what *is* the object in the above examples, the answer must be: the accusative with infinitive as a whole (*you to stay*, *me to wait*, *boys to be quiet*, etc.).

1. It will now be seen that the construction of 39*a* (*She saw him lift the latch*) occupies a position midway between that of 39*b* and 41. *Him* may, indeed,

---

[1] *To ask* and *to request* may take an infinitive with *to*: *Did he ask to see me? He requested to be allowed to go.* In other respects, however, they do not go with the verbs of 41.

[2] Wyld, *Universal Dictionary*, s.v. *hate* vb.

be interpreted as the object of *saw*, but its connection with *lift* is so close that the accusative-with-infinitive as a whole has an equal claim to be regarded as the object.

2. The same construction is found with *there*: *I don't want there to be any trouble.* (Cf. A. S. Hornby, *A Guide to Patterns and Usage in English*, § 14 C.)

42. Some of the verbs of 31, notably *to allow* and *to permit*, are sometimes, like those of 41, followed by an acc. with inf. with *to* in which the 'accusative' can hardly be interpreted as the object of the preceding verb. This is especially (though not exclusively) the case when it does not denote a person.

He allowed the secret to ooze out.[1]
He permitted himself to be drawn into the conspiracy.[1]

The same construction is used after *to cause*, *to mean* (in the sense of 'to want'), *to suffer*, and two or three other verbs.

Sun and rain cause the grass to grow.
I did not mean you to hear it.
They would not suffer her to remain.

Unlike those of 41, however, these verbs may also occur in the construction described in 31 n. (cf. 52).

The secret was allowed to ooze out.
You were not meant to hear it.
She was not suffered to remain.

43. Another group of verbs, mainly such as serve to express an opinion or a perception (*to believe*, *to declare*, *to deny*, *to imagine*, *to perceive*, *to suppose*, *to understand*, etc.), may take an accusative with infinitive with *to* in literary English,[2] but are usually followed by a dependent clause in spoken English. The infinitive is nearly always *to be* or *to have been*,[3] followed by a predicative noun

---

[1] Note that *let* (with an acc. with plain inf.) is also possible here, and would be preferred in spoken English; similarly in the example with *suffer*. Instead of *cause the grass to grow* spoken English would prefer *make the grass grow* (cf. 18).

[2] By 'literary English' is meant the English of writers and orators in so far as it differs from the language as commonly spoken. 'Spoken English' includes written English in so far as the latter does not differ from the language as commonly spoken. In the present instance, therefore, the accusative with infinitive is uncommon in spoken English, but the dependent clause is by no means uncommon in informal writing.

[3] With other verbs a dependent clause is the rule in literary English as well:
I believe (that) he has told us the truth.

or adjective; the analysis is much the same as after the verbs of 42.

I believe it to have been a mistake.
I believe (that) it was a mistake.
I declare this to be my firm intention.
I declare (that) this is my firm intention.
Most people supposed him to be dead.
Most people supposed (that) he was dead.

The infinitive construction also occurs after *to feel* and *to see* when these verbs denote mental, not physical perceptions, and after *to know* in the sense of 'to be aware' (cf. 18).

I felt (saw) the plan to be all wrong.
I felt (saw) (that) the plan was all wrong.
They knew the man to be a liar.
They knew (that) the man was a liar.

There is an example of *to hear* followed by an acc. with *to be* in Kruisinga's *Handbook*[5], § 285; but this construction is rare even in literary English. In the sense 'to perceive with the ear' *to hear* may take the construction described in 18; in that of 'to be informed' it may take a dependent clause, as in

I hear (that) Mr. Jones has gone.

44. A few words of comment would seem to be called for on the constructions found after the following verbs:

a. After *to expect* English uses either an acc. with inf. with *to*, or a dependent clause, both in the sense of 'to look forward to' and in that of 'to look for as due.'[1]

I expect him to come.
I expect (that) he will come.
I expect you to be punctual.
I expect that you will be punctual.

The accusative is of the kind analysed in 42, though, like the verbs of 40 and 41, *to expect* may also take an infinitive with *to*:

I expect to see him to-morrow.

b. After *to find* in the sense of 'to discover by trial' COD offers a choice of four constructions: *I find it pays*, *pay*, or *to pay*, or *that*

---

[1] COD s.v. The construction illustrated by the fourth example seems to be less usual, however.

it pays.[1] The second of these belongs under 18, the third under 43 (except that the infinitive is not *to be*).

c. Note the accusative with infinitive after *to leave* in the sense of 'to allow (person, thing) *to* do something without interference' (COD), or 'to rely on to do' (Wyld).

I'll leave him to solve the problem for himself.
He left his wife to deal with the creditors.

The construction may be classified with those of 42.

d. A similar construction occurs after *to trust*:

I would not trust that man to leave the money alone.

45. Attention should be paid to the ACCUSATIVE WITH PASSIVE INFINITIVE,[2] which is used when the person performing the action denoted by the infinitive is either not mentioned or denoted by an adjunct with *by*. It occurs after many of the verbs mentioned in 31, and in 41–44. The analysis is the same as in 42.

The captain ordered the flag to be hoisted.
If you would like a list of new books to be sent regularly to you, kindly ask for it.
He believed his intentions to have been misrepresented by his enemies.

1. After the verbs of 42 we also find the construction described in **112**: *If you would like a list of new books sent to you . . .* Cf. 112, 2.

2. After *to let* the passive infinitive is used without *to*: *You cannot let the house be neglected like that.*

Nominative with Infinitive

46. As was pointed out in 31 the infinitive with *to* may occur in constructions with verbs like those of 18 and 31 in the passive. On the analogy of the active construction, this is known as the NOMINATIVE WITH INFINITIVE, the traditional term 'nominative' standing for the stem of a noun or of a demonstrative or indefinite pronoun, as well as for the subject form of a personal pronoun (*I*, *he*, etc.) (cf. 37).

---

[1] *To pay* in the sense of 'to yield an adequate return'.

[2] i.e. with *to be* (or *to have been*) plus the perfect participle of a transitive verb. Cf. 117 ff.

Unlike the accusative with infinitive, the nominative with infinitive never[1] occurs without *to*.

47. The nominative with infinitive construction occurs with the verbs *to hear*, *to feel*, *to see* (not with *to watch*); *to make* (= 'to cause'); *to find*, *to know* (in the sense of 'to experience'). Compare the somewhat longer list of 18.

The ship was seen to heel to starboard.
He was made to repeat everything.
He has never been known to lose his temper.

48. Here are some examples of the construction with the verbs of 31 in the passive:

We were not allowed to visit the patient.
I was asked to sit down.
He was persuaded to withdraw his resignation.
The public are requested not to walk on the grass.

See also 42.

49. The nominative with infinitive also occurs with the verbs of 43.

It is believed to have been a mistake.
The man is known to be a liar.
He was supposed to be dead.

Unlike the corresponding active construction, the nom. with inf. with these verbs is not restricted to literary English. Thus even a schoolboy may say: *We're not supposed* (= allowed) *to play games on Sundays.*[2]

The verb *to say*, which never takes an acc. with inf., occurs quite frequently with the nom. with inf.:

He is said to be a miser.

50. The construction is not uncommon either with *to expect* and *to leave* (cf. 44).

Am I expected to believe this?
The future was to be left to take care of itself.[3]

51. As with the accusative with infinitive (45), the infinitive in some

---

[1] With the single exception of *to let* (*fall*, *go*, *slip*, cf. 17): *The opportunity was let slip*. Cf.: *One remark let fall suddenly by the boy. . . .* (E. A. Robertson, *Four Frightened People*, Ch. II); *I was let see him* (COD s.v. *let*[2]).
[2] In this case the restriction of the infinitive to *to be* (43) does not hold.
[3] *Oxford English Dictionary* (abbrev. OED) s.v. *Leave* v.[1] 5 b. Cf. 32.

of the above-mentioned cases may itself be passive (i.e. *to be* or *to have been*, plus the perfect participle of a transitive verb).

The flag was ordered to be hoisted.
The victim is believed to have been poisoned.

52. The nominative with infinitive hardly ever occurs with the verbs of 41, perhaps because their meaning requires a personal, not merely a grammatical, subject. An instance like the following, to be found in the OED s.v. *know*, v., p. 744, bottom of the 3rd column, strikes one as exceptional:

. . . the kind of fact which is usually wanted to be known about the thing or person in question.

For + Acc. with Infinitive

53. It was said in 37 that the accusative with infinitive usually depends on a preceding verb. In English it may also depend on a noun or an adjective, especially when these are used predicatively. In this case it is preceded by *for*. Other languages mostly use a dependent clause.

It became the custom for people to go out of town for the week-end.
I think it is high time for something to be done.
It was unusual for anyone to call after ten.
This house is much too small for us to live in.

54. As with the ordinary acc. with inf., two types are to be distinguished:

a. The 'accusative', which is the subject of the following infinitive, stands to the (predicative) noun or adjective in the relation of an adjunct; other languages may similarly use the equivalent of *for* + acc. with inf.

It is bad for him to smoke.[1]
Have you got some paper for me to draw on?
It's all very well for *you* to speak like that.

This type corresponds to an acc. with inf. like *We cannot force them to stay*, in which the acc. may be interpreted as the object of the preceding verb. There may be a slight pause after the acc. (*It is bad for him | to smoke*).

---

[1] COD s.v. *for*.

b. The accusative can only be interpreted as the subject of the following infinitive; other languages use a dependent clause.

It is wicked for him to smoke.[1]
Everybody said it was madness for me to go.
He was quite willing (He was anxious) for the experiment to be repeated.
It is better to hear the rebuke of the wise, than for a man to hear the song of fools. (Ecclesiastes 7 : 5.)

This type corresponds to an acc. with inf. like *I don't want him to smoke*, in which the accusative can only be interpreted as the subject of the following infinitive. There is no pause after the accusative, though there may be a slight break after the predicative noun or adjective: *It is wicked / for him to smoke.*[2]

Care should be taken not to mistake an instance of type *b* for one of type *a*. Thus, when Skeat, in a note to *Piers Plowman*, Passus III, 174, writes: *It is a mark of respect for Meed to address the king in the plural number*, the respect is meant for the king, not for the Lady Meed; the break comes after *respect*, not after *Meed*. With a passive infinitive (3rd ex. of *b*) we always have to do with type *b*.

55. A variant of this construction occurs when the leading noun is the subject, *for* + acc. with inf. the nominal predicate.

The tendency in these songs is for the refrain to occupy a more prominent place.
The rule was for women and men to sit apart.

It is obvious that this construction belongs to type *b*.

56. We also have type *b* when *for* + acc. with inf. is used as the subject of a sentence.

For a commoner to marry a nobleman's daughter was a thing unheard of.
For Britain to isolate herself from Europe to-day would mean to disinterest herself in trade with Europe.[3]

57. The uses so far described run parallel to those of the infinitive with *to* as discussed in 25, 26 and 35. Like the infinitive with *to* (27), the *for* + acc. with inf. construction may also express purpose.

He pushed the door open for Jack to enter.
I will send you some views of our village for you to show your wife and daughter.

---

1 COD s.v. *for*.
2 There is no such break after *to want* and the other verbs of 41.
3 Note how this example (quoted from E. H. Carr, *Conditions of Peace*, p. 200) seems to contain an admixture of type *a*: it may be interpreted as: 'For Britain, isolation from Europe would mean loss of European trade.'

The policeman blew his whistle for the cars to stop.
She rang for the table to be cleared.

As in 27 and 28, the idea of purpose may shade off into that of result or condition.

He imagined he had only to step on Portuguese soil for the people to rise and throw off the Spanish yoke.
Production must soar; and for production to soar (= if production is to soar, 33) individuals must have some incentive to work harder.
But for the plea to be effective, it was necessary above all that the work should be widely read.
(J. W. H. Atkins, Introduction to *The Owl and the Nightingale*, p. lxxiii.)

58. From the fourth example of 57 it appears that *for* + acc. with inf. may depend on a preceding verb. After verbs that normally take the preposition *for*, the meaning of purpose may be weak or even absent.

We were waiting for the door to be opened.
She longed for him to say something.
I should not care for (= like) that man to be my doctor.

59. There is a tendency, especially in American English, to use the *for*-construction after verbs and adjectives that do not normally take that preposition.

I want very much for my son to be happier than I have been.
The fireman showed them the bell. He told them that when the bell rang, it meant for them to get out of the way. (Cf. 57.)
We'd be proud for you to dine with us.

Note that in the first ex. the verbal predicate and the 'accusative' are separated by intervening words. Cf. the following ex. from Onions, *An Advanced English Syntax*, § 60: *I desire nothing more than for you to come.* In both cases, too, the construction with *for* seems to express less purposeful determination than the one without; cf.: *I want my son to be happy*; *I desire you to come.*

60. The *for* + acc. with inf. construction frequently alternates with a dependent clause with *should* (cf. 172).

The rule was for women and men to sit apart.
The rule was that women and men should sit apart.

Anaphoric *to*

61. Verbs, nouns and adjectives that may take an infinitive with *to* (22 ff.) may be followed by *to* without an infinitive to refer to a preceding verb or verbal group. The construction is described by OED as 'a frequent colloquialism'.

> Don't go unless you have to (want to).
> She opened the window, though I had told her not to.
> I'd like to come, but I have not time to.
> They shouted to him to jump the ditch, but he was afraid to.

Anaphoric *to* does not seem to occur after *for* + accusative (53 ff.).

In the third and fourth examples one might also say or write: *but I have not time*; *but he was afraid*. The addition of *to*, however, makes the reference to the preceding verb or verbal group more definite. Cf.:

After supper he suggested they should go to a movie, but she refused. 'You go (606) if you want to', she said. 'I don't care to.'
Somerset Maugham, *Creatures of Circumstance* (Star Editions, p. 301).

CHAPTER TWO

GERUND AND PRESENT PARTICIPLE

62. Words derived from a verb stem by means of the suffix *ing* may be used in a variety of meanings and functions, according to the contexts in which they occur.

In the first place, such words may be used as VERBAL NOUNS, i.e. as nouns with a verbal MEANING. Thus in *Reading and writing are now common acquirements* (OED); *I am fond of smoking.*

In addition to its verbal meaning, such a form in *ing* may have verbal FUNCTION: it may take an object or be qualified by an adverb, as in *I am fond of smoking a pipe*; *He educated himself by reading widely.*

Nouns in *ing* with verbal meaning, or with verbal meaning and function combined, are called GERUNDS.

1. Cf. the definition of COD: 'English verbal noun in *-ing* when used distinctly as part of verb.'

2. In groups like *a human being, the Chrysler* [ˈkraizlə] *Building,* the character of the words in *ing* is purely nominal, the former being synonymous with *person* or *creature*, the latter with *house* or *edifice*. Such nouns are not called gerunds.

63. In the second place, such words may be used as VERBAL ADJECTIVES, either attributively, as in *a burning house, playing children,* or predicatively, as in *the house was burning, the children are playing on the lawn.* In this case they are called PRESENT (or IMPERFECT) PARTICIPLES.

In groups like *an amusing story, a charming hostess, a daring attempt,* the words in *ing* are purely adjectival, being synonymous resp. with *comical* or *funny, delightful,* and *bold.* Similarly in predicative use, as in *the story was very amusing, she was perfectly charming.* Such adjectives are not called present participles.

Gerund

64. A gerund may exhibit all the syntactic properties of a noun. Thus it may be preceded by an article, a possessive or demonstrative pronoun, a noun in the genitive, or an adjective, or followed by a noun-adjunct with *of* (or another preposition). It may function as the subject, object or nominal predicate of a sentence, and form part of a prepositional adjunct.

His handling of the situation was masterly.
He was waked by an insistent tapping on his door.
I detest all this quibbling.

See also the examples in the preceding and following sections.

The gerund is also used as an adjunct to a predicative noun or adjective in sentences with introductory *it*: *It was a difficult business lowering the long boats into the tossing sea*; *It's been a great pleasure showing you the sights of London*. Cf. 378 f.

65. A gerund may also exhibit the syntactic properties of a verb. Thus it may be qualified by an adverb or adverbial phrase, and in the case of a transitive verb may govern an object. It may also take a subject of its own (see 73). It may be used in the perfect tense (*having written*) and in the passive voice (*being written*). In most of these cases other languages use an infinitive.

He began reading slowly and in a clear voice.
Scamping your work is hardly the way to get on.
Of making many books there is no end. (Ecclesiastes XII. 12.)
He was suspected of having embezzled large sums of money.
I object to being treated like a child.

66. It will be noted that the gerund shares many of its syntactic properties with the infinitive with *to*. Thus both may occur as the subject, object or nominal predicate of a sentence (cf. 35 and 64), though only the gerund can take noun-qualifiers. Both may be qualified by an adverb or adverbial phrase, take an object or a subject (cf. 38 ff.), and be used in the perfect tense and the passive voice. It will, therefore, be necessary to define their respective territories.

67. The gerund is used, to the exclusion of the infinitive,[1] in the following cases:

---

[1] Though not necessarily to the exclusion of other constructions. *To deny*, for instance, may be followed by a clause: *I deny that it is so.*

a. as part of a prepositional adjunct.

b. as an object or adjunct to a number of verbs (some of them followed by adverbs) and verbal phrases, of which the principal are:[1] *to avoid, to burst out,*[2] *to deny, to detest, to enjoy, to escape, to fancy,*[3] *to finish, to give over* or *up, it's no good, (I) cannot help, to keep (on), to leave off, to mind* (in negative and interrogative sentences), *to postpone, to put off, to resent, to stop*;

c. as an adjunct to the adjectives *like* and *worth*, which may also take non-verbal noun-adjuncts, and after the phrase *there is no.*

> *a.* The doctor began by feeling my pulse.
> The sun is near setting.
> Without saying good-bye, he took his hat and walked out of the house.
> How (what) about trying to do it my way?
> *b.* As we lived in the same town, I could hardly avoid meeting him from time to time.
> Denny denied knowing anything of their plan.
> She enjoyed hearing him talk.
> Have you finished cooking?
> I've given up trying to pronounce his name.
> It's no good talking to him.
> I could not help asking where he had left his wife.
> The little girl kept (on) looking at me.
> I wish you would leave off smoking.
> Would you mind opening a window?
> We cannot postpone (put off) answering that letter any longer.
> For goodness' sake, stop talking![4]
> *c.* Lovely morning, isn't it? — Yes; doesn't look like lasting, though.
> He has a few pictures that are well worth looking at.
> There's no accounting for tastes.

The gerund[5] is frequently used after *as well as* (= besides):

> The author describes four different styles of standard English pronunciation, as well as including a text with dialogue in Cockney.

68. After a number of other verbs and verbal phrases either the gerund or the infinitive may occur. The principal are:[6] *to begin,*

---

[1] A fuller list may be found in Poutsma's *Grammar*², I, Ch. XIX.

[2] Nearly always *to burst out crying* (*laughing*). The nominal character of the form in *ing* is doubtful. Cf. 104.

[3] In the imperative, as an exclamation of surprise: *Fancy meeting you here!*

[4] In *He stopped to look about him, stopped* means *stood still* or *ceased* (whatever he was doing), and *to look* is an adjunct of purpose (cf. 27). Cf. also *he went on talking* (= he talked and talked) and *he went on to say* (= next he said).

[5] See n. 2.

[6] For a fuller list see Poutsma, *Grammar*², I, Ch. XIX, § 20.

to cease, to continue, to dislike, to dread, to fear, (I) cannot or *could not forbear,*[1] *to hate, to intend, to like, to love, to neglect, to prefer, to propose, to purpose* [ˈpəːpəs], *to recollect, to remember, to start, to try, it's (of) no use.*

After *to continue, to dread, to fear, to intend* and *to neglect* the infinitive is more frequently used than the gerund, especially in spoken and informal written English. On the other hand, the gerund is commoner after *cannot* or *could not forbear, to recollect, to remember.* After *to propose*[2] and *to purpose* the two constructions seem to be about equally frequent. On the difference between them in the case of *it's no use* see *English Studies,* XXXIII, 2, April 1952, 90–91.

After *to remember* the infinitive refers to the future, the gerund to the past:

I must remember (= not forget) to ask him.
I remember seeing her when she was a little girl.

In the same way one may say:

I shall never forget seeing her stand on the balcony of the palace.

To try takes a gerund when it means 'to make an experiment', an infinitive when it means 'to make an attempt'.[3]

To make a living, he had tried writing, painting, and various other things, but had failed in all.
Try to keep perfectly still for a moment.

69. With the other verbs of 68, too, it is often possible to find a reason for the use of either form.

When a gerund is used after *to begin,* this verb usually expresses a deliberate act; otherwise an infinitive is mostly preferred.[4]

a. On his return to England he began studying law.
Now don't begin eating them at once.
b. He began to realize that he had made a mistake.
Suddenly it began to rain.
I felt I did not begin to understand her.[5]

---

[1] After *to forbear* not preceded by *cannot* or *could not,* an infinitive with *to* is the rule: *I forbear to enter into details.*

[2] On *to propose* see Poutsma, *Grammar*², I, Ch. XIX, § 19.

[3] On the construction with *and* (*try and remember*), see 663.

[4] Cf. Kruisinga, *Handbook*⁵, § 378, and Poutsma, *Grammar*², I, Ch. XIX, § 20.

[5] American, but spreading in England. *Begin* is here pronounced with strong stress and rising intonation. Craigie's *Dictionary of American English* defines this meaning as: 'to make any, or the least approach (*to* be or do something).'

A similar distinction applies to the use of the gerund or the infinitive after *to cease*.

a. On account of the snow, the tramcars ceased (*or* stopped) running at eight o'clock.
b. The German Empire has ceased to exist.

According to COD, *to start* normally takes a gerund, the infinitive with *to* being colloquial or vulgar. From the examples collected by Poutsma and Kruisinga, however, it appears that there is little to choose between the two constructions in this respect. In the sense of 'to take up' the gerund would seem to be indicated, for reasons to be stated presently.

You must have had a busy time since you started cycling.[1]

'Since you started to cycle' would probably be taken to refer to a special trip. Cf. also the first (authentic) example of *to begin* + gerund given above.

70. This suggests another distinction between the gerund and the infinitive as objects; it applies especially to *to hate*, *to like*, *to dislike*, and *to prefer*. After these verbs the infinitive is mostly used with reference to a special occasion, the gerund being more appropriate to a general statement.

a. She hated shopping.
b. I hate to disappoint you, but . . .
a. Do you like going to concerts? — That depends on the kind of concert.
b. Would you like to have a look at my stamps?
a. On the whole I prefer walking to cycling.
b. You can take the 8.20, unless you prefer to stay another night.

The distinction also frequently holds good when either form is used in the function of a subject or nominal predicate. Cf. Sweet, *A New English Grammar*, Part II, Syntax, § 2326.

a. Going to fairs and markets was one of his favourite pastimes.
b. I have not been to America, but to go there is one of my ambitions.

Compare also the two following quotations:

We moved off silently. I was inaudibly cursing the pawang,[2] who had

[1] Quoted by Poutsma, *Grammar*², I, Ch. XIX, § 20, from Jerome, *Three Men on the Bummel* (publ. 1900).
[2] A native guide.

made drawing back impossible for me,[1] long before we reached the appointed spot. *Climbing* into the tree was not as difficult as *walking*: it was soon over, and one could choose where one's weight came on the foot.

E. A. Robertson, *Four Frightened People*, Ch. VI.

Canton is safe — if one has a house as powerful as the Lin clan, of whom all governors are afraid; but the reign of terror is such at Samshui that we just had (cf. 166.2) to come away. *To stay* would have been folly.

Nora Waln, *The House of Exile*, Penguin ed., p. 244.

The former does not exactly contain a general statement, but comparison with the latter will show that the character of the infinitive is more definite than that of the gerund. The gerund may have something of the durative character proper to the participle in *ing*.

1. An attentive reader will come across many instances, however, where the distinction attempted here does not apply. Thus in *The Squire's Story* by Mrs. Gaskell[2] (*Sel. Short Stories*, Oxf. Univ. Press, I, p. 210) we find: 'Mr. Higgins, however, preferred engaging two lads out of Barford' — where one might have expected *to engage*. To substitute the infinitive for the gerund, however, would be to spoil the rhythm of the sentence,[3] and this may be the reason why Mrs. Gaskell — without thinking about the matter, no doubt — wrote it as it stands.

2. The following quotation from Dickens, *Nicholas Nickleby*, Ch. X, illustrates what is said in 69 and 70:

'I will try to please, uncle', replied Kate; 'indeed I —'
'Don't begin to cry,' growled Ralph; 'I hate crying.'

71. After *to need*, *to require* and *to want* the gerund varies with the passive infinitive. In this case the grammatical subject of the finite verb is at the same time the logical object[4] of the gerund.

a. That needs no accounting for.
b. These quotations need to be checked.
a. That young man will require looking after.
b. Teachers require to be warned against shouting.
a. Your house badly wants painting.
b. He wants to be watched.

The gerund after these verbs is probably commoner than the

[1] With an infinitive the clause would run: who had made *it* impossible for me *to draw back* (cf. 378).

[2] [ˈgæskəl]. — Mrs. G. is best known as the author of *Cranford* (1853).

[3] Note the use of the infinitive in this sentence! (Cf. 35.)

[4] In *Your house wants painting*, *your house* is the grammatical subject of *wants*, but the logical object of *painting*, because the house undergoes the action of painting.

(passive) infinitive. It is the only form used after *to bear* = *to be fit for*:

His language won't bear repeating.

72. An infinitive with *to* is the rule after most verbs not mentioned in 67 and 68; see the chapter on the infinitive. It is the only possible construction in adjuncts of purpose (27). Compare the following sentences:

To acquire (or: acquiring) a really good pronunciation is a matter of patient effort.
To acquire (not: acquiring) a really good pronunciation, it is necessary to go to England.

A gerund after a preposition may vary with *to* + infinitive as an adjunct to certain nouns and predicative adjectives (cf. 25, 26). Thus *opportunity* may be construed either with *of doing* or *to* do (COD); Wyld, s.v. *honour*, gives *may I have the honour* (of doing, to do, something); either *He was surprised to see me*, or, less closely connected, *surprised at seeing me*. Cf. also Am. *They aim to save something every month*, Engl. *They aim at saving something every month* (*American College Dictionary*).

73. Like the infinitive (cf. 40, 41), the gerund in a given sentence or clause may refer to the same agent (or subject) as the finite verb, or each may refer to a subject of its own.

In the latter case the gerund is usually preceded by the stem of a noun or indefinite pronoun, or by a possessive pronoun. The equivalent in other languages is usually a clause.

a. He was accustomed to eating a big breakfast.
b. We were accustomed to uncle (Jack, his) eating a big breakfast.
a. I don't like leaving home for a fortnight on end.
b. I don't like everybody (your) leaving home for a fortnight on end.

In literary English a preceding noun is frequently put in the genitive;[1] in initial position, before a gerund functioning as the subject of a sentence, the genitive is generally used in all styles of English; but cf. 102. (On such a construction as *That's Dr. Gwynne's doing* see 292 and 311.)

Parliament objected to the Government('s) being given a free hand.
John('s) coming home to-morrow will make all the difference.

On the other hand, in non-initial position the object form of a

[1] At least, when it admits of being used in the genitive; see the chapter on Nouns.

personal pronoun is often used instead of a possessive pronoun, especially in colloquial (i.e. informal spoken) English.

What's the use of me going there?
Mother hates us eating peas with a knife.

The object form is common after *to prevent* and *to stop*, both of which may also be construed with *from*. A genitive or possessive pronoun (without *from*) is more literary.

There is nothing to prevent us (from) getting married.[1]
Better stop him (from) getting into mischief, before it's too late.

Compare the following quotation (distinctly colloquial!):

All the same, I'm all *for every one doing* what they want. I should be jolly sick if any one *stopped me bug-hunting*.[2]
Rose Macaulay, *Orphan Island*, Tauchnitz ed., p. 188.

74. The genitive (or possessive pronoun) is always used in *of*-adjuncts to nouns, when the noun is the logical object of the gerund (cf. 71). The construction occurs chiefly in literary English. The *of*-adjunct may also be used predicatively.

I found him absorbed in a scheme of his partner's devising (= devised by his partner).
The dinner was of aunt's own cooking (= had been cooked by aunt herself).

The construction also occurs with other nouns denoting action: *an opera of Purcell's composition* (= composed by Purcell); *a passage of his own authorship* (= written by himself).

Present (or Imperfect) Participle

75. The traditional name PRESENT PARTICIPLE is open to the objection that the verbal form it denotes does not necessarily refer to the present, just as a 'past' participle need not refer to the past. The alternatives, viz. 'imperfect' and 'perfect' participle, are prompted by the consideration that a form like *going* usually expresses an incomplete action, a form like *gone* a completed one. But, as will be seen, participles in *ing* do not *always* express incomplete actions, just as those in *ed* (or the corresponding

[1] Or: *to keep us from getting married*, in which case *from* cannot be omitted.
[2] i.e. collecting insects.

irregular forms) do not always express completion.[1] So long as no name has been invented that covers all the uses of these forms it is, perhaps, better not to discard the traditional terms.

As a general rule, a present participle expresses an action or a state simultaneous with that expressed by the predicate of the sentence; see, however, 83.

76. In attributive use an English present participle usually corresponds to a present participle in other languages.

As a child he had once been rescued with great difficulty from a burning house.
With trembling hands he opened the mysterious envelope.

77. The present participle may be used in a construction analogous to that illustrated in 18, after *to hear*, *to feel*, *to see*, *to watch*, and after *to have*. The construction may be denoted as the ACCUSATIVE WITH PRESENT PARTICIPLE. The present participle may be regarded as a predicative adjunct[2] to the object of these verbs, with the same reservation, however, as was made in 41 with regard to the analysis of a sentence like *She saw him lift the latch.*

She heard him coming downstairs, whistling (82) all the time.
He felt his heart beating wildly.
From my study window I could see (or: watch) the ships sailing in and out of the harbour.
I cannot (or: won't) have you doing nothing all day.
In five minutes he had them all laughing.

Here is a clear case of a present participle as a predicative adjunct after *to find:*[3]

When at last he returned home, he found his wife dying.

78. In the above examples the present participle refers to an action represented as being in progress and having a certain duration. In the corresponding construction with the plain infinitive (18) the action is not viewed as in progress, but merely referred to as such, either because the speaker or writer considers its duration irrelevant, or because it actually occupies but a moment.

---

[1] Cf.: *Seating myself, I began to read* (83), and: *a smooth-spoken rascal* (107).
[2] See 592.
[3] Cf. 44*b*; also Kruisinga, *Handbook*[5], § 107.

The difference is one of what is called ASPECT.[1] The aspect expressed by the present participle (in the examples of 76 and similar cases) is called IMPERFECTIVE or DURATIVE; that expressed by the infinitive in the corresponding construction is called PERFECTIVE.

In *She heard him come downstairs* the infinitive shows that the duration of the action is regarded as irrelevant; in the following quotation (from one of Conan Doyle's Sherlock Holmes stories) the infinitive (*get away*) denotes an action that takes only a moment.

> Now it was on these stairs that young Mr. Cunningham stood and *saw the two men struggling* just where we are. Old Mr. Cunningham was at the window — the second on the left — and he *saw the fellow get away* just to the left of that bush.

Compare also the following paragraph about Seymour [ˈsiːmɔː] Hicks, the actor:

> The accomplishment of the man! The tricks! the diabolical cleverness! *Watch him listen*, for example. There is no more difficult or less understood art on the stage than this one of listening, and when you *have seen Seymour listening*, you have seen the whole thing, inside out, upside down, backwards.
>
> Beverley Nichols, *Twenty-Five*, Ch. XXI.

1. Sometimes the distinction is one between completion and incompletion: *I saw him walking across the road* (on the way across, incomplete); *I saw him walk across the road* (from one side to the other, complete).

2. In the construction with the present participle the emphasis on the noun or pronoun (at least after a verb of perception) is usually greater than in that with the infinitive. Thus *Have you ever seen Barbirolli conduct?* is roughly equivalent to 'the conducting of Barbirolli', whereas *Have you ever seen Barbirolli conducting?* means 'B. when he is conducting'. Compare from this point of view the examples of 18 and 77, together with 41.1.

79. An accusative with present participle (but without the alternative construction with a plain infinitive) is also found after *to catch*, *to keep*, *to leave*, *to send*, *to set*, *to start*, and one or two other verbs.

> Take care he does not catch you napping.[2]

---

[1] For a detailed treatment of Aspect see Kruisinga, *Handbook*[5], §§ 304–335, and Visser, *Syntax of the English Language of St. Thomas More*, §§ 243–249; for a brief, but pointed, discussion, Sapir, *Language*, p. 114. — The difference between the two aspects mentioned here may be graphically represented by a line ▬▬▬ for the imperfective, a dot ● for the perfective aspect.

[2] Cf. COD s.v. *nap*[1].

Never keep a lady waiting.
His remark left me wondering what he was driving at.
If I were you, I would send him packing.[1]
A few words caught in passing set me thinking.
He tried to start the engine running.

Note the occasional use of an accusative with present participle after *to want*: *you don't want people thinking* you *did it*.

80. The verbs that take an accusative with present participle may also stand in the passive (cf. 46 ff.), a construction that may be denoted as NOMINATIVE WITH PRESENT PARTICIPLE.

The ship was seen heeling to starboard.
He admitted that he had been caught napping.

81. A present participle may follow the noun or pronoun it qualifies; in this case it is used in a semi-predicative function. Together with any accompanying object or adjunct, it is usually equivalent to an attributive clause. Cf. 581 ff. and 703.

a. Do you happen to know the number of men (those[2]) playing?
He is one of the best fellows going.[3]
b. Members wishing to resign (= who wish to resign) are requested to notify the hon. secretary[4] before January 1st.
It was impossible not to see the distance separating (that separated) masters and men. (Cf. 77.)

82. A present participle (with its object or adjunct, if any) may be equivalent to an adverbial clause, chiefly of time, reason, or attendant circumstances. As in the examples of 81*b*, spoken English usually prefers a subordinate clause.

Arriving (= when he arrived) at the station, he found his train gone.
Not knowing (=As she did not know) what to do, she applied to me for advice.
She wrote him a friendly letter, thanking him for his help, and sending him her best wishes.

In such sentences, where there is a clear break between the participle (with the words accompanying it) and the rest of the sentence, the participle group forms what is called a FREE ADJUNCT.[5] (See 611.)

---

[1] Cf. COD s.v. *pack*[2]. [2] Cf. 422. [3] Cf. COD s.v. *going*.
[4] An hon(orary) secretary is one who is not paid for his work.
[5] A free adjunct does not necessarily contain a participle. Cf.: *An orphan at six*, he was brought up by a distant relative. — *To sum up*: twelve persons killed, twenty wounded, and considerable material damage done.

A present participle in a free adjunct may be preceded by a conjunction:

While reading I fell asleep.

83. A present participle group in a free adjunct may be practically equivalent to a co-ordinate clause. In such cases the participle may express an action anterior or posterior to that denoted by the finite verb;[1] its aspect is not always clearly durative, often the reverse. Spoken English mostly uses a co-ordinate clause.

Seating myself I began to read (= I sat down and began to read).
Entering a covert [ˈkʌvə], she walked along a ride.
Young men by the dozen came up, asking her to dance.

84. In a number of expressions the present participle in a free adjunct does not refer to any particular word in the sentence that can be considered its subject. This is called the UNRELATED PARTICIPLE construction, to distinguish it from the RELATED PARTICIPLE instanced in 81–83. (Cf. 115.)

Generally speaking, he didn't like boys.
Granting this to be true, what follows?
Considering his abilities, he should have done better.
That is not so bad, considering (sc. the circumstances) (COD).

85. An unrelated participle may be practically equivalent to a preposition or a conjunction.

Barring accidents he ought to make Capetown in two days.
He asked me concerning (= about) my health.
I think we shall win, providing[2] (that) John is well enough to play.
Supposing[3] we lose, what then?

86. A present participle in a free adjunct is sometimes preceded by a noun or pronoun functioning as its subject. This is called the ABSOLUTE[4] PARTICIPLE construction. It is especially frequent in literary English; spoken English usually prefers a dependent clause. As with the construction of 82, the relation implied may be one of time, reason or attendant circumstances (*a*); as in the

---

[1] A finite [ˈfainait] verb is one expressing or implying tense, number, person, and mood. The non-finite forms are the infinitive, the participles, and the gerund.

[2] Or *provided*.

[3] Or *suppose*.

[4] The term 'absolute' indicates that the participle is not dependent on the subject of the finite verb.

examples of 83, the two parts of the sentence may be practically co-ordinate (*b*). (Cf. 116.)

a. The authorities having arrived (= When the authorities had arrived) and taken the seats reserved for them, the ceremony began.
None of those present having any further remarks to make (= As none of those present had . . .), the chairman closed the meeting.
Human nature being what it is, perhaps the outcome was inevitable.
They had many talks with the natives, the guide acting as interpreter.
b. On the old man's death, the property was divided, the greater part going to the elder son, the remainder to the younger.

Compare also the phrase *weather permitting*,[1] where the meaning implied is one of condition.

1. Note that between the fourth example and the fifth there is only a gradual difference.

2. On absolute participle adjuncts introduced by *with* (*It's ever so pretty with all the trees coming out*) see 614.

87. When the subject of the absolute participle is a personal pronoun of the 1st or 3rd person, the nominative is used.[2]

We spent most of the summer in a cottage we had rented together with some friends of ours, they occupying the front room and the attic, and we having the rest at our disposal.

If the summer was still to come, an absolute infinitive with *to* would take the place of the present participle (cf. 27). Cf. also 32.1.

We were going to spend most of the summer in a cottage we had rented together with some friends of ours, they to occupy the front room and the attic, and we to have the rest at our disposal.

Progressive

88. What was said in 78 of the imperfective or durative aspect of the present participle also applies to its predicative use, as in *The ships were sailing out of the harbour.* This construction (*to be* + present participle together forming the verbal predicate)[3] is known as the PROGRESSIVE, because it usually denotes an action or an activity as in progress.

---

[1] Also *funds permitting*, and similar combinations.

[2] In familiar English the object form may occur: *We continued to swear undying friendship, me feeling no end of a hypocrite.*

[3] Cf. 577 n.

To distinguish them from the progressive, the other forms of the verb (*sail*, *sails*, *sailed*; *has sailed*, *will sail*, etc.) will be denoted collectively as the 'simple' form.

89. Most English verbs have a complete conjugation in the progressive as well as in the simple form. The difference between the two may be seen from the following examples.

1*a*. What are you reading? — Oh, some trash I picked up at a bookstall.
b. I seldom read French.

2*a*. When she returned to the dining-room the guests had left, and the servants were clearing the table.
b. My car only just cleared the lorry in the lane.[1]

3*a*. I have been paying and receiving calls almost every day for the last fortnight.
b. I have paid several calls during the last fortnight.

4*a*. In another year I shall probably be growing tea in Ceylon [siˈlɔn].
b. When I am older, I shall grow a beard and moustache.

The difference between the examples marked *a* and those marked *b* is similar to that between the present participle and the infinitive discussed in 78. The *a* sentences express the continuity of an action, the *b* sentences do not. In 1*b* the simple form is used because the duration of the action is irrelevant; 2*b* refers to an action that takes only a moment. The difference between *She heard him coming downstairs* and *She heard him come downstairs* is, therefore, paralleled by that between *He was coming downstairs* and *He came downstairs*.

As regards the other tenses, 3*a* emphasizes continuity, 3*b* describes the action as having been completed. The difference between 4*a* and *b* is similar to that between 1*a* and *b*.

1. The difference may sometimes be formulated as one between a general truth on the one hand, and an actual occurrence on the other. Cf. *The sun rises in the east and sets in the west*, and *Look! the sun is rising*. — Another contrast is that between an activity of which no end is foreseen, and another of limited duration. Cf.: *I live at Amsterdam*, and *I am staying with my uncle*. See also 131, 132.

2. The character of the progressive may be described as 'dynamic', that of the simple form as 'static'. See an article by Th. Satchell in *English Studies*, XXI (1939), 214–217; also one by A. S. Hornby in *English Language Teaching*, May 1949 ('The Progressive forms are still gaining ground.' — 'The essence of the Progressive Tenses is *incompletion*.') There is an

[1] Wyld, *Universal Dictionary*, s.v. *Clear* vb.

excellent analysis of the use of the progressive in the present tense by A. G. Hatcher in *Language* (Journal of the Linguistic Society of America), 27/3, July–Sept. 1951, 254–280.

90. In the case of certain verbs which in themselves express continuity or duration there seems to be little difference of meaning between the simple and the progressive forms. For instance, in newspaper accounts of weddings we find both *The bride wore a dress of white silk* and *The bride was wearing a dress of white silk.* The verbal-adjectival character of the present participle makes the progressive more descriptive here than the purely verbal character of the simple form. Compare also *He looks ill* and *He is looking ill*; *I feel tired* and *I am feeling tired*; and see 91.

To want, to wish, and *to like* mostly occur in the simple form;[1] still we find, by the side of *I want some stamps — Are you wanting a lawn-mower, by any chance?* and by the side of *I wish I'd never seen him — He sold his house because he thought he would get a good price for it; now he is wishing he had kept it.* Cf. also *How do you like this?* and *How are you liking your new job? I hope* (*I'm hoping*) *to see you soon.* In cases like these, the progressive has a more colloquial ring than the simple form.

91. The 'dynamic' character of the progressive (see 89.2) makes it particularly suitable for use in descriptive and in emotional contexts. Thus in the sentence about tea-planting in Ceylon (89, 4*a*) the speaker is drawing a mental picture of himself as he will be a year hence. Similarly in the sentence about paying and receiving calls, whereas the one with the simple perfect merely states a fact.

At the same time, in the sentence with the progressive just referred to there is perceptible a feeling of weariness of the interminable round of social duties. Similarly indignation and annoyance are implied in sentences like the following:

What are you thinking of?[2]
Who has been tampering with that lock?

92. Either the descriptive or the emotional character of the progressive (or sometimes both) is often in evidence in sentences with *always* or its synonyms (*constantly*, *perpetually*, *for ever*, etc.). The

[1] In *The head of the statue is wanting* the participle is purely adjectival (= *absent, missing*); cf. 98.

[2] Said with strong stress (and a sharply rising intonation) on *are*. Without this special stress (but with high level pitch for *what*) the sentence simply asks for information.

repetition expressed in such sentences may be either 'descriptive' or a source of irritation or similar feelings.

> Father was always saying that there was no place like home.
> She was constantly complaining of the cold.
> Peter says he saw a ghost last night.— Peter is always seeing ghosts, or pretending to, at least.
> He's for ever finding fault with whatever I do.[1]

As appears from the third example, the addition of *always*, etc., may induce the use of the progressive of verbs that would normally take the simple form. Cf. also *Do you doubt my word?* (93)—*You're always doubting my word.*

93. Though most English verbs have a complete conjugation in the progressive as well as in the simple form, the ratio of frequency between the two is by no means the same with all.

Some verbs, on account of their meaning, do not normally occur in the progressive. *To contain*, for instance, expresses an essentially 'static' idea: *The box contains* (or *contained*) *books*; it does not denote an activity in progress. Other verbs which, for the same or similar reasons, rarely occur in the progressive are to *believe*, *to belong*, *to deserve* (cf. 98), *to hate*, *to know*, *to love*, *to mean*, *to own*, *to please*, *to possess*, *to prefer*, *to recognize*, *to remember*, *to resemble*, *to satisfy*, *to seem*, *to sound*, *to suffice*, *to suit*, *to surprise*, *to understand*.

A number of verbs rarely occur in the progressive in what may be called their central meaning, but may take the construction in a collateral or subsidiary sense. Compare the following examples:

> 1*a*. Do you see that house over there?
> *b*. I am just seeing my friend off.
> I shall be seeing him to-morrow.[2]
> 2*a*. I hear you won a prize recently?
> *b*. Jane is hearing Mary her lesson.
> I am hearing (= attending) lectures at the University.
> 3*a*. I forget (= cannot remember) his name.
> He forgot to shave.

---

[1] Palmer, *op. cit.*, § 302.

[2] The future progressive often represents an action as something that may be expected in the natural course of events. See 89 (the example about Ceylon); also Poutsma, *Grammar*, II, Ch. LII, § 17, and Palmer, *op. cit.*, p. 153 top. As A. S. Hornby (*A Guide to Patterns and Usage in English*, p. 214) points out, a statement like the 2nd ex. of 1*b* might be followed by something like: *Is there anything you'd like me to tell him?*

b. I am forgetting my French.
Dear me, I'm forgetting my umbrella!
4*a.* Do you mind (= object to) letting me get out first?
b. Aunt Mary is minding (= looking after) the children.
5*a.* I think (i.e. I am of opinion) (that) we had better take his offer.
He seems to think I'm too old.
b. What are you thinking of? (Cf. 91.)
He seems to be thinking the matter over.
6*a.* That's a very funny story.
b. I suppose you think you're being funny? (i.e. saying or doing something funny.)

Even in their central meaning verbs like *to hear* and *to see* may occur in the progressive to express development by degrees: *I'm hearing it better now*; *I'm seeing it more clearly now*.

94. Some transitive verbs may occur in the progressive in an intransitive or passive sense. The present participles chiefly used in this way are *doing*, *owing*, *shaping*; *binding*, *cooking*, *printing*, and one or two others describing similar processes.

Anything doing?[1]
He paid all that was owing.
The boy is shaping (=developing) satisfactorily.
The potatoes are cooking.

The following is from a letter from a London bookseller dated Feb. 28, 1947:

Granville-Barker's 'Othello' is binding and we will send a copy when ready. I say 'binding' but no London binders[2] is working at present, no electric power.

Tillyard's 'Elizabethan World Picture' is reprinting, we also keep this on order.

The limited use of this construction is well explained by Prof. Paul Christophersen in *English Studies* XXXIII, 3, June 1952, 140–141. — While the following quotation probably represents normal English: 'As a result of delays, mostly political in origin, the bus terminus has already been four years building.' ('Dublin after Twenty Years', in *The Listener*, June 5, 1952, p. 916), in other contexts (and with other verbs) a passive construction would be preferred: 'A new bus terminus is being built.'

95. By way of anticipation, the present (or, in reported speech or thought, the past) tense of the progressive may be used to express a (usually near) future or an intention. The verbs used in this way include *to arrive*, *to come*, *to go*, *to leave*, *to sleep*, *to stay*; *to*

[1] Short for *Is there anything doing?*
[2] Cf. 279.

dine, to lunch; *to issue, to publish*; *to wear*; *to do*; *to play*. The time of the action is often indicated by an adverbial adjunct.

Is Jack coming to-night?
I am going there next year.[1]
When are you leaving?
Are you staying here till next week?
Chatto & Windus are publishing his novel in the autumn.
What are you wearing to-morrow?
What are you doing next Sunday?
I am playing tennis this afternoon.

'Have we nearly done?' Underwood asked. 'Because I'm dining.' (i.e. I'm dining out to-night.)

Cole, *The Murder at Crome House*, Penguin ed., p. 80.

'Satterthwaite,' he said, 'I'm leaving here to-morrow for good.'

. . . .

'It's the Only Thing To Do,' he said, obviously speaking in capital letters. 'I shall sell this place . . .'

. . . .

'Cut your losses — it's the only way . . . Youth to youth . . . They're made for each other, those two . . . I shall clear out . . .'
'Where to?' asked Mr. Satterthwaite.

A. Christie, *Three Act Tragedy*, p. 47.

The shadow of Flora fell on Rosamund.
'I've been sent,' she said, 'to fetch you. It's bedtime. I believe you are sleeping at the Yams.'

R. Macaulay, *Orphan Island*, Tauchnitz ed., p. 126.

'I'm not coming to this service,' William said to Charles and Rosamund. 'I shall catch crabs and filefish in the pools.'

Ibid., p. 259.

We have the same anticipatory meaning in *Coming!* — said in reply to a summons even when we are not yet on our way. Cf. *I'm just coming*, and similar examples in Palmer, *op. cit.*, § 621.

1. The difference between the examples of the use of the progressive (*I'm leaving*, *I'm not coming*) and those of the construction with *shall* (*I shall sell this place*, *I shall clear out*, *I shall catch crabs*) seems to be that, whereas in the former the future is represented as connected with the present in the speaker's mind, in the latter the future is thought of as such. *I'm not coming to this service* expresses the speaker's determination *now*; *I shall catch crabs* denotes what he will do an hour hence.

2. The fact that the progressive form of the present tense may express the speaker's determination now is well illustrated by such sentences as *I'm not paying a pound for an article that is worth no more than ten shillings*; *I am not accepting any excuses*; *I am not letting him get away with that story.*[2] But

[1] Palmer, *op. cit.*, § 303.

[2] i.e. tell it with impunity.

C*

it is not always determination that is expressed, as witness such sentences as *I am having my holidays in July this year*; *I am going up to London next week*; *I am sitting for my matriculation examination in June*. These all show a present arrangement about the future which has been made either by the speaker himself or by some one else with his agreement or acquiescence.

96. The progressive of *to go* may be followed by the infinitive of almost any other verb to denote a near future or an intention.

I'm going to see him to-morrow.[1]
He said he was not going to let others reap the benefit of what he had done.
It's going to rain.

97. The present participle is also used predicatively with a number of intransitive verbs denoting motion or the reverse, viz. *to come*, *to go (out)*, *to lie*, *to sit*, *to stand*.

The ships came sailing into the harbour.
Menelaus went looking for Helen.[2]
The two men went out fishing.
He lay meditating on the problem.
Sophia sat waiting on the sofa.[2]
Don't stand there arguing (COD).

After *to go* (*out*) the present participle does not, as after the other verbs, denote an action simultaneous with that of the finite verb; like some of the participles of 95, it expresses purpose.

98. As was said in 88, we have to do with a progressive only when *to be* + present participle together form the verbal predicate of the sentence. This rules out (*a*) cases where the predicative form in *ing* is purely adjectival in meaning (63); note especially those followed by *of*; (*b*) cases where the two are not closely connected, the present participle functioning as an adjunct.

a. He is deserving (= worthy) of praise.
Be sparing (= economical) of your epithets.
b. The door opened, and there was his mother waiting for him.
The train was ten minutes late leaving that station. (Cf. 104.)
He saw high elms behind the hedges, and vaguely thought how happy[3] boys would be climbing there. (G. K. Chesterton, *The Man Who Was Thursday*, Ch. XIV.)

Note that in the examples under *b* there is often a slight break before the participle.

---

[1] Palmer, *op. cit.*, § 303.
[2] Kruisinga, *Handbook*[5], § 84.
[3] Strong stress and rising intonation.

Verbal Forms in *ing* not derived from Verb Stems

99. A number of verbal forms in *ing* are not derived from verb stems, but from nouns, interjections, or words denoting sounds. Some of them are nonce-words, i.e. spontaneous creations by a speaker or writer, coined for the occasion. Now and then such a form in *ing* may give rise to other verbal formations, such as an infinitive, a present or a past tense, but this is exceptional. Cf. 802.

In the following examples both the gerund and the present participle are represented.

> As boys they used to go nutting and bird's-nesting together.
> What's the use of all this oh-ing and dear-dearing?

Then we heard the voice of Mrs. Mardick *sergeant-majoring* the truant few who were enjoying the first breath of cool air instead of dressing up.
E. A. Robertson, *Four Frightened People*, Ch. II.

We sank in over the knees, when the boughs to which we clung bent under the sudden weight; and the ooze bubbled up on each side, opening a million tiny stinking mouths as gas bubbles rose with a soft '*plup-plup*'*-ing* from disturbed matter decomposing below. *Ibid.*, Ch. V.

The action, moreover, of these later scenes is exceptionally dependent upon *to-ings and fro-ings.*[1]
Granville-Barker, *Prefaces to Shakespeare*, 1st Series, p. 154.

Gerund or Present Participle?

100. As the distinction between present participle and gerund is made on the basis of function, not on that of outward form, there are cases where it may offer some difficulty.

In some of these the difficulty is only apparent. Thus in *a dancing doll* (= doll that dances) or *a running man* (= a man who runs) we have to do with present participles, in *a dancing-master*[2] (= a teacher of dancing) or *a running competition* (= a competition in running) with gerunds. That the distinction is a real one is also proved by the difference in stress and intonation. In *a dancing doll* the participle and the noun have even stress; the participle is

[1] i.e. a continual going to and fro.
[2] On the use of the hyphen see 831.

pronounced on a high level tone, the noun on a falling tone. In *a dancing-master* the noun has weaker stress than the gerund; the group of gerund plus noun is pronounced on a falling tone. Cf. also, for instance, *growing children* with *growing pains* 'neuralgic pains in limbs of the young' (COD).

101. Instances of the construction discussed in 73 (stem of noun or indefinite pronoun, or object form of personal pronoun, plus gerund) may at first sight be sometimes hard to distinguish from constructions with a present participle as a predicative adjunct (77) or in a semi-predicative function (81). A moment's reflection, however, will usually show whether one has to do with a present participle or a gerund. If we compare *I can't understand a clergyman going to a cinema* with *She was surprised to see a clergyman going to a cinema*, or with *The letter was found by a clergyman going to a cinema*, it will be clear that, while *going* in the second example is equivalent to *go* (77), in the third example to *who was going* (81), no such substitution is possible in the first example, though in literary English *a clergyman's* might be substituted for *a clergyman*.

Again, if *I hate any one listening when I'm telephoning* is compared with *I hate being disturbed when I'm telephoning*, it will be seen that *listening* (like *being*) is a case of the gerund after *to hate* (68), with the stem of an indefinite pronoun for its subject (73).

102. Another type of ambiguity, hinted at in 73, is illustrated by the following quotations and resolved by the last two of them.

It may be a mystery; it may be as simple as bread and cheese. *The body not being robbed* looks interesting, but . . .
E. C. Bentley, *Trent's Last Case*, Penguin ed., p. 23.

The car stopping gave me a bit of a jar — in both senses . . .
G. D. H. & M. I. Cole, *The Murder at Crome House*, Penguin ed., p. 218.

Strangers overhearing us matter**s** nothing. They assume that we are joking. But what would matter, even unto death, is this, that . . .
G. K. Chesterton, *The Man Who Was Thursday*, Ch. VI.

In turn she was anxious about him, and *two people worrying about each other*, with little or no external diversion, brew**s** a deadly atmosphere.
E. F. Benson, *Charlotte Brontë*, p. 260.

103. Cases like those discussed in 73 may be compared with the (accusative with) infinitive construction after *to want*, *to wish*, *to like*, *to hate* (40, 41).

Infinitive:

	One Subject:		Two Subjects:
A.	I want to stop.	B.	I want you to stop.
	I wish to stay.		I wish mother to stay.
	I like to be quiet.		I like boys to be quiet.
	I hate to talk of it.		I hate people to talk of it.

Gerund:

C.	I don't mind going.	D.	I don't mind you[1] going.
	I remember reading the poem.		I remember mother reading the poem.
	I don't like looking ridiculous.		I don't like boys looking ridiculous.
	I hate losing my temper.		I hate people losing their tempers.

It will be clear that A is to B as C is to D. If the addition of another 'subject' (*you*, etc.) to A does not prevent the group *to* + verb stem (*to stop*, etc.) in B from being called an infinitive, there is no reason why the similar addition of a 'subject' to C should prevent the form in *ing* in D being called a gerund.

104. That the distinction between present participle and gerund may be a valuable help in the analysis of certain constructions may be seen from the discussion of the sentence *You must find it rather dull living here all by yourself* in *English Studies* XXV (1943), 15–16, 80–81 and 109. (Cf. 408*d*.)

On the other hand, there is no denying that there are cases where the distinction is not, perhaps, impossible, but where a decision either way is at any rate not wholly convincing. It is, no doubt, justifiable to call the verbal forms in *ing* present participles[2]

---

[1] Or *your*; but in that case there is, of course, no need to explain that *going* is a gerund.

[2] Compare, though, Sweet's uncertainty in dealing with such constructions in his *Syntax*, §§ 2333, 2334, and, indeed, in his whole discussion of what he calls 'half-gerunds'.

in *They were busy packing*, *She spent the afternoon writing letters*, *He tears his coat climbing trees*; but one gradually becomes less sure when considering examples like the following:

For recreation they amused themselves *translating* together the Greek Anthology into Latin verse.

Ch. Hollis, *Sir Thomas More*, p. 18.

They have some difficulty *getting* all the employers, especially the smaller ones, to conform to the adopted scale of wages.

J. B. Priestley, *English Journey*, Tauchnitz ed., p. 241.

The lock of the door had been broken for some time and there was no point *executing* repairs on a house where no one lived.

A. Gilbert, *The Man who was too Clever*, p. 209.

In the last quotation, *there was no point executing repairs* is to all intents and purposes equivalent to the commoner *there was no point in executing repairs*; and it seems a little futile to call the form in *ing* by a different name in either case. Similarly in *He wasn't long* (*in*) *making up his mind*, *I lost no time* (*in*) *talking*. While, of course, we have gerunds in the sentences with prepositions, it is perhaps better to denote the *ing*-forms without prepositions merely as adjuncts to verbs or verbal phrases, and to refrain from labelling them any further.

Again, there is little to choose between such combinations as *He went on laughing*, *He kept* (*on*) *laughing*, *He continued laughing*. In the latter two the form in *ing* may be analysed as a gerund because it functions to some extent as an object to the transitive verbs *keep* (*on*) and *continue*. *To go on*, on the other hand, as an intransitive verb cannot take an object; yet the affinity of *He went on laughing* with the other combinations is obvious. In such cases the difficulty of the distinction is in inverse proportion to its relevance or reality.

105. Some of the difficulties dealt with above are caused by the fact that, though in the majority of cases verbal forms in *ing* naturally fall into one of two clearly marked categories, their formal identity has favoured the development of certain uses that do not easily fit into either. These uses are not sharply differentiated from either the present participle or the gerund, but pass into them by almost imperceptible gradations. They are among the most interesting features of the English verbal system, but in no way invalidate the traditional classification,[1] which is based on the recognition of a distinction inherent in the language itself and evident to any one going beyond the surface criterion of outward form.

---

[1] Cf. the following remark, apropos of another grammatical distinction, in Kruisinga and Erades, *An English Grammar*, I, i, 7th ed., p. 28 (6th ed., p. 17): 'It is not always possible to distinguish rigidly between prepositional objects and prepositional adjuncts, nor is this necessary. . . . There is no reason for the student to be distressed or even surprised at this; he should realize that making distinctions necessarily entails creating doubtful cases and that speech, like life of which it is a function, cannot be cut up into small fragments, each fitting into its own special pigeon-hole.'

CHAPTER THREE

PAST PARTICIPLE — PASSIVE VOICE

106. The merits and demerits of the terms PAST and PERFECT PARTICIPLE have been discussed in 75.

As the present participle is identical in form with the gerund, so the past participle of all regular and some irregular verbs is identical with the past tense (or preterite), and is to be distinguished from it by its function in the sentence.

Like certain quasi-participial forms in *ing* (*amusing*, *charming*, etc.), some past participles may be purely adjectival in meaning. Such are *distinguished* (*a distinguished* [= eminent, famous] *guest*), *fixed* or *set* (*a fixed* or *set* [= steady] *stare*), *pleased* (*I am very*[1] *pleased* [= glad] *to meet you*), *surprised* (*I was surprised to hear it*), *tired* (*my tired* [= weary] *limbs*), etc. Like the *ing*-forms, these words may also, of course, occur as real participles: *he had distinguished himself by great gallantry*, etc.

107. In attributive use the past participle of a transitive English verb usually corresponds to a past participle in other languages. The meaning is usually (*a*), though not always (*b*), passive; i.e. the person or thing denoted by the noun has usually undergone the action expressed by the participle.

a. As far as the eye could reach nothing was to be seen except the blackened ruins of deserted villages.

b. A well-read clergyman; a smooth-spoken rascal; an outspoken critic. The notion of an unread Shakespeare (i.e. that Sh. was not a man of wide reading) is still widely prevalent in England.

E. M. W. Tillyard, *Shakespeare's Problem Plays*, p. 41.

108. The attributive use of the past participles of intransitive verbs is mainly limited to some of the so-called mutative verbs, i.e. those denoting a passing from one place or state to another.[2] The

[1] Note the use of *very*, which is not used before words with clearly verbal meaning.

[2] Cf. Poutsma, *Grammar*, II, Ch. XLV, § 16*b* and Ch. LVII, § 31. Also Kruisinga, *Handbook*[5], §§ 44, 45, 47.

meaning is naturally active; i.e. the person or thing denoted by the noun has performed the action[1] expressed by the participle.

The abode of the fallen angels.
The returned prodigal was received with icy indifference.
The birds saluted the risen sun.

Other examples are: *the abdicated Emperor of Austria*; *the newly arrived* (not: the arrived) *visitors*; *his deceased* (= *dead*) *partner*; *the departed guests*; *an escaped convict*; *the exploded bomb*; *a faded colour*; *a retired business-man*; *the vanished* (not: the disappeared) *jewels.* Some are less clearly mutative, though they do imply motion: *the assembled company*; *a travelled man.*

109. In predicative use the past participle of a transitive verb may express the state or condition resulting from the action indicated by the verb. The verb connecting the participle with its subject is usually *to be* (*a*), but may also be one of the verbs *to appear*, *to feel*, *to lie*, *to look*, *to remain*, *to seem* (*b*).

a. The village was quite deserted.
None of his poems are preserved.
I am glad those letters are written at last.
b. The village appeared (lay, looked, seemed) quite deserted.
He felt thoroughly disappointed.
The door remained locked.

1. Note the use of *to stand* in expressions like *I stand* (= am) *prepared to dispute it* (COD), *I stand corrected* (= accept correction), *he stood convicted* (was found guilty) *of robbery*. The first of these is rather an instance of 106 n. (*prepared* = ready).

2. Under *do* v. t. & i. COD gives: '(p. p. & perf.) complete, bring to an end, (*it is, I have, done*)'; but with a personal subject we may also find a form of *to be*: . . . *a man who seems certain* (26, 3rd par.) *to make a great deal of history before he is done* (*Times Literary Supplement*, Oct. 31, 1952, p. 703).

3. Note the use of *to come* with a past participial adjective in *un-* to denote an undesirable condition: *My shoe laces have come undone* (= *loose*). (A. S. Hornby, *A Guide to Patterns and Usage in English*, p. 122.)

110. In the examples of 109 the past participles, though implying action, chiefly denote resultant CONDITION. Some of them are almost equivalent to predicative adjectives (*deserted* = *empty*; *preserved* = *extant* [eks'tænt]).

When the idea of ACTION predominates, the group *to be* +

[1] See p. 58, n. 1.

past participle forms the category of the PASSIVE VOICE, which will be dealt with in 117 ff.

His letters were written by a secretary.

On the difference between a past participle expressing action and one expressing condition, see also 113.1.

111. The predicative use of past participles of intransitive verbs is not very common in English, *to have* + past participle being usually preferred.

You cannot eat that jelly; it is (has) not nearly set yet.
The moon was (had) set and it was very dark.

COD s.v. *spring*[1], v. i. & t.*: (t. & i. of wood) split, crack, as *bat* is* or *has sprung, have sprung my racket.*

Gone is frequently used predicatively in the senses of *dead*, *tired*, or *lost*. In the former two senses *to have* cannot be substituted; in the last, substitution of *to have* affects the meaning of the participle.

My grandfather has been dead and gone [ˈdednˈgɔn] these twenty years.
The horse was too far gone to be able to gallop.
His money was gone and his health broken (109).

But:

I was told that Tom had gone to America.

In semi-predicative use (without an auxiliary) participles of mutative verbs occur more frequently. Thus a writer on English ballads in a discussion of the folk tradition lying behind them, speaks of 'a mythology once quite coherent but *become* fragmentary through the passage of time'. (M. J. C. Hodgart, *The Ballads*, 1950, p. 35.)

112. The past participles of transitive verbs may be used as predicative adjuncts (cf. 592) to the objects of verbs like *to see*, *to hear*, *to feel*; *to find*, *to get*, *to make*; *to like*, *to want*, *to wish*, *to order*. The construction may be denoted as ACCUSATIVE WITH PAST PARTICIPLE.

He had seen villages evacuated, bridges blown up and railways destroyed.
I will see her avenged.
He heard his name called.
He felt his eyes dazzled by a blaze of light.[1]
He was greatly surprised to find himself elected president.

---

* i.e. verb intransitive and transitive. *Bat* = cricket-bat.

[1] OED s.v. *Feel* v. 9b.

We must get the laws obeyed.[1]
He got his wrist dislocated.[1]
By sheer force of personality he succeeded in making himself obeyed.
The queen said she wished the performance stopped.

The reservation made in 77 applies to the above examples of the accusative with past participle as well. After *to find* we may again have to do with a real predicative adjunct: *He found the house deserted.*

1. Unlike the accusative with infinitive and the accusative with present participle, the accusative with past participle has no passive counterpart; there is no parallel with a past participle to *He was seen to fall* and *He was seen falling*. That there *is* such a parallel after *to leave* (*to leave no stone unturned* = to try every possible means; *no stone was left unturned*) is probably because we have to do with a real object here. Cf. also: *He was reported killed*; *the ship must be considered lost.*

2. After *to like, to want, to wish,* and *to order*, the ACCUSATIVE WITH PASSIVE INFINITIVE (45) also occurs. The shorter construction is usual after *to want*: *I want it done at once*, which sounds more peremptory than the construction with *to be* (*done*). A similar distinction may often be observed in the case of *to wish* and *to like*; cf. *I don't like such subjects discussed* (COD), and *I should like this subject to be discussed at our next meeting.* After *to order*, the shorter construction seems to occur chiefly in American English, where it may even occur with the finite verb in the passive (cf. n. 1): *He would not recant and was ordered banished from the lands of Massachusetts.*

Note that in all the examples of 112 (as in those of 109) the past participle expresses a RESULT. This explains its use after *to want* and verbs of similar meaning, where the execution of the wish expressed is regarded as a matter of course.

113. Special attention should be paid to the use of the accusative with past participle after *to have* expressing causation. As in the examples of 112, the person performing the action denoted by the participle is either not mentioned, or indicated by an adjunct with *by* (cf. 45).

I had the house painted inside and out.
If he won't behave, I'll have him locked up by the police.

The same construction is used after *to have* in the sense of *to experience, to suffer.*

He had his licence taken away for reckless driving.
You'll have your house broken into one of these days.

---

[1] COD s.v. *get*[1]. Cf. 124.

1. The difference between a past participle expressing action (as in the above examples) and one expressing condition (as in 109) is well brought out by the following quotation:

Thoughtful people are puzzled by the appearance life presents to them. Their hour-to-hour experiences do not satisfy them and are felt to convey a false impression. The impression is both *impoverished* and *unordered,* and they wish to have it *enlarged* and *interpreted.*

E. M. W. Tillyard, *Shakespeare's Problem Plays*, p. 27.

We might apply the distinction of 89.2 to the participles in the last sentence, and say that, in this context, *impoverished* and *unordered* are 'static', *enlarged* and *interpreted* 'dynamic'.

The construction also occurs with *to have* in the sense of *to hold, to possess*, and in the sense of *to get.*

The Romans had the Persian army virtually surrounded.
That's where he has you beat.
I have my paper all written.
The operation may be expensive, and I have no money saved.
I always have (get) him clean-bowled first ball.

When the object follows the past participle, we usually have the category of the (plu)perfect tense, which will be dealt with in **140** f.

He had saved a little money.

2. Note the neutral meaning of *to have* in a sentence like the following: *It was the quiet time of day—the top of the bus had very few seats occupied.* (Agatha Christie, *Cards on the Table*, Pan Books, p. 96.)

114. Like the present participle (81), the past participle may follow the noun or pronoun it qualifies. In this case it is used in semi-predicative function, and usually equivalent to an attributive clause.

Do you happen to know the number of men (those[1]) killed?

For more examples see 703.

115. Like the present participle (82), the past participle of transitive and a few intransitive (108) verbs may be used in free adjuncts.

Worn out by hunger and fatigue the fugitives at last reached the coast.
Arrived at the station, he found his train gone.

Granted may be used as an unrelated participle (cf. 86):

Granted that he did say so . . . (Wyld).

116. Like the present participle (86), the past participle of a transitive verb may be used in the absolute participle construction.

---

[1] Cf. 422.

All things considered, it is not such a bad bargain.
This done, he locked his door and went to bed.

For more examples see Kruisinga, *Handbook*[5], § 61.

On absolute participle adjuncts introduced by *with*, see 614.

Passive Voice

117. As was indicated in 110, a verbal group consisting of one of the forms of *to be* plus the past participle of a transitive verb may denote an action undergone by the subject of the sentence. The construction is known as the PASSIVE VOICE,[1] or simply as the PASSIVE. It is especially used in sentences in which it is unnecessary or undesirable to mention the agent,[2] though the agent may be expressed by means of an adjunct with *by*. The verbal meaning of the group may also be brought out by adjuncts expressing other adverbial relations, such as time, manner, cause or instrument.

My car has been requisitioned.
William the Silent was proclaimed a traitor by Alva.
Further details will be announced to-morrow.
Sugar is sold by the pound.
(Cf. Sugar is sold out (109).)

1. In cases where 'an action undergone by the subject' seems a somewhat forced definition, the passive may be said to express what 'happens' to the subject. Cf.:

Several men were drowned; their bodies were washed ashore.

2. On passive sentences introduced by *There* see 684.

118. The passive is used of a number of verbs which, while being primarily intransitive, may be used as causatives. Some of the commonest are *to fly*, *to run*, *to stand*, *to walk*. Cf. 584.2.

How many persons have been flown to New Zealand this year?
Cheap trains will be run on Sundays.
This bottle must not be stood close to the fire.
Horses should be walked for some time after a race.

119. The predicate of a passive sentence may consist of a form of *to be* + a past participle (whether of a transitive or an intransitive verb) followed by a preposition, if participle and preposition are

---

[1] Latin: *vox passiva*. Opposite: active voice.
[2] i.e. the person or thing that performs or causes the action.

so closely associated as practically to form a unit (or, in other words, as to be equivalent to a transitive participle). Some of the commonest groups of this type are *to be cared for* (= tended),[1] *to be come to* (= reached), *to be laughed at* (= ridiculed), *to be listened to* (= heard), *to be looked upon* (= regarded), *to be relied on* (= trusted), *to be sent for* (= called), *to be talked of* (= discussed), *to be thought of* (= considered). The stress is on the participle.

> Has any decision been come to?
> He could always be relied on to pull his weight.
> A doctor must be sent for at once.
> His mysterious death was talked of for years afterwards.
> Rescue was not to be thought of.

Compare: *They had come to a decision*; *We sent for a doctor*; *People talked of his mysterious death.*

The construction is also found with a few intransitive verbs accompanied by a local preposition, even though, in the corresponding active sentences at any rate, the preposition is less closely associated with the verb.

> My new hat has been sat on.
> The bed had not been slept in.

Compare: *Someone has sat on my new hat*; *Nobody had slept in the bed.*

120. The predicate of a passive sentence may also consist of a form of *to be* + past participle followed by a noun plus a preposition so long as this group can be regarded as a unit (or, in other words, as equivalent to a single transitive participle). Some of the commonest groups of this type are *to be taken advantage of* (= utilized), *to be paid attention to* (= heeded), *to be taken care of* (= tended), *to be found fault with* (= criticized), *to be set fire to* (= ignited), *to be made fun of* (= ridiculed), *to be lost sight of* (= overlooked), *to be put a stop to* (= stopped). The stress is on the noun. Similarly: *to be got rid of* (= removed).

> His weakness was taken undue advantage of.
> They promised us that the child should be taken care of.
> The rick had been set fire to (= set on fire) by a tramp.

---

[1] It is not suggested that the equivalents given are in every respect identical in meaning and range with the prepositional groups.

He could not bear being made fun of.
Some things had been lost sight of.[1]
This silly business must be put a stop to.
The troublesome customer was quietly got rid of.

Compare: *They took undue advantage of his weakness*; *You must put a stop to this silly business.*

With some of these groups an alternative passive construction occurs, with the noun as subject: *Undue advantage was taken of his weakness*; *Little attention was paid to this warning*; *No fault was found with my suggestions.* The alternative construction is found especially (but not exclusively) when the noun is preceded by a qualifying word.

121. On comparing the examples of 117–120 with the corresponding active sentences, it will be found that the subjects of the passive constructions correspond to the (direct or prepositional) objects[2] of the active constructions.

HE was ridiculed (laughed at, made fun of).	They ridiculed (laughed at, made fun of) HIM.

The subject of a passive sentence may also correspond to the INDIRECT object of the active sentence. In this case we may speak of the INDIRECT PASSIVE.

I have been offered a mastership at Rugby.
(Cf.: They have offered ME a mastership at Rugby.)
SHE was furious at being denied admittance.
(Cf.: They denied HER admittance.)
You will be given twenty-four hours to consider your decision.
The boy was found employment in a newspaper office.
We have been saved (spared) a great deal of trouble.

The direct object in sentences with an indirect passive (*a mastership*, *admittance*, etc.) is known as the RETAINED OBJECT.

122. In the active sentences corresponding to sentences with an indirect passive the indirect object usually denotes a person, the direct object a thing.

When it is desired to predicate something about the latter, a

---

[1] Poutsma, *Grammar*, II, Ch. XLVII, § 26; quoted from Galsworthy, *Forsyte Saga*, II, iv, 159. Compare, on p. 160 of the novel: 'And further . . . it was not generally recognised by Forsytes that . . .'

[2] In the last examples of 119, *my new hat* and *the bed* are rather (parts of) prepositional ADJUNCTS (cf. 105, note, and 595).

passive construction may be used with the subject corresponding to the DIRECT object. In that case the (pro)noun denoting the person is usually preceded by *to* when more or less emphatic; American English, however, frequently dispenses with the preposition (cf. 596).

The mastership was offered to Mr. Jenkins.
It was given him on condition that he would take up his duties immediately.
It was an honor never before accorded a woman.[1]

1. Alternative passive constructions may also occur with verbs taking two direct objects. Compare the following quotation:

The last three questions I was asked were: 'Do you play football?' 'Which game?'[2] 'Any good at it?' The answers to the first two were easy, but the last was a poser. *It was asked me* by the inquisitor sitting immediately on my right.

E. Hamblock, *British Consul*, London 1938, p. 25.

2. It should be noted that in English no sentence or clause, whether active or passive, ever begins with a (non-prepositional) indirect object. If the latter is given front-position, it is preceded by *to*: *To Mary Queen the praise be given.*[3]

123. The non-finite forms of the passive (*to be seen*, *being seen*, etc.) have been illustrated in the preceding chapters. Note especially the use of the passive infinitive after *to be* (33):

Such men are to be pitied.
The porter was nowhere to be found.

It remains to point out that the passive infinitive may vary with the active infinitive as an adjunct to nouns and pronouns, especially after *there is* and *there was*. In spoken English the shorter form would usually be preferred. (Cf. also 34 n.)

There was no time to lose.
There was no time to be lost.
There is a lot of work to do.
There is a lot of work to be done.

Occasionally a difference of meaning between the two constructions

---

[1] See G. Kirchner, 'The Verbs with Direct and Indirect Object Reexamined', *English Studies* XVIII (1936), 1 ff. — Strictly speaking this example belongs under 114; it may, however, easily be converted into a passive voice proper: *This hono(u)r had never been accorded a woman.*
[2] i.e. Association ('soccer' [ˈsɔkə]) or Rugby.
[3] Coleridge, *The Rime of the Ancient Mariner.*

may be observed. Thus *There was nothing to see* means virtually 'nothing worth seeing', whereas *There was nothing to be seen* means either 'nothing there at all', or 'nothing visible' (owing, e.g., to fog).

The passive only is used in:

There is nothing to be had here.[1]

---

124. Besides *to be, to get* may occur as an auxiliary of the passive. It expresses the getting into a state or situation denoted by the participle; in other words, it has a mutative meaning, which distinguishes it from the ordinary passive. (Cf. 112.)

Another of our new cups got broken last night.
One of his fingers got squeezed in the door.
It's time he got married.

In the last example, there is really no question of any one undergoing an action; *got married* is practically equivalent to the intransitive *married.*

125. *To become,* which usually takes a complement expressing a state or condition the subject passes into (*He became famous, they had become acquainted in Boston*), is occasionally followed by a past participle denoting action, and may then be said to be a kind of auxiliary of the passive. (Cf. 109.)

The whole world is rapidly becoming Americanized.[2] (Cf. 117.1.)

The difference between *to get* and *to become* as auxiliaries of the passive may be expressed by the terms 'perfective' and 'durative' (cf. 78).

---

[1] OED s.v. *Have* v. 14.

[2] J. B. Priestley, quoted by H. T. Svartengren in an article in *Moderna Språk*, Dec. 1948.

CHAPTER FOUR

PRESENT, PAST, AND PERFECT TENSES

126. English grammatical terminology has a special word, TENSE, to denote two verbal forms (past and present) and an equal number of verbal groups (perfect and future) whose main function it is to denote the TIME at which an action[1] takes place. Three of the tenses (past, present and future) are named after the time-sphere usually indicated by them. The so-called perfect tense is mostly a special case of the present.

The future tense will be dealt with in **185** ff.

127. For the form(s) of the present tense, see **2**, **4**, **6–8** and Appendix; for those of the past tense **5**, **9**, **10**, **11** and Appendix. On the perfect tense see the last paragraph of **113**.

128. The use of the simple PRESENT TENSE in English is more restricted than in other languages. For one thing, actual duration, which may be implicit in the simple tense-form in other languages, is expressed by the progressive in English (**88** ff.).

129. In the second place, though in many languages the simple present tense may be used with reference to future time, this use is less common in English, where it is limited to cases in which a future action is considered as part of a programme already fixed.[2] It is hardly possible to give a complete list of the verbs used in this way, though the future-present is especially common with those which denote a coming or leaving.[3] Sentences of this kind usually contain an adverb or adjunct expressing future time.

---

[1] As elsewhere in this book, 'action' is used to denote whatever may be expressed by the verb. Cf. OED s.v. *Action*, 1d.

[2] Palmer, *A Grammar of Spoken English*, § 288*e*.

[3] Poutsma, *Grammar*, II, Ch. L, § 83.

We start to-morrow.
He comes back next week.
The train leaves at 6.30.
We dine at the Joneses' to-night.
Classes don't begin until Monday morning.

But:

I'll (= I will) come again next Friday (188).
All leave will be cancelled to-morrow.

Note the use of the present tense when asking for instructions:

What do I do next? Stand, or sit down?
Where do we go now?

130. Thirdly, to denote an action or a state beginning at some time in the past and continuing up to the moment of speaking, English requires the perfect tense (known in this function as the CONTINUATIVE PERFECT; see 140).

We've known each other for years.
I've been living here since 1928.
How long has he been unconscious?

131. The uses of the simple present tense that English shares with other languages (apart from that described in 129) may be roughly distinguished as the NEUTRAL, the ITERATIVE, and the ACTUAL PRESENT.

The NEUTRAL PRESENT is used when no particular time is thought of; hence (but not exclusively) in general statements.

The Thames rises in Gloucestershire [ˈglɔstəʃ(i)ə].
Dogs make better pets than cats.
Do you sing? — A little.
It says in the Bible that we should bear one another's burdens.

132. The ITERATIVE PRESENT refers to an action repeated at intervals, the repetition being usually denoted by an adjunct like *every day*, *twice weekly*, *always . . . in summer*, etc. Like the neutral present, it is often used in general statements.

I get up at six every day.
This paper appears twice weekly.
We always go to the seaside in summer.

133. The ACTUAL PRESENT denotes an action[1] occurring at the moment of speaking or writing. In English the simple actual present is limited to those cases that do not require the progressive.

[1] Cf. p. 58, n. 1.

I see an aeroplane.
The headmaster wants to speak to you.
Guess what I have in my pocket.
It is very cold.

What is known as the HISTORIC OR DRAMATIC PRESENT is sometimes used in vivid narrative of past events. Cf. 735.

He enters the room, seizes the burning object, and flings it out of the window. The next moment . . .
'No,' he says, 'I don't think I can help you.'

134. The present tense is used in subordinate clauses dependent on a main clause expressing or implying future time.

We shall go as soon as you are ready.
Don't get off the tram till it stops.
Let's go to a café when the concert is over.

135. There is a good deal of difference between the distribution of the PAST and PERFECT TENSES in English and other languages, the perfect tense being often used in other languages where the past tense (or PRETERITE) is required in English. This is the case when attention is drawn to the time at which an action or event took place in the past; hence especially in questions beginning with *when?* (sometimes with *where?*), and in sentences with adverbial adjuncts answering such questions.

When (where) did you see him last?
(Cf. Where have you been all the time? (130).)
Twenty aeroplanes were shot down yesterday.
I received his letter a week ago.
My father was born in Ireland.
Did you come by tram or by bus?

1. The exclusion of the perfect tense from the past time sphere does not apply to the perfect infinitive:

Twenty planes are said to have been shot down yesterday.

2. In subordinate clauses English sometimes uses a preterite where other languages would use a pluperfect. Thus in the following quotation from the *Daily Telegraph*, May 2, 1952: 'For the second time in three months Oxford City Police are investigating the disappearance of a young woman *who hired a horse* from a local riding stables.' (cf. 341) — the italicized words would be rendered in Dutch, for instance, by *die een paard had gehuurd.*

136. The PAST TENSE may be used with ITERATIVE meaning (cf. 132).

We always went to a pantomime at Christmas.
Whenever he went abroad, he took his son with him.

On the use of the past tense to report a present tense in indirect speech see 769.

137. The preterite may be used in subordinate clauses to express something desirable or conceivable. In this case its function is not to express a contrast between past and present time (so that the term 'past tense' is better avoided), but between reality and desirability or mere supposition. This is usually called the MODAL[1] PRETERITE.

> It's high time somebody held his tongue.
> I'd rather you paid me now.
> Suppose we went to a show.

138. The modal preterite is frequently used after *I wish* expressing 'an unrealized or unrealizable desire' (OED), and after *if*, *as if* (also, in literary English, *as though*), in clauses denoting a condition not likely to be fulfilled, or a state of things contrary to reality. In these cases the subjunctive[2] (*I* or *he*) *were* is often used instead of *was* (cf. 219).

> I wish I knew the fellow's name.
> If I were you, I should go and tell him.
> He acts as if he owned the place.
> It isn't as if she did not know him.

139. Except in the cases discussed in 153, 160 and 182, English does not use the modal preterite in head-clauses, *should* and *would* with a plain infinitive being used instead.

> If I got the chance, I should go to South Africa.
> If you had not helped them they would still be in London.

140. The PERFECT TENSE usually denotes an action that falls within the time-sphere of the present. Its uses are mainly three: (*a*) the CONTINUATIVE PERFECT; (*b*) the RESULTATIVE PERFECT; (*c*) the PERFECT OF EXPERIENCE. All three occur with transitive verbs (113) as well as with intransitive (111).

The continuative perfect has been described in 130. It often corresponds to a present tense in other languages.

English shares with other languages the use of the RESULTATIVE PERFECT, which denotes a past action connected, through its result, with the present moment.

> I've bought a new car.
> (Cf. I bought a new car last week (135).)

---

[1] On the meaning of 'modal', see 222.

[2] See 214 ff.

Look what you've done.
(Cf. Remember what you promised Jack.)
Twenty years have passed since we first met.

1. We have a use intermediate between the continuative and the resultative perfect when the reference is to a period of time that is not yet over.

I've been to the pictures twice this week.
(But: I went to the pictures twice last week (135).)

2. To indicate completed activities in the immediate past the perfect tense with the adverb *just* may be used:[1]

George has just gone out.
It has just struck twelve.

3. In spoken English *I've got* is often equivalent to *I have*: *Guess what I've got in my pocket* (cf. 133). In a sentence like *He's got* (= obtained) *what he wants,* however, we have to do with a resultative perfect.

4. Cf. the following sentences from *Flowering Wilderness* by John Galsworthy (Tauchnitz ed., p. 274): *Wilfred has gone* (111, 140). *He went this morning* (135). *He is not coming back* (95).

141. The PERFECT OF EXPERIENCE expresses what has happened, once or more than once, within the speaker's or writer's experience. It is not unknown in other languages, at least in head-clauses, though an adjunct expressing repetition is usually added. Similar adjuncts may be added in English.[2]

I have sat for hours on the river bank on a fine summer's day, waiting for a fish to bite.
When I have asked a London policeman the way, I have invariably received a polite answer.
Men's hairs have grown grey in a single night.
We have caught shotten fish one night, and the next they have been full of spawn. (OED s.v. *Shotten* 3.)

142. Like the present tense (134) the perfect may be used in subordinate clauses dependent on a main clause expressing or implying future time.

Wait till I've finished my coffee.
As soon as I have saved £20,000 I shall retire from business.

143. The PLUPERFECT (*had* + perfect participle) answers partly to the past tense, partly to the perfect. It may be said to represent a shifting back of these tenses into the (more distant) past.

---

[1] See A. S. Hornby, *A Guide to Patterns and Usage in English*, p. 98.
[2] For further information see *English Studies* XIV (1932), 11–20; also R. W. Zandvoort, *Collected Papers* (1954), 106–121.

144. In the following examples the pluperfect represents a past tense (or preterite) shifted back.

I was told that twenty aeroplanes had been shot down the day before (135).
They had always been to a pantomime at Christmas (136).
He wished he had known the fellow's name (138).

In a conditional clause the MODAL PLUPERFECT may be used without the conjunction *if*, and with the auxiliary verb at the head of the clause. The construction is mainly literary. Cf. 176.

If I had known you were here, I should have come at once.
Had I known you were here, I should have come at once.

145. In the following examples the pluperfect represents a perfect tense shifted back:

They had known each other for years (130).
I asked her how long the man had been unconscious (130).
She told me she had bought a new hat (140).
They had been to the pictures twice that week (140.1).
The inspector had noticed that when Trent had picked up a strong scent he whistled faintly a certain melodious passage (141).

146. With the verbs *to expect*, *to hope*, *to intend*, *to mean*, *to suppose*, *to think*, *to want*, the pluperfect expresses that the hope, intention, etc. did not materialize.

I had hoped to catch the 8.30, but found it was gone.
She had intended (meant, wanted) to call, but was prevented by a headache.

The same idea may be expressed by a perfect infinitive after the preterite of these verbs: *She intended* (*meant*) *to have called*. Like the preterite in the examples of 137, the perfect infinitive is here used modally. Cf. also 135.2.

The perfect infinitive may also express non-fulfilment in other cases:

We were to have met (32) at ten, but she cancelled the appointment at the last moment.
He was clever enough to have been a doctor.[1]

[1] Kruisinga, *Handbook*[5], § 580.

CHAPTER FIVE

AUXILIARIES

147. The Oxford English Dictionary defines an AUXILIARY as 'a verb used to form the tenses, moods, voices, etc. of other verbs.' It goes on to say:

They include auxiliaries of periphrasis, which assist in expressing the interrogative, negative, and emphatic forms of speech, viz. *do* (*did*); auxiliaries of tense, *have*, *be*, *shall*, *will*; of mood, *may*, *should*, *would*; of voice, *be*; of predication (i.e. vbs. of incomplete predication which require a verbal complement), *can*, *must*, *ought*, *need*, also *shall*, *will*, *may*, when not auxiliaries of tense or mood. (OED s.v. *Auxiliary*, B. *sb*., 3).

Have and *be*[1] as auxiliaries of tense, and *be* as an auxiliary of voice have been treated in the preceding chapters. In the present chapter we shall deal with *can*, *may*, *must*, *shall*, *will* (cf. 6 and 11) in their various meanings and functions; with *have* as an auxiliary of incomplete predication; with *do*; with *need*; and, for reasons which will appear, with *dare*, *ought*, and *used* [ju:st].

1. On the concept of MOOD, see the next chapter; in the quotation from OED it is used in the sense of MODALITY.

2. The opposite of 'auxiliary' is 'notional verb', 'principal verb', or 'verb of full meaning'.

148. In some languages the equivalents of *can*, *may*, *must*, etc. may be used as full predicates, especially in sentences implying some kind of motion, or with the equivalent of *have* understood. English requires a complementary infinitive, or uses a different construction.

I've asked Madge too, but she cannot come.
Must you go out to-night?
May I have the paper for a moment?
It isn't allowed.

---

[1] By *be* as an auxiliary of tense the OED probably means its use as an auxiliary of the Progressive (88 ff.), which is sometimes treated as part of the system of tenses.

The construction occurs in English in the saying *Murder* (or: *truth*) *will out.*

In cases like *I will do what I can* the complementary infinitive (*do*) can be supplied from the head-clause.

Can (*Could*) — *May* (*Might*)

149. *Can* usually expresses power, ability or capacity.

She can (= knows how to) make her own dresses.
We can call for you at nine.
Can you hear what he is saying?
I cannot [kɑːnt] promise anything.

In cases like the following *can* (*be*) expresses what a person or thing is occasionally capable of (mostly something unpleasant[1]):

Children can be very trying.
The English climate can be pretty grim in winter.

150. *Can* sometimes expresses permission. In this case it may be used as what COD calls a 'mild imperative'; also in requests. Note, besides, *cannot* (negative of *may*, 155), to express prohibition.

You can go now.
You can have the book when I have finished it.
Can I have some more bread, please?
You cannot play football in England on Sundays, though you may, of course, on Saturdays.

151. In interrogative and negative sentences corresponding to affirmative sentences with *may* (155), *can* inquires after possibility (*a*), *cannot*[2] expressing impossibility (*b*).

a. Can this be true?
b. It cannot be true.

Emphatic *can* in questions may express puzzlement or impatience:

What *can* he mean?
Where *can* he have got to?

152. *Could* may refer to the past in the meanings defined in 149.

She could (= knew how to) make her own dresses.
It was so dark we could see nothing.
Mary could be pretty trying when a child.

---

[1] Cf. the examples in Kruisinga's *Handbook*[5], § 655. Pleasant qualities are not excluded, however: *She can be charming.*

[2] Note the spelling as one word. In America *can not* is often written as two words (like *may not*, etc.).

In past-time contexts, *could* may report *can* in indirect speech or thought.

He said I could go (150).
Could it be true, she wondered? (151).
What *could* he mean? (*ibid.*).

153. In present-time contexts *could* is frequently used as a modal preterite (137). As such, unlike the modal preterites of verbs of full meaning (139), it may occur in simple sentences and in the head-clauses of compound sentences.

Modal *could* may be used in sentences with a conditional adjunct or clause expressed or understood (*a*); in the sense of 'feel inclined to' (*b*); also in polite requests (*c*).

a. I could come earlier, if necessary.
I could not promise anything (less direct than: I cannot promise anything (149)).
b. I could laugh for joy (COD).
c. Could you lend me a shilling?
Could I have some more bread?

154. With reference to the past, *could have* is used modally.

I could have laughed for joy.
Nobody could have foreseen such a calamity.

As in 146, the perfect infinitive (*have laughed*, *have foreseen*) expresses non-fulfilment.

155. In affirmative sentences, *may* may express possibility (note its use in the definitions of 150, 152, 153, etc.). As stated in 151, *can* is used in the corresponding interrogative and negative sentences.

I may be away from home to-morrow.
He may have been hurt (= Perhaps he was hurt; cf. 135.1).
You may take a horse to the water, but you can't make him drink.

In sentences in which the idea of possibility is mixed with that of uncertainty the negative is expressed by *may not*.

The report may be true.
It may or may not [ˈnɔt] be true.

May is similarly used in questions, with a suggestion of condescension or superiority on the part of the speaker:[1]

And who may *you* be?

---

[1] A. S. Hornby, *A Guide to Patterns and Usage in English*, p. 222.

156. Possibility and uncertainty may also go together in other cases:

The handwriting may be his, but the signature certainly isn't.

The last example implies admission or concession. This is even more clearly the case with a sentence like

Progress may be slow, but it is sure.

In an example like the following *may* expresses what is apt to occur:

You may walk miles without seeing a house (COD).

Note the use of *may* and *might* in *as*-clauses after a subjunctive or infinitive (20): *be that as it may*; *try as he might*.

157. *May* is the usual auxiliary to express permission.

You may come back whenever you like.
May I come and see you?

Note that the negative of *may* in this sense is usually *must not* (164) or *cannot* (150). A light prohibition is expressed by *may not* (*You may not smoke here*). Cf. 163.

May sometimes expresses what is reasonable:

We may expect a good harvest.

158. In exclamatory simple sentences (*a*) and, more frequently, in object clauses (*b*), *may* is used to express a wish.

It also occurs in final clauses (chiefly in literary English) (*c*), and (to express uncertainty) in concessive clauses (*d*).

a. May you live to repent it! (COD).
b. I hope he may succeed.
I will pray that your brother's life may be spared.
c. Leave the book here, (so) that I may read it. (Cf. 633.)
d. Whatever faults he may have had, dullness was not one of them.

159. In past-time contexts, *might* is used in senses corresponding to most of those of *may* discussed above. The case is often one of reported speech or thought.

The handwriting might be his, but the signature certainly was not (156).
Progress might be slow, but it was sure (*ibid.*).
One might walk miles without seeing a house (*ibid.*).
He assured me I might come back whenever I liked (157).
He thought we might expect a good harvest (*ibid.*).
He hoped his boy might succeed (158).
He brought me the book (so) that I might read it (*ibid.*).
He was afraid lest (or: that) his attitude might be misunderstood (*ibid.*).

On *lest* (which is little used in spoken English), cf. 633.

160. In present-time contexts, *might* is used as a modal preterite. It differs from *may* in implying greater reserve on the part of the speaker. Like modal *could*, it may occur in simple sentences and in the head-clauses of compound sentences.

The report might be true, you know (155).
The whole thing might turn out a disappointment.
Might I trouble you for a match? (157; cf. 153 *c*.)
We might ask him to be chairman.

The last example embodies a mere suggestion. *We could ask him to be chairman* (cf. 153*a*), on the other hand, means that the speaker and his associates would be in a position to do so, if they chose.

161. With reference to the past, *might have* is used modally. The perfect infinitive expresses non-fulfilment (154).

It might have been worse.
You might have asked me if I had no objection.

162. As *can* and *may* have no participles and no infinitive, they do not occur in the perfect and future tenses. If necessary, the sense of *can* defined in 149 (first par.) is expressed by the perfect or future tense of *to be able*:

Will he be able to attend the meeting to-morrow?
We have been unable to trace his address.

In the present tense *can* is usually preferred, though *am* (*are*, *is*) *unable* is not uncommon. *Was* (*were*) (*un*)*able* is found rather frequently; it may express the idea of competence or capability more explicitly than *could* (which, besides, is often used modally). Cf. 168.

He concluded that I was able to take care of myself (OED).

163. Permission may similarly be expressed by the indirect passive (121) of *to allow* or *to permit*. The latter are also regularly used in the past tense, as *might* expressing permission is practically restricted to indirect style (159, 4th ex.).

Nobody was allowed to be out after ten.
Shall we be permitted to use a dictionary?

In the present tense *may* is usually preferred, though *am* (*are*, *is*) *not allowed* is not uncommon (cf. 157).

Instead of *to be allowed*, *to be supposed* is sometimes used, chiefly to soften down a prohibition:

We're not supposed to talk in the dormitory (49).

Must — Ought — Should

164. *Must* usually expresses a necessity, frequently a command, sometimes a probability or a conclusion. With *not* it expresses a prohibition.

We must all hang together, or we shall all perish.
You must come earlier to-morrow.
He must be seventy now.
You mustn't [mʌsnt] touch the pictures, Jack (157).

Necessity is less emphasized in the following examples (from COD):

We must [mst] see what can be done.
I must ask you to retract that.
You must know . . . (i.e. I now tell you).

Absence of necessity is expressed by *need not* (206):

You need not come early to-morrow.

165. In past-time contexts (chiefly in reported speech and thought) *must* may be used in the meanings defined in 164.

The situation was highly critical: they must all hang together, or they would all perish.[1]
He told us we must all be ready at nine.

In such contexts *must* may also serve to denote some foolish or annoying action or some untoward [ʌnˈtouəd] event.[2]

At a time when everybody was in bed, he must needs turn on the wireless.
Just as I was getting better, what must I do but break my leg? (COD).

166. As *must* is virtually limited to the present tense, necessity is often expressed by *to have* (*to*) or *to be obliged*, the latter when the idea of compulsion is prominent and with a personal subject.

I had to repeat the message twice before he understood it.
We shall have to hurry up or we shall be late.
The crew were obliged (or: had) to leave the sinking ship.

Both also occur in the present tense; compare, for instance:

He has (got) to be in by ten.[3]

1. Note also the following COD definitions: 'be burdened with, as *I had my work to do*; be obliged, as *I had to do my work*'.

---

[1] 'Reporting reflection made at the time' (COD).
[2] Kruisinga, *Handbook*[5], § 684.
[3] Wyld, *Universal Dictionary*, s.v. *have* 6. — But a direct *command* would be expressed by 'You must be in by ten.'

2. For an example with stressed *had* (and corresponding emphasis on the idea of compulsion) see the 2nd quotation on p. 29.

167. *Ought* and *should* are modal preterites expressing moral obligation or desirability. *Ought* is, as a rule, more emphatic than *should.* With reference to the past, *ought to have* and *should have* are used, the perfect infinitive, as in 154 and 161, expressing non-fulfilment.

> You ought to be ashamed of yourself.
> It ought to have been done long ago (COD).
> I do not see why you should apologize.
> I (you, he) should really have been more careful (COD).

Ought and *should* may also express strong probability.

> Don't you think Eclipse ought to win the Derby ['dɑ:bi]?
> If it's a story by P. G. Wodehouse ['wudhaus], it should be amusing.

1. *Ought* is called a modal preterite on the analogy of *should,* although there is not, as in the case of *should, could* and *might,* a present tense form to contrast it with.

2. *Should* is used in instructions and corrections in which *must* would sound too peremptory.

> Applications should reach us before May 1st.
> She gives the writer's name as Johnson; this should be Johnstone.

168. Attention should be paid to the difference between (*a*) *had been able* and *could have,* (*b*) *had had* (*had been obliged*) and *should* (*ought to*) *have.* The former of each pair expresses a fact:

> As he had not been interrupted he had for once been able to finish his work in time.
> As he was too busy, he had unfortunately had to decline the invitation.

The latter denotes what would have been possible or proper:

> I could easily have come if you had let me know.
> He should not have made such a fuss about nothing.

Shall — Should

169. *Shall* [ʃəl] is used in the second and third persons to express the will (command, promise, threat) of the speaker or writer; also, in the first and third persons, to ask after the will of the person addressed. In case of opposition to the will of the speaker, and at the end of a clause, *shall* is strong-stressed [ʃæl]; *shan't* [ʃɑ:nt] (= *shall not*) always is.

Any one found guilty of robbery shall be shot at once.
You shall have the book to-morrow.
Shall I [ʃl'ai] open a window?
He refuses to go? I tell you he *shall* go.
Johnny hopes you'll let him steer from time to time. — All right, he shall.
Thou shalt not steal.
You've been lazy, you shan't have any sweets.

On *shall* as an auxiliary of tense, see 185.

170. In slightly archaic English *shall* is used to denote a hypothetical experience, where ordinary English would prefer *may* or *will*.

After knowing him for years you shall suddenly discover that your friend's nose is slightly awry [ə'rai].[1]

171. In formal (*a*) or slightly archaic (*b*) style *shall* is used modally (i.e. to express purpose, desirability or contingency) in dependent clauses. Ordinary English would use the present tense in *b*.

a. It has been decided that the second reading shall not be opposed.[2] (Cf. 169.)
b. Do whatever shall seem good to you.[3]
May God be with us when that day shall come.

172. *Should* [ʃəd] is used in dependent clauses, after the past tense of a verb expressing will. (Cf. 169.)

He gave orders that the strangers should be hospitably entertained.
Theseus ['θi:sju:s] commanded that the prisoners should be taken to Athens.
He promised me that the message should be sent at once.

1. After a head-clause expressing a command, this construction alternates with (*for* +) accusative with infinitive (cf. 45 and 60): *He gave orders for the strangers to be hospitably entertained; Theseus commanded the prisoners to be taken to Athens.*

2. On *should* in head-clauses, see 167; also 191. Compare the following specimen of reported speech; note, however, that what the duchess actually said was probably: 'You (shall) either marry him or you (shall) go into a convent' (cf. 129).

The duchess was determined not to stand any more nonsense, and when she told Pilar of the proposal added that she had shilly-shallied long enough. She must (165) either marry him or she should go into a convent.
'I'm not going (193) to do either the one or the other,' said Pilar.
Somerset Maugham, *Creatures of Circumstance* (Star Editions, p. 138).

---

[1] OED s.v. *Shall* 9. See also *English Studies* XIV (1932), p. 78 (R. W. Zandvoort, *Collected Papers*, p. 120 f.).
[2] Kruisinga, *Handbook*[5], § 1546. [3] Onions, *An Advanced English Syntax*, § 65.

173. *Should* is often used, in all persons, in clauses dependent on an expression of feeling or opinion, with the predicate of the head-clause either in the present or in the past tense.

I am surprised that you should have been so foolish.
It is strange that he should refuse to see her.
It seemed incredible that he should be the same man I knew twenty years ago.
Nothing more unlucky, I sometimes think, could have befallen Chaucer than that he should have been christened 'the father of English poetry'. Livingstone Lowes, *Geoffrey Chaucer*, p. 1.

The use of *should* in these clauses indicates that their contents, though referring to undoubted facts,[1] are viewed, not merely as facts, but as things exciting our surprise, regret, or disapproval.

174. The use of *should* described in 173 should be distinguished from that of the same auxiliary in clauses dependent on a sentence (negative, interrogative, or hypothetical) expressing possibility, or expectation.[2] In such cases the clause in which *should* occurs contains a statement contrary to fact. Cf. 651, 2nd ex.

It was impossible that this should continue for long.[3]
It was not to be expected that they should surrender without a struggle.

175. *Should* may be used in final clauses referring to the past, after (*so*) *that* and *lest*.

Copies of the Bible in English were deposited in the churches so that all should be able to read the Scriptures in the vernacular [vəˈnækjulə].
I hid it lest he should see it.[4]

Might, in similar contexts (159), suggests possibility, in conformity with the fundamental meaning of *may* (155); *should* more directly expresses purpose, in conformity with the fundamental meaning of *shall* (169).

---

[1] Cf. the following quotation from The Times Weekly Edition, 7/6, 1918, in Kruisinga's *Handbook*[5], § 710: *Unlike Mr. Justice Darling, we are disposed to treat with the utmost gravity* the fact *that such charges* should *even be possible.* Also the OED definition (s.v. *Shall 22c*): 'In expressions of surprise or its absence, approval or disapproval of some present or past fact.'

[2] OED s.v. *Shall 22d.*

[3] Kruisinga, *Handbook*[5], § 709. Of the examples in this paragraph, nos. 1, 4 and 5 refer to facts, 2, 3 and 6 to non-facts.

[4] Wyld, *op. cit.*, s.v. *lest.*

176. *Should* is also used in conditional clauses expressing contingency.

If you should see him, give him my regards.
Should he ask for references, tell him to apply to me. (Cf. 144.)

Should is similarly found in relative clauses with conditional meaning:

Any one who should wish to come will be welcome.

For more examples see Kruisinga's *Handbook*[5], § 707.[1]

177. Besides the cases already discussed, *should* is used with reference to the past in dependent clauses similar to those taking *shall* according to 171.

He was authorized to do whatever should seem good to him.
He promised to come back as soon as the war should be over.

178. *Should* is used in rhetorical questions in a sense approximating to that of 167.

Why should he obey an order given him by a perfect stranger?
Where is Mary? — How should I know?
I won't pay the fine. — Why should you?
(Cf. There is no reason why you should.)

Note a similar use of *shall* in literary English:

Who shall say whether he acted wisely or no?

Will — Would

179. *Will* [wil] may express the will, wish or consent of the subject (cf. the definition of *shall* in 169). It is especially used in this sense in negative and interrogative sentences, and is mostly strong-stressed. (Cf. also 500, 1st ex.)

Come when you will (COD).
Will you do me a favour?
I won't have you go hungry.
Won't you come in?[2]
They have to obey, whether they will or not.

Special stress is laid on *will* in case of opposition to the will of the subject (cf. 169):

I *will* be obeyed (Wyld).

On *will* as an auxiliary of tense, see 185.

---

[1] Though the reference to § 703 had better be replaced by one to § 708, 2.
[2] *Won't you* is often used for invitations.

180. *Would* [wud] is similarly used with reference to the past, mostly in negative sentences, *would not* being equivalent to *refused to.*

He would not tell us where the money was hidden.
The wound would not heal (COD).
They had to obey, whether they would or not (Wyld).

181. *Will* and *would* may express habit or repetition, especially what is or was characteristic under certain circumstances (*a*); also a natural propensity (*b*). The spoken forms in this case are [wil] and [wud], as in 179 and 180; they are strongly stressed (*c*) when special emphasis is intended. In sense *a* [1] also occurs.

a. She will (or: She'll) sit there for hours,[1] waiting for her son to come home.
Now and then a blackbird would call.
When pressed for an answer, he would say that it was none of his business.
b. Boys will be boys.
Accidents will happen.
c. You *will* have your way.
He *will* have his little joke.
He *would* get in my light.

In the examples of (*c*), *will* and *would* at the same time express a certain degree of volition.[2] Note, though, that *will* in *You will have your way* expresses a different shade of meaning from that of the same auxiliary in *I will be obeyed* (179); also that *He would get in my light* expresses the annoyance of the speaker.

1. Repetition stated merely as a fact is not expressed by *will* or *would*: *He often wrote to his parents*. But: *He would write for hours at a time*. Cf. 211.

2. Strongly stressed *would* and *would not* are used somewhat sarcastically in sentences like: *He tore his new trousers the first time he had them on. — He would.* (= that was to be expected.) — *I don't understand this book. — You wouldn't.* (= I did not expect you would.)

182. *Would* and *would have* are also used modally; cf. 192. Note the use of *would* after *to wish*, when there are two different subjects, and when the sub-clause implies some degree of volition. (Cf. 138.)

---

[1] This use of *will* seems to be unusual in the first person singular, where the equivalent would be *I often sit there for hours*. (Cf. Kruisinga, *Handbook*[5], § 722.) *I would sit there for hours*, on the other hand, is all right. The reason is probably that *will* and *would* imply observation of others, or of oneself in the past.

[2] 'Exercise of the will; power of willing' (COD).

a. I would ask you to reconsider your decision.
Would you pass the salt?
I wish people would not talk so much.
b. She would have done anything to make amends.

Note, however (cf. 168 and 183):

He had wanted to know who owned the place, but nobody had been able to tell him.

183. Apart from the cases discussed above, volition is usually expressed by the verb *to want.*

I want to see the manager.
Mother wants you to come home.

Other words and phrases of related meaning are *to like* and *to be willing* (which expresses readiness).

I should very much like (= I very much want) to come, but I am afraid I shall be too busy.
I am willing to help you, provided you first try to help yourself.

184. Attention should be paid to the use of *to will* (3rd pers. sing. present tense *wills*, past tense and past participle *willed*) as a notional verb, to express an unalterable decision (said esp. of *God* or *Fate*), or 'to control by means of the will' (Wyld).

God wills (willed) that man should be happy (COD).
A mesmerist may will a patient to think himself well (*ibid.*).

Future Tense

185. An action or state belonging to a future time-sphere may be expressed by *shall* [ʃəl] + plain infinitive in the first person, *will* [1] + plain infinitive in the second and third. When used in this way, these groups are said to form the FUTURE TENSE.

In questions, either *shall* [ʃæl, ʃəl] or *will* [wil, l] may be used in the second person, though *will* is commoner.

I'm afraid I shan't [ʃɑ:nt] have time to finish the book.
When shall we see you again?
We shall all be back before dark.
You will see that I am right.
Shall (will) you be in for dinner?
A week's holiday will do you good.
They will not (won't) find it so easy as they think.

1. In American, as in the English of Scotland and Ireland, *will* is used in all persons of the future tense (cf. H. L. Mencken, *The American Language*,

4th ed., pp. 199–201). In Southern English, too, constructions like *I'm afraid I won't have time*, and *I would like to say . . .* (192) are fairly common.

2. In the 2nd and 3rd persons, the future may express an assumption (cf. 190 and 192): *It will be unnecessary to give further examples.*

186. In indirect style, with a preterite in the head-clause, *should* [ʃud, ʃəd] and *would* [wud, wəd, əd] are similarly used to form the past future.

> I *told* you I should not be in for dinner.
> He wrote to say that he would be back on Friday.

The past future occasionally occurs apart from indirect style:

> He was fifty-nine years of age, and would be sixty next year.[1]

187. In literary English *shall* and *should* are sometimes used in indirect style in the second or third person to report *shall* in the first person.

> He says he (you say you) shall never manage it (COD) ['I shall never manage it.'].
> He wrote to say that he should be back on Friday ['I shall be back . . .'].

Will and *would* are the usual forms, however.

188. The idea of futurity is often combined with that of the will or intention of the speaker or writer. In this case *shall* is used in the second and third persons (see 169), *will* in the first person.

> I will (I'll) do what I can.
> We won't detain you any longer.

189. When used as auxiliaries of the future (185), *shall* and *will* may also express volition.

> I shall say what I like.
> You will wait here till I come back.

The former example expresses determination; in the latter obedience is taken for granted. A less domineering attitude towards the person addressed is implied in a sentence like

> You will understand that this is strictly confidential.

which denotes a confident assumption on the part of the speaker.

190. A verbal group consisting of *shall/will* + *have* + past participle constitutes the FUTURE PERFECT.

---

[1] Jespersen, MEG IV, 19.4(1).

I shall have finished my work by five o'clock.
The snow will have disappeared before the end of April.
Next Monday I shall have been staying in England for three years.

In the 2nd and 3rd persons, the future perfect may also express an assumption (cf. 185.2 and 192).

You will have heard that I am going to America.
The invitations will have been sent out by now.

191. In the head-clauses of hypothetical statements (i.e. statements dependent on a condition) English uses *should* and *would* with a plain infinitive, in the same way as for the past future; also *should/would* + *have* + past participle, like the similar group for the future perfect.

I should certainly take the job if it were offered me.
He would not have made that mistake if he had consulted a dictionary.
I should do it, if I were you. (Cf. 139.)

192. When no condition is expressed, *should/would* with a plain infinitive may be used to make a polite or modest statement, or to ask a polite question. Cf. 182. The last example expresses a tentative assumption (cf. 185.2 and 190).

I should (would, 185) like to go for a walk.
Would you be good enough to post this letter for me?
It would (occ. should) seem that such was his intention. (Cf. 44, 1st par.)
What's that valley called, I wonder? — Oh, that would be the Wye Valley.

193. It may not be superfluous to point out that what is usually known as the Future Tense is not the only means to express an action or state belonging to a future time-sphere (185). The student is referred to 32 (*We are to be married next week*), 95 (*Is Jack coming to-night?*), 96 (*I'm going to see him to-morrow*), 129 (*We start to-morrow*). Of these constructions, the simple and the progressive present are limited to special groups of verbs, whereas the infinitive after a form of *to be* primarily expresses an arrangement. The *going to* construction may denote pure futurity (*It's going to rain*), though with a personal subject it often implies intention; this, however, may also be the case with the Future Tense with *shall/will* (*I shall punish you severely if you do that*). The following remarks from *Living English Structure* by W. Stannard Allen (Longmans, Green & Co., 1947) deserve consideration:

As a simple affirmative statement of intention, with no external circumstances (time, condition, reason, etc.) mentioned, the future tense is rare; where the futurity depends on the external circumstances, 'going to' is rare.

Examples: *a.* He will sell his house (rare).
b. He's going to sell his house (normal).
a. He'll sell it if you ask him (normal).
b. He is going to sell it if you ask him (rare).

To Do

194. *To do* is used as a notional verb, chiefly in its non-finite forms and with a neuter pronoun-object (*something*, *nothing*, *this*, *that*, *it*, *what?* etc.).

He whistled, for want of something better to do.
That will do.
What are you doing?
Look what you've done!
It did me good to see him again.
The book does him little credit.

Note, among other idiomatic uses, *done* = finished: *it is*, *I have*, *done* (COD).

195. The weak-stressed finite forms of *to do* may be used as substitutes for a preceding notional verb.

He cultivated his garden, as he did his music, with the utmost attention to detail.

In examples like the following, *to do* refers to the preceding verb with its adjuncts:

I strongly disapprove of his conduct. — We *all* do.
Who made that noise? — *I* did.

196. In comparative clauses without an object this function of *to do* occurs more frequently than in some other languages.

If you saw the truth as clearly as I do . . .
He knew more about it than we did.

Cf. the following type of clause (see also 632.2), with stress on *do*:

I am not surprised, knowing them as I do.

With a phonetically weightier second subject, however, English often dispenses with *to do* as well.

He knew more about it than most people.

197. The stressed forms of *to do* are occasionally used in combination with *so* to refer to a preceding verb with its adjuncts. This use is more frequent with the non-finite forms than with the finite, and is commoner in written than in spoken English.

Those wanting to take the oath in the old way may do so.
People who deceive us once are capable of doing so again.
I remember him opening the letter and trembling all over as he did so.

To do in similar constructions may also be followed by *it*: *I remember seeing him throw the letter into the fire and asking him why he did it.* In such a case *to do* is used as a notional verb with a neuter pronoun object (194). Note that *it* is more definite in its reference than *so*, which is, of course, really adverbial (cf. 425).

198. The strong-stressed finite forms of *to do* are used, without or with a plain infinitive, in sentences contrasting two aspects[1] of a verbal action (negative-affirmative, potential-actual, etc.).

He promised to send me the letter, and he did (send it).
I don't know what you mean by that; but I do know that I want a decision now.
They told me I could not see him that day; but I did (see him).

When the preceding statement contains an auxiliary other than *to do*, or the copula *to be*, the same contrast may be expressed by repeating the auxiliary or copula with strong stress in the second part of the sentence.

You think I cannot support myself, but I'll show you I can (support myself).
We rather expected him to be in a sombre mood, and he was.

199. Strong-stressed *do* may be merely emphatic, without expressing a contrast.

You do look pale.
You did give me a fright.
Oh, do come! It's going to be such fun.
If you won't think me rude, I'll take one of these cigars. — Do, by all means!

1. Emphatic *do* may be used as an imperative before *be*: *Do be quiet.* This expresses an urgent request rather than a command.

2. Another auxiliary, or the copula *to be*, may also be strongly stressed for emphasis.

Oh, but you simply *must* come.
You *are* an ass.

200. The finite forms of *to do* are used in combination with a plain infinitive in questions, and especially in negative sentences with enclitic *not*. Negative *do* is usually stressed; interrogative *do* may

[1] This word to be taken in its general sense, not in that of 78.

be either stressed or unstressed when initial; otherwise it is usually unstressed.

Do you ([du ju] or [dju])[1] want to see the headmaster [ˈhedˈmɑstə]?
What does it[2] matter?
What did he tell you?
She did not know what to say.
Don't go yet.

On the use of *to do* in appended questions, see 656.

201. *To do*, in the function just described, is not used:

a. in questions beginning with the subject (unless they are also made negative by *not*);

b. in dependent questions (unless they are also made negative by *not*);

c. with most auxiliaries, and with the copula *to be*.

a. Who killed Cock Robin?
b. He asked me how much Latin I knew.
c. I have not seen him for ages.
I will not (won't) go there.
It isn't true.

But: *Who doesn't know that he is a miser?* And in the negative imperative of *to be*: *Don't be silly*. (Cf. 199 and 607.)

1. *To do* is used with the verb *to have* in the sense of *to obtain* or *to receive* (*Did you have an opportunity to go there? Do they often have visitors?*); *to experience* (*Did you have any luck? Did you have a good time?*) or *to cause* (*Did he have a house built?*); sometimes in that of *to be obliged* (*Do I have to pay for this? I did not have to pay anything*). Similarly with names of meals: *We don't have lunch before midday*; and with *have* in the sense of *eat* or *drink*: *Do you have coffee for breakfast? — To do* is not used with *to have* in the sense of *to possess*: *Has she blue eyes? I have not any matches*; *Have you money in the bank?* — Note the difference between: *Do you have much time for golf?* (i.e. habitually), and: *Have you (got)*[3] *time for a round of golf on Saturday afternoon?* (specific occasion).[4] This distinction applies to most uses of *to have* in the PRESENT tense; hence *Have they visitors to-day? Did*-forms are possible, beside *had*, in all senses of *to have* as a full verb, including *to possess*. — In American English the restriction to HABITUAL actions in the present tense does not apply. An American may, therefore,

---

[1] But *Do you* [ˈduː ju] *want to see the headmaster?* — if the person addressed seems unable to make up his mind.

[2] [ˈwɔt dəz it] or [ˈwɔts it]. Sometimes written *What's it matter?*

[3] Cf. 140.3.

[4] See *English Language Teaching* (Published by the British Council), I, 2 (Nov. 1946), p. 48; *ibid.* IV, 6 (March 1950), 156–163.

ask: *Do you have any children?* An Englishman, on the other hand, would say: *Have you any children?* (Cf. G. V. Carey, *American into English*, pp. 22–23.)

As an auxiliary of tense, *to have* never takes *to do*: *I have not seen her for ages.*

2. On the use of *to do* with *to dare, to need,* and *use(d) to,* see 203 ff., and 212.

3. *To do* is often absent in sentences containing the negative phrase *not at all* (mostly in final position): *It was clear that the idea pleased him not at all* (perhaps slightly more emphatic than *the idea did not please him at all*).

4. Note also the absence of *to do* in phrases like *I know not how*; *I doubt not*; *If I mistake not*; and in questions like *How comes it that ——?* *What says the almanac?*

202. The use of *to do* in questions (200) makes it possible for the subject to precede the principal verb, which is the normal word-order in English; in questions beginning with the subject (201*a*) the normal word-order can be preserved without *to do.*

A similar purpose is served by the unstressed finite forms of *to do* in sentences beginning with a negative adjunct, and sometimes, also, with another emphatic word. The construction is commonest in literary English. Cf. 690.

Not for an instant did she lose her head.
Rarely does it happen that the harbour is frozen up as late as February.
Well do I remember the day.

1. In less rhetorical style one would say: *She did not lose her head for an instant*; *It rarely happens that . . .*; *I can well remember the day.* In the constructions with front-position of a negative or other emphatic word we have inversion of the normal order subject-verb, in so far as the auxiliary precedes the subject.

In sentences with another auxiliary, or with the copula *to be, to do* is not used (cf. 201*c*): *Rarely had it happened . . .*; *Never shall I forget . . .*; *Only thus is it possible to maintain . . .*; etc.

2. For further information on the uses of *to do,* see an article in *English Studies,* XXIV (1942), 1–16 (reprinted in R. W. Zandvoort, *Collected Papers,* pp. 122–141).— Mention may be made here of the occasional use, in literary English, of *did* to emphasize a contrast between past and present (cf. 198). E.g.: *An even more doubtful story attempts to explain the figure of a wailing woman, which haunts, or did haunt, the banks of the River Goyt near Marple Hall.* (Christina Hole, *Haunted England.*)

To Dare and *To Need*

203. *To dare* and *to need* have certain characteristics which enable them to be grouped with *can, may,* etc. as auxiliaries of predication.

When followed by a complementary infinitive, their third person singular present tense as a rule takes no *s*; the following infinitive frequently does not take *to*; nor do they always require *to do* in interrogative sentences and in negative sentences with *not.*

204. After the present and the past tense of *to dare*, the plain infinitive is always used in interrogative sentences and in negative sentences with enclitic *not* that are formed without the auxiliary *to do* (*a*). In other contexts (*b*) usage varies.

a. How dare you speak to me like that?
She dare not ask for a rise, for fear of losing her job.
He dared not return to the house.
How dare you come here?[1]
b. We shall see whether you dare keep your word.
He hardly dared speak to her.
I hardly dare to think of it.
As soon as he dared to leave his hiding-place, he visited his sick wife.

1. *Dare* forms a compound with *say* in *I daresay* 'am prepared to believe, do not deny, = very likely (often iron.)' (COD).

But she's really very sorry for what she's done. — Oh, I daresay.

2. *Dared not* is usually pronounced [dɛənt], and sometimes written without the second *d*, when the time-sphere is sufficiently clear from the context.

He was in such a temper that I daren't ask questions.
He would have liked to protest, but he dare not.

205. After the infinitive *dare* (usually preceded by an auxiliary), and especially after the past participle *dared*, the infinitive is more commonly used with *to* than without; *daring* (present participle or gerund) is always followed by *to*.

I did not dare look up.
Nobody would dare to suspect him.
I should not have dared to ask for such a thing.
She shook her head again, not[2] daring to speak.

206. What has been said of *to dare* also applies to the present tense of *to need*. Cf. 164.

He need not worry; everything will be all right.
Need I come again?

---

[1] A number of examples have been taken from an article on 'The Infinitive after *To Dare*' by G. Mulder in *Neophilologus* XXII (1934), 25–48 Some of Mr. Mulder's conclusions have also been adopted.
[2] *Daring* is usually preceded by *not*.

Need is used as a past tense in reported speech, and in combination with *have* + past participle (cf. 146).

I assured him that he need not worry.
We need not have hurried after all.

207. In the sense of *to have* or *to require* (cf. 71), *to need* takes an infinitive with *to*. The third person sing. pres. tense is *needs*.

One needs to be careful.[1]
He did not need to be told twice.
In Holland, bicycles need to be catered for seriously.[2]

208. As to the use or absence of *to do*, with *to dare* there are three possible constructions in negative sentences with *not*: *He dare(d) not return*; *He (does) did not dare (to) return.* The choice between them would often seem to depend on whether a longer or a shorter group of words is required in the context, though the periphrastic construction seems to occur more frequently in the past tense than in the present: *He daren't return*; *He did not dare (to) return.* — *Don't* is always used in the negative imperative: *Don't you dare to touch me.*

In interrogative use, *to dare* is almost limited to rhetorical questions of two types. Those beginning with *How* never take *to do* (*How dare you speak to me like that?*); they express indignation. The other type is more or less menacing in tone, and begins with *Do*: *Do you dare to tell me that you did not know?*[3] Examples of interrogative *dare* in other persons than the second are rare; note the type *Dare I ask you to join me?*,[4] where periphrasis would be impossible.

As regards *to need*, *to do* is used in the cases described in 207.

209. Both *to dare* and *to need* may take (pro)noun objects, the former in the sense of *to challenge* or *to face*, the latter in that of *to require.*

I dare you to contradict me.
To dare the perils of the London streets.
What you need is a good rest.

---

[1] Wyld, *op. cit.*, s.v. *need* vb.
[2] Kruisinga, *Handbook*[5], § 638, 2. Cf. also § 631.
[3] Mulder, *loc. cit.*, p. 36. Mr. M.'s only other example contains an infinitive without *to*.
[4] *Ibid.*, p. 32.

Used (*to*)

210. *Used* [ju:st], followed by *to* + infinitive, is used [ju:zd] to contrast past and present (*a*), often with the idea of habit or repetition implied (*b*). It is grouped with the auxiliaries on account of its subordination to the following infinitive.

a. I used to [ˈju:stə] think that all Belgians spoke French, but I know better now.
There used to be a house there.[1]
b. On my way to school I used to pass a bookshop.

211. Habit or repetition in the past may also be expressed by *would* (181). The difference between *would* and *used to* is *a.* that *used to* does not necessarily express repetition; *b.* that whereas *used to* implies appreciable extent in the past, the action or state expressed by *would* + inf. may cover a very brief space of time or be just momentary (cf. 181, 2nd ex.); *c.* that *would* usually implies personal interest, whereas *used to* is more objective.

He would spend every penny he earned on books.

This, as Kruisinga (*Handbook*[5], § 745) rightly says, 'suggests a picture of the past'; *used to* would sound more matter of fact:

He used to say that one place was as good as another.

The following sentence from Sweet, *A Story of Two Englishmen*, quoted by Poutsma (*Grammar*[2], I, Ch. I, § 54) may seem to show that in some contexts there is little to choose between *would* and *used to*: *They used to nod to one another when they met, and now and then they would exchange a word or two.* Still, it may be that *would* is used in the second half because it denotes something more *occasional* than *used to* (cf. A. S. Hornby, *A Guide to Patterns and Usage in English*, § 51 e).

212. In questions and in negative sentences with enclitic *not*, *used* may be separated from *to*,[2] though even then it is pronounced [ju:st]. *Used not* is usually pronounced [ju:snt] and sometimes written without *d* (cf. 204.2).

Used he always to go out into the garden after dinner?
He used not (or: usen't) to answer.

In colloquial (i.e. informal spoken) English, periphrastic forms with *did* occur; [ju:stə] is then written *use to.*

[1] Wyld, s.v. *use* vb.
[2] Some examples of *used* separated from *to* in affirmative sentences may be found in Kruisinga's *Handbook*[5], § 648.

Did he use to take the bus?
He didn't use to [ˈjuːstu] answer.

213. The above use of *used to* is easily distinguished from that of *to be used* (= accustomed) *to*, as in

I am not used to [ˈjuːstə] this sort of thing (COD).
I am not used to being spoken to like that (Wyld).

In the construction with an infinitive, the difference between *used to* and *had been used to* may be very small:

He was glad that the count began to come more often to Florence than he had been used to [ˈjuːstu].
W. Somerset Maugham, *Creatures of Circumstance* (Star Editions, p. 124).

CHAPTER SIX

MOOD AND MODALITY

Subjunctive

214. The structure of a language is to a large extent conditioned by its system of formal oppositions. Thus, to anticipate the following chapters, we have in English the formal oppositions illustrated by such pairs as *boy* — *boys*, and *boy* — *boy's*; among the personal pronouns we have the pairs *I* — *we*, and *I* — *me*, and the set of three *he* — *she* — *it*. It is around such oppositions that the grammatical system of the language is to a large extent built up.

215. Similar formal oppositions among the verbs are *play* — *plays* and *play* — *played*; cf. also the set of three *am* — *is* — *are*.

The pair *play* — *plays* has been shown to represent the opposition between the third person singular present tense on the one hand, and the other persons of the singular plus those of the plural on the other. In literary English, however, it also represents an opposition on a different plane: the third person singular of a verb may occur either with or without *s*; the form without *s* is known as the SUBJUNCTIVE, the one with *s* as the INDICATIVE, and the difference is said to be one of MOOD.

216. The subjunctive may be used in nominal sub-clauses depending on a main clause expressing will or wish, either by means of a verb or by a noun of similar meaning. It is indifferent whether the verb in the main clause is in the present or in the past tense; as a matter of fact, examples of the latter are by far the most frequent.[1]

> Miss Dorothy L. Sayers has passed to us your letter of June 22nd and has asked us to thank you for your suggestion that she come over to Holland to lecture next Autumn or Winter.

---

[1] The quotations in sections 216–218, and the first quotation of 219, are from authentic written or printed sources.

Lodge suggested that White show it in strict confidence to Balfour, Clemenceau, and Nitti.
Joanna had insisted that he come.

The opposition subjunctive—indicative may be felt potentially in other persons than the third singular if the conditions are otherwise the same:

When Pierre insisted that they quit the house . . .[1]
As we passed through Pevensey he suggested that we stop and have a look over the castle.

217. The subjunctive is also found in adverbial clauses, chiefly of open condition[2] (*a*), or of concession (*b*).

a. So long as a volume hold together, I am not much troubled as to its outer appearance.[3]
The inventor may, if he live in London, or visit that city, search the files of the Patent Office.[4]
b. Though everyone desert you, I will not.[5]

218. The formal opposition subjunctive—indicative is especially marked in the case of *to be*, where *be*, in all persons of the singular and plural, stands in contrast to *am* — *is* — *are*. The following quotations correspond to those of 216 and 217:

a. An army lieutenant demanded that the flag be lowered.
b. If two angles of a triangle be equal to one another . . .

Be may also open a concessive clause:

Be that as it may, little had been said about her husband.[6]

219. Another formal opposition, also covered by the terms subjunctive—indicative, is that between *were* and *was* in the first and third persons singular of the *past* tense of *to be*. Connection with past *time*, however, exists, if at all, only after a main clause with a verb in that tense:

She looked as though she were fainting.[7]

---

[1] Same source as preceding quotation. — This use of the subjunctive is especially common in American sources, from which the second, third and fourth quotations of this section are taken.
[2] A clause of 'open' condition says nothing as to whether the condition is, or is not, likely to be fulfilled. Cf. 636. [3] Kruisinga, *Handbook*[5], § 1535.
[4] Schut and Zandvoort, *Eng. Spraakkunst voor Gymnasia*, II, p. 142.
[5] Onions, *An Advanced English Syntax*, § 58.
[6] Kruisinga, *Handbook*[5], § 1532.
[7] Onions, § 154. — That the idea of time is inessential, appears when the verb in the main clause is in the present tense: *She looks as though she were fainting.*

In most other cases, *were* is indifferent as regards time, and only expresses IRREALITY:[1]

> I wish it were over. (Cf. 138.)
> If I were you, I should go.

Cf. also the stereotyped phrase *as it were.*

220. The subjunctive is further found in a number of traditional phrases, such as *Suffice it to say* . . .; *Heaven forbid* (*that* . . .); *God bless you*; *God save the King*; etc.

221. If it be asked what the subjunctive in the above instances expresses, the answer is threefold.

In those of 216, the first example of 218, and those of 220 the subjunctive expresses a WISH; in this sense it may be called an OPTATIVE.

In those of 217, and in the second and third examples of 218, the subjunctive expresses POSSIBILITY; in this sense it may be called a POTENTIAL.

In those of 219, the subjunctive expresses UNREALITY; in this sense it may be called an IRREALIS [iriˈeilis].

Of the three, the irrealis (*were*) only is in common use in spoken and ordinary written English, the optative (apart from some of the phrases of 220) and the potential being practically confined to literary English. The optative as used in the instances of 216 and the first example of 218 has a somewhat wider currency in American English; an English author would probably have written *Joanna had insisted that he* should *come* (172). In the cases of 217, spoken and ordinary written English use either the indicative (all three examples), or *should* + plain infinitive (2nd and 3rd exx.).

It will be clear, therefore, that from the point of view of the structure of present-day English, the opposition subjunctive—indicative is of comparatively little importance.

---

222. Of far greater importance for the structure of present-day English is the opposition *play*(*s*) — *played* in the function described

[1] Cf., however, the quotation in 281, where the subjunctive (*if the day were fine*) expresses a supposition (cf. 217). This use is mainly literary; in ordinary English the clause would probably have run: *if it was a fine day.*

in 137 and 138. As there explained, the function of the preterite in the sub-clauses of sentences expressing something desirable or conceivable, or denoting a wish or a condition not likely to be fulfilled, is not to express a contrast between present and past time, but between reality and desirability or (im)possibility[1] (the so-called MODAL[2] PRETERITE). In the cases of 219 it coincides with the opposition subjunctive — indicative. For examples, see the sections referred to.

223. When the preterite of an auxiliary is used with modal function, it is called an AUXILIARY OF MODALITY. See especially the uses of *should* described in 167 and 176, that of *would* described in 182, and that of *might* described in 160. In

If I were to tell you all I know, you would be amazed.

were is an auxiliary of modality, a modal preterite, and a subjunctive all in one.

An auxiliary of modality is not necessarily a preterite; cf. the examples with *may* in 158; also 171.

224. On ADVERBS OF MODALITY, see 722.

---

[1] Cf. OPTATIVE and POTENTIAL in 221.
[2] *Modal* [moudl] is derived from *mode*, which, as a grammatical term, used to be another form of *mood*. See Appendix, p. 344.

PART II

NOUNS

INTRODUCTORY

A. Regular Nouns

225. An English noun normally has the following forms:

a. the stem: *boy*, *girl*, *ship*, *ass*;

b. the stem + sibilant-suffix: *boys/boy's/boys'* [bɔiz]; *girls/girl's/girls'* [gə:lz]; *ships/ship's/ships'* [ʃips]; *asses/ass's/asses'* [ˈæsiz].

As appears from the examples, [iz] is used after stems ending in a sibilant, [z] in other cases, except after breathed consonants, [s] after breathed consonants, except sibilants. Cf. VERBS, 1. — For the spelling, see 227. On words like *Chinese*, see 921.

226. The stem of an English noun is used in the following functions:

a. to denote the singular as distinct from the plural number: *I met a boy — I met some boys.* In this case the noun is usually preceded by an article or another attributive word.

b. attributively (589), no matter whether one or more specimens are meant: *a boy scout — boy scouts*; *the slave-trade*; *a five-pound note*; *a holiday course.*

c. collectively: *to shoot quail and duck*; *he spared neither man, woman nor child* (thus often in enumerations).

227. The stem + sibilant-suffix is used in the following functions:

a. to denote the plural as distinct from the singular number: *Boys will be boys.*

[iz] is spelt *es*; if the stem ends in *e* in the spelling (e.g. *horse*), *s* only is added.

[z] and [s] are spelt *s*.

On spellings like *ladies* (sing. *lady*), *heroes* (sing. *hero*), see Appendix, p. 338.

b. as a genitive singular: *the girl's father*, *the ship's captain*, *an ass's head.*

The spelling is nearly always *'s* (cf. 246).

c. as a genitive plural: *the boys' parents*, *ships' officers.*

The spelling is *(e)s'* (that of the plural followed by an apostrophe), but *'s* with the nouns discussed in 235, 236 and 237.

Many nouns take the sibilant-suffix in function *a* only.

228. Compound nouns usually add the sibilant-suffix to the last element: *fellow-travellers* (*fellow-traveller's*, *fellow-travellers'*); *schoolmasters* (*schoolmaster's*, *schoolmasters'*), *bedrooms*, *broomsticks*; *man-eaters* (*man-eater's*, *man-eaters'*); *onlookers* (*onlooker's*, *onlookers'*); *handfuls*; *good-for-nothings* (cf. 806).

229. Noun-adverb compounds derived from verb-adverb combinations add the plural suffix to the noun: *goings-on*, *lookers-on*, *passers-by*, *runners-up*.

A genitive-suffix is added to the last element: *looker-on's*, but examples are rare.

230. Compounds consisting of a noun followed by a prepositional adjunct usually add the plural suffix to the noun, but the genitive-suffix to the last element: *fathers-in-law*,[1] but *my father-in-law's*[1] *house*.

The genitive-suffix is always added to the last element of a word-group: *the Prince of Wales's birthday*, *Miss Mansfield's wedding*. This is known as the GROUP-GENITIVE. Cf. also *anybody else's opinion* (549).

In groups of the latter type the plural ending is added to the title in formal English, to the proper name in more familiar style: *the Misses Mansfield*, *the Miss Mansfields*. But usually *the two Mr. Forsters*; *Messrs.* [mesəz] *Forster* would be taken to be the name of a firm.

231. In groups with *kind of*, *sort of* (*this kind of tool*, *that sort of speech*), *kind of* and *sort of* are often felt to be subordinated in meaning to the following noun. In that case the plural ending is added, at least in familiar English, not to *kind* or *sort*, but only to the last word of the group: *these kind of tools*, *those sort of speeches*.

What kind of trees are those?

In literary English we also find *all manner of* (*benefits*, etc.).

---

[1] Stress on *father(s)*. — See Jones, *An English Pronouncing Dictionary*, s.v. *jack-in-office*, *jack-in-the-box*, *jack-in-the-green*.

Kind and *sort* take the plural ending after *all*: *all kinds of men, all sorts of people.* The same applies in non-colloquial English to *kind* and *sort* preceded by other qualifiers: *these kinds of tools, those sorts of speeches.*

A genitive-ending would, as usual, be added to the last word of the group: *that kind of student's idea of work, those kind of people's notions of honesty.*

232. When *kind* or *sort* are of equal importance with the following noun, they take the plural ending, the following noun being usually in the singular.

What kinds of cherry flourish best in this region?

B. Irregular Nouns

233. A number of nouns ending in a breathed spirant ([s], [f], [θ]) voice the spirant before taking a plural suffix.

a.	house	[haus]	—	houses	[hauziz]
b.	calf	[kɑ:f]	—	calves	[kɑ:vz]
	half	[hɑ:f]	—	halves	[hɑ:vz]
	loaf	[louf]	—	loaves	[louvz]
	knife	[naif]	—	knives	[naivz]
	life	[laif]	—	lives	[laivz]
	wife	[waif]	—	wives	[waivz]
	leaf	[li:f]	—	leaves	[li:vz]
	sheaf	[ʃi:f]	—	sheaves	[ʃi:vz]
	thief	[θi:f]	—	thieves	[θi:vz]
	elf	[elf]	—	elves	[elvz]
	self	[self]	—	selves	[selvz]
	shelf	[ʃelf]	—	shelves	[ʃelvz]
	wolf	[wulf]	—	wolves	[wulvz]
c.	bath	[bɑ:θ]	—	baths	[bɑ:ðz]
	path	[pɑ:θ]	—	paths	[pɑ:ðz]
	oath	[ouθ]	—	oaths	[ouðz]
	mouth	[mauθ]	—	mouths	[mauðz]
	youth[1]	[ju:θ]	—	youths	[ju:ðz][2]
	truth	[tru:θ]	—	truths	[tru:ðz][2]
	sheath	[ʃi:θ]	—	sheaths	[ʃi:ðz][2]
	wreath	[ri:θ]	—	wreaths	[ri:ðz][2]

[1] In the sense of 'young man'.

[2] Also regularly: [ju:θs], [tru:θs], [ʃi:θs], [ri:θs]. On *cloth(s)* see Jones, *An English Pronouncing Dictionary*.

It will be noticed that all these nouns, with the exception of those ending in [lf], contain a long vowel or a diphthong.

In the genitive singular the sibilant-suffix is added to the stem in a breathed spirant: *a thief's confession.*

In the genitive plural the sibilant-suffix is added to the stem in a voiced spirant: *thieves' slang.*

The following nouns in [f] form their plural either without or with voicing of the spirant: *hoof* [hu:f] — *hoofs* [hu:fs] — *hooves* [hu:vz]; *scarf* [skɑ:f] — *scarfs* [skɑ:fs] — *scarves* [skɑ:vz]; *wharf* [wɔ:f] — *wharfs* [wɔ:fs] — *wharves* [wɔ:vz]. — *Beef* [bi:f] has a plural *beeves* [bi:vz] in the sense of 'ox(en), esp. fattened, or their carcases' (COD).

234. Two nouns take the breathed plural suffix (spelt *ce*[1]) irrespective of the final sound of the stem: *die* — *dice* [dais];[2] *penny* — *pence* [pens]. The latter also drops the vowel of the second syllable before the plural suffix.

Pence is used collectively, expressing an amount: *Take care of the pence, and the pounds will take care of themselves*; *twopence* [ˈtʌpəns], *threepence* [ˈθrepəns] or [ˈθripəns], *sixpence* [ˈsikspəns]; but *eighteen pence* [ˈeiti:n ˈpens], after a medium-stressed syllable.

When individual coins are meant, the regular plural *pennies* is used: *She gave me my change in pennies.*

Sixpence as the name of a coin has a plural *sixpences.*

Die and *penny* do not normally occur in the genitive.

235. *Ox* has a plural *oxen*; the genitive singular, when it occurs, is *ox's* [ˈɔksiz] (cf. COD s.v. *rump*).

Child [tʃaild] has a plural *children* [ˈtʃildrən, ˈtʃuldrən, ˈtʃldrən], a genitive singular *child's* (*child's play*), and a genitive plural *children's* (*the children's hour*).

236. Some nouns have two stems, differing in their vowels, one of which replaces the stem + sibilant-suffix in the function of the plural: *a man* — *two men.*

---

[1] For more examples of final [s] spelt *ce*, cf. the plural nouns *lice* and *mice* (236), the singulars *ace, dace, pace, ice, price*, and the adverbs *once, twice, since, hence, thence, whence.*

[2] 'Small cube used in games of chance': *to play at dice, a dice-box.* Acc. to Wyld (*Universal Dictionary*) 'the pl. *dice* is far oftener used than the sing., which is hardly ever heard, *dice* being felt as a collective. *Die* is generally avoided, and *one of the dice* substituted for it.' In the sense of *engraved stamp for coining* the regular plural *dies* [daiz] is used.

The functions of the genitive (singular and plural) are expressed by the respective stems + sibilant-suffix: *a man's voice*, *men's clothing*.

man	[mæn]	—	men	[men]
woman	[ˈwumən]	—	women	[ˈwimin]
goose	[gu:s]	—	geese	[gi:s]
tooth	[tu:θ]	—	teeth	[ti:θ]
foot	[fut]	—	feet	[fi:t]
louse	[laus]	—	lice	[lais]
mouse	[maus]	—	mice	[mais]
dormouse[1]		—	dormice	
titmouse[2]		—	titmice	

237. Compounds in *-woman*, and a few trisyllabic compounds in *-man*, form their plurals (and genitives) in the same way: *Englishwoman* [ˈiŋgliʃˌwumən] — *Englishwomen* [ˈiŋgliʃˌwimin]; *sandwich-man* [ˈsænwidʒˌmæn] — *sandwich-men* [ˈsænwidʒˌmen].

Most nouns in *-man*, however, whether trisyllabic or disyllabic, distinguish the plural from the singular in the spelling only: *Englishman/Englishmen* [ˈiŋgliʃmən]; *alderman/aldermen* [ˈɔ:ldəmən]; *footman/footmen* [ˈfutmən].[3] Similarly *the footman's* [ˈfutmənz] *livery* — *the footmen's* [ˈfutmənz] *liveries.*

A plural form *gentlemen* [ˈdʒentlˌmen] is sometimes used, especially in addressing an audience: *Ladies and gentlemen!*

238. Groups or compounds with *man* or *woman* for their *first* element to indicate sex usually pluralize both parts: *man friend — men friends*; *man-servant — men-servants*; *woman doctor — women doctors* (but *man-eaters*, *woman-haters*, etc., in accordance with 228).

Sometimes the second element only is pluralized, especially after *woman*: *woman clerks* or *women clerks*. Cf. 296.

Cf. also *gentlemen farmers*, *yeomen farmers*, where the distinction is a matter of spelling only.[4]

---

[1] 'Small rodent.'

[2] 'Small bird.'

[3] When no connection with the word *man* is felt, the plural is formed by the addition of the sibilant-suffix: *German(s)*, *Roman(s)*.

[4] and where the first nouns do not denote sex, but social position.

C. Nouns with only one Number Form

239. Some nouns have only one number form. Thus many abstract and material nouns never take a plural suffix: *courage*, *despair*, *haste*; *bran*, *coke*, *slag*.

The same applies to many collective nouns, such as *cattle*, *clergy*, *police*. On the construction of these nouns, see 755.

Cf. also 266 (*brace*, *gross*).

With the exception of *clergy*, these nouns do not normally occur in the genitive either.

240. Among names of animals, *deer* and *sheep* never take a plural suffix: *a herd of deer*, *twenty sheep*.

The genitive chiefly occurs in certain combinations: *deer's eye* (American horse-chestnut), *deer's foot* (a kind of grass), *sheep's eyes* (amorous glances), *a sheep's head*, *a wolf in sheep's clothing*. Cf. 286.

241. Some nouns never occur without a plural suffix; they are known as *pluralia tantum* (sing. *plurale tantum*) Such are *riches*, *thanks*, *tongs*. See Appendix, p. 340.

That the final sibilant is felt as a plural ending is shown by the facts that it varies with the final sound of the stem (225); that these nouns, in the function of a subject, take a plural predicate (*Where are the tongs?*) and plural attributive words (*Many thanks!*); and that they are referred to by plural pronouns (*his riches and the way he had acquired them*).

On nouns that always take the plural suffix in one of their meanings (*colours* = flag, etc., but also plural of *colour* = hue) see Appendix, p. 340.

242. Some other nouns in *-s* are usually construed as plurals, though the singular construction also occurs: *Alms are given to the poor* — *The beggar asked for* (*an*) *alms*; *The bellows need* (sometimes *needs*) *mending* — *A bellows is chiefly made of leather*; *All possible means have been adopted* — *Every means has been tried*; *The headquarters of the Army were at Windsor* — *Macbeth did not direct his battles from a remote headquarters*. Cf. 751 and 763.

243. Others again are usually construed as singulars: *Mathematics is* (sometimes *are*) *not his strong point*; *measles is a disease*; *the place became a shambles* (COD).

Gallows is always construed as a singular (*a gallows was erected*), so that the final sibilant can hardly be looked upon as a plural ending. Still, the form *gallowses*, to denote more than one specimen, is usually avoided, which seems to show that the word is not entirely dissociated from the group discussed here.

Though there is, of course, a singular noun *work*, the compound *gas-works* always has the *s*-suffix; it may denote one or more specimens: *There was a gas-works* (*There were two gas-works*) *in the town*.

244. The nouns discussed in 241–243 do not normally occur in the genitive (but cf.: *at the gallows' foot*).

D. Plurals and Genitives of Classical Nouns

245. Classical nouns often keep their classical plural forms: *alumnus*[1] — *alumni* [əˈlʌmnai]; *crisis* [ˈkraisis] — *crises* [ˈkraisi:z]; *larva* — *larvae* [ˈlɑ:vi:]; *phenomenon* [fiˈnɔminən] — *phenomena* [fiˈnɔminə]. For more examples see Appendix, p. 341.

Some have an English as well as a classical plural, the English form being naturally preferred in familiar speech: *cactus* — *cacti* [ˈkæktai]/*cactuses*; *index* — *indices* [ˈindisi:z]/*indexes*;[2] *memorandum* — *memoranda*/*memorandums*.[3]

Others have become completely naturalized and always take the English plural suffix: *irises* [ˈaiərisiz], *orators* [ˈɔrətəz], *prospectuses*, *specimens*, etc.

On foreign words of non-classical origin see Appendix, p. 341.

246. Classical names in a sibilant mostly use the stem (with an apostrophe added in writing) in the function of the genitive: *Achilles'* [əˈkili:z] *death*, *Æschylus'* [ˈi:skiləs] *plays*, *Euripides'* [juˈripidi:z] *personality*, *Menelaus'* [meniˈleiəs] *wife*, *in Socrates'* [ˈsɔkrəti:z] *lifetime*, *Theognis'* [θiˈɔgnis] *poems*, *Zeus'* [zju:s] *decision*, *Aeneas'* [iˈni:æs] *father*, *Catullus' villa*, *Lucretius' poem*; and similarly *St. Barnabas' Day* (June 11), *for Jesus' sake*.

Some writers prefer the full form of the genitive of classical names not ending in [i:z]: *Aeneas's father*, *Catullus's villa*.

---

[1] In England, a pupil of a school or university; in the U.S., mostly in the plural, and with reference to graduates (*Harvard Alumni Magazine*).

[2] Acc. to OED, *indices* is the usual plural form in connection with mathematics and science, and in the sense of 'sign' or 'indication', *indexes* being found at the end of a book.

[3] Abbrev. *memo*, pl. *memos* [ˈmemouz].

CHAPTER ONE

USE OF THE NUMBER FORMS

247. As stated in 226, the stem of a noun is used to denote the singular as distinct from the plural number, the stem + sibilant being used, according to 227, to denote the plural as distinct from the singular.

This, of course, applies only to names of persons and animals, and of things that are countable. Such nouns are usually called CLASS-NOUNS. They include many words for more or less abstract ideas, such as *hour*, *mile*, *walk*, *ride*, *mind*, *hope*, *virtue*, etc.

1. Class-nouns are sometimes used, without either a plural suffix or an article, in a generalized or abstract sense. Cf. '. . . the dramatist may give him a general idea of the pattern of *event*' (Clifford Leech, *Shakespeare's Tragedies*, p. 53); '. . . that experience must be judged in the light of a norm and that the consequences of a violation of *norm* must be taken into account' (R. H. Heilman, *This Great Stage*, p. 205). — Cf. also *party*, in the sense of 'system of taking sides on public questions' (COD): the king is above party; 'Party is in England a stronger passion than love, avarice, or ambition' (OED s.v. 6b), but the word may also be used in a neutral, or even in a favourable sense).[1]

2. Names of authors (or other well-known people) may be used in the plural, preceded by the definite article, in the sense of 'people like': '. . . heartened too, no doubt, by the spectacle of Lady Gregory's gay and gentle comedies, they came crowding in: the Pádraic Colums and William Boyles and T. C. Murrays, each with his own story to tell, . . .' (M. Mac Liammóir, *Theatre in Ireland*, p. 15.) The same applies to titles of plays (or novels, etc.): 'For as these gentlemen looked about them at the English life they were to portray with such gusto in their *Ways of the World* and their *Schools for Scandal*, . . .' (*Ibid.*, p. 6; note the possessive pronouns.)

248. A singular class-noun preceded by a definite article (322) may denote a class of persons, animals or things thought of as a single entity.

The Mallard or Wild Duck is a resident British bird.

---

[1] Cf. also the last ex. of 470.

It may also stand for an abstract idea for which the thing denoted by the class-noun serves as an instrument:

The pen (= writing, the written word) is mightier than the sword (= fighting, war).

249. The plural of some abstract and material nouns may be used to express intensity, great quantity or extent.

Against his express wishes.
Tossed between hopes and fears.
The sands of the desert.
The waters of the lake.
The moon was already bright in the heavens.

Another instance is *woods*, which may correspond to 'forests', but is often rather equivalent to 'forest', as in the following sentence from Sweet's *Primer of Spoken English*, p. 63: *The man seized Webb without saying a word, and pulled him after him through the woods.* (Cf. 944.) Cf. also Wyld's *Universal Dictionary* s.v.: *to ride through the wood(s).*

250. Some abstract and material nouns occur in the plural to denote different kinds or degrees of the idea expressed. Thus *alcohol, tobacco, of different strengths*; *coffees*, *teas*, *wines*, *soils*.

Cf.: When I placed upon the tiny counter of a village post-office letters addressed to Camembert and Gorgonzola, the post-mistress said: 'But they're cheeses!' (i.e. kinds of cheese). They were no more to her; and, I suspect, to most of us. (Cecil Hunt, *Talk of the Town, The Place Names in Our Language*, London, 1951, Foreword.)

251. In familiar and slangy English plural names of things are sometimes used as names or nicknames for persons professionally connected with them. Thus *boots*, for the hotel-servant who cleans boots; *buttons*, for a liveried page; *carrots*, for a red-haired person; *chips*, for a ship's carpenter; *Guns*, for the Gunnery Officer of a destroyer; *Sparks*, for a wireless operator. In *Torps*, for the Torpedo Officer, and *props*, for the property-man in the theatre, *s* is added to shortened forms.

The latter also applies to pet names or nicknames derived from shortened names of persons, such as *Babs* for *Barbara*, *Wedders* for Wedderburn, *Wimbles* for Wimsey, and *Mr. Chips* for Mr. Chipping (the hero of a well-known story of public-school life), where *-s* is a hypocoristic (888) rather than a plural ending. — Cf. *turps* = oil of turpentine, on which OED observes: 'the final *-s* appears to be collective'.

252. In American English names of seasons, days and parts of the day are often used in the plural (or at least with the *s*-suffix) to denote repeated occurrence:

He was accustomed to working nights (Engl.: at night).
. . . the heat that's descended on us. One expects it here summers (Engl.: in summer).

---

253. As stated in 226*b*, the stem of an English noun may be used ATTRIBUTIVELY (cf. 792 ff.), no matter whether one or more specimens are meant. This applies to groups of two separate nouns as well as to compounds; the border-line between these two types is often difficult to draw.[1] The following cases may be distinguished.

254. Groups of the type *boy scout*(*s*), *girl guide*(*s*), *lady doctor*(*s*), whose first element serves to indicate sex, inflect the last element only. Cf. 238 and 228.

255. With *the boy scout movement* we pass over to type two: a noun (*scout*), in spite of its plural meaning, takes the singular form as an attributive adjunct to another noun (*movement*). Other examples are *the slave-trade*, *a negro insurrection*, *a stamp collector*, *a dog show*, *a man-eater*, *a tooth-brush*, *soldier speech*, *an all-purpose room* (= *a room used for all purposes*).

256. Type three is a special case of type two: the attributive noun, denoting an amount, a weight, a measure, etc., is preceded by a numeral higher than one, which otherwise requires the plural suffix: *five pounds*,[2] but *a five-pound note*; *ten miles*, but *a ten-mile walk*; *twopence halfpenny*, but *a twopenny-halfpenny stamp.*[3]

257. Type four consists of compounds whose first element otherwise takes a plural suffix, either invariably (241), or generally, or in

---

[1] This also appears from the spelling, the same collocation being sometimes written as two separate words (*head master*), sometimes with a hyphen (*head-master*), sometimes as a single word (*headmaster*). In the majority of cases usage is fairly settled; thus always *boy scout*, but *bookcase*. (Note the difference in stress; but *head*(-)*master* is always even-stressed, no matter how it is spelt.)

[2] But in slang: *five quid*. Similarly *ten bob* = ten shillings.

[3] In Northern English, however, the usual form is *a twopence-halfpenny stamp*.

one of its meanings. Examples of the first group are (*a game of*) *billiards*, but a *billiard-table*; *the Balkans*, but *the Balkan peninsula*; *munition-workers* (make *munitions*); of the second: *oatmeal* (*oats*), *an ash-pan* (*ashes*), *a sweepstake ticket* (*sweepstakes*), *a holiday course* (held during the *holidays*), *barrack-life* (life in *barracks*); of the third: *a spectacle-case* (to wear *spectacles*), *a card-sharper* (to play [at] *cards*), *sight-seeing* (the *sights* of London).

258. There is a tendency, however, for words usually taking a plural suffix to keep the suffix in attributive position. Thus always *an alms-house*, *an arms depot*, *a bellows-mender*, *the Forces programme* (BBC during World War II), *a gallows-bird*, *a goods-train*, *the points* (*rationing*) *system*, *a savings-bank*. Usage is divided in cases like *Trades Union(s)* beside *Trade Union(s)*; *profits tax* and *profit tax*; *scissors-grinder* by the side of the more usual *scissor-grinder*; *trousers-pocket* by the side of *trouser-pocket*; *customs duties* by the side of *the Custom-house*.

On the other hand, we always find *the United States Government*; *British Industries Fair*; *Films Quota Act*; *the Young Turks Party*; *a two-thirds majority*.

Note *British Book Exhibition* beside *Book Exhibitions Department*, both from a letter by a British Council Representative.

259. The use of the noun-stem in a COLLECTIVE sense (226*c*) is common among sportsmen[1] (though not confined to them) with reference to wild animals. Thus *to shoot duck*; but *a farmer raises ducks*. Similarly *to catch fish*, *trout*, *salmon*, *mackerel*, *cod*; *fowls* (= *hens*) *in a farm-yard*, but *snares for wildfowl* [ˈwaildfaul]; *herds of antelope*, *buffalo*, *giraffe*, *zebra*.

Many of these nouns also occur with the plural suffix. Those that are (nearly) always used without include *grouse*, *wildfowl*; *carp*, *cod*, *haddock*, *mackerel*, *perch*, *pike*, *trout*, *salmon*.

260. Note that these stems may be preceded by a numeral: *six mackerel*, *a few antelope*. When the number is small, the collective meaning may be less evident:

He caught two salmon and three trout.

When different species are meant, the plural suffix is used:

A book on American fresh-water fishes.

[1] i.e. persons fond of hunting, shooting, or fishing.

261. The collective noun-stems mentioned in 259 may take a plural predicate and plural attributive and anaphoric[1] words. Cf.:

> There were many fish at that time of the year, and the best time to catch them was during the night.

262. They may also be used in a MATERIAL sense:

> We had salmon for lunch and duck for dinner.

263. Names of plants may also be used collectively without a plural suffix, though they do not take a plural predicate or plural attributive and anaphoric words (cf. 261).

> Oak and beech began to take the place of willow and elm.
> The short grass was rich with white violet and snowflake and cyclamen [ˈsikləmən].
> A rocky bluff overgrown with large cactus.
> The first of the poppies appeared beside the last of the wild narcissus.

As appears from the last two examples, the collective use of the noun stem sometimes makes it possible to avoid the dilemma of the classical or non-classical plural of Latin names of plants (245).

264. Other nouns whose stems are used in a collective sense are *craft*[2] (= ships, boats), *aircraft*[2] (= aeroplanes), *horse* (= cavalry), *foot* (= infantry). *Horse* and *foot* in this meaning are now less common than they used to be.

These nouns are construed as plurals.

> Eighty odd craft made up their fleet.
> Two of our aircraft are missing.
> Light horse.

265. Nouns like *coal*(*s*), *coin*(*s*), *fruit*(*s*), *hair*(*s*), may be used in the stem-form as collectives, and in either the singular or the plural to denote single specimens: *put some more coal on the fire—a few coals are still glowing*; *his hair is grey—he has some grey hairs.*[3]

266. Nouns denoting a fixed number fall into two groups. *Brace* (= two) and *gross* never take a plural suffix.[4]

> Several brace of partridges.
> Ten gross of buttons.

---

[1] An anaphoric word refers to some word already mentioned, as *them* in the following example, and in the last example of 241.

[2] But (*air*)*craft* may also denote a single specimen.

[3] Cf. K. Brunner, *Die englische Sprache*, II, pp. 19–20.

[4] *Brace* may take a plural suffix in other senses; cf. COD.

Others take no plural ending when preceded by a definite numeral, or by *several* or *a few*:

> Two dozen eggs.
> Several dozen figs.
> A few score yards.
> Threescore years and ten (Psalm XC. 10).
> Five hundred years.
> Six million inhabitants.

But:

> (Some) dozens of aeroplanes.
> Scores of people.
> Many thousands were killed.

After a definite numeral, *pair* is found both with and without the plural suffix: *three pair(s) of gloves.*

Foot is sometimes used after a numeral higher than one, especially when followed by another numeral: *six foot three* or *six feet three* (*sc.* inches) (COD); also *six foot* (or *feet*) *tall.* Note also *ten stone* ('weight of 14 lb. or of other amounts varying with the commodity', COD). — Cf. p. 99, n. 2.

267. Plural names of objects consisting of two equal parts, such as *tongs* (241), *bellows* (242), *spectacles* (257), *scissors*, *trousers* (258), etc., are often preceded by *pair of* to enable them to take a word expressing number. *Pair* in this function is called a NUMERATIVE.

> I wouldn't touch it with a pair of tongs.
> He boasted only two pair(s) of trousers.

Bellows is also found without a numerative: *a bellows*; cf. 242 and 243.

268. Other numeratives are *head* (before collective names of animals, esp. *cattle*), *piece* and *bit* before abstract and collective nouns. *Head* never takes a plural suffix in this function, but *piece* and *bit* do.

> Twenty head of cattle (game, sheep, oxen).
> What a piece of luck!
> Various bits of news.

CHAPTER TWO

USE OF THE GENITIVE

A. The Genitive Singular

269. As was indicated in 227, the genitive suffixes are used far less freely than the plural suffix. They are also used less freely in spoken English than in written English.

270. In all kinds of English, nouns denoting persons, whether proper names or class-nouns, may occur in the genitive singular. (On the GROUP-GENITIVE, see 230.)

I shall be back in time for mother's birthday.
Jack's bicycle is in the shed.
The dog at once knew his master's voice.

271. Names of animals are also used in the genitive.

It is difficult to explain a bird's notes in writing.
His partner took the lion's share of the profits.

272. Names of things[1] are not as a rule used in the genitive, at least in non-literary English. One exception is formed by nouns denoting time, including some that are really adverbs.

We never had a moment's rest.
Mother is worrying about to-morrow's dinner.

Nouns denoting distance may be used in the genitive when followed by a headword (i.e. the noun qualified by the genitive) related in meaning: *at a yard's distance* (cf. 298).

273. Several nouns denoting things are used in the genitive in set phrases; they cannot be freely combined with other nouns, or used in other than special meanings. Thus *to keep a person at arm's length*, but not, e.g., **his arm's skin*; *a pin's head* = something very small; *a needle's eye* = least possible aperture (but: *Her eye-sight was poor*

[1] By names of 'things' are meant all nouns that do not denote living beings.

— *she could not find the eye of the needle*). For a list of such phrases, see Appendix, p. 342.

Ship's can be combined with almost any other noun: *ship's cabin*, *ship's captain*, *ship's company*, etc.

274. In more or less literary English other names of things (esp. of such as have human associations) may occur in the genitive. Thus *England's greatness*, *London's history*, *for his country's good*, *the city's* (or *the City's*) *representatives*, *the Church's doctrine*, *the world's judgment*, *the play's title* (*ending*, *significance*, etc.; thus often in books on Shakespeare); *at the table's foot*, *at the water's edge*, etc. Cf. 371.

In spoken English the less affective *the greatness of England*, *the history of London*, etc., would generally be used;[1] this is also the ordinary construction in written English.

---

275. The examples given so far all illustrate the ATTRIBUTIVE GENITIVE, which is grammatically subordinated to its headword.[2]

English also makes frequent use of the INDEPENDENT GENITIVE, i.e. the genitive without a headword. In the cases discussed in 276 the headword may be supplied from the context, and the genitive is only semi-independent; in that of 277 (POST-GENITIVE) there is a headword, but what is subordinated to it is the group *of* + genitive, not the genitive by itself; in that of 278 only (LOCAL GENITIVE) there is no headword at all.

276. The headword need not be repeated if it occurs earlier or later in the sentence.

She put her arm through her mother's.
He had read all the Waverley novels, and many of Marryat's.
Chambers's is the only Encyclopaedia that is always up to date.
Maggie's was a troublous life.

---

[1] See H. Svartengren, 'The -*'s*-Genitive of Non-Personal Nouns in Present-Day English,' *Studier i Modern Språkvetenskap*, Vol. XVII (1949), 139–180. Also R. W. Zandvoort, 'Notes on the Genitive', *English Studies*, Vol. XXV (1943), 65–79 (reprinted in *Collected Papers*, pp. 142–160).

[2] On a construction in which the attributive genitive alternates with the definite article, see 394. On cases in which it alternates with an attributive noun-stem, see 589, 805.

With a form of *to be* the genitive in this construction may come to be used PREDICATIVELY.

Whose is this umbrella?—I think it's father's.

277. The attributive genitive always precedes its headword in English.

The only case when an English genitive may be said to follow its headword is when it is the principal part of an *of*-adjunct to a preceding noun. The headword may be qualified by an article,[1] a numeral or a pronoun, or used in the plural without a qualifying word. When the noun in the genitive introduces a new idea, both it and its headword are stressed (*a*); when it has been mentioned before, only the headword is stressed (*b*). The construction is known as the POST-GENITIVE.

a. I gave him an old raincoat of my brother's.
This is that picture of Turner's that he is always talking about.
It was no fault of the doctor's.
I am staying with friends of Mary's.
b. This realism of Carlyle's gives a great charm to his writings.

The post-genitive (not the headword!) is limited to nouns denoting persons and specifying particular individuals.

278. The genitive of a proper name, or of a noun denoting trade or relationship, may be used to denote a building or business (church [and, by extension, parish], shop, school, house, hospital, etc.) with which the bearer of the name is somehow connected (whether as owner or as patron, founder, etc.).

This kind of genitive occurs especially in prepositional adjuncts of place, but, with the exception of nouns denoting relationship, may also be used in other functions (subject, object, etc.). It may be called the LOCAL GENITIVE.[2]

Old St. Paul's was burnt down in 1666.
Her father was vicar of St. Andrew's.
Where did you buy that tie? — At Selfridge's [ˈselfridʒiz].

---

[1] The definite article occurs chiefly when the headword is further specified: *the picture of Turner's that I like best*.

[2] It is sometimes called the 'absolute' genitive; but this term is apt to lead to confusion with the word as used in 'absolute' participle construction (86), and with the 'absolute genitive' in Greek. See also *English Studies*, Febr. 1944.

Would you like to see Madame Tussaud's [ˈmædəm təˈsouz]?
There was a tobacconist's at the corner.
I am dining at my uncle's to-night.

279. It stands to reason that a form thus freely used ceases to some extent to be felt as a genitive. As a result, the apostrophe is generally omitted in names of department stores, publishing firms and the like (*Harrods*, *Woolworths*, *Longmans*, *Cooks*). This, together with the collective character of such names, explains why they are usually construed as plurals.

Harrods are offering bargains in remnants.

280. It is sometimes said that in the above construction a word like *house*, *shop*, *church*, etc., is 'omitted'. This may have been true at the time when the local genitive first came into use; but an Englishman of the present day who speaks of *St. Paul's*, or *Selfridge's*, or *a tobacconist's*, or *at my uncle's*, is not conscious of 'omitting' anything. Neither is it correct to say that in cases like *St. Paul's* or *a tobacconist's* the word 'church' or 'shop' is 'understood': *St. Paul's* as such denotes a church, just as *a tobacconist's* as such denotes a shop.

281. When there are two ways of denoting a place (*St. Paul's — St. Paul's Cathedral*; *Guy's — Guy's Hospital*; *at my uncle's — at my uncle's house*), the shorter is usually the more familiar, the longer the more formal way. This accounts for the use of *house* in the following quotation from J. M. Mackail's *Life of William Morris* (London, 1911, Vol. I, p. 217), a quotation which illustrates two other uses of the genitive as well.

After he ceased to live at Queen Square in 1872, he very often went to lunch at the Faulkners' house a few doors off. He went along, if the day were fine, without a hat and in his French workman's blouse; and a new housemaid of the Faulkners' when she let him in thus dressed for the first time, went down to the kitchen in some perplexity, describing him to the cook as the butcher.[1]

282. In the case of shops the local genitive denotes the shop from the customer's point of view (*Sutton's*, or *Sutton, the butcher's* [230];

[1] *His French workman's blouse* is an instance of the classifying genitive discussed in 286 ff. On *a new housemaid of the Faulkners'* see 277, and the sections on the Genitive Plural. — If the Faulkners themselves had been out of town, *house* could not very well have been dispensed with; but there is no suggestion of this in the context.

the confectioner's; *at my tailor's*) — just as, for instance, *Guy's* as the name of a London hospital will be used primarily by the medical students frequenting it. But suppose one were describing to a friend a street accident that had recently occurred, one would say, for instance, *Do you see that butcher's shop over there?* — because the butcher's function as a caterer for his customers has nothing to do with it.

283. *St. Paul's*, *Guy's*, *the butcher's*, then, are more or less familiar designations used primarily by those connected with the places in question (as church-goers, medical students, customers, etc.). So long as this connection is understood such forms can be used as almost any part of a sentence (subject, object, etc.; see 278). In *I am dining at my uncle's to-night* the connection is that between host and guest, and becomes apparent from the context only. Consequently, whereas in *the tobacconist's was closed* the function of the tobacconist as a tradesman is immediately clear, no such definite idea would be suggested by, say, **My uncle's is at Hammersmith.* This explains why the local genitive of names of relationship is limited to such contexts as in the example given above; in other words, why it is not often used as the subject or object of a sentence.

284. Department stores, on the other hand, like *Harrod's*, *Gamage's*, *Selfridge's*, are nearly always denoted by the local genitive; there is no current alternative such as *Harrod's stores.* As modern developments they have not, as a rule, had the more formal, old-fashioned type of name (genitive + headword) applied to them. Since these forms are hardly ever combined with a headword it is only natural that the apostrophe should usually be omitted (cf. 279).

The apostrophe is also regularly dropped in some names of towns called after their patron saints: *St. Andrews*, *St. Albans*, *Bury St. Edmunds.* The reason is that they are never followed by a headword, though this is owing to their antiquity, not, as in the case of *Harrods*, etc., to their modernity.

---

285. Combinations of an attributive genitive plus headword fall into two groups, according as the noun in the genitive refers to a particular person or thing, or denotes the class or kind to which the person or thing denoted by the headword belongs.

Examples of the former group are *my mother's picture, the man's voice, England's greatness.* This is called the SPECIFYING GENITIVE.

286. On the other hand, *sheep's eyes* (240) are not the eyes of one particular sheep, but a *kind* of eyes (or glances); *a giant's task* is a *kind* of task; *a summer's day* such a day as one expects in summer. Cf. also *a busman's holiday,*[1] *a butcher's shop, child's play, a clergyman's son, a doctor's degree, a farmer's wife, a fool's errand, a lady's maid, a planter's life, widow's weeds; a bird's nest, a cat's paw, a horse's head, a robin's egg, a wolf in sheep's clothing; a death's head, a shilling's worth, a stone's throw, a world's fair.*

This is called the CLASSIFYING GENITIVE.

287. Whereas groups consisting of a specifying genitive plus headword usually have even stress, those with a classifying genitive usually have uneven stress (strong for the genitive, medium for the headword), with a greater difference of pitch between genitive and headword than is the case with a specifying genitive. Cf. *my ˈmother's ˈpicture* and *a ˈdoctor's deˌgree.*

288. Semantically as well as phonetically[2] groups with a classifying genitive are more closely connected than those with a specifying genitive; in fact, apart from the spelling, many of them[3] are hardly distinguishable from compounds.

There are a few examples of compounds with a connective *s* which is neither felt nor written as a genitive ending: *brakesman* (Am. *brakeman*; cf. 805), *craftsman, draughtsman, helmsman, kinsman, statesman, tradesman*; *bridesmaid, heartsease* (= *pansy*); and, with a suggestion of the genitive plural, *beeswax, ratsbane* (see COD).

289. A number of classifying genitives differ from those just discussed in that the groups of which they form part are usually pronounced with even stress. Among them are many combinations with *ship's* (cf. 273): *a ship's carpenter, the ship's doctor, ship's papers,* etc. Also with genitives of nouns denoting time: *a day's work, a good night's rest.*

It should be observed that in these examples the headword is more prominent, phonetically as well as semantically, than in those of 286. Thus we

[1] a holiday spent in one's regular work.
[2] i.e. from the point of view of *meaning* as well as of *pronunciation.*
[3] Compare, however, 289 and 304.

may distinguish *a day's work* from *a day's wages*;[1] but *a doctor's degree* is to be distinguished from *a master's degree* or *a bachelor's degree*. Similarly *the ship's doctor* (cf. *the ship's cook, the ship's carpenter*, etc.), but *a butcher's shop* (cf. *a grocer's shop*).

290. The close connection between a classifying genitive and its headword causes any attributive words preceding the genitive to refer to the group as a whole, not to the genitive by itself.

He took his doctor's degree at Edinburgh.
The children were playing with their doll's house.
Morris in his French workman's blouse[2] (281).
We have done a good day's work.

An attributive word preceding a specifying genitive refers to the word in the genitive: *my mother's picture*. This is the surest test to tell a specifying from a classifying genitive.

291. On comparing examples of the classifying with those of the specifying genitive it will be seen that the two do not cover exactly the same ground. On the one hand, the specifying genitive is the 'freer' of the two, because it is as a rule less limited in its choice of headwords than the classifying genitive of the same noun. Thus *child's* as a specifying genitive can take a great many headwords: *the child's father, mother, parents, health, clothes, toys, feelings*, etc., etc. It will be difficult, however, to find anything like the same number of examples in a classifying function: *child's play, a child's part* (child's portion of inheritance), *her child's* (= childlike) *face*, almost exhaust the possible combinations.

On the other hand, especially with names of animals and names of things, a classifying genitive may be current in cases where a specifying genitive would hardly be used, at least in spoken and ordinary written English: *a lark's egg, a lark's nest*, but *the song of the lark* (see 300); *a stone's throw* (*from the house*), but *the size of the stone. The lark's song* or *the stone's size* would be possible in literary English only.

---

[1] 'And yet', said Scrooge, 'you don't think *me* ill-used, when I pay a day's wages for no work.' (*A Christmas Carol in Prose*, St. I.)

[2] Here *French* qualifies *workman's*, the two together qualify *blouse*, and *his* qualifies the whole group. Graphically, the connections may be represented thus: *his* [(*French workman's*) *blouse*].

292. The number of possible relations between a specifying genitive and its headword, regarded from the point of view of meaning, is practically unlimited. If the headword denotes an object, the genitive may denote the possessor, and we may speak of a POSSESSIVE GENITIVE: *my uncle's car*. If the headword denotes an action, the genitive may denote the agent: *the new member's maiden speech*; *that's Dr. Gwynne's doing*. In this case we may speak of a SUBJECTIVE GENITIVE. The OBJECTIVE GENITIVE is not very usual in ordinary English, which prefers, for instance, *the murder(ers) of Caesar* (311) to *Caesar's murder(ers)*, the construction being rather more frequent when the genitive may be interpreted as one of possession (*Helen's lover, Sylvia's admirers*).[1]

There is no need to label the many possible relations not covered by these three terms; cf. *the king's son*, *Dickens's works*, *yesterday's mail*, *for George's sake*, *the little boy's tears*, *life's little ironies*, *my mother's illness*, *my mother's picture*, etc., etc.

B. The Genitive Plural

293. Genitives formed from plural names of persons[2] not ending in a sibilant-suffix (235, 236, 237) are used in the same way as the genitive singular.

> The men's faces were keen and intelligent, but the women's were dull (270, 276, 285).
> The place was alive with happy children's voices (286).
> Freshmen's beer parties.

294. The specifying genitive plural of other names of persons and animals can be used when the context leaves no doubt as to its identity. It is commoner in written than in spoken English.

> As a solicitor I have to consider my clients' interests in the first place.
> The horses' heads were turned from the fire.
> She had eyes quite unlike her parents' (276).
> The Morrises were friends of my grandparents' (277).
> We are dining at the Johnsons' to-night (278, 281).

295. In groups with a classifying genitive the genitive usually takes

---

[1] Cf. the last paragraph of 301.

[2] The genitive of plural names of animals not formed by a sibilant-suffix (*geese's*, *mice's*) is theoretically possible, but occurs very rarely.

the plural form when the number of persons (animals or things) denoted by the word in the genitive is greater than that denoted by the headword: *a ladies' committee, the Ladies' gallery* (in the House of Commons), *a prisoners' camp, a thieves' den, a wasps' nest*. Hence also *ladies' committees, prisoners' camps, thieves' dens, wasps' nests*.

When the number of persons, etc., denoted by the genitive is the same as (or less than) that denoted by the headword, we naturally find *'s* in the singular (*a butcher's shop*). The plural is spelt either *butcher's shops* or *butchers' shops*; the former spelling is in accordance with the rule that compounds (cf. 228) inflect the *last* element. Similarly *farmer's wives* or *farmers' wives, labourer's cottages* or *labourers' cottages, lady's maids* or *ladies' maids, bird's eggs* or *birds' eggs*, etc.

Analogy with the latter group is responsible for such occasional spellings as (*a*) *wasp's nest*(*s*), (*a*) *lover's quarrel*(*s*) in the case of words belonging to the former.

Similar uncertainty prevails in the plural of such a group as *a printer's error*, which is spelt either *printer's errors* or *printers' errors*.

296. In the type of word-group discussed in the first paragraph of the last section we sometimes find the genitive singular *man's* or *woman's* instead of the plural *men's* or *women's*, especially with a headword in the singular. Thus *a man's club* by the side of *a men's club*; *a woman's college* by the side of *a women's college*. This seems to be to some extent a matter of 'sound-symbolism': the singular forms are preferred because they have a more 'manly' sound,[1] though the 'pull' of the plural form of the headword usually induces the genitive plural (*men's clubs, women's colleges*).

We sometimes find (*a woman in*) *men's clothes* by the side of *man's clothes*. Cf. also *gentleman's outfitter* (Wyld), though here the difference is only one of spelling (cf. 238).

297. Nouns denoting time (272) may also occur in the genitive plural, though the apostrophe is not always written (or printed).

[1] Students reluctant to accept this explanation in the case of *woman's* may be referred to Jespersen's *Modern English Grammar*, Vol. II, p. 194.

We had (a) five minutes' talk before breakfast.
It's nearly two hours' walk.
He owed me several months' rent.
In ten or twenty years time.

298. Names of measures or values may occur in the genitive plural if they are followed by a headword related in meaning. (Cf. 272, and *a shilling's worth*, 286.) The apostrophe is sometimes omitted.

The fox ran by at less than a hundred yards' distance[1] from where I stood.
He had chosen a shawl of about thirty shillings' value.
A thirty miles march.

299. The alternative construction discussed in 256 (*a ten-mile walk, a five-minute talk*) differs from that of 297 and 298 in being, as a rule, more distinctly classifying (i.e. it denotes a *kind* of [talk]). Cf. also *a ten-day visit, a ninety-nine year building-lease* (Kruisinga, *Handbook*[5], § 912).

C. Genitive and *Of*-Adjunct

300. In the linguistic consciousness of speakers and writers of English the genitive is associated with certain uses of the adnominal[2] *of*-adjunct. Thus *his master's voice* is felt as nearly equivalent to *the voice of his master*; *the play's title* (274) is a possible alternative to *the title of the play*; though a word-group like *the skin of his arm* could not be replaced by **his arm's skin* (273).

We will therefore ascertain, on the one hand, what is the difference, if any, between the two constructions in cases where both may occur and, on the other, when the *of*-adjunct is used to the exclusion of the genitive (or vice versa).

301. With proper names (270) the genitive is commoner than the *of*-adjunct, the latter being chiefly used for the sake of balance.

---

[1] *Feet* never takes the genitive ending: *at a hundred feet distance*. This might prompt the question whether *yards'* is to be understood as a genitive or as a mere plural, the more so as the apostrophe is sometimes omitted. The fact, however, that the (undoubted) genitive is used in the singular (*at a yard's distance*) supports the interpretation of *yards'* as a genitive; besides, the mere plural is not very common in attributive function.

[2] An 'adnominal' adjunct is one attached to, and qualifying, a noun.

Thus *John's father*, but *the father of John and Mary*; *James's reign*, but *the reign of James the Second*; *Shakespeare's plays*, but, on a title-page, *The Works of Shakespeare*; *Dickens's novels*, by the side of *the novels of Charles Dickens*.

It should be noted that the position after the headword usually gives more prominence to the proper name than the position before the headword, which is the only one possible for a word in the genitive. Thus *the novels of Charles Dickens* draws attention to the name of the author, whereas *Dickens's novels* emphasizes *novels* at least as much as *Dickens's*. Hence *The Life and Death of Jason*; *Morris studied Icelandic under the guidance of Mr. Magnússon.*

If the headword requires an indefinite article, the *of*-adjunct is the only possible construction: *He was a great admirer of Chaucer.* Also in: *They were great admirers of Chaucer.*

302. Names of relations that occur without a preceding attributive word — *(grand)father*, *(grand)mother*, *uncle*, *aunt* (270) — nearly always prefer the genitive-construction to the one with an *of*-adjunct: *mother's birthday*.

When these words are preceded by a possessive pronoun, English continues to prefer the genitive, except for the sake of special emphasis, when an *of*-adjunct may be used.

> Illness prevented him from attending his mother's funeral.
> The death of his uncle, coming almost immediately afterwards, was a new shock to him.

303. With other names of persons in the singular (270) the choice between the SPECIFYING genitive and the *of*-adjunct is usually determined by the same considerations as in the case of proper names. This may be illustrated by another quotation from J. W. Mackail's *Life of William Morris* (Vol. I, p. 20):

> In an unpublished story written fifteen years later, the description of his hero's boyhood has many passages in it which are unmistakably drawn from his own experience. The dreams which mingle with the healthy life of a boy, the first beginnings of thought, of sentiment, of romance, are touched[1] in these passages from knowledge and vivid recollection.

In *his hero's boyhood*, *boyhood* is the principal idea; that the story had a 'hero' may almost be taken for granted. Hence the use of

[1] i.e. described.

the genitive, in the less emphatic position before the headword. At the beginning of the second sentence, the principal idea is still that of *boy*(*hood*); hence the *of*-adjunct — *the healthy life of a boy* — with *boy* in the emphatic end-position, and, incidentally, parallelism with *the first beginnings of thought*, etc.

304. CLASSIFYING genitives are mostly inseparable from their headwords, so that there can, as a rule, be no question of replacing them by an *of*-adjunct. Thus always *a doctor's degree, a lady's maid*, etc. In some cases, where the connection between genitive and headword is less close, an *of*-adjunct may occur: *a clergyman's son — the son of a clergyman*; *a planter's life — the life of a planter.*

That classifying genitives of the latter type are separable from their headwords also appears from a quotation like the following, where the headword is not repeated the second time:

'Not me.' He was very emphatic. 'I've had enough of it. A steward's life's no good.' — 'Not even a smoke-room steward's, in a first-class ship?' — 'No, sir.' (J. B. Priestley, *English Journey*, Tauchnitz ed., p. 20.)

305. The specifying genitive exists by the side of the *of*-adjunct in the case of the names of the larger and more familiar animals. Thus *the elephant's trunk — the trunk of the elephant*; *his horse's tail — the tail of his horse.* Spoken English usually prefers the latter construction, especially in the case of the smaller and less-known species (*the wings of a butterfly*).

What was said above of the classifying genitive also applies to names of animals: it would be very unusual to say, e.g., *the egg of a robin* instead of *a robin's egg*, and impossible to replace *a cat's paw* ('person used as tool by another') (sometimes written *catspaw*; cf. 288 n.) by 'the paw of a cat'.

306. With names of things the *of*-adjunct is the rule, with the exceptions noted in 272, 273, 274 and 286. Examples will be unnecessary.

307. An attributive genitive with the headword mentioned before (276) may be replaced by an *of*-adjunct preceded by *that* or *those*: *She put her arm through that of her mother*; *He had read all the Waverley novels, and many of those by*[1] *Marryat.* Cf. 423.

[1] The usual preposition in an adjunct denoting authorship.

A *that of*-adjunct is unusual in initial position; it would hardly be used in the sentence about the encyclopaedia (276).

308. An *of*-adjunct is unusual as an equivalent of a predicative genitive (276).

309. The 'post-genitive' is itself part of an *of*-adjunct. It differs from an ordinary *of*-adjunct in suggesting a subject-object relation between the word in the genitive and its headword: *a friend of Mary's* implies that Mary has a friend or friends; *that picture of Turner's*, that Turner painted the picture. *He was a great admirer of Chaucer*, on the other hand, does not suggest *Ch. has many admirers*, but *He greatly admired Ch.* Hence the post-genitive would not be possible in a sentence like *Though not perhaps a lovable woman, she was an admirable nurse of the sick child.*

See the discussion of this point by P. A. Erades in *English Studies*, August 1952.

310. The local genitive (278) being, not an adjunct to another noun, but what Jespersen (*Modern English Grammar*, Vol. V, 1.31) calls a 'primary', cannot be replaced by an *of*-adjunct, although it may form part of one (*vicar of St. Andrew's*).

311. It has already been said (292) that an *of*-adjunct is more usual than an objective genitive: *the murder(ers) of Caesar*.

On the other hand, the (subjective) genitive is the rule before a gerund in such a construction as *that's Dr. ˈGwynne's doing*.

312. The relation between the genitive and the *of*-adjunct is the same in the case of the plural genitives discussed in 293 as in that of singular names of persons (303).

313. The same is true of the specifying genitive plural of other names of persons and animals in *written* English (294).

Spoken English usually prefers an *of*-adjunct (*the interests of my clients*), as a sibilant-suffix in attributive position generally suggests to the ear the singular number (*my client's interests*). This is not necessarily so with such a word as (*grand*)*parents*', the singular being infrequent; hence the third and fourth examples of 294 are not necessarily confined to written English, though for the third *unlike those of her parents* may be substituted.

The local genitive plural (*at the Johnsons'*) is also quite common in spoken English, an *of*-adjunct being out of the question for the reason stated in 310.

314. After what has been said in 304 it will be unnecessary to explain why classifying plural genitives (295) have no *of*-equivalents.

315. The same holds good for the nouns denoting time discussed in 297 (*several months' rent*).

316. Names of measures and values may also form part of an *of*-equivalent: *at a distance of less than a hundred yards*, *a shawl of the value of about thirty shillings.*

No such equivalent exists for *a shilling's worth*, which forms a closer unit than *thirty shillings' value.*

317. To sum up, it may be said that the genitive is the rule, to the exclusion of an *of*-adjunct, *a.* with *father*, *mother*, *uncle*, *aunt* not preceded by a possessive pronoun; *b.* with classifying genitives; *c.* with nouns denoting time, whether singular or plural; *d.* as a post-genitive, whether singular or plural; *e.* as a local genitive, whether singular or plural; *f.* as a subjective genitive before a gerund; *g.* in a number of set phrases.

The genitive alternates with an *of*-adjunct, with varying ratios of frequency, *a.* with proper names; *b.* with other names of persons in the singular (apart from classifying genitives); *c.* with names of animals in the singular (*ditto*); *d.* in *written* English, with plural names of persons and animals (*ditto*), with certain names of things (274), and in the objective relation (292); *e.* with some names of measures and values.

The *of*-adjunct is the rule, to the (entire or practical) exclusion of the genitive, *a.* with names of things (with the exceptions noted above); *b.* in *spoken* English, with a noun in a plural sibilant-suffix (apart from classifying, local and post-genitives, and from such a word as *parents'*).

Many *of*-adjuncts are not associated with the genitive at all; cf. *a glass of water, a house of cards, a man of tact, her scamp of a husband.*

CHAPTER THREE

USE OF THE DEFINITE ARTICLE

318. A noun may be preceded by a monosyllable called a DEFINITE ARTICLE.[1] Its use in English is more restricted than in some other languages.

The definite article, written *the*, is [ði] before vowel sounds, [ðə] (in rapid speech [ð]) in other cases. There is also a stressed form [ði:], often italicized in print, which is chiefly used when the word is pronounced by itself (e.g. in slow dictation, or when casting about for a substantive), and in the cases discussed in 321.1.

319. The definite article may be used before singular as well as plural nouns. It may be separated from its noun by one or more other words: *the next house*, *the most unreliable man I've ever met*, *the three-year-old prizes*.[2] English does not, however, go to such lengths here as Dutch and especially German.

The definite article may also be used with a noun in the specifying genitive; not, however, with its headword. Thus in *the King's enemies* the article belongs to *King's*, not to *enemies*. When used with a classifying genitive the article belongs to the whole group: *the barber's shop*.

320. In the majority of cases, the definite article denotes that the following noun refers to a special person, animal or thing as distinct from others of the same kind. Thus when we read: *The evening was quiet: there was no wind* — it is understood that the writer means the evening of the particular day described in his story. In a sentence like *The age of Elizabeth saw the defeat of the Armada and the rise of England as a great sea-power*, the nouns *age*, *defeat* and *rise* are

[1] In most of its uses (for an exception see 321.1) the definite article may be called a proclitic (cf. p. 4, n. 1).
[2] Stress on *three*. (Prizes for three-year-old horses. Cf. 226.)

specified by the adjuncts *of Elizabeth*, *of the Armada*, *of England*. In the fable of the wolf and the dog, as told by Sweet,[1] the two animals are introduced at first as *a wolf*, *a dog*, and are then spoken of as *the wolf*, *the dog*: *One night a wolf fell in with a dog. The wolf was all skin and bones, while the dog was as fat as he could be* — meaning, of course, the particular wolf and the particular dog mentioned in the fable. Similarly, *the birds are singing* implies 'the birds around us or near us'.

If a special name is needed, this may be called the SPECIFYING function of the definite article.

321. We have a special case of this function of the definite article when class-nouns like *lord*, *king*, *tower*, *house*, *river*, etc., are understood to refer to a person or thing *unique* in their own sphere. Thus *the Lord* = God; *the King* (*sc.* of England); *the Tower* (*sc.* of London); *the House* (*sc.* of Commons); *the river* (in London: the Thames; elsewhere it may be the Severn, the Trent, etc.).

1. If any one in his ignorance were to ask, for instance, 'which river?', the answer might be '*the* [ði:] river', i.e. the only, or the principal, river in the neighbourhood; and the same with 'the Tower', 'the King', etc.

Strong-stressed *the* [ði:] can be used in a similar function before other class-nouns: she was *the* landlady (i.e. the typical landlady); it is *the* boot for present wear (i.e. the ideal boot).

2. An English informant has noticed in recent years the use of a strongly stressed *the* pronounced as the unstressed form [ðə] but with emphatic articulation, *and retaining the short vowel.* This is used in precisely the same manner as that given above: [ˈðə ˌrivə]. Our informant has noticed this usage mostly among academic people; also in BBC programmes.

The restriction 'in their own sphere' is all but superfluous in cases like *the Bible*, *the Armada*, *the sun*, *the moon*, *the earth*, *the sky*.

322. As was pointed out in 248, a singular class-noun preceded by the definite article may denote a class of persons, animals or things thought of as a single entity. Here is another example:

The early twentieth century was sometimes called the age of *the child.*

With collective nouns and plural class-nouns the definite article emphasizes the idea of collectivity, suggesting that of 'the whole

[1] *Syntax*, § 2014. The other examples in this section are taken resp. from Kruisinga and Erades, *An English Grammar*, 7th ed., § 387 and from Kruisinga, *A Handbook of Present-Day English*, 5th ed., § 1173.

body of . . .', as in *the nobility and gentry*, *the dissenters and catholics*, *the Russians do not like the Germans* (Sweet, *Syntax*, § 2030).

This may be called the CLASSIFYING function of the definite article. It is also found before adjectives used as nouns (778, 780, 781): *the blind*, *the unusual*.

323. In a number of phrases the definite article has a weakly demonstrative force, corresponding to *this* or, more frequently, *that*.

> Tell him I am busy at the moment.
> I could not remember it at the time.
> He said: 'See you later', or something of the kind.
> How much are these melons? — Sixpence, and cheap at the price.

324. Apart from its use before nouns, the definite article is found before adverbial superlatives (though these also occur without it), and before ordinal numerals in dates and titles, where it is usually suppressed in writing.

> At (the) worst our lives are safe. (See also 563, 5th ex., and 789.)
> Charles II (read: Charles the Second).
> May 10th, 1940 (read: May the tenth).

325. The definite article (or at least a word identical in form) has an adverbial function before comparatives, indicating degree or amount.

> The more he gets, the more he wants (569).
> That makes it all the worse.

---

326. With few exceptions the use of the definite article in English, as discussed, agrees with that in other languages.

In a number of cases, however, where other languages require a definite article, English dispenses with it.

327. *Man* and *woman* take no definite article when used in a collective or abstract sense.

> Man cannot live by bread alone.
> The garden seemed untouched by the hand of man.
> The old dispute over woman's alleged inferiority to man.

The same applies to *mankind* and *humanity*.

328. Abstract nouns like *history*, *art*, *life*, *literature*, *love*, *antiquity*, and scores of others, take no article unless applied to a special case.

Note that *English literature*, *life at sea*, *old age*, and similar combinations, though specified as compared with *literature*, *life*, *age* without any qualification, are yet sufficiently general in meaning to dispense with the article.

> The Renaissance is one of the most interesting periods in the history of architecture, and, indeed, of art in general.
> Caesar protected Italian agriculture.
> Life begins at forty.
> [But: The book gives a very good idea of the life of an airman.]

329. No article is used before plural class-nouns used in a general sense.

> After the removal of the disturbers events moved swiftly.
> [But: The events of the next three days are best described in his own words.]
> Members are requested to pay their subscriptions before September 1st.
> His father was the kindest of men. (Cf. 790.)
> The lion is the king of animals.

The same is true of the collective noun *people*.

> People began to wonder what he was up to.
> [But: The young people appear to be enjoying themselves.]

330. Names of meals hardly ever take an article, unless specially qualified.

> Dinner is ready, sir.
> We can talk it over at lunch.
> At the dinner given in honour of the French ambassador the Lord Mayor made an important speech.
> Will you bring in the tea? (i.e. the tea we are waiting for.)

331. Nouns like *school*, *church*, *prison*, *hospital*, *table*, *bed*, take no article when we think of the use made of the building or object.

The article is used when we refer to the building or object as such.

> School begins at half past eight.
> He once hit a ball right over the top of the school.
> Coulson was in hospital for five weeks before he could be tried.
> He put shrewd questions as to the financial position of the hospital.
> I'm getting old, and bed's the place for me.[1]
> The bed was a big four-poster.

In the sense of 'the clerical profession' *Church* takes the definite article (and a capital *C*): *to go into the Church* = *to take holy orders*.

---

[1] D. Sayers, *Busman's Honeymoon* (1937), p. 413.

332. Names of seasons mostly behave like abstract nouns, though the definite article may be found even in general statements.

Winter is the best time for reading.
The first time I was in America was in the autumn (American: fall) of 1923.
They keep a few cows there in the summer.

333. A few nouns denoting time, especially in connection with school life (*term*, *break*, *prayers*, *hall* = dinner; also = *prep*-[*aration*]) are used without the article.

The same applies to *day*, *night*, *morning*, *evening*, *dawn*, *twilight*, *dusk*, when used in an abstract or general sense (*night*=darkness, etc.), and in some prepositional adjuncts.

Come to me during break, will you?
Term[1] was drawing to a close.
Her hair was (as) black as night.
We always got up at dawn.
He had not a soul to speak to from morning to night.[2]

334. Nouns like *day* (and the names of the days of the week), *night*, *week*, *month*, *year*, preceded by *next* or *last* take no definite article, except sometimes when starting from a point of time in the past or future.

The banns are going up next Sunday.
I met him at a concert last week.
The next day she was still feeling weak and giddy.

335. Proper names denoting persons, places and countries preceded by an adjective usually take no definite article.

Tiny Tim was a cripple.
Medieval London was a picturesque, but not a very healthy place.
Our civilization owes a heavy debt to that of ancient Greece.

In *Tiny Tim*, *Old Jolyon*, *little Dick*, etc., the adjective almost forms part of the proper name; such combinations occur chiefly in familiar style. When the adjective is more independent, the group is preceded by the definite article.

The cruel Macbeth had Macduff's wife and children murdered.

---

[1] But: *early in the term*, i.e. the particular term spoken of.
[2] English, like some other languages, usually dispenses with the article in enumerations. Cf. also *between finger and thumb*; *from head to foot*; *sceptre and crown*; *lock, stock, and barrel*. Cf. 783.

336. Concrete[1] nouns like *Heaven,*[2] *Hell,*[2] *Paradise*; *Parliament, Congress*; and abstract nouns like *Fortune,*[2] *Fate*[2], *Nature*[2], *Providence*, all of them used more or less as proper names, take no definite article.

The road to Hell is paved with good intentions.
Fate had decided otherwise.

Cook and *nurse*, like *father, mother, aunt*, etc., take no article in the sense of 'our cook', 'our nurse'.

Cook has given notice.
Nurse is cross.

337. Names of buildings, parks, squares, streets, etc., consisting of a proper name (denoting either a person or a place) and a class-noun take no definite article. Cf. *Buckingham Palace, Trafalgar Square, Hyde Park, Waterloo Bridge, Westminster Abbey, Salisbury Plain, Windsor Forest.*

By the side of these there are a number of names with the article: *The Albert Hall, the Victoria Embankment, the Thackeray Hotel.* Sometimes both types exist: (*the*) *High Street*, (*the*) *Brighton Road.* Cf. 796.

338. As stated in 324, usage varies as regards the definite article before an adverbial superlative (*a*).

Before a predicative superlative the absence of the definite article is the rule (*b*).

a. Wheat grows best in the south of England.
b. He turned against the very people who had been kindest to him.

No definite article is generally found before *most* (*of*) in the sense of *the majority of, the greater part of.*

Most people prefer to take the line of least resistance.
Most of the arable land was under cultivation.

339. It is impossible to mention here all the cases in which English dispenses with the definite article. Many of them belong to idiom rather than to grammar. Cf. *to pay court*; *to lose heart*; *to call a thing to mind.*[3]

---

[1] '(Gram., of noun) denoting a thing as opposed to a quality, state, or action, not abstract' (COD).

[2] Also written without a capital letter.

[3] For more examples see Kruisinga, *Grammar and Idiom*, 4th ed., § 29 ff.

It should be noted that there are also a few instances of the opposite phenomenon, where an English noun with a definite article corresponds to a noun in another language without. This is sometimes (but by no means always) the case with nouns qualified by an adjunct with *of.*

> To the great amusement of the children he performed a few conjuring ['kʌndʒəriŋ] tricks.
> At the request of his widow there were no speeches.

But we find *under* (*the*) *command of*, *under* (*the*) *cover of*, *in* (*the*) *face of* (= despite), *in* (*the*) *presence of* and other phrases both with and without the definite article; and always *in case of* (= *in the event of*), *within reach of*, *by way of*; etc.

CHAPTER FOUR

USE OF THE INDEFINITE ARTICLE

340. Another monosyllable that may precede a noun is the INDEFINITE ARTICLE. Its use in English is less restricted than in some other languages.

The indefinite article is [ən], written *an*, before vowel sounds, [ə], written *a*, in other cases. There are also stressed forms, [æn] and [ei], used when the word is emphasized or pronounced by itself, e.g. in slow dictation, or when casting about for a substantive.

341. The indefinite article is only used before singular nouns, including such words as *alms*, *barracks*, *bellows*, *gallows*, *gas-works*, *headquarters*, etc., which, though plural in form (cf. 242 and 243) may be singular in meaning.[1] It may be separated from its noun in the same way as the definite article: *a young dog*, *a very high temperature*, *a never-to-be-forgotten experience*.

The indefinite article may also be used with a noun in the specifying genitive: *a friend's house*. When used with a classifying genitive the article belongs to the whole group: *a butcher's shop*.

342. The principal function of the indefinite article is to denote that we have to do with a single specimen of the class of persons, animals or things indicated by the noun (often with the implication that any other specimen of the same class would have done just as well).

> A bus stopped close to me and so I climbed to the top of it, let it mount a hill and leave most of the town behind, and got off near a golf-course.

See also the second indefinite article in the first quotation of 343 and the first indefinite article in the last quotation. If a special

[1] Note also: . . . a young woman who hired a horse from *a* local *riding stables* (full quotation in 135.2).

name is needed, this may be called the INDIVIDUALIZING function of the indefinite article.

343. Sometimes the function of the indefinite article is rather to assign a person, animal or thing to a special class or kind. This is the case with the third and fourth indefinite articles in the first of the following quotations, and with the second indefinite article in the last.[1]

> Less than a year before I had produced a play there at the Repertory Theatre; though I doubt if this can count as *a* visit, for my days and nights were spent either trying to keep awake in the theatre or trying to go to sleep in the hotel, *a* pitiful state of mind and body well known to all dramatic folk.

> On two previous visits I had been given a dinner at the University Club. *A* very jolly little club it is too, where they know how to turn Liverpool into something like summer, at least for one evening.

This may be called the CLASSIFYING function of the indefinite article.

344. The difference between the two functions just described may be made clearer by turning the instances given of each into the plural. In that case we have to substitute plural nouns preceded by a word like *some*, *a few*, or a definite numeral, for those belonging to 342, but plain plural nouns for those belonging to 343. Suppose Mr. Priestley had been conducting a party too large for a single bus, and suppose the ride had taken them through a stretch of hilly country, he might have written something like this: *Two buses* (or *A number of buses*) *stopped close to us and so we climbed to the top of them, let them mount some hills* (or *a number of hills*), etc. On the other hand, in the relevant parts of the quotations of 343 we should expect: *though I doubt if these can count as visits*; *Very jolly little clubs they are too.*

Compare also the examples given in Sweet's *Syntax* §§ 2043–45: *they sailed on till they came to an island/they sailed on till they came to some islands* (or *a group of islands*); but *a hill is the opposite of a valley/hills are the opposite of valleys.*[2]

---

[1] The quotations in this section are from J. B. Priestley, *English Journey*, Tauchnitz edition, pp. 242 and 243; that in 342 is from the same book, p. 143.

[2] *A hill* in the first quotation from Priestley belongs to 342 because it denotes a single specimen; in that from Sweet it belongs to 343 because it denotes a feature of the landscape assigned to a special class.

345. It should, perhaps, be pointed out that the indefinite article is not confined to class-nouns. It may precede abstract nouns (*a pitiful state of mind*), even such as do not occur in the plural (239): *an almost superhuman courage.* The noun in such cases is usually qualified by an adjective or an adjunct: *with a courage generally not found in a boy of that age.*

346. A special case of 342 is when an indefinite article is used before a personal proper name preceded by a title; it is then equivalent to *a certain*: *a Mr. Jones* (also *a certain Mr. J.*, *one Mr. J.*), but without the title only *a certain Jones, one Jones*).

This should be distinguished from such a case as *Every budding cricketer should not believe himself a Hobbs*, i.e. a player like Hobbs, which belongs to 343.

347. The first indefinite article in the first quotation of 343 shows that it is sometimes used in a weakly numerical sense (= *one*). Other instances occur after *not* (*not a word, not a trace, not a hair of your head shall be touched*); in *a hundred* (*a thousand*) = *one hundred* (*one thousand*); in *it costs a penny* (*a shilling, a pound*); *one at a time*; and in a number of phrases where other languages use the stressed numeral.

> Rome was not built in a day.
> He emptied the glass at a draught.
> Men, women and children, in a word, the whole population of the parish had turned out to welcome the new vicar.

We may also include a few expressions where the indefinite article is equivalent in meaning to *the same.*

> They were much of a size.
> Birds of a feather flock together.

348. As stated in 340, English makes a less restricted use of the indefinite article than some other languages.

As a general rule it may be said that English uses the indefinite article before singular predicative nouns (581 ff.), and in adjuncts introduced by *as* and *for*.

> You *are* an ass, to miss such a splendid opportunity.
> I want to be an officer.[1]
> As a coach he was a great success.
> He was hanged for a pirate.

[1] In the plural: *They want to be officers* (344).

349. Like other languages English dispenses with the indefinite article before predicative nouns denoting a profession, office, etc., that is normally held at one time by one person only.

Dr. Arnold was headmaster of Rugby.
As mayor of this town it is my privilege to welcome you.

350. The indefinite article is usually dispensed with in *of*-adjuncts to words like *office*, *post*, *rank*, *title*. As in the case of 349 there is in these expressions no idea of numbers.

He was given the post of deputy keeper of the archives [ˈɑːkaivz].
In a short time he rose to the rank of major.

351. Predicative nouns are often used without an indefinite article when a contrast between different capacities of a person is expressed or implied.

Mr. Boyd is Irishman first, critic next.[1]
Mr. Andrew Lang makes a study of Dumas as writer and as man.[1]

Similarly after *to turn*:

In 1882 Morris turned socialist.[2]

But: *No two of his friends agree in their view of the steps by which he became a convinced Socialist.* (J. W. Mackail, *Life of William Morris*, II, p. 79.)

352. As with the definite article (only in reverse order) it is hardly possible to mention here all the cases in which English uses an indefinite article and some other languages dispense with it. Several instances belong to idiom rather than to grammar. Cf.: *He has a right to it*; *He has a turn for mathematics.*[3]

There seem to be hardly any examples of the opposite phenomenon,[4] though there are a few expressions where an indefinite article in English corresponds to a definite article in some other languages: *for a change*; *he expressed a desire to see me.*

353. In conclusion, attention may be called to the distributive function of *a*(*n*): *once a day*, *twice a year*; *a penny an ounce.*

---

[1] Kruisinga, *Handbook*[5], § 1397.
[2] Cf. *In summer milk is apt to turn sour.*
[3] For more examples see Kruisinga, *Grammar and Idiom*, 4th ed., § 25. Note that after *without* a singular concrete noun takes the indefinite article (*he came without a hat*). Cf.: *to act without hesitation.*
[4] Cf. (*a*) *part of it was spoilt* (COD).

PART III

PRONOUNS

CHAPTER ONE

PERSONAL PRONOUNS

354. English has three classes of personal pronouns, denoting, respectively, the person(s) speaking (first person); the person(s) spoken to (second person); (an)other person(s) or thing(s) (third person).

355. The personal pronouns of the first and third persons have distinct forms, *a.* for the singular (*I*, *he/she/it*), and for the plural (*we*, *they*); *b.* for the 'nominative' (*I*, *he*, *she*, *we*, *they*), and for the 'oblique' (*me*, *him*, *her*, *us*, *them*). *It* does not distinguish nominative and oblique.

The third person singular has distinct forms for the 'masculine' (*he/him*), for the 'feminine' (*she/her*), and for the 'neuter' (*it*).[1]

The second person (*you*) makes none of these distinctions.

In prayer (as in the Bible and the Liturgy), and sometimes in poetry, *thou* is used for the second person nominative singular, *thee* for the oblique.

In similar style *ye* occurs for the second person nominative plural; also in the exclamation *ye gods!*

On the verbal forms used with *thou*, see Appendix, p. 336 f.; on weak forms, *ibid.*, p. 342 f.

356. The pronoun of the second person may be used vaguely to denote some one (often the speaker himself) to whom something happens, or may happen, in the ordinary course of events.

> It was not a bad life. You got up at seven, had breakfast, went for a walk, and at nine o'clock you sat down to work.
>
> You never can tell.

---

[1] In other words, the personal pronouns distinguish *a.* PERSON; *b.* NUMBER (except *you*): *c.* CASE (exc. *you* and *it*); *d.* GENDER (3rd p. sing. only).

357. In cases where *I* or *me* would sound too assertive (hence often in the style of authors, editors and critics) the pronouns of the first person plural may be used to denote a single person (the so-called editorial *we*).[1]

We are convinced that this book supplies a long felt want.

In colloquial English *us* is sometimes used instead of *me*, especially after an imperative:

Let's[2] have a look.

358. The pronouns of the first person plural may be used to denote the speaker or writer and those associated with him (his audience, readers, etc.). Cf. 526.

But we must not forget that it was their energy that made the undertaking possible at all.
We are all apt to believe what we wish to believe.[3]

359. *They* may refer to people in general, especially in the phrase *they say*:

They say it's going to be another cold winter.

360. The NOMINATIVE forms are chiefly used as the subject of a sentence, the OBLIQUE forms in other functions.

As nominal predicates, especially after *it is* (*was*) or *that is* (*was*), spoken English uses the stressed oblique forms: *it's me*, *that's him*, *if I were her*. Written English as a rule prefers the nominative forms (*she saw that it was he*), though *it is I* is often felt to be pedantic.

Me is also used in exclamations: *ah me! dear me!*

Note the frequent (though usually deprecated) occurrence of the phrase *between you and I* (=*between you and me*).

361. After *as*, *but* (= except) and *than* the nominative is the usual form in parallelism with the subject, though spoken English also uses the oblique. Cf. 680.

She is as tall as I (me).[4]
No one can do it but he (him).
You are much better off than they (them).

---

[1] It properly belongs in *unsigned* articles (COD).
[2] This is the only case in which [ʌs] is shortened to [s]. Otherwise the weak form is [əs]: *Give us a cigarette, there's a good fellow.* — The imperatives are usually pronounced on a higher tone than the rest of the sentence.
[3] What is called 'wishful thinking'.
[4] Stress on *tall*, not on *as*.

Before a nominative, *as*, *but* and *than* function as conjunctions; before an oblique they function as prepositions.

Except usually functions as a preposition:

They are all out except me.

362. The unstressed oblique forms are used REFLEXIVELY (i.e. with reference to the subject) in prepositional adjuncts, chiefly of place. Cf. 407 and 411.

We had nothing but the sky above us and the sea around us.
He looked behind him to see if anyone was watching.
They carried all their belongings with them.

---

363. The personal pronouns of the third person are chiefly used anaphorically, i.e. to refer to an idea in the speaker's mind, usually expressed by a preceding noun (cf. p. 101, n. 1).

The choice of a pronoun of the third person singular depends, roughly speaking, on whether the reference is to a living being (*he/him* or *she/her*) or to a lifeless thing (*it*); but this principle may be crossed by other considerations.

He and *she* may also be used 'deictically' (413), i.e. to point out a person: Who is *he*? (i.e. the person going or standing there). In this case they are given strong stress. *It* is not used in this way, being replaced by *that*: What's *that*?

364. *He* (*him*) are used chiefly to refer to male[1] persons.

Where's father? — Here he comes.

Occasionally *he* (*him*) refer to a child or baby when the sex is unknown or a matter of indifference.

A baby should have one bath every day and if strong he may have two.
COD *s.v. swing*: *s. child* &c., work the s. in which he sits. (Cf. 368.)

365. *He* (*him*) may also refer to male animals and to animals whose sex is a matter of indifference.

The horse[2] was rather restive at first, but he soon became more manageable.
I must try and kill that fly. — Got him [ˈgɔtim].

For the ordinary person dogs are presumed to be 'masculine' and cats 'feminine'.

---

[1] 'Male' and 'female' are distinctions of sex, and refer to human beings and animals; 'masculine', 'feminine' and 'neuter' are grammatical distinctions (355) and refer to nouns and pronouns.

[2] '(esp.) adult male h., stallion or gelding' (COD).

366. *He* (*him*) are occasionally used with reference to plants or to artificial objects, to express affection or familiarity. A few examples from printed sources are given by Curme, Kruisinga and Poutsma. Sweet (*Syntax* § 1960) instances *watch*, *pipe* (to smoke with). See also a passage, too long to quote here, in J. B. Priestley, *English Journey*, Tauchnitz Edition, p. 239, bottom, and cf. the following quotation from *Everybody's Weekly*, Oct. 11, 1952, p. 12: *He* (*all railway engines are hes*) *was built in Leeds*, etc.

367. In literary English *he* (*him*) are sometimes used with reference to lifeless things, such as *sun*, *river* (and names of rivers), *mountain* (and names of mountains), *oak*, *Love*, *Death*, *Time*, *War*, etc. This usually implies a greater or smaller degree of personification, which in the case of abstract nouns is often indicated by a capital.

Death will come when he is least expected.

368. *She* (*her*) are used chiefly to refer to female persons.

Have you heard from your sister lately? — I had a letter from her this morning.

This gipsy child has gone with her nomadic family to Kent, to join the thousands of Londoners who travel out from the East End for the fruit and hop picking.

The Observer, Sept. 7, 1952 (photograph of a little girl). (Cf. 364.)

369. *She* (*her*) may also refer to female animals whose sex is not a matter of indifference.

The mare whinnied when she saw her master.
A hen with a dozen chickens around her.

370. *She* (*her*) are occasionally used with reference to plants and, rather oftener, to artificial objects, to express affection or familiarity.

Among the latter are *ships*, by whatever names they are called (*boats*, *frigates*, *schooners*, *submarines*, etc.); also *engines* (cf. 366), *trains*, *motors*, *balloons*, *aeroplanes*, etc., whose main characteristic feature is movement.

The *Good Hope* was a three-master built in 1890. She was lost with all hands in a gale off the coast of France.
'Contact!' — the magic word which at aerodromes means: 'Start her up!'[1]

---

[1] This example shows that the idea in the speaker's mind is not necessarily expressed by a preceding noun.

Compare also the following quotations:

'Jack has the honour of ringing the oldest bell we have,' added the Rector. 'Batty Thomas was cast in 1338 by Thomas Belleyetere of Lynn; but she gets her name from Abbot Thomas who recast her in 1380 — doesn't she, Jack?'

'So she do, sir,' agreed Mr. Godfrey. Bells, it may be noted, like ships and kittens, have a way of being female, whatever names they are given.

Dorothy Sayers, *The Nine Tailors* (Albatross ed.), p. 24.

I shall be glad enough to get back to the dye-house at Leek to-morrow. I daresay you will notice how bad my writing is; my hand is so shaky with doing journeyman's work the last few days: delightful work, hard for the body and easy for the mind. For a great heap of skein-wool has come for me and more is coming: and yesterday evening we set our blue-vat the last thing before coming here. I should have liked you to see the charm work on it: we dyed a lock of wool bright blue in it, and left the liquor a clear primrose colour, so all will be ready for dyeing to-morrow in it: though, by the way, if you are a dyer, you must call it *her*.

J. W. Mackail, *Life of William Morris*, Vol. I, p. 318.

25 July. The vat was coming round all day; she seemed to be doing well at 6.30, when I left; a coppery scum was coming on the surface.

Ibid., p. 356.

It will be seen that this use of *she* and *her* belongs to the language of what may be called 'insiders'; though their use with reference to ships is current in wider circles, no doubt because ships are familiar to more people than bells or (the contents of) dye-vats. Compare what was said in 283 on the use of independent genitives like *Guy's*, *the butcher's*, etc.; the use of *St. Paul's*, which is not really limited to 'insiders' (in this case, church-goers), may be compared with the freer use of *she* (*her*) with reference to ships.

371. In literary English *she* (*her*) are sometimes used with reference to lifeless things, such as *moon*, *sea*, *earth*, *country* (and names of countries), *city* (and names of cities), *the Church*; and to abstract ideas such as *Nature*, *Fortune*, *Science*, *Liberty*, *Mercy*, *Peace*, etc. Cf. 274.

England at that time was not the maritime power she has since become.
To know nature is to love her.

If it be asked why *sun* should be 'masculine' and *moon* 'feminine', the answer is that in this, as in many (not in all) of the examples given in 367 and 371, it is the gender of the corresponding Latin noun that decides (*sol* m., *luna* f.; *natura*, *fortuna*, *libertas*, etc., all of them feminine). But *Death*, e.g., is 'masculine' in spite of the feminine gender of *mors*, because it is thought of as something strong and terrible, like *War* (cf. *mercy*, *peace*, which suggest ideas of gentleness).

372. *It* is used chiefly to refer to lifeless things.

Is this house your own? — Yes, I bought it in 1938.
Please shut the door. — It *is* shut.

The plants and objects mentioned in 367 and 370 are referred to by *it*[1] by those who are not 'insiders', or when there is no occasion for familiarity. Even *ship* and its synonyms are sometimes treated as 'neuter'.

The boat was attacked by a constant fire from both banks as it drifted along.

The same applies to the nouns mentioned in 367 and 371 in ordinary English: *Death will come when it is least expected*; *England is unable to feed itself* (406); *To know nature is to love it.*

373. *It* may refer to animals; it usually suggests less familiarity than either *he* or *she*.

We found the dog with a long snake in his mouth, and shaking it furiously.

374. Similarly *it* may refer to a child or a baby when the sex is unknown or a matter of indifference. See the first and second stanzas of Wordsworth's *We Are Seven.* Hence in talking to an adult as if he were a baby:

'Poor Frank! Was all the beef gone? Did it get nothing but bread and cheese and gingerbeer?'

G. B. Shaw, *Mrs. Warren's Profession.*

375. Finally, *it* may refer to nouns denoting a number of persons when the group is thought of collectively (cf. 753 and 754): *Give the public full information so that it may judge for itself.*

---

376. 'Gender', in English, is mainly a matter of the choice of one of the three personal (or possessive) pronouns of the third person singular to refer to a preceding noun (REFERRING GENDER). As has been shown, with a not inconsiderable number of nouns, this gender differs according to context and point of view, so that it is hardly possible to say whether such a noun 'is' masculine, feminine or neuter.

[1] or, in other words, treated as 'neuter'.

There is no such thing in English as 'attributive gender', by which nouns are classified according to the definite articles and/or attributive words used before them; cf. French *le toit, la chambre*; German *der Turm, die Tür, das Haus*; Dutch *de deur, het* ('*t*) *huis*, etc.

---

377. The idea referred to by *it* may also be expressed by a preceding word-group (esp. one containing an infinitive with *to*) (*a*), or by a clause or a sentence (*b*).

> *a.* I am trying to get a taxi. — You won't find it easy.
> *b.* I hope you understand that this is a matter of months, not of weeks? — Yes, you've made it quite clear.
> I hear that John has given up football. — I rather expected it; he was never very keen.
> Father is quite well again, fortunately. — I am very glad of it.

As will be seen, the idea referred to by *it* is not always expressed by the actual words of the preceding group, clause or sentence. In the second example of *b*, for instance, what the speaker expected is that John *would* give up football; indeed he might have said: *I rather expected he would.*

Verbs like *to know, to forget, to try, to tell, to remember* usually do not take *it* to refer to a preceding clause or word-group. Cf. Poutsma, *Grammar*, II, Ch. XXXII, § 22 ff.

> Peter is coming home to-night. — Yes, I know.
> My number is 4035.[1] — I'll try and remember.

Note, however:

> I'm not a young man, and I know it.

On the use of *so* to refer to a preceding clause or word-group see 424 ff.

378. The word-group or clause referred to by *it* may also follow.

> *a.* You won't find it easy to get a taxi.
> It was not easy to get a taxi.
> *b.* He made it clear that it was a matter of months.
> It was clear that it was a matter of months.

As will be seen, *it* as an object may refer to a following infinitive or to a following clause introduced by *that* when there is an intermediate predicative adjective.[2] In the second and third examples

---

[1] Four—O [ou]—Three—Five.

[2] The construction also occurs with a predicative noun (*I think it my duty to warn you*) or a prepositional adjunct (*He has it in his power to kill you*). After *to hear* we find the past participle *said* or a synonym: *I have heard it said that they are paying no dividend this year.*

of 377*b* it would not be used if the clause followed (*I rather expected that John would give up football*; *I am very glad that your father is quite well again*); and the same with an infinitive: *Would you like to come with us for a picnic to-morrow?*

Before a clause introduced by *if* or *when* a few verbs (*appreciate, understand*; *like, love*) take *it* as an object: *Why don't you appreciate it when people are nice to you?* — *How would you like it if I boxed your ears?*

To take it = *to assume* is followed by a *that*-clause: *May I take it that you will sign the document?*

379. In the odd examples of 378 *it* functions as an object, in the even examples as a subject. *It* in this construction is usually called a 'provisional' object (or subject), the infinitive or clause being called the 'real' or 'logical' object (or subject). It cannot be denied, however, that there is something forced about this analysis, and that the infinitive or clause rather completes the meaning of the preceding head-clause, so that there is something to be said for parsing it as a complementary adjunct, or. a complementary clause, rather than as a 'logical' subject or object. Cf. 64 n. and 652.

380. In a few instances of a construction otherwise similar to that just described, *it* is usually dispensed with. This is the case with a small number of set phrases, the principal of which are *to think fit* (*right, proper*), *to see fit*. Verb and adjective form a close group, with the stress on the adjective.

After ten years' devoted service he thought fit to discharge her without a pension.

381. *It* also refers forwards in sentences beginning with *it is* or *it was* in order to give prominence to some part of them. Cf. 627.

It is the work of these twelve years which gives Bunyan a place in English literature.

It was riding to hounds that my son met him.

The construction also serves, not merely to emphasize, but to identify:

This time it was not the woman who was to blame.

382. *It* refers backwards as well as forwards in sentences giving a person's name or identity.

My bag was carried for me by a man I am sure I must have seen before.
I wonder if it was James, our old gardener.
Go and see who it is who rings. — It is John and Mary.

But to describe a person whose identity is known, *he*, *she* or *they* is used.

Mrs. Clement is a neighbour of ours. She is a very nice woman.
They are very nice people.

For a fuller discussion see an article by P. A. Erades in *English Studies* XXX, 299–308, Dec. 1949.

383. With some verbs *it* is used as a 'formal' subject or as a 'formal' object, referring either to some vague notion, or to nothing at all.

As a FORMAL SUBJECT *it* precedes verbs and verbal phrases denoting weather conditions (*it snows*, *it was raining*, *it is warm to-day*).

Note its use before the verb *to blow* accompanied by a noun:

On the night of the 15th it blew a heavy gale.

It is also used in expressions of time and distance (*it is three o'clock*, *it is six miles to Oxford*) and other impersonal statements:

It says in the Bible that all men are liars.

384. *It* occurs as a FORMAL OBJECT, *a.* in phrases like *to fight it out*, *to have it out*, *let him have it hot*; *b.* after verbs (esp. imperatives) like *to chuck*, *to go*, *to hang* (imperative only), *to hop*; *c.* after nouns used as verbs meaning either 'to behave like the person indicated by the noun', or 'to avail oneself of the vehicle or public building indicated by the noun'; and after the adjective *rough* used as a verb, meaning 'to do without the ordinary conveniences of life'.[1]

Most of these expressions are colloquial, those under *b* even slangy. In those under *a* there may be a vague reference to some such idea as 'quarrel'; see also the first of the following examples.

a. The Ayes [aiz] have it.
b. Chuck it, Charley!
Hang it all, I don't want to stand here all day.
Look at those boys fighting![2] My word, they *are* going it!
Hop it, old thing, you're in the way here.

---

[1] On formal *it* in *of*-adjuncts, see 782.
[2] In American English also: *Look at those boys fight!* (cf. 18.2).

Run for it, Jack!
If you're found out, you'll catch it.
c. William lorded it over the other servants.
She was queening it over the younger girls.
They tube it to Hampstead or tram it to Kew.
We tried hotelling it.
I am quite prepared to rough it.

385. In literary English anaphoric *it* (363) may be strongly stressed, chiefly when placed in opposition to another (pro)noun. Cf. Poutsma, *Grammar*, II, Ch. XXXII, § 3*a*; also the present work, 277, 2nd paragraph, 3rd sentence.

In slangy English strong-stressed *it* (often italicized in print) is used as what may be called a formal nominal predicate, in the sense of 'the ne plus ultra' (COD).

For barefaced lying you really are *it*.

Compare also:

Doggerel rhymes for counting out, that is, finding out who is 'it' in a game, are very common.

Note the use of stressed *it* in the sense of 'what we had been waiting for all the time':

There were huge maps on the walls, hand-drawn. The men who had drawn them had already been in sealed camps for six weeks. This, we thought, was it. This was it, at last. At last, we were going to know where it[1] was to be.

Alastair Barthwick, 'Ten Years Back: The Normandy Landing', *The Listener*, June 17, 1954, p. 1036.

[1] unstressed.

CHAPTER TWO

POSSESSIVE PRONOUNS

386. From a functional point of view the possessive pronouns (*my*, *your*, *his/her/its*, *our*, *their*) may be looked upon as the genitives of the corresponding personal pronouns. From a formal point of view this is true of *its* only. It will be seen, however, that these 'genitives' often behave differently from the genitives of nouns. For one thing, they are only used as specifying, not as classifying adjuncts (285, 286); for another, whereas genitives can usually be substituted for *his*, *her*, and for personal *their* (*their father* — *the children's father*), they cannot, as a rule, be substituted for *its* and for non-personal *their* (*their branches* — *the branches of the trees*).

1. In prayer (as in the Bible and the Liturgy), and sometimes in poetry, *thy* and *thine* (before a vowel or *h*) are used for the second person singular.
2. On the weak forms of Possessive Pronouns, see Appendix, p. 343.

387. Another set of possessive pronouns consists of the forms *mine*, *yours*, *his*, *hers*, *ours*, *theirs*. They are known as 'independent' possessives (to distinguish them from the 'attributive' possessives of 386), and will be discussed in 395 ff.

In the second person singular *thine* is used in the same style as *thy*. — *Its* as an independent possessive hardly ever occurs.

388. *Your* may be used in the same general way as *you* (cf. 356).

As you go upstairs, the wall is on your left.

It is also used, often with a half-humorous or contemptuous implication, before a noun denoting a person to be taken as typical rather than individual.

No one so fallible as your expert in handwriting.
Your facetious bore is the worst of all.

This use of *your* has a somewhat archaic flavour.

389. 'Editorial' *our* corresponds to the similar use of *we* (357).

In our opinion this is the best novel of the year.

390. Like *we*, *our* may be used in a general sense (358 and cf. 526).

It is often best to rely on our own efforts.

391. The use of *his*, *her* or *its* is on the whole governed by the same considerations as that of *he* (*him*), *she* (*her*) or *it*, as explained in 363–375.

392. Note the use of a possessive pronoun before nouns denoting some part of the body, an article of clothing, or something else belonging to a person. In those marked *b* other languages often use an oblique or reflexive personal pronoun denoting the person affected.

a. In his right hand he carried a stick.
She waved her handkerchief in token of farewell.
b. That man once saved my life when I was a boy.
He bit his lips, but said nothing.

393. In similar cases English often uses a definite article when the person is not the subject of an active sentence; also in a number of idiomatic phrases.

He was shot through the heart.
The ruffian dealt him a sound whack on the head with his cudgel.
Scrooge had a cold in the head.
He became very red in the face.

It will be seen that the definite article in these examples is used in adjuncts of place. (Cf. 362.) In the following sentence *with his hand* is an adjunct of attendant circumstances, and a definite article would be impossible.

The thief was caught with his hand in the pocket of his victim.

394. Sometimes English has two constructions. Thus we can say either *I looked him in the face* or *I looked in his face*; the former draws more attention to the person affected. For the same reason we say *The dog bit him in the leg*, but *the dog licked his hand*.

There is the same alternative with the attributive genitive of a personal noun. Thus we can say either *He looked the man straight in the face*, or *He looked straight in the man's face*. Similarly *He kissed the girl on the forehead*; but *He kissed the Queen's hand*.[1]

---

395. In cases parallel to those discussed in 275 and 276 English uses the independent possessives (387). In the following

[1] Kruisinga, *Handbook*[5], §§ 837, 838.

examples the headword may be supplied from the context (275):

> She put her arm through mine.
> Ours is the only clock in the village that is always right.
> His was a complex character.[1]
> Whose is this umbrella? — I thought it was yours.

The independent possessives are also used to avoid having two possessive pronouns before a noun: *his family and mine*.

396. The independent possessives are also used in the same way as the post-genitive (277). They are usually unstressed in this construction (*a*), but may take contrasting stress (*b*). The construction may be denoted as the post-possessive.

> *a.* I gave him an old raincoat of mine.
> He hated that pride of hers. (Cf. 416.)
> *b.* It was no fault of *theirs*.

As with the post-genitive (cf. p. 105, n. 1) the definite article occurs chiefly when the headword is further specified:

When I got back home I sent him a copy of a book of mine, and at once he sent me the water-colour sketch of his, of one of the Tyne bridges, that I liked best, though I am sure it was his own favourite too.
J. B. Priestley, *English Journey*, Tauchnitz ed., pp. 314–5.

The independent possessives are not used in the local sense discussed in 278 ff.; cf. *at (to) my house, at your house, at your place*, etc.

397. The independent possessives are used, but only after the corresponding personal pronoun, to denote a person's family.

> With best wishes for you and yours.

Yours also occurs in polite formulas at the end of letters: *Yours truly* (or *Truly yours*), *Yours sincerely*, etc.

---

398. The various relations between a specifying genitive and its headword distinguished in 292 may also exist between a possessive pronoun and its headword: *my car*, *his maiden speech*, *that's her doing*, *his murderess*, *her lover*, *your mail*, *for their sake*, *life and its little ironies*, etc.

The objective possessive occurs more frequently than the

[1] More literary than *His character was a complex one* (512). Similarly *Mine is a long and sad tale.*

objective genitive: *her readers*, but usually *readers of Jane Austen*; *his murder*, but usually *the murder of Caesar* (cf. 311).

---

399. As with the genitive of nouns (300 ff.), though to a far more limited extent, an *of*-adjunct sometimes occurs with a meaning similar to that of a possessive pronoun.

With reference to persons this applies (*a*) to a number of set phrases, (*b*) to some occasional combinations. In both the *of*-adjunct (or at least the context in which it is used) often expresses some special feeling (despair, distrust, disdain, hate, pity, etc.).

a. That cough will be the death of me one of these days.
I did not like the look of him.
She could not for the life of her remember his address.
Anything is good enough for the like(s) of you.
I hate the very sight of them.

b. They were slaughtered in youth; and the parents of them have gone lonely, the girls they would have married have grown grey in spinsterhood and the work they would have done has remained undone.

J. B. Priestley, *English Journey*, Tauchnitz ed., p. 172.

I hope it may come to seem yet more strange that Lyly should have had to wait so long for his due. The neglect of him is, I think, partly referable to his depreciation[1] by Collier.

R. W. Bond, *Complete Works of John Lyly*, vol. I, p. V.

400. With reference to things, an *of*-adjunct with a meaning similar to that of a possessive pronoun is somewhat commoner. It is frequently used without any emotional connotation; cf., however, phrases like *The pity* (*the shame*, *the injustice*) *of it!*

It is not difficult once you have caught the trick of it.
He struck a match, and then another, and by the light of them looked for his watch.
It was only a small village but quite attractive. The name of it was Shipton.
On the face of it[2] it sounds quite reasonable.
The main street ran downhill, with a Baptist chapel at the end of it.
This scarf is made of silk, and the colour of it is mauve. (BBC, early 1948.) [See also the quotation of 342.]

---

[1] Cf. 398. Note that the meaning of the *of*-adjunct in this quotation is objective, that in the preceding quotation possessive.

[2] *On its face* would suggest a literal application (*The child fell on its face*). In many cases (*the trick of it, get the hang of it, the long and the short of it*) substitution of the possessive pronoun would be impossible.

Just as the genitive of names of things occurs chiefly in literary English (274), so the substitution of *its* or *their* for *of it* (*of them*) (*by their light, at its end*) would sometimes give the sentence a less colloquial turn. But the parallel must not be pressed too far; even with reference to things an *of*-adjunct with *it* is far less common than one with a noun.[1]

---

401. An attributive possessive may be followed by *own* to emphasize ownership (*a*), or to express or imply a contrast (*b*).

> *a.* I will not be dictated to in my own house.
> My own flesh and blood to rebel!
> *b.* Why don't you use your own pen instead of always borrowing mine?
> She cooks her own meals (COD).[2]

402. The combination may also be used as an emphatic post-possessive (cf. 396).

> She had always wanted a room of her own.
> As they had no children of their own, they had adopted an orphan.

403. As appears from the examples of 401, *own* is always preceded by a possessive pronoun (apart from the construction mentioned in 405). The only exception is in the expressions *own brother*, *own sister* 'with both parents the same' (COD), *own cousin* = *first cousin*:

> He is own cousin to the King of Denmark.

404. *My* (*your*, etc.) *own* may, like the independent possessives (395), be used with a preceding headword understood.

> I need not borrow your pen any more, I have brought my own.

In a sentence like the following, however, *his own* means *his private property*, and no headword is understood:

> The last instalment of the mortgage [ˈmɔːgidʒ] was paid off, and the house was all his own.

---

[1] Cf. Sapir, *Language*, p. 176: 'It is significant that *theirs* is hardly ever used in reference to inanimate nouns, that there is some reluctance to so use *their*, and that *its* also is beginning to give way to *of it*.'

[2] 'Expressing idea of personal activity rather than possession' (Wyld).

405. *Own* is also, though less frequently, added to the attributive genitive of a noun.

He is a bit of a spoilt child: mother's own darling.
The King's Own Scottish Borderers.[1]

---

[1] Name of an infantry regiment.

CHAPTER THREE

COMPOUND PERSONAL PRONOUNS

406. Compound personal pronouns are formed by the addition of *self* (plural *selves*) to the possessive pronouns of the first and second persons, and to the oblique form of the personal pronouns of the third person.

PERSON	SINGULAR	PLURAL
First:	*myself*	*ourselves*
Second:	*yourself*	*yourselves*
Third:	*him/her/itself*	*themselves*

On *oneself* see 526.

407. The compound personal pronouns are used reflexively to express identity between what may be roughly described as the subject and the object. They may be either weak-stressed or strong-stressed.

When weak-stressed they may occur (*a*) as direct objects; (*b*) as indirect objects; (*c*) after prepositions.

a. As a boy Napoleon distinguished himself by his application to mathematics.
He said nothing, but helped himself to some more strawberries.
I expect you to behave yourself.
b. He gave himself a great deal of trouble.
She made herself some tea.
c. He was muttering to himself that his new dinner-jacket was missing.

Verbs taking a reflexive pronoun as a direct object are called reflexive verbs. Some of them never take another kind of object, e.g. *to avail oneself* (of an opportunity), *to perjure* [ˈpəːdʒə] *oneself*, *to pride oneself* (on something), etc. Others can take another object, but not in the same sense, e.g. *to apply oneself* (to a task), but *to apply a new method*. Others again can take a non-reflexive object without any difference of meaning: *to wash oneself — to wash one's hands*.

408. The compound personal pronouns are pronounced with strong stress on the second element when a contrast is intended.

In this case they may occur (*a*) as direct objects; (*b*) as indirect objects; (*c*) as the nominal part of the predicate (583); (*d*) after prepositions.

a. She knew him better than he knew himself.
b. I gave him better food than I allowed myself.
c. That poor boy was myself.
I'm not quite myself these days.[1]
d. They seem very fond of talking about themselves.
You must find it rather dull living[2] here all by yourself.

409. The strong-stressed compound personal pronouns may stand in apposition to a noun or to a simple personal pronoun. In this case they are used either after the predicate and the object (if any) (*a*), or immediately after the noun or pronoun to which they belong (*b*), to denote that a certain person or thing and no other is meant.

a. I offered to carry the parcel myself.
The manager decided to answer the letter himself.
b. Peter felt that he himself was growing smaller and smaller.
What does William himself think of it?

The noun or pronoun to which the compound personal pronoun stands in apposition is usually the subject of the sentence. It may, however, be the object, as in the following quotation:

'And did you see much of him after that?'
'Well — a fair amount. He asked me to parties and things like that. They were rather fun.'
'But you didn't like him himself?'
'No, I thought he was a shivery kind of man.'
Agatha Christie, *Cards on the Table*, Pan Books, p. 41.

410. A strong-stressed compound personal pronoun may also be used, in a sense almost identical with that of the corresponding simple personal pronoun, in combination with a noun, with which it is linked by *and*, *like*, or another connecting word. The group may serve as the subject or object of a sentence; it may also be preceded by a preposition.

My sister and myself were the only ones not down with the flu.
He said it would be best to send my brother and myself away out of danger.
There had always been complete understanding between his father and himself.
To a poor bookworm like myself such a blow is irreparable.

[1] COD s.v. *himself*: *he is not himself* (not in normal state of body or mind).
[2] A present participle, not a gerund. Cf. 104.

In these examples the corresponding simple personal pronouns (*My sister and I*, *my brother and me*, etc.) would also be quite possible; but it will usually be found that in contexts where the compound pronoun is used, the person to whom it refers has been mentioned before.

411. After the prepositions *among* and *between*[1] the compound personal pronouns may be used in a reciprocal sense (= *each other*).

They were always quarrelling among (between) themselves.[2]

Note that the simple personal pronouns also occur, in conformity with 362:

The three mates divided the watches among (between) them.[3]

Among (*between*) *themselves* (with stress on *themselves*) would imply that others were excluded.

On various idiomatic uses of *among* and *between*, with compound as well as simple personal pronouns, see Poutsma, *Grammar*, II, Ch. XXIV, § 22 f.

---

[1] *Between* is not restricted to a relation to *two* points, etc. See an article by A. Bolbjerg in *English Studies*, Aug. 1949; also OED s.v. *Between*, V. 19.

[2] Stress on quarrelling.

[3] Stress on the preposition.

CHAPTER FOUR

DEMONSTRATIVE PRONOUNS

412. There are four demonstrative pronouns in common use: *this*, plural *these*; *that*, plural *those*.

This and *these* refer to what is near in space, time or conception, *that* and *those* to what is farther off.

1. *This* and *that* agree with the English definite article in not distinguishing gender (see 376).

2. On *yon* and *yonder* as demonstrative pronouns, see COD.

413. The demonstrative pronouns may be used to point out or mention something for the first time. This is sometimes called their DEICTIC [ˈdaiktik] function. (For the etymology of this word see COD.)

> Look at this picture!
> I am afraid I shan't get it finished this week.
> See those horses?
> Do you remember that time we went up to town together?

Note the use of *this* and *these* in adjuncts of time meaning 'just past':

> I have been asking for it this (or: these) three weeks.

Note also that *this evening*, *summer*, etc., may refer to a near future, as appears from OED s.v. *This*, II. 1: '*This morning, this afternoon, this evening* now always mean "the morning (etc.) of to-day" (whether past, present, or future).' Cf. also the famous saying of Wm. Pitt, on hearing the news of the battle of Austerlitz: 'Roll up that map; it will not be wanted these ten years.'

414. The demonstrative pronouns may also be used anaphorically, i.e. to refer to something mentioned before, the difference between *this* (*these*) and *that* (*those*) being similar to that explained in 412.

> When he had ceased talking, 'Why is he telling me all this?' she wondered.
> Texas and Arizona did not form part of the Union then. These territories were not added until much later.
> My great-grandmother used to wear a crinoline, but that was in the time of Queen Victoria. Ladies' clothes were very unpractical in those days.

415. In some cases *this* refers to what is to follow, *that* to what precedes. This is illustrated by the two following quotations:

In the French official estimates of the money to be expended by foreign nations at the Paris Exhibition of 1937 Germany heads the list with forty million francs, followed (in this order) by Italy, the U.S.S.R., Belgium, the United States, and Great Britain.

Hamblock, *British Consul* (London, 1938), p. 13.

His account of formative influences — Burne-Jones, Japanese prints and Greek vases, in that order — strikes one as just.

The Times Literary Supplement, Jan. 17, 1929, p. 43/2.

416. The demonstrative pronouns, especially in their deictic function, are often used with emotional connotation. The kind of feeling implied (affection, vexation, contempt, disgust, etc.) depends upon the situation.

I am not interested in this planning business.
(Policeman speaking:) 'Now then, what's all this?'
He hated that pride of hers[1] (396).
How he used to love these old villages of ours.[1]
He's one of those so-called modern artists.

Compare also such well-known advertising slogans as *Kill that fly!*; *keep that schoolgirl complexion*; *that Kruschen feeling*; and book titles like *This Freedom* ('this much-vaunted f.'), *This Modern Poetry* ('that everybody talks about'), *This Salzburg* ('S. as a musical centre and everything connected with it'; cf. Shakespeare's affectionate *This England*).

Note the more matter-of-fact *this country* = England; in many other languages the place of *this* would here be taken by the possessive pronoun of the first person plural.

417. Emphatic *that* is sometimes found in the sense of *such* (*a*). In colloquial English it is also used adverbially, to qualify an adverb or an adjective.

He was wounded to that degree that he resigned (COD).
I will go that far, but no farther.
I'm that hungry I could eat a dog.

Note the (literary) use of emphatic *that* (= *something*), after *to have* or *to be* and (usually) before a prepositional adjunct of place, as antecedent to an attributive clause: *He had that in his eye which forbade further trifling* (COD); *There was that about the place which filled me with a sense of utter dreariness*

[1] Note how *these* goes with *ours*, *that* with *hers*.

(OED); *they have that for which the richest blind man alive would give all that he has* (Kruisinga, *Handbook*[5], § 1565). This use of (emphatic) *that* should be distinguished from that described in 421.

418. In most of the above examples the demonstrative pronouns are used attributively.

When used substantively, *this* and *that* usually refer to things.

What do you think of this?
That's an excellent idea.
That's why I don't trust him.

419. With *to be* as a copula (583) *this* and *that* may also refer to persons, *this is* being especially used as a formula of introduction or identification.

This is my father. These are my friends, Gwynneth and Nancy.
This is the B.B.C. Home and Forces programme. Here is the news,[1] and this is A.B. reading it. (Second World War.)
That's the new mayor.

Cf.: *This is where he lives,* where *this* is roughly equivalent to *here.*

420. *These* and *those* when used substantively may refer to persons as well as to things.

If you like almonds, have some of these.
Are those your children?
Who are those passing?

The demonstrative pronouns in sentences with *to be* agree in number with the noun they refer to.

These are my friends.
Are those your children?

421. *That* and *those* may be used as DETERMINATIVE pronouns, i.e. as antecedents qualified by an attributive clause.

Determinative *that* is usually followed by an attributive clause introduced by *which*; the reference is exclusively to things. When *that* is not anaphoric (414), the construction is literary, and spoken English uses *what* for *that which.* In other cases determinative *that* alternates with the more colloquial *the one.*

That which (= what) promised happiness once, is now fraught with misery.
He drew his chair nearer to that (= the one) on which Nicholas was seated.

---

[1] Cf.: *That is the end of the news.*

422. Determinative *those*, when not anaphoric, is usually followed by an attributive clause introduced by *who*; the reference is exclusively to persons. The construction is especially found in general statements. — Cf. also 81 and 114.

Anaphoric *those* in this construction may also refer to things, the relative, if any, being *which* or *that*.

> Those (= People) who live in glass houses should not throw stones.
> There are (I know) those (= people, some) who would not stir a finger to help him.
> These cherries are not so good as those we had last year.

1. In literary English the singular of *those who* is *he* (*she*) *who, him* (*her*) *who*: *He who steals once is for ever a thief*; *All things come to him who waits.* Spoken English would prefer *A man who, any one who.*

Conversely, *they* (*them*) *who* is little used, except when the two pronouns are separated: *They laugh best who laugh last* (also *He laughs best who laughs last*).

2. Determinative *that* and *those* are sometimes followed (at a distance) by a present or past participle: '*Sidewalk* is the usual term in most parts of America for that part of a street reserved for pedestrians.' — 'Those compounds ending in *where*.' — Cf. 423, last ex.

423. Anaphoric *that* and *those* may also be qualified by a prepositional adjunct (usually with *of*), or by an adjunct beginning with a participle.

> My aunt's portrait was hung beside that of my uncle.
> Let us now compare Keats's odes with those by Shelley.
> John enters by the door opposite to that opening into the garden.

In the first and second examples *that* (*those*) with its adjunct might be replaced by a genitive (*beside my uncle's, with Shelley's*; cf. 307); in the third *that* is equivalent to *the one.*

424. In some constructions the adverb *so*, when used anaphorically, is similar in meaning to anaphoric *it* or *that* (occasionally *this*).

To begin with, an example from COD showing anaphoric *so* in a purely adverbial function: (*he*) *did not get it by force & ought not to be so deprived of it.* Here *so* clearly means *in that way.*

425. Attention has already been called (see 197) to the use of *so* after stressed (chiefly non-finite) forms of *to do* to refer to a preceding verb with its adjuncts.

> Those wanting to take the oath in the old way may do so.

As was pointed out there, *it* after *to do* is more definite than *so*:

My advice is that you send him an apology, and that you do it at once.

That in a similar construction is more emphatic than either, though not necessarily strong-stressed. It suggests a less close connection between two statements, or two parts of a statement, than *it*.

I am going to shoot that cat. — Don't do that; it has not done you any harm.

426. With reference to the nominal part of a predicate, *so* is used with verbs like *to be* (especially in its non-finite forms), *to remain, to seem*; it may also occur as a predicative adjunct to an object (592), and immediately after an adverb.

He had been weak but he would[1] be so no longer.
His income was insufficient, and likely to remain so.
She is ill and he thinks himself so.
The great bulk of the people were either half starved or wholly so.

It does not occur in this construction (it cannot refer to an adjective or to a word in a similar function), but *that* occasionally does.

They must be very curious creatures. — They are that (= they are indeed).

427. In spoken English the use of the constructions *to do so* and *to be so* is more limited than in literary English. Thus the first example of 425 might be expressed less officially by something like *If you want to take the oath in the old way, you may*. Similarly *so* would be omitted in ordinary English in a sentence like the following quoted by Poutsma, *Grammar*, II, Ch. XXXII, § 28 f.: *Don't call me censorious, Mark; you know I am not so.*

So is never used in confirmative and reactive questions (656).

You're not hungry, are you?
Oh, you're hungry, are you?
I'm awfully hungry. — Are you?

Neither is it used after questions that may be answered by *yes* or *no* (cf. 601).

Are you hungry? — (Yes,) I am. — (No,) I am not.
Do you believe in ghosts? — (Yes,) I do. — (No,) I don't.

---

[1] Direct speech: *I will.*

428. *So* is similarly used after verbs like *to say*, *to think*, *to hope*, *to suppose*, *to believe*, etc. In this case it refers to the whole of a preceding sentence.

Will your sister be coming to-night? — I think so.
It would be nice if the doctor would let me go out next Sunday. — Let's hope so.
Is the last train gone? — Yes, I'm afraid so.

Compare the following examples with *it* and *that*:

The child is nine years old, though you'd hardly think it.
He thinks the war will be over before Christmas. — They all think that.

429. *So* often has front-position, accompanied by emphasis on another word in end-position. The latter may be either verbal or nominal. When it is verbal, the auxiliary of the preceding sentence is repeated, with a change of person and/or tense, if necessary, or a form of *to do* is used as a substitute (see 198), the whole construction (*so* + pronoun + verb) serving to confirm the preceding statement[1] (*a*). Cf. 670.

When the emphasis is on a nominal word (noun or pronoun), the predicate of the preceding sentence is applied to another subject (*b*). Cf. 673.

a. You have called me an adventurer. So I am.[2]
But you ought to have warned her beforehand. — Well, so I did.
b. 'I come from Yorkshire', he said. 'So do I', she replied.
Peter is of age, and so is John.

It will be noted that the use of *so* with *to do* is the same as that described in 425, while its use with *to be* agrees with that described in 426. With other auxiliaries the function of *so* is similar to that after *to do*: *He says he can play cricket. — So he can.*

It does not occur in this construction, partly for the reason given in 426 (with *to be*), partly because it does not occur initially as an object (with *to do*).

Emphatic *that* may occur in construction (*a*) (though not in the sense referred to in note 1).

It was a horrid place. — That it was (= indeed it was [cf. 426, last ex.]).[3]

---

[1] Sometimes to express surprise: *Your glass is empty. — So it is.*

[2] *Am* is here repeated from the original statement of the person addressed: *You are an adventurer*, or words to that effect.

[3] Contrary to what Kruisinga says in his *Handbook*[5], § 1163, *so* would be equally possible here, only it would be less emphatic (and less colloquial).

430. The word referred to by *so* in the construction described in 429 is sometimes repeated after the auxiliary for more emphasis.

a. 'You were mentioning the degeneracy of the age, madam.' — 'Oh, ay, we were. So it is degenerate, sadly; but that'll keep. Now to business.'[1]
b. 'Paulina is at least sincere, don't you think?' — 'So is Tessa sincere.'
Is your wife any better? — No; she sleeps badly, and so do I sleep badly.

431. In conclusion, attention may be called to the use of *so* after *if*. As in the construction of 428, *so* here refers to a preceding sentence. In the negative its place is taken by *not*.

He may be innocent; if so, why did he give himself up? If not, why didn't he try to escape?

Similarly *how so? why so?*

---

432. *Such* may be classed with the demonstrative pronouns on account of its meaning; it *indicates* kind or degree: *Such men are dangerous.*

Its meaning is often completed by an adjunct with *as* or a clause with *that*.

Such beauty as hers (or: Beauty such as hers) is rare.
She had such a fright that she hardly survived it.

The adjunct with *as* may contain an infinitive with *to* indicating a result:

His indifference is such as to make one despair.

Such is followed by an indefinite article before singular class-nouns.

433. Pronounced with high pitch and strong stress, *such* in attributive position before a noun has an intensifying meaning, sometimes indicated by italics in print.

Tom is *such* a darling.
We had *such* fun.

434. On the other hand, with its correlative *as* (but always without an article) *such* may function as what Stoffel[2] calls a 'down-toner'.

His education, such as it was, was finished by the time he was fifteen.
Such money as he earned was spent on spirits and tobacco.

---

[1] R. Macaulay. *Orphan Island*, Tauchnitz ed., p. 90.
[2] C. Stoffel, *Intensives and Down-toners, a Study in English Adverbs.* Heidelberg, 1901.

435. The substantive use of *such* is chiefly literary. Note the determinative *such as* with reference to persons, meaning *those who* (*such as sit in darkness*, COD).

Also its anaphoric use, similar to *that*: *I may have offended, but such was not my intention* (*ibid.*).

For further uses of *such* see COD.

CHAPTER FIVE

INTERROGATIVE PRONOUNS

436. English has three interrogative pronouns: *who*, *what* and *which*.

437. *Who* asks after persons only.[1] Unlike the personal pronouns of the third person *he/she*, *they*, it does not distinguish sex or number, and may be the subject or nominal predicate of a singular as well as of a plural verb. It agrees with these pronouns in having an oblique form *whom* (cf. *him*, *them*); and it agrees with *it* in having a genitive *whose*, with a spelling even more unusual than that of *its*.

438. *Who* may introduce independent as well as dependent questions.

> Who did that?
> Who is that knocking?
> Do you know who did it?
> Do you know who they are?

Who also agrees with the personal pronouns in being only used substantively. It also occurs at the head of exclamatory sentences.

> Who would have thought it![2]

439. The outward similarity between the oblique forms *whom*, *him* and *them* does not mean that they also agree in use; for whereas *him* and *them* are essential elements of the language, *whom* exists almost exclusively on paper, *who* being used instead in the spoken language (and often in the written language as well).

Whom occurs as an object, and is regularly written after a preposition: *Of whom are you thinking?* In spoken English,

[1] Occasionally after domestic animals, e.g. (to a dog): *Who did that?*

[2] The sentence might also be followed by a mark of interrogation, and would then be interpreted as a rhetorical question. The meaning would be practically the same.

however, the preposition would usually be put after the predicate, and the sentence would run: *Who are you thinking of?*

Note that in the function of an indirect object, *who(m)* is accompanied by *to.* Cf. 453 and 596.

To whom did you give the letter?
Who(m) did you give the letter to?

One reason why *who* is preferred to *whom* in natural English (*Who[m] did you see?*) is probably its position at the head of the sentence, which is usually occupied by the subject (*Who was it you saw?*). The student is strongly recommended to read the discussion of this question in Sapir's *Language*, pp. 166–174.

440. *Whose* occurs fairly frequently, also in the spoken language. It is mostly used attributively; but, like the independent possessive pronouns (395), it may also be used predicatively.

Whose umbrella is this?
Whose is this umbrella?

441. *What* has no special oblique form, and no genitive. It is used substantively as well as attributively.

When used substantively, *what* asks after things. Compare *it* in most of its uses (372 ff.), and *that* used substantively (418), all of them ending in *t*.

As a subject *what* can only take a singular verb; but with a nominal predicate in the plural it may be followed by *are* or *were*. Like *who*, it may introduce independent as well as dependent questions.

What are you doing?
I asked him what he was doing.
What'll you have?
What's up here?
What are the best books on the subject?
What does it matter?[1]
What's your name?
What do you call that flower?[2]
What are you doing that for?

442. As a nominal predicate *what* may be used with a subject denoting a person, when a description or classification is asked for. (See Sweet, *Syntax*, § 2119.)

[1] With *to care* (*What do I care?*), *to matter, to signify, what* is an adverb rather than an object.

[2] *What* is a predicative adjunct (592) here (cf. *We call it a daisy*).

What is man?
What is he — is he a lawyer?

But to identify a person, *who* is used:

Who is he? (363 n.)—He is the new curate.

443. *What* is used attributively with nouns denoting persons as well as things.

What languages do you know?
He asked me what languages I knew.
What woman would not have done the same?
What word of six letters begins with p and ends with e and means attractive?
What name, please?

444. To ask after the kind or sort to which a person or thing belongs, English uses *what kind of*, *what sort of*; literary English also *what manner of* (cf. 231).

What kind of man is he?[1]
What sort of apples are those?
What manner of man art thou?[2]

445. Attributive *what* is also used in exclamatory sentences, in the sense of 'how great or strange or otherwise remarkable for good or ill' (COD). The following noun takes the indefinite article if it would also take the article when used as a nominal predicate.

What a fool you are!
What a pity! (Cf. It's a pity.)
What nonsense! (Cf. It's nonsense.)
What manners!
What pretty cups those are on that shelf!

Exclamatory *what* may also be used substantively:

What was their astonishment to see the whole building on fire.

What! followed by a question may be used as an interjection expressing surprised remonstrance.

What! No plum-pudding at Christmas?

446. The use of *which* (which has no special oblique form and no genitive) is more restricted than that of *what*. It has a selective meaning; it assumes a group, and implies a contrast between the members of the group that are meant and those that are not

[1] The same idea may be expressed by *What is he like?*
[2] Coleridge, *The Ancient Mariner*, l. 577.

meant[1] — or to use an old, if incomplete, definition, it selects one or more out of a definite number.

Here are some examples of attributive *which*:

Here is a letter from my lord to my lady. — From which lord to which lady?
Which way shall we go?
Say which chapter you prefer.
He knows (on) which side his bread is buttered.

447. *Which* may also be used substantively, with reference to a person or thing mentioned in the same sentence.

In sentences of type *a*, a choice is proposed between two alternatives.

In those of type *b* (with *of*), there are no alternatives, and *which* has its ordinary selective function.

a. Which would you rather have been, Livingstone or Stanley?
Which is it to be, black or white?[2]
b. Which of you is George Washington?
Which of these three will you have?

448. Foreign students should be warned against an excessive use of attributive *which*. When the meaning is not clearly selective, English uses *what*. See the examples of 443.

Even where a selection is made, *what* is sometimes preferred if *which* would be too definite or specific.

Will you decide what men shall live, what men shall die?

Here *which men* would create the impression of a definite number. Besides, *what* is collective here, *which* would be individualizing.[3]

Similarly, *who* is sometimes found instead of *which* when the idea of selection is (or seems to be) added by way of afterthought.

Who (439) do you love best, Daddy or Mummy?

Before *of* + (pro)noun *who* has a more personal meaning than *which*; it also forms a less close group with the following adjunct. Cf.:

But perhaps it is premature to talk of failure. Fail the play does (19, 198), when read: but who of its judges have seen it acted? Not I at any rate; and I suspect that it acts far better than it reads (584.3).

E. M. W. Tillyard, *Shakespeare's Problem Plays*, p. 89. (About *All's Well that Ends Well.*)

---

[1] Cf. Sweet's *Syntax*, § 2120, and Kruisinga, *Handbook*[5], § 1701.

[2] The reference is to coffee.

[3] For an example where the use of *what* by the side of *which* seems to be due to the need for variety, see 519, second ex.

In the following quotation from *I, Claudius*, by Robert Graves, the *which*'s emphasize Sulpicius' exact knowledge of details:

If I ever wanted some out-of-the way information, such, for instance, as the laws of succession to the chieftainship among one of the Alpine tribes against whom my father had fought, or the meaning and etymology of their outlandish battle-cry, Sulpicius would know what authority had treated of these points, in which book, and from which shelf of which case in which room of which library they were to be obtained.

449. For various phrases and constructions with *who*, *what* and *which* the student may be referred to the *Concise Oxford Dictionary*.

Here we will only draw attention to the curious type of three-word groups, in which the same pronoun occurs, first as a subject, then as a nominal predicate. The following examples and explanations are taken or adapted from COD:

He knows who's who	: who and what each person is.
A Who's Who[1]	: a list with description of notables.
He knows what's what	: he knows a good thing from a bad.
Which is which?	: which of two etc. given persons etc. corresponds to one of given descriptions etc., and which to another?

450. Interrogative *who*, *what* and *which* may be emphasized by the addition of *ever*, which some authorities (e.g. COD) insist should be written as a separate word after an interrogative. It may express surprise, bewilderment, annoyance, despair, etc. This use of *ever* is distinctly colloquial.

Who ever can it be?
What ever does he want?
Which ever Brown do you mean?

After *which*, *ever* seems to be rare; which is, perhaps, intelligible after what was said in 448. It is also rare after the declined forms of *who*.

[1] As a title, printed *Who's Who* (for 1951, etc.).

CHAPTER SIX

RELATIVE PRONOUNS

451. *Who* and *which* also occur as relative[1] pronouns at the head of an attributive sub-clause, i.e. one qualifying a noun or pronoun (the 'antecedent') in the main clause.

452. Relative *who* agrees with interrogative *who* in referring to persons only (occ. to domestic animals), in not distinguishing sex or number, and in having the declined forms *whom* and *whose.* It differs in being used as a subject only, not as a nominal predicate.

I wish I knew the man who wrote that book.
My uncle, who will be seventy to-morrow, is still a keen sportsman.

Both *who* and *which* occur as relatives after *child* and *baby*; cf. 364 and 374.

453. Relative *whom* occurs as an object and after prepositions in literary English. As an indirect object, it is accompanied by *to*: *This is the man to whom I gave the letter* (cf. 439 and 469).

Occasionally a different preposition is required: *the man* for *whom I bought this tie* (*I bought him a tie*); *Mr. D.*, against *whom she bore a grudge* (*She bore him a grudge*). Cf. 596.1.

Unlike interrogative *whose*, relative *whose* may refer to things, at least in literary English.

The only consonants whose notation[2] requires special notice are the following.

454. Relative *who* differs from interrogative *who* in being pronounced with weaker stress and lower pitch. Compare: *Who*[3] *said so? — I asked him who*[3] *had said so. — The man who*[4] *said so*; and similarly with *whom* and *whose.*

---

[1] '(Gram.) referring, & attaching a subordinate clause, to an expressed or implied antecedent . . ., (of clause) attached to antecedent by r. word' (COD).

[2] Or: *of which the notation,* or: *the notation of which.*

[3] [hu:]. [4] [u].

455. The difference defined in 454 makes it possible to distinguish between interrogative and relative *who(m)* in sub-clauses. Thus we have interrogative *who* in a sentence like the following:

There was a longer fight about who should be king.[1]

In sentences like the following, however, though there is no antecedent, and the reference is, therefore, quite general, *who(m)* is to be regarded as a relative, not as an interrogative, pronoun:

I have said it; and let who will deny it.
It is much in the king's power to summon whom he will, to take the advice of whom he will.[1]

Who as an independent relative (*Who breaks pays*) is now archaic, except in clauses opening with the stem of a verb: *Deny it who may*. Cf. 156 n.

---

456. Relative *which* differs considerably from interrogative *which*. It has no selective meaning; and, with one exception (457), it cannot refer to persons.

The task which confronted him had to be faced alone.
Westminster Abbey, which is one of the oldest churches in Great Britain, contains the graves of many famous Englishmen.

457. Relative *which*, like interrogative *what* (442), may be used as a nominal predicate with reference to a person, when a description or classification is intended.

He looked like a lawyer — which he was.

458. In written English relative *which* may be followed by a noun (such as *time*, *size*, *idea*, etc.) summarizing or repeating part of the main clause.

It rained all night and all day, during which time the ship broke in pieces.
A 5 × 4[2] camera (which size is now the most popular).

459. Relative *which* may also refer to a preceding sentence or part of a sentence.

The decision was postponed, which was exactly what he wanted.
I have known men far more able than Bowles, but not half so interesting, which is quite a different thing.

---

[1] Kruisinga, *Handbook*[5], § 1050.
[2] five by four.

A clause of this type is sometimes interpolated in the sentence referred to by way of parenthesis.

> They also had, which was of importance to some of them, an heroic past.[1] (Cf. 472, 2nd ex.)

460. As in the case of *who* (454), relative and interrogative *which* differ in stress and intonation. This distinction can be used here, too, to tell interrogative from relative *which* in sub-clauses. It should be noted, however, that *which*, when used analogously to *whom* in the third example of 455, retains its selective meaning.

> He might see a reason for his friend's strange preference or bondage (call it which[2] you please).[3]

461. When the antecedent is a collective noun denoting persons, relative *who* (with a plural verb) is used when the individuals forming the group are thought of, *which* (with a singular verb) when the group as such is meant. (Cf. 753.)

> He joined the party[4] who were walking before him.
> He joined the party[5] which was in power.

Both *which* and *who* occur as relatives after names of countries: *Russia, which* . . ., or *Russia, who* . . . The verb is singular in either case.

---

462. Of the two examples given of the use of relative *who* (452) and *which* (456), the former in each case contains a clause restricting the reference of the antecedent to one or more particular persons or things, and, therefore, called a RESTRICTIVE clause; the latter contains a clause which does not restrict the reference of the antecedent, but gives further relevant information about it; such a clause is called a CONTINUATIVE or AMPLIFYING clause.[6]

Restrictive clauses are subordinate to the clause containing the antecedent; continuative clauses are more independent: their contents might often be expressed by an independent statement.

---

[1] The commas before and after the interpolated clause might be replaced by parentheses.

[2] Cf. p. 156, n. 2.

[3] Kruisinga, *Handbook*[5], § 1075.

[4] i.e. group.

[5] i.e. political party.

[6] The two kinds of clause are also known as 'defining' and 'non-defining'. On clauses that do not easily fit into either category, and on the use of *that* in such clauses, see 619 ff.

This distinction is marked by a different intonation, and by the pause preceding the latter kind of clause, no such interval separating a restrictive clause from its antecedent.[1]

It may also be pointed out that a sentence with a restrictive clause contains a single statement, one with a continuative clause containing two statements.

463. By the side of *who* and *which* English employs a relative particle[2] *that*. It differs from *who* and *which* in three respects: it occurs chiefly in restrictive clauses;[3] it may refer to personal as well as non-personal antecedents; it is never preceded by a preposition, though it may open a clause with a preposition at the end. As a part of speech, it is intermediate between a relative pronoun and a conjunction.

Like *which*, it has no special oblique form and no genitive; nor does it distinguish sex or number.

> You are the very boy that I have been looking for.
> This is the house that Jack built.

464. Like relative *who* and *which*, relative *that* is unstressed: [ðət]. Still, *who* and *which*, with their distinct vowels [u] and [i] and their restriction to either persons or things, are weightier words, not only phonetically but also semantically.[4]

This may explain why, on the whole, *who* is more usual than *that* with reference to persons, whereas *that* is more usual than *which* with reference to things.

That is especially used with reference to persons in clauses that are distinctly classifying, consequently in such as define an antecedent qualified by a superlative, or by *any* or *only*.

> You are a man that can understand.
> Newton was one of the greatest men that ever lived.
> Ask John, or any other boy that was there.

465. *That* is used, to the exclusion of *who*, in the function of a nominal predicate. This reminds us of the somewhat similar use

[1] The presence or absence of such a pause is marked in writing and in print by the presence or absence of a comma before as well as after the sub-clause.
[2] Cf. p. 4, n. 2.
[3] See p. 162, n. 6.
[4] Cf. p. 108, n. 2.

of *which* (457); but *that*, of course, only occurs in this function when the clause is restrictive.

I let him have it — fool that I was — without asking for a receipt.

466. *That* is the usual relative when the antecedent denotes both a person and a thing; also, for reasons of euphony, after interrogative or exclamatory *who*.

The men and manners that he describes will be unfamiliar to most of his readers.
Who that ever came into personal contact with him could help liking him?

On the semi-relative use of *as* and *but* see 624 and 625.

---

467. Restrictive clauses are often joined to their antecedents without an intervening relative. In such cases the relation of the antecedent to the verbal predicate of the sub-clause may be that of a direct or indirect object, a prepositional object, a nominal predicate, or an adverbial adjunct.

I did not meet any one I knew personally.
This is the man I gave the ticket to.
Is this the book you were looking for?
Your father is not the man he was.
He went back the way he had come.

468. When the antecedent is the subject, the absence of a relative occurs only after a head-clause introduced by *it is* (*was*), *that is* (*was*), *there is* (*was, were*). The construction is mainly colloquial.

It isn't everybody can do that. (Cf. 381.)
That was her shadow passed the window.
There was a man asked for you, sir.

There is may also be part of the restrictive clause; this construction is not limited to colloquial English.

It's the best book there is on the subject.

The absence of a connecting word is not peculiar to attributive clauses. Compare:

I *told* you (that) I could not come.
I was so tired (that) I could hardly stand.

This is a syntactic feature sharply differentiating English from some other languages.

469. Much of what has been said in 456–468 may be summarized by the following syntactic variants, which form a descending series as regards formality of style.

This is the house of which I spoke.
This is the house which I spoke of.
This is the house that I spoke of.
This is the house I spoke of.

---

470. Dependent questions introduced by *what* are often divided by only a thin partition from similarly constructed clauses with no interrogative meaning. Compare:

I asked him what he had found.
He gave me what he had found.

A clearly interrogative meaning, as in the first example, will be marked by stronger stress and higher pitch; cf. 455 and 460. This is well brought out by a passage from *The Sunday Times* quoted in Kruisinga and Erades, *An English Grammar*, Texts, IX:

It (viz. the whirr of a lawn-mower) gently amuses the mind with speculations as to where the machine now is as the sound recedes or grows in volume: at what point it will stop for the grass to be emptied from the receptacle: how good that grass must smell!

Here *where* and *what* are clearly interrogative, and pronounced on a high pitch and with strong stress; *how* is exclamatory with most of its pitch and stress transferred to *good*.

When the meaning is clearly non-interrogative, *what* may be classed as an independent relative, i.e. one without an antecedent; compare again 455. It may introduce a subject clause, an object clause (see the second example above), a predicative clause, or a clause preceded by a preposition.

What is one's man meat is another man's poison.
But that is not what you promised us!
After what you have told me I think you ought to see a doctor.

1. The close affinity between interrogative and non-interrogative *what*-clauses is partly due to the fact that they have the same word-order.

2. *What* may be the subject of a plural verb (cf. 749):

What chiefly *count* at the election are the shibboleths of party (247.1).

471. Relative *what* may be used attributively; the following noun usually denotes a thing. In some cases its meaning is more or less depreciatory (cf. 434).

I shall receive what letters I please.
I gave him what help I could.

This depreciatory meaning may be made explicit by the addition of *little.*

I gave him what little help I could.

It may also be expressed by non-attributive *what*:

We did our own cleaning, what there was of it.

472. Relative *what* may refer to a following sentence or part of a sentence. (Cf. 459 on *which* in a similar function.)

Yes, I have the letter; and, what's more, I mean to keep it.
Fortunately, Mr. Mayfield was at home and, what was rarer, disengaged.

A clause of this type is sometimes interpolated:

He wore, what was then very uncommon in this country, a loose brown linen blouse. (Cf. 459, 3rd ex.)

---

473. *Who, which* and *what*, compounded with *ever*, are used as independent relatives. These compounds, which are very indiscriminate in meaning, may introduce noun-clauses and concessive adverbial clauses. (Cf. 450.)

a. Whoever comes will be welcome. Whoever said so, it is false.
b. He would eat white bread or brown, whichever could be got with least thought or trouble.
The result will be unsatisfactory, whichever side wins.
c. Do whatever you like.
Whatever happens, whatever friends we may offend, we shall have done our duty.

1. It will be noticed that *whichever* and *whatever* may be used substantively as well as attributively, and that *whichever* is selective (cf. 460).

2. *Ever* may also be added to *what* in the depreciatory meaning discussed in 471:

The Irish party has lost whatever claim it had to speak for the people of Ireland.

3. These compounds are always stressed on the second element.

4. Note the emphatic forms *whosoever, whichsoever, whatsoever*: *Let me warn you, whosoever you are. . .*; *for no reason whatsoever*. — Forms in *-soever* also alternate with the forms in *-ever* mentioned in 630, 631 and 640. They are rarely used in colloquial speech.

474. *Whatever*, in the sense of *at all*, may be added to a noun or pronoun in a negative context.

> There is no doubt whatever about that.
> No one whatever[1] would accept (COD).

---

[1] Not *whoever*!

CHAPTER SEVEN

INDEFINITE PRONOUNS

475. The pronouns discussed in this chapter express various degrees of indefiniteness (*some*, *any*, *one*, etc.). Some of them might be called 'distributive' rather than 'indefinite' (*each*, *every*, *either*); but grammatical terms should not be multiplied unnecessarily.

476. *Some* may be singular as well as plural.

In the singular it may mean, (*a*) a particular but unknown or unspecified (person or thing); (*b*) a certain quantity of (something).

a. Some [sʌm] fool[1] has locked the door.
I must have read it in some book or other.
b. Can we have some milk?
He waited for some time.

477. In the plural *some* denotes an indefinite number. When stressed, it implies contrast.

He lived at Oxford for some years.
Have some more grapes.
Some [ˈsʌm] people detest Wagner [ˈvɑːgnə] (other people . . .).

478. In the examples hitherto given *some* is used attributively. It may also be used substantively to denote a number of persons (*a*); or followed by an *of*-adjunct with a singular material or abstract noun, or a plural class-noun (or pronoun) denoting persons or things (*b*).

a. Some say yes, and some say no.
b. Some of the milk had turned sour.
Some of what is said misses the point.
Some [sʌm] of us would like to see some [s(ə)m] further proof.

479. *Some* is also used before numerals, meaning 'approximately'.

We were some [s(ə)m] sixty in all.

---

[1] *fool* with higher pitch than *some*. The reverse is the case in *Some fool!* =what a fool! (slang).

480. *Any* [ˈeni] is especially common in negative, interrogative and conditional contexts. Like *some*, it may be either singular or plural. It may also take an *of*-adjunct; but it is not often used substantively.

I cannot see any [unstressed!] difference between them.
Are there any old prints in the house?
Let me know if you want any of us.
Complaints, if any, to be addressed to the management.

In an affirmative sentence it may be practically equivalent to an indefinite article:

The story of a family can be as fascinating as any [unstressed!] novel.

481. Though *any* is more usual in the contexts mentioned above, *some* is by no means uncommon. The difference between them may be expressed by saying that *any* is negative or non-committal, whereas *some*, though indefinite, is positive in meaning.

Thus *some* is used in questions that are really polite substitutes for commands, or to which an affirmative answer is expected; *any* being employed in questions that ask for information, without seeming to take either an affirmative or a negative answer more or less for granted.

Can we (Could we, Cannot we, Could not we) have some [s(ə)m] milk?
Have you any [unstressed!] milk?
Can't we talk of something[1] else? (= Let's talk of something else.)
What's the matter? Has something[1] happened?

Something in the last question shows the speaker's anxiety on seeing the expression on the face of the person addressed; even before his question is answered, he is almost sure that something *has* happened. *Has anything happened?*, on the other hand, would sound more indifferent, as if the speaker hardly cared what the answer would be.

482. *Any* is also used as an adverb of degree before a comparative in a negative or interrogative context.

So they went home without being any [unstressed!] (the) wiser.

483. Strong-stressed *any* is used in affirmative contexts in a meaning that invites comparison with *every*. It may be paraphrased by 'no matter which (who or what)'.

---

[1] These examples anticipate what will be said about compounds of *some* and *any*.

a. Any chemist will tell you it's poison.
He may come (at) any moment.
b. He comes here every day.

The difference may be expressed by saying that *any*, in this sense, stands for A *or* B *or* C, etc.; *every* for A *plus* B *plus* C, etc.

---

484. *Every* is only used attributively, and before singular class-nouns. It may be said to add up the individual members or elements of a definite or indefinite group. It always refers to more than two.

England expects every man to do his duty.
Every word of it is false.

It also occurs before word-groups denoting recurrence in time or space, even such as contain a plural noun. The following instances are taken from the *Concise Oxford Dictionary*, which the student should also consult on the other indefinite pronouns.

He comes here every other day; every three days (every third day); every now and then (every now and again).

We may add *every few miles*, *every other mile*, etc.

485. *Every* may be used before an abstract noun, in the sense of 'all possible'.

He had every reason to be satisfied.
There is every indication that it was a put-up job.

---

486. *Every* leads on to *each*, which takes the members of a definite group one by one, without adding them up. Like *every* it is used attributively before singular class-nouns; but it may also be used substantively, and followed by an *of*-adjunct. It may refer to two or more. Cf. 496 and 545.

Each student had a separate room.
He shook hands and had a few minutes' talk with each of us.
How much are these oranges? — A penny each.

---

487. On the other hand, *every* requires delimitation from *all*.

All may be used attributively as well as substantively, in the singular as well as in the plural. As an attributive singular it is used before abstract, material and other nouns to express quantity, and may be roughly paraphrased by 'the whole (of)' (*a*). As an attributive plural it is used before plural class-nouns, in the sense of 'without exception' (*b*). In both cases *all* may be followed by a definite article, or by a possessive or demonstrative pronoun; cf. 492 n., and 712.

As a substantival singular *all* may be paraphrased by 'everything' (*c*); as a substantival plural by 'everybody' (*d*). In either case it may take an *of*-adjunct; in case *c* it is not often used without an adjunct or clause.

a. We cannot stay here all day.
All his money was gone.
Why should they have all the fun?
b. All students should register before October 1st.
Are all these books yours?
c. All[1] I know is that the thief was never found.
I should like to give him something, that's all.[1]
Don't give him all of it!
d. All agree that he has behaved splendidly.
And so say all of us.

488. *All* may be compared with *every* in case *b* (*all students — every student*), *c* (*that's all — that's everything*) and *d* (*All are agreed — Everybody is agreed*). The difference is that *all* takes the members of a group collectively, whereas *every* individualizes.

Attributive *all* differs, not only from *every*, but also from the other indefinite pronouns hitherto dealt with, in being capable of being followed by another attributive word (487). It may also be followed by the substantive demonstrative pronouns *this* and *that*: *all this*, *all that*.

1. *All*, in function *d*, may stand in apposition to a personal pronoun: *They all agreed. . . .* Unlike *all this* and *all that*, these combinations are separable: *They were all agreed. . . .* With a word between them, neuter *all* (function *c*) may also follow a demonstrative pronoun: *That's all very well, but . . .*

2. Instead of attributive plural *all* followed by another attributive word (487) we sometimes find *all of*, esp. in American English.

All of our students have registered.
All of these books are mine.

Similarly (*Am.*) *all of the time*, (*Brit.*) *all the time*.

[1] Here *all* means 'the only thing', rather than 'everything'.

489. In negative contexts *all* may resemble *any* (*whatever*).

His sincerity was beyond all doubt.
He hated all interference.
He had lost all interest in his surroundings.

490. *All* is also used adverbially, meaning 'wholly'.

They were all covered with mud.
He says it is all right, but I believe it is all wrong.[1]
The end came all too soon.
If it's all the same to you. . . .

This meaning should not be confused with that in a sentence like the following, where non-adverbial (plural) *all* is also separated from the subject:

They were all (or: all of them) covered with mud.

In the singular, *all* could only be adverbial:

He was all covered with mud.

---

491. English has three indefinite pronouns (*both*, *either*, *neither*) that are used only with reference to *two* (persons or things).

492. *Both* can be used in the same ways as plural *all* (487*b* and *d*).

Both men were found guilty.
Both these books are mine.
Both agreed that the matter had better be dropped.
They have asked both of us to come.
They both accepted the invitation. (488.1.)
We have both been invited.
Both of his feet were frozen. (488.2.)

A definite article is less common after *both* (*both* (*the*) *men*) than after *all* (*all the men*). This is only natural, as there is a real difference in meaning between *all men* (in general) and *all the men* (with reference to a particular number); but *both* in itself refers to a particular number.

493. *Both* is usually stressed. In unstressed position *two* is used:

The girls are going to Wales for the holidays, and the two boys are going to a camp.

494. *Both* is used adverbially in the sense of 'with equal truth in both cases' (COD). Cf. 679.

She is both dead and buried.

---

[1] There is a play on words here: *all wrong* is not really the opposite of *all right* in the usual meaning of this phrase.

495. *Either* (= one or other of two) stands in much the same relation to *any* as *both* to *all*. Like *any*, it occurs especially in negative and interrogative contexts, and, when used in affirmative contexts, means 'no matter which'. Cf. 756.

There is no lamp at either end.
Have you seen either of them?
Either of you can go.

Cf. the COD definition of *cross voting*: 'when in Parliamentary divisions etc. some of either or each side vote against their own party'.

496. In more or less literary English *either* also occurs in the meaning 'each of two'. Spoken and ordinary written English usually prefer *each* or *both*, except in such combinations as *on either side*, *at either end*.

At either end of the street was a lamp.
The houses on either side were tall and big.

497. *Either* is used adverbially to introduce an alternative.

He is either drunk or mad.
Either you or I will have to go.

It is also used with a negative, (*a*) in the sense of 'any more than the other', (*b*) in the sense of 'for that matter'.

a. If you do not go, I shall not either.[1]
b. There was once a time, and not so long ago either[2] . . .

---

498. *Either* can be negatived by prefixing *n*: *neither*, i.e. 'not either, not the one nor the other'. Cf 756.

Truth may lie on both sides, on either side, or on neither.
Neither description (neither of these descriptions) is correct.

499. *Neither* is also used adverbially to deny an alternative:

He is neither drunk nor mad.
Neither you nor I (Neither of us) can go.
That's neither here nor there.

In the sense of 'any more than the other' (*a*), it is equivalent to *not . . . either*, though it usually has front-position:

a. If you don't go, neither shall I.

[1] Quoted from COD, which omits sense *b*.
[2] Quoted from Kruisinga's *Handbook*[5], § 1232, which omits sense *a*.

In colloquial (some might say uneducated) English it is sometimes used in the same meaning as *either*:

> *b.* There was once a time, and not so long ago neither . . .

In sense *a*, *neither* often corresponds to *so* in similar affirmative sentences (cf. 429*b*):

> 'I don't come from Yorkshire', he said. — 'Neither do I', she replied.

In this function, *neither* can be replaced by *nor* or *no more*: *Nor do I*. — *No more do I*.

---

500. *Either* stands in much the same relation to *any* as *neither* to *none*. *None* is not, however, used attributively (except in archaic diction; see Wyld and COD); on the other hand, it occurs in many cases where it does not lend itself to comparison with *neither*.

It may either stand by itself (*a*), or refer to a single or plural noun or pronoun that has been mentioned before (*b*), or that follows in an *of*-adjunct (*c*).[1] The verb may be singular or plural, according to the sense required, and the noun to which *none* refers need not be a class-noun. (Cf. *one*, 502.)

> *a.* None are so deaf as those that *will* not hear.
> *b.* You have money and I have none.
> Sounds there were none.
> *c.* None of us knew where the man had gone. (Cf. *neither*.)
> His understanding was none of the clearest.
> It's none of your business.

501. *None* is also used adverbially, before a comparative, and before *so* or *too*. Cf. adverbial *all* and *any*.

> I am none the better for it.
> I am none so fond of him.
> The pay is none too high.

---

502. The various uses of *one* may be classified from two points of view:
(*a*) with regard to their more or less clearly numerical meaning;
(*b*) with regard to whether they refer to persons as well as things, or to persons only.

---

[1] *An English Grammar*, by Kruisinga and Erades, 7th ed., § 428.

In all its uses *one* refers exclusively to persons or things that are countable, i.e. to such as are denoted by class-nouns, not by abstract or material nouns (cf. 247, 2nd par.).

503. The strictly numerical use of *one* (*one man in ten*, *one is enough*), need not be dwelt on here. It may, of course, refer to persons as well as things.

The first step in the pronominal direction is taken when strong-stressed (*the*) *one* (whether substantive or attributive) is used with *the* (or *an*)*other* expressed or understood.

He poured tea into two collapsible cups, and passed one to Rodney.[1] (Implication: keeping the other himself.)
On one occasion, the Fabii offered to conduct the war.[1] (Implication: On another occasion . . .)
The speech of the Prime Minister in the one House, and of Lord Curzon in the other, . . .[1]
Joan and Mary are so much alike that I sometimes cannot tell (the) one from the other.[2]
According to Jim, life was just one damn thing after another.

504. There is a similar (though sometimes weaker) implication when strong-stressed *one* is followed by an *of*-adjunct.

Then one of us hit on the idea of asking a policeman.
One of the signatures was illegible.

505. The contrast implied in the foregoing uses of *one* is absent in non-prepositional adjuncts of time like the following. (Note that an indefinite article in such an adjunct would require *on* before it.)

One summer evening I had gone for a stroll in the park. (Cf. On a summer evening. . . .)

506. Strong-stressed *one* may be used attributively with the meaning of 'only' or '(a) single'. In this case it is usually preceded either by a definite article or by *no* or *any*.

---

[1] The first two examples are taken from Kruisinga's *Handbook*[5], §§ 1257 and 1258, where, however, the implication here pointed out is overlooked, and *one* is simply called a numeral. The third is from § 1326, where many examples are given with *the other* expressed. — On the difference between *another* and *the other*, see 544.

[2] In this case, viz. when *the one* is used substantively with reference to a person (not, of course, when it refers to a thing) there is also a genitive *the one's*: *He did not know which to admire most, the one's courage or the other's self-denial.*

It is the one way to do it.
No one[1] man is equal to it.
It is not restricted to any one[1] rank or class.
They cried out with one voice: Crucify him!

507. Medium-stressed *one* is used in constructions outwardly similar to that of 504. The partitive meaning of *of* is here weakened to the same extent as the stress on *one*.

We must meet again one of these days.
He is one of the richest men in England.

---

508. Medium-stressed *one* may be used as a substitute for a preceding class-noun. The reference may be to persons as well as to things.

I lose a neighbour and you gain one.
'Can you play the piano?' — 'A little.' There was one in the room.

509. Anaphoric *one* may be qualified by an adjunct or a clause; in this case it is determinative as well (421).

The year has been one of great political unrest [ˈʌnˈrest].
After the death of his old gardener he engaged one who had been strongly recommended to him by a friend.

510. So far the uses of English *one* and of the corresponding words in some other languages have run fairly parallel, but from now on they part company.

Anaphoric-determinative *one* may be preceded by a definite article (cf. 421). The reference may still be either to persons or to things.

He drew his chair nearer to the one (= that) on which Nicholas was seated.
Which master do you mean? The one[2] with a beard?

511. By now the numerical meaning of *one* is so far weakened that a plural form *ones* may be used in the case of 510.

The cleverest boys at school are not always the ones (= those) who succeed best in after life.

1. Occasionally *ones* occurs in the function described in 509:

   The faults in this *Dictionary* are mainly ones of presentation. (RES 1941, p. 499.)

2. The plural of non-determinative anaphoric *one* (508) is *some*. Cf. 344.

   Do you like nuts? There are some on the sideboard.

---

[1] Strong stress!   [2] Not *that*; cf. 421.

512. Anaphoric *one* may also be qualified by an immediately preceding adjective (with an indefinite article before it in the singular).

The difference between a good walker and a bad one is that one (503) walks with his heart and the other with his feet.
I want a pound of those cherries. Pick me out some good ones, will you?

In this function *one* is weak-stressed.

When the group: indefinite article + adjective + *one* is used predicatively, the equivalent in other languages is usually a predicative adjective without an article:

His task was a heavy one.

513. Anaphoric *one* after a definite article or an adjective is usually called a PROP-WORD. The reason is that definite articles, and adjectives denoting one or more specimens of a class,[1] cannot stand by themselves, and need a word to support them.

In the case of two adjectives expressing a contrast, the prop-word is often dispensed with, especially after a monosyllable at the end of a sentence or clause.

Crime and poverty exist in the New World as well as in the Old.
He meant to attain his object by fair means or foul.
My right hand was in my mother's left.

As the anaphoric prop-word *one* is sometimes felt as rather colloquial (cf. also 421), the noun referred to is sometimes repeated after the second adjective, especially in the case of persons. (Cf. Poutsma, *Grammar*, II, Ch. XLIII, § 12*a*, and Jespersen, MEG II, 10.95.)

It's as easy to marry a rich woman as a poor woman.
An Oxford man will differ all his life from a Cambridge man.[2]

514. Usage varies as regards the employment of the prop-word after comparatives, though again it is often dispensed with after comparatives expressing or implying a contrast.

I had to go to school in my old boots, while my tidier ones were re-soled.
I doubt if it is wise always to praise the younger son in the presence of the elder.

515. After a superlative the prop-word is more often dispensed with than not.

The English climate is, according to pessimists, the worst in the world.

---

[1] Adjectives denoting a whole class of persons can, and do, stand by themselves: *the young, the rich*. See 778 ff.

[2] The circumstance that *man* is here felt as part of a compound may also account for its repetition.

This applies to so-called 'relative' superlatives; after 'absolute' superlatives with *most* (=*very*, cf. 571), *one* is regularly used.

His collection of stamps is a most valuable one (512).

516. The prop-word is rarely used after *own*; cf. 513 and 514.

If there is any difficulty about cars, I can bring my own.

When *my* (*his*, etc.) *own* means 'my (his) private property' (404) there is, of course, no question of *one* being 'omitted'.

I am not a tenant of this house; it's my own.[1]

517. What was said in 512 of an adjective preceding *one* also applies to nouns used as adjectives (cf. 792 ff.).

Five penny stamps and three twopenny-halfpenny ones, please.
The house was a corner one.

The fact that a noun is followed by *one* in itself goes to show that it is used as an adjective. The second example shows such a converted noun used in a predicative group; though by the side of, for instance, *My visit is a business one*, it is also possible to say *My visit is strictly business*, in which the converted predicative noun is 'supported' by an adverb.

518. The prop-word *one* may also occur after *this* and *that*, making it possible for them to refer, not only to things, but also to persons (418).

If you will take this chair, I will take that one.
Few poets can be so obscure as this one.

Similarly after *such a* (cf. 432 n.):

The cell was such a one as a convict would now disdain to inhabit.[2]

519. *One* is occasionally used after interrogative *which* and *what*, making it possible to distinguish the singular from the plural.

Aren't these shells pretty? I'll give you one (some: 511.2) if you like. Which one(s) will you choose?
A good judge knows what years of which wines[3] to avoid and what ones to order.

520. Lastly, the anaphoric prop-word *one* is occasionally found after *each*, *every* and *other*; and after *first*, *second* and *third*.

---

[1] Kruisinga, *Handbook*[5], § 1300.
[2] Poutsma, *Grammar*, II, Ch. XLIII, § 20*b*.
[3] Cf. p. 158, n. 3.

He built several houses, each (one) more expensive than the former.
If each smooth tile had been a blank at first . . . there would have been a copy of old Marley's head on every one.[1]
If you don't like this cigar, take another (one).
My uncle's house is the first (one) on the left.

For a discussion of the principles underlying the use or non-use of the prop-word *one* see F. T. Wood, 'Some Observations on the Use of the Prop-Word *One*', in *English Language Teaching*, Winter 1952.

---

521. We now come to those uses of *one* that refer exclusively to persons. They can be divided into two groups: (*a*) those in which *one*, like *some* (476), refers to a *particular* person; (*b*) those in which *one*, like *any* (480), refers (in appearance if not in reality) to nobody in particular.

522. In case (*a*) *one* is never used by itself, but always accompanied by a word, an adjunct or a clause qualifying it.

This qualifier may either precede or follow. In the former case the qualifying word is usually an adjective, with *one* after it as a prop-word. This use of *one* differs from that discussed in 512 in *not* being anaphoric. In many (not in all) cases it belongs to the literary language.

The Holy One (God).
The Evil One (the Devil).
He is a knowing one.
The little ones have gone to bed.
The great ones of the earth.
He saw two herds of zebra (259), but did not shoot: there were so many little ones[2] among them.

The similar use of *one* after *any*, *every*, *some*, *no* will be discussed in 537 ff.

523. Personal *one* may also be *followed* by an adjective; in this case it ceases, of course, to be a 'prop-word', but takes on a determinative function. (Cf. *something big* in 701*c*.)

---

[1] *Every* cannot dispense with the prop-word *one*; though it does not often occur with it. This use of *every one* is to be distinguished from that discussed in 538.

[2] In spite of appearances, *ones* is *not* anaphoric here. *Young ones* would have conveyed practically the same meaning. Both are applied to children as well as to young animals.

He behaved like one mad.
He lay like one dead.

The construction is mainly literary; ordinary spoken and written English would prefer *He behaved like a madman* [ˈmædmən]; *He lay like a dead man* [ˈded ˈmæn].

524. Personal *one* may be followed by a personal proper name, with or without a title. Cf. 346.

I bought it from one (Mr.) Stephens.

525. Personal *one* is clearly determinative (and non-anaphoric!) when it is followed by an adjunct or a clause. The construction is mainly literary, non-literary English preferring *a man*, *a person*, or some such word. Cf. Poutsma, *Grammar*, II, Ch. XL, §§ 152 and 195*a*.

He was one of really superior intelligence.
Scrooge was not one[1] to be frightened by echoes.
It may be well to give some account of one who exercised so much influence over many kings.[2]

1. It will have been observed that, whereas the anaphoric prop-word *one* sometimes has a colloquial ring (513 n.), the non-anaphoric personal *one* is often (not always) literary.

2. *One* in this function is referred to by *him* (*her*) and *his* (*her*): *He was one who did not care what happened to him*; *She was not one to spoil her children*. Cf. 526.

---

526. The last use to be discussed is that of personal *one* as an indefinite pronoun properly so called[3] (521*b*). It is defined by COD as 'any person, esp. the speaker, spoken of as representing people in general'. It is weak-stressed, and is referred to by *one*, *one's*, *oneself* (cf. 525.2). *One's* and *oneself* also occur without reference to a preceding *one*.

One should always do one's duty.
One must allow oneself a rest from time to time.
The book gives one a good idea of life in the tropics.

1. In American English the correlatives of *one* are often *he* — *him* — *himself* — *his*.

---

[1] But Dickens wrote *a man*. In this idiom *one* is not exclusively literary.
[2] Kruisinga, *Handbook*[5], § 1268.
[3] One might also, with Fowler (MEU, p. 402) call it an 'impersonal' pronoun.

In comparing the American and British types of English speech one should always be sure that he has selected his examples from the same social classes in the two countries.

The construction is occasionally found in British English, especially in more or less archaic style.

2. As in the case described in 525, *a man* may be used as an equivalent of indefinite *one*: *What can a man do in such a case?* (COD s.v. *man*[1].)

527. Sometimes, in a sentence with *one*, the emphasis is on 'the speaker' (or writer) rather than on 'people in general'. In such cases *one* becomes a substitute for *I* or *me*, either from modesty or affectation.

Of the following examples, the former still comes within the definition of 526; the latter does not, and illustrates a use of *one* that many people would regard as a mannerism. (Cf. Fowler, MEU, pp. 402–403.)

a. One does not like to refuse an old friend.
b. He asked me to review his new novel. Of course one did not like to refuse, but . . .

528. It may be useful to point out that *one* is used only in more or less general statements. In other cases English mostly uses the passive:

He was asked all sorts of indiscreet questions.
It was decided to make further inquiries before coming to a final decision.

Compare also 117, 356, 358 and 359.

This is not to say that the passive voice in English is never used in general statements. Cf. *It's not done* (or *It isn't done* = *it is bad form*).

---

529. Instead of passing from *none* to *one*, we might have passed from *none* to *no*. Indeed, a consecutive treatment of the indefinite pronouns is difficult, as there are all sorts of cross associations. Thus we shall have to discuss *no* in connection with *not a*.

530. Unlike *none*, *no* is always used attributively. It is, first of all, used in the straightforward sense of 'not any', with which it often alternates, the latter being more frequent in colloquial English.

There are no letters to-day.
There are not (aren't) any letters to-day.

In this function *no* often negatives the whole sentence rather than the noun it qualifies.

531. *No* is often used in what is called 'litotes' [ˈlaitoti:z], i.e. 'the expressing of an affirmative by the negative of its contrary' (COD), as *no small* for *great*. The word negatived may be an adjective or a noun. In many cases either praise or blame is implied.

The stranger's movements were watched with no little suspicion.
He's no great talker.
Hers was no common talent.
She is no fool.
I am no angel.
He's no gentleman.

532. *Not a* may, like *no*, be used by way of litotes (*a*); but it often means just what it says, neither more nor less (*b*).

a. The evening was not a success.
Augustine was not a Gregory (i.e. he was inferior to him).
b. I am not a philosopher.
I'm a fiddler, not a soldier.

I am no philosopher would sound like self-depreciation; *I am not a philosopher* is (or at any rate may be) a neutral statement of fact. In the second example of *b*, *not a* is used to express a contrast; *no* would be impossible here.

Where blame is intended, *not a* may express a more emphatic denial than *no*: *He's not a gentleman.* But combinations like *no fool* and *no angel* are hardly ever expressed otherwise.

533. *Not a* is used, to the exclusion of *no*, for the sake of emphasis; *a* is here equivalent to *one* (347).

Not a word to any one, mind.
Not a sound was heard.

Cf. the following quotation:

The depot ship is ready with securing wires, and as the submarine comes alongside somebody asks: 'Did you see anything?' 'Not a thing', is the reply.
Nothing seen on this patrol, or perhaps upon the next; . . .
Life Line, by Charles Graves (1941, p. 92).

Cf. also: *I didn't hear a thing*; *There wasn't a thing to see.*

534. Like many of the other indefinite pronouns, *no* may be used adverbially. This is especially the case before comparatives in *-er*, whether of adjectives or adverbs. The adjective in this construction is usually predicative, and there are many cases of litotes.

His French is no better than (i.e. as bad as) mine.
I can wait no longer.

Spoken English often prefers *not any* to *no*: *I cannot wait any longer*. In initial position this substitution is impossible:

No sooner had he said it than he was sorry.

535. *No more . . . than* is often used to express a strong denial, *no less . . . than* by way of an intensifier.

He is no more a lord than I am.
It is no less than a scandal.

On the other hand, *not more . . . than* means: *as . . . as*, with the emphasis on the second adjective.

I was not more surprised than indignant.

536. Note the difference in meaning and intonation between

There were no less than (= as many as) fifty people present.

and

We shall need not less than fifty members.

Compound Indefinite Pronouns

537. The difference between *some* and *any* also applies to their compounds *somebody* — *anybody*; *some one* — *any one*;[1] *something* — *anything*; and to the adverbs *somehow* — *anyhow*; *somewhere* — *anywhere*.

With *every* are similarly formed *everybody*, *every one*, *everything*, and the adverb *everywhere*; with *no*: *nobody*, *no one*, *nothing* (though this is hardly felt as a compound); and the adverb *nowhere*.[2]

538. The compounds with *-body* and *one* denote single persons. They may take a genitive-suffix:

To everybody's surprise, the balloon disappeared behind the clouds.

It will be unnecessary to say that those in *-thing* do not.

[1] In spite of being usually spelt as two words, *some one* and *any one* are compounds as well as *somebody* etc.; but cf. 539.

[2] On other adverbial compounds, such as *anyway*, *everyway* (sometimes written as two words), *nohow*, *noway*(*s*), see Wyld and COD.

539. The difference between the compounds with *-body* and those with *one* is that the latter are as a rule more individualizing. Compare the following sentence quoted by Poutsma from Thackeray's *Vanity Fair*:

> Everybody admired her there: everybody danced with her: but no one proposed who was worth the marrying. (Stress on *no*.)

Here *everybody* takes the men in the room collectively, a meaning already inherent in *every*, but more clearly brought out by *everybody* than by *every one*; whereas *no one* refers to individuals more clearly than *nobody* would have done.

As a result of their meaning, the compounds with *-body* cannot take an *of*-adjunct. (See 541.)

540. The personal compounds with *one* discussed above are not to be confused with such combinations as are mentioned in 520. In the latter, *one* functions as an anaphoric prop-word, and may refer to persons as well as to things. It may also occur after *each*, whereas *each one* is but rarely used in the function discussed in 538 and 539.[1]

541. *Every one* etc. may also be used in a function analogous to that of *one* mentioned in 504, though in these combinations *one* is not necessarily strong-stressed.

> Every one of her books was a success.
> Any one of us could do that.

Compare also *no one*, *any one*, etc., with *one* in the meaning of 'single', as described in 506. Apart from this, *none* (500) is more usual than *no one* before a prepositional adjunct.

> None of her books was a success.

542. *Any*, *each*, *every* and *no* are sometimes followed by *man*, the combination being practically equivalent in meaning to *anybody* or *any one*, etc. It is, however, regularly spelt as two words.

> Cicero saw as clearly as any man what was wrong with the state of Rome.
> He was answerable to no man for his acts.

Everyman [ˈevrimæn] is spelt as a single word as the title of the

[1] That *each* cannot form a compound with *body* will be understood on comparing 486 and 539. *Each thing* occurs only with *thing* as an independent noun.

English version of the Flemish morality *Elckerlijc*, and in the name *Everyman's Library*.

The above-mentioned combinations may also occur with *man* in its full nominal meaning: *England expects every man to do his duty*. Cf. *What Every Woman Knows* (title of a play by J. M. Barrie).

543. *Something*, *anything* and *nothing* are also used adverbially. Only a few examples will be given here; for fuller details COD or some other dictionary should be consulted. Cf. also 612, last ex.

It was shaped something like a cigar.
My tobacco is nothing like[1] so good as yours.
He looked anything but pleased.

Note the difference between *anything but* (=not at all) and *all but* (=nearly):

The job is all but finished.

---

544. Attention has already been drawn (in 503) to the use of (*the*) *one* . . . *the* (or *an*)*other* as correlatives. It remains to say that (*the*) *one* . . . *the other* is used when speaking of two (persons or things), *one* . . . *another* when speaking of more than two.

There is the possibility of considerable gain on the[2] one hand, and the risk of detection on the other.
She went in vain from one shop to another.

See also the examples given in 503.

545. *One another* (without any intervening words) is also, like *each other*, used in a reciprocal sense. The second word may take a genitive-ending.

Though they lived in the same street, they rarely saw one another (each other).
The two women flung themselves into each other's arms.
Bear ye one another's burdens. (Galatians 6: 2.)

For a discussion of the difference between *each other* and *one another* see P. A. Erades in *English Studies*, Aug. 1950; also S. Potter, *ibid.*, Dec. 1953.

546. *Other* may also be used correlatively with preceding *some*.

Some idiot or other has been scribbling on the window-pane.

---

[1] *like* pronounced with strong stress and rising tone.
[2] In this expression, *the* is hardly ever omitted.

547. When not used correlatively, *other* may be attributive or substantive. In the latter function it may take a plural and/or a genitive suffix.

The others had nothing to do with it.
He looked anxiously into the other's face.
Whatever he did was done for others' good.

In the second example spoken English would probably prefer *the other man's face* (cf. 542); in the third, *for other people's good.*

548. *Another* may mean 'an additional (one)':

Try another pear.
She smoked first one cigarette and then another.

549. After interrogative and compound indefinite pronouns, after *not much* and *little*, and after *somewhere* and *anywhere*, the idea of 'in addition', or 'alternatively', is expressed by *else*. Cf. 230.

What else could I do?
Is there anything else you want?
The food was little else than bread and potatoes.
Cannot we go somewhere else?

---

550. On some other words often classified among the indefinite pronouns, such as *(a) certain*, *(a) few*, *(a) little*, *many*, *much*, *(n)aught*, *(n)ought*, *same*, *several*, etc., the student may consult the *Concise Oxford Dictionary*, or such detailed grammars as Kruisinga's and Poutsma's.

Attention may be drawn to the use of *people* and *things* as indefinite words, as in the following quotation from Galsworthy's *Man of Property* (Part I, Ch. VII, 2nd par.):

He never asked her for her company. It was not his habit to ask people for things!

See also COD s.v. *thing*, and 701*c*.

PART IV

ADJECTIVES AND ADVERBS

INTRODUCTORY

551. As a linguistic category ADJECTIVES are related to, and have to be distinguished from, nouns and pronouns on the one hand, adverbs on the other.

They differ from nouns in that they do not take the sibilant suffixes that are used to form the plural and the genitive; they may pass into nouns by what is known as Conversion (see 770 ff.).

They may be subordinate to nouns in what is known as their attributive use (589, 591), or form part of nominal predicates (583, 591), or function as predicative adjuncts (592).

552. Attributive adjectives have a good deal in common with attributive pronouns (possessive, demonstrative, interrogative, relative, indefinite), though some of these (*this/these*, *that/those*) have distinct forms for the singular and the plural. Unlike the attributive pronouns, however, they do not in themselves enable their leading nouns to dispense with the use of an article (cf. *my horse — the old horse*).

The analogy may be extended to the predicative use of some of these pronouns: *the book is mine — the book is old.*

553. In function, attributive adjectives resemble ADVERBS qualifying adjectives; cf. *true greatness — truly great.*

Similarly, predicative adjectives resemble adverbs qualifying verbs; cf. *he was* (*looked*) *cheerful — he spoke cheerfully.*

In these and many other cases, the suffix *-ly* (949) distinguishes adverbs from adjectives, though sometimes the form without *-ly* is used for both: *a dead dog — dead tired* (cf. 953).

554. On the use of adverbs as adjuncts to verbs, adjectives and adverbs, see 593.

COMPARISON

555. There is one set of suffixes that is peculiar to adjectives (and to some adverbs), viz. *-er* and *-est*, which can be added to most monosyllabic and many disyllabic adjectives (and to some monosyllabic and disyllabic adverbs) to express CONTRAST OR SUPERIORITY.

When two persons or things (or two groups of persons or things) are compared or contrasted as bearers of a certain quality, we use the form in *-er*, the so-called COMPARATIVE, with reference to the person(s) or thing(s) that excel(s) (*John is cleverer than Peter*).

When a person or thing[1] is compared or contrasted with a group of persons or things, we use the comparative if the person or thing that excels is represented as *excluded* from the group (*John is cleverer than the other boys*), the form in *-est*, the so-called SUPERLATIVE, if he or it is represented as *included* in the group (*John is the cleverest of the boys*).

1. A simpler, though less comprehensive definition is given by A. S. Hornby in *English Language Teaching*, Summer 1953, p. 140: 'The comparative is used when one object or group is compared with another and separate object or group. The superlative is used when we refer to one object or group that forms a part of a larger group or collection.'

2. As Jespersen (MEG VII, 11.61) observes, 'it is important to insist on the fact that in ordinary usage the superlative does not indicate a higher degree than the comparative, but really states the same degree, only looked at from a different point of view.'

3. The comparative is occasionally used, esp. in literary English, with reference to a person or thing *included* in a group of *two*: *John is the taller of the two*. See Poutsma, *Grammar*, II, Ch. XXX, § 33.

In the case of adverbs, the comparison or contrast usually concerns two or more different actions.

556. Adjectives and adverbs of ONE SYLLABLE usually take *-er* and *-est*: *great — greater — greatest*; *soon — sooner — soonest*. This also applies to the endingless adverbs discussed in 953: *He could not speak any plainer*.

Adjectives of TWO SYLLABLES may take *-er* and *-est* if the resulting

[1] Or more than one person or thing (*John and Peter are cleverer than the other boys*).

comparative or superlative has only one syllable after the word-stress, or at most two, the first of which is very short. This is the case with:

a. adjectives stressed on the last syllable: *polite — politer — politest*; similarly with *complete, obscure, profound, sincere,* etc.

b. adjectives with a second syllable in syllabic [l], which ceases to be syllabic when followed by a suffix containing a vowel (cf. 949): *able, noble, simple, subtle,* etc.

c. adjectives in *-er*, *-ow*, *-some* or *-y*: *tender, hollow, handsome, happy.*

d. a few other adjectives: *civil, common, cruel, pleasant, quiet, stupid, wicked,* besides the adverbs *early* and *often.*

1. *Long, strong* and *young* have medial [ŋg] in the comparative and superlative: [ˈlɔŋgə], [ˈlɔŋgist], etc.

2. The spelling follows the usual rules for *y>i* and the doubling of final consonants: *gayer/happier, greatest/hottest.* See Appendix, p. 338 f.

3. When combined with negative prefixes, the above-mentioned types of adjectives may also take *-er* and *-est*: *impoliter, ignobler, unhappiest, unpleasantest,* etc., though *more impolite, most unhappy,* etc., are often found instead (see next paragraph).

557. With other adjectives and adverbs contrast or superiority are usually expressed by means of the adverbs *more* and *most*, placed before the adjective or adverb: *recent — more recent — most recent*; *difficult — more difficult — most difficult*; *nobly — more nobly — most nobly*; *easily — more easily — most easily.*

The terms 'comparative' and 'superlative' are also applied to these word-groups.

558. We sometimes find *more* and *most* where, according to the rules given above, we should expect *-er* and *-est*. Thus a heavy final consonant group in an end-stressed disyllabic adjective may be an objection to using the suffixes; hence sometimes *more* (*most*) *exact* rather than *exacter* (*exactest*). According to Jespersen (*Essentials of English Grammar*, § 22.31), 'sometimes the superlative in *-est* is in frequent use (*correctest, solidest, stupidest*), while the comparative in *-er* is rarer'. This might be worth testing.

According to COD, *wrong* is compared by means of *more* and *most*, and has no comparative as an adverb (*go* ~).

559. Another reason for the use of *more* or *most* may be parallelism with an adjective or adverb requiring *more* or *most*, or preceded by *less* or *least*:

London is the most wealthy and one of the least commodious capitals in the world.[1]

560. When a comparative in *-er*, or a superlative in *-est*, is combined with one formed with *more* or *most*, the form with the suffix usually precedes.

His knowledge is both deeper and more extensive than mine.

561. Sometimes the suffixes are used for humorous effect where one would have expected *more* or *most*:

'Curiouser and curiouser!' cried Alice.[2]
You're the confoundedest jay that ever lived.[3]

562. The suffixes are not used with two classes of adjectives, even though their form would seem to allow it:

a. with such as are only used predicatively: *afraid, alive, aloof.*[4]

b. with participles, even if purely adjectival in meaning: *pleased, surprised, tired.*[5]

Some other adjectives do not allow of comparison at all, on account of their meaning: *only*, *unique*, *whole*, etc.

563. A number of forms in *-er* and *-(e)st* show various deviations as compared with the simple adjective or adverb. They are: *far — farther/further — farthest/furthest*; *late — later/latter — latest/last*; *old — older/elder — oldest/eldest.* Here the regular forms (including *farther*) express the same fundamental meaning as the simple form, the irregular forms expressing a meaning of their own: *further* = additional (though it may be synonymous with *farther* in referring to space or time); *at the furthest* = at the latest; *latter* is the opposite of *former* (see below); *last* is the opposite of *first* (and cf. *last week*,[6]

---

[1] Kruisinga, *Handbook*[5], § 1780.
[2] Trace this quotation, and see what follows it.
[3] Kruisinga, *Handbook*[5], § 1783.
[4] Occasionally used attributively: *an aloof air*.
[5] *Tireder* occurs very occasionally.
[6] Opp. *next week*. *Next* is often regarded as an irregular superlative of *near*, with which, however, it has no connection semantically (the *next* station says nothing as to proximity), and very little phonetically. *Near* has only regular degrees of comparison: *nearer, nearest*.

etc.); *elder* and *eldest* are especially found before names of relationship (never predicatively), to indicate seniority. Note that *latter* and *elder* are only used as comparatives of contrast (568) (opp. *former* and *younger*).

Closed till further notice.
The side farthest from the enemy.
As Lord Grey's son and successor says, the book[1] is a sketch, not a picture; 'the latter', he hopes, 'may follow later'.[2]
At last he spoke.
Expect me on Wednesday at (the) latest. (Cf. 324.)
My eldest son; my oldest friend.
Elder Statesmen (cf. COD).
John is older than I.

564. Other forms in *-er* and *-(e)st*, one comparative in *-re*, and two without any suffix, have no *phonetically* related simple forms at all, although most of them are associated with a simple adjective or adverb *semantically*. They are: (*good/well*) — *better* — *best*; (*bad/ill*) — *worse* — *worst*; (*much/many*) — *more* — *most*; (*little* = not much) — *less* — *least*;[3] to which may be added *former* and *rather* (= sooner), and, perhaps, *first*.

Which do you like best, Scott, Dickens or Thackeray?
She made a living as best she could.
If the worst comes to the worst, we can go to America.
He is no more mad than I am.
She was not more surprised than angry. (Cf. 535.)
Shakespeare was said to have small (= little)[4] Latin and less Greek.
In former times people often travelled on horseback.
Erasmus and More first met when the former was on a visit to England.
I'd rather stop now.

1. When *little* is used to denote size or age (*little children*) it usually implies some personal feeling on the part of the speaker, which does not lend itself to expressions of contrast or superiority by means of a comparative or superlative (*littlest* is found very occasionally). Mere smallness is expressed by *small* — *smaller* — *smallest*.

2. *Less* and *least* refer to quantity, plural number being expressed by *fewer* and *fewest*. Still we find: *Less people go to church than to theatres* (Wyld); *Less than a hundred people were present.*

3. A form *lesser* occurs in the sense of 'minor' in such expressions as *The Lesser Bear*, *the lesser evils of life* (COD).

[1] Probably a biography. [2] Kruisinga, *Handbook*[5], § 1750.

[3] *Less* and *least* sometimes refer to *size*; cf. the COD definition of *shrub*: 'Woody plant of less size than tree', and the definition of *needle's eye* in 273.

[4] This use of *small* is now archaic.

565. There are three comparatives in *-er* derived from adverbs of place, without a corresponding superlative in *-est*: *inner*, *outer* and *upper*. They only express contrast, not superiority: *an inner wall*, *the inner man*; *an outer room*, *the outer world*; *his upper lip*, *the upper ten*.

Utter (= complete) is not connected with an adverb either phonetically or semantically: *utter misery*; as an adverb: *utterly miserable*.

Nether (cf. *beneath*) is somewhat archaic: *nether garments*, *the nether world*.

566. The forms mentioned in the last section can have *-most* [-moust], [-məst] affixed to them to form superlatives: *innermost*, *outermost*, *uppermost*; *uttermost*, *nethermost*. By the side of these we find *inmost*, *outmost*, *upmost*; *utmost* is commoner than *uttermost*.

There are a few more similar forms, either with or without *-er*: *furthermost*;[1] *foremost*, *hindmost*. Some are derived from nouns indicating position: *bottommost*, *topmost*.

> He penetrated to the inmost depths of the jungle.
> She showed the utmost reluctance to reply.
> Devil take the hindmost!
> The topmost twig of the tree.

567. Compounds of the types *kind-hearted*, *fine-looking* may add the suffixes to the first element: *a kinder-hearted*, *finer-looking man I never met*. In some combinations, however, the connection between the two elements is too close for them to be separated by a suffix. Hence, though we find *our oldest-established institutions*, we always say *She wore the most old-fashioned kind of clothes*; and similarly *more narrow-minded* (by the side of *a stronger minded woman*[2]), *most far-fetched*, *his most well-to-do parishioners* (Sweet).

568. As stated in 555, a comparative or superlative may express either CONTRAST (a) or SUPERIORITY (b). The difference will appear from the following examples.

> *a.* How slow you are! Try and be a little quicker.[3] (Contrast expressed.)

---

[1] There is a form *furthermore* = moreover, but this is a compound, and unconnected in meaning with *furthermost*.

[2] Jespersen, MEG VI, 24.18.

[3] Kruisinga, *Handbook*⁵, § 1734.

The younger generation. (Contrast implied.)
Roughage: the coarser kinds or parts of fodder or food (*American College Dictionary*).
The lower classes.
A poorer-class family.
His upper lip.
The youngest son was an engineer.[1]
b. John is even more musical than[2] his sister.
Gradually she grew calmer.[3]
All the stories were funny, but yours was the funniest of all.
He is happiest when left alone.[4]

Note that superiority implies contrast, and that the comparatives and superlatives of *b* either express a higher degree of a quality than is shown by another person or thing (odd examples), or by the same person or thing at different times (even examples).[5]

Note the (mainly literary) use of the superlative preceded by a possessive pronoun: *She smiled her sweetest* (= as sweetly as she could), *the drummers thumped their loudest.* (See also 789.) In meaning this construction approaches that described in 571.

569. To express that two qualities increase or decrease at an equal rate, the comparative of contrast, preceded by adverbial *the* (325), is used in two parallel clauses (*a*).[6] Another construction is with the conjunction *as* (*b*).

The construction may be denoted as the COMPARATIVE OF PROPORTION.

a. The longer I think of your proposal, the less I like it.
The more the merrier.
b. He became more cautious as he grew older.
As he grew older, he became more cautious.

A sentence of the latter type may also contain an adverbial clause without a comparative: *As he grew up, he became more cautious. As*-clauses do not express such a close causal connection as those with *the . . . the . . .*

570. To express that a quality increases or decreases at an even rate, the comparative of superiority is repeated, the two identical forms being connected by *and.*[7] When the comparative is formed by *more*, the adjective or adverb is put only at the end of the group.

[1] *Ibid.*, § 1742.
[2] Note that only a comparative of superiority can be followed by *than.*
[3] Kruisinga, *Handbook*[5], § 1735.
[4] *Ibid.*, § 1742.
[5] *Ibid.*, § 1735.
[6] *Ibid.*, § 1737.
[7] *Ibid.*, § 1740.

This construction may be denoted as the COMPARATIVE OF GRADATION.

> He ran faster and faster.
> Life was becoming more and more difficult.

571. *Most* is sometimes used before an adjective or adverb to indicate a high degree, in much the same sense as *very*. This is traditionally known as the ABSOLUTE SUPERLATIVE, though it has nothing to do with comparison.

> Everybody has been most kind.
> I once tasted the flesh of a young lioness and found it most palatable.
> He behaved most rudely.[1]

---

572. Besides the comparative of superiority (568), we may distinguish a comparative of inferiority (*a*), a comparative of equality (*b*), and a comparative of inequality (*c*).

> *a.* John is less musical than his sister.
> *b.* Is John as musical[2] as his sister?
> *c.* John is not so (or: as[3]) musical as his sister.

---

[1] *Ibid.*, § 1777.
[2] Stress on *musical*, not on *as*.
[3] *So* especially when *not* is stressed; also after *quite* (*not quite so large as*).

PART V

SENTENCE STRUCTURE

CHAPTER ONE

THE SIMPLE SENTENCE

573. An oral or written communication is made up of one or more units, each of which contains a complete utterance formed according to a definite pattern. Such units are called SENTENCES.

In writing, the beginning and end of a sentence are indicated resp. by a capital letter and by a full stop, or a note of exclamation or interrogation. In speaking, the beginning and end of a sentence are marked off from any preceding or following sentence by a pause, the intonation, especially at the end of a sentence, often contributing to the effect.

Cf. Gardiner's definition (*The Theory of Speech and Language*, p. 98): 'A sentence is a word or set of words followed by a pause and revealing an intelligible purpose.'

574. A sentence may consist of one or more words. Examples of one-word sentences are such exclamations as *Thanks!* — *Bother!* — *Good!* — *What!* (445) — *Fire!* — *Rain!*; imperatives such as *Stop!* —*Look!* (cf. a closely similar use of adjectives and adverbs like *Quick!* or *Quickly!* — *Steady!*); and vocatives, such as *Mother!* — *Jack!* (cf. *Hallo!* used, like the vocatives, to draw a person's attention).

Other, non-exclamatory (or not necessarily exclamatory) examples are: *Yes.* — *No.* — *True* (as a formula of concession). — *Perhaps.* — *Certainly.* — *Impossible.* — *Tired?* — *Hungry?* — *Rain?* — *What?* (= what did you say?)

One-word sentences are, as a rule, intelligible only in connection with a particular situation, or with a statement made (or a question asked) in another sentence (usually by another speaker). Cf. *Why don't you smoke?* — *Smoke? I never do.*

575. The last remark also applies to similar utterances consisting of more than one word: *Thanks awfully! — Dear me! — Poor dog! — Hurry up! — Look out! — What a joke! — Nothing doing! — Not at all. — By all*[1] *means. — Very likely. — Not on your life! — He a gentleman! — His father dead?*

576. In some of the examples of 575 there is to be discerned a splitting up of the utterance into two nuclei [ˈnjuːkliai]: *Nothing doing. — He a gentleman! — His father dead?* The meaning of such a sentence depends on the relation between the two parts. (*Thanks awfully*, or *Very likely*, on the other hand, contain only one nucleus, *awfully* and *very* merely serving to intensify the meaning of the other word.)

577. Most sentences of more than one word consist of two nuclei, one indicating the person or thing about whom or which a statement is made (or a question asked), the other containing the statement or the question asked.

The word (or words) indicating the person or thing referred to is (are) called the SUBJECT of the sentence; that (those) containing the statement (or the question) the PREDICATE.

In the following examples the subject is italicized, the non-italicized word(s) forming the predicate.

The term 'predicate' is sometimes restricted to the VERBAL part(s) of the statement, or to the group of copula plus noun or adjective discussed in 583. To prevent ambiguity, the term 'verbal predicate' may be used to denote the verbal part(s) of the statement.

Nothing doing.[2, 3]
He a gentleman![3]
I see.[3] (377 n.)
You don't say so![3]
Twenty people were killed.
The dogs barked furiously.
My sister married young.
After some time *they* saw a light.
There was *no wind.*
To advance was difficult, *to retreat* impossible.
Who saw the victim last?

---

[1] Stress on *all*.
[2] 'Slang announcement of failure or refusal of request' (COD).
[3] See the last remark of 574.

Where is *the station*?
Has *she* been ill?
Does *your brother* play tennis?
Will *waiting* do him any good?

As will be seen, the subject is usually a noun (often preceded by an article or another determining word) or a pronoun; it may also be a nominal part of a verb, i.e. an infinitive with *to* or a gerund (cf. 14).

578. Sentences expressing weather conditions or time are formed on the same pattern, with meaningless *it* (383) serving as a 'formal' subject.

Is *it* raining?
It was about midnight.

579. As appears from the examples, the predicate may consist of one or more words, one of these being usually a finite verb (cf. p. 35, n. 1). Besides the finite verb the predicate may contain one or more non-finite forms closely connected with the finite verb (*don't say*, *were killed*, *has been*, etc.). It will be found that in such verbal groups the non-finite form is usually the most important of the two as regards meaning.

580. At this point three things should be observed: *a.* that the two-nucleus type of sentence, with a predicate consisting of or containing a finite verb, is the usual one in statements and questions intelligible by themselves; *b.* that this type also occurs in sentences fully intelligible only in connection with a particular situation, or with a statement made in another sentence (*I see*); *c.* that a one-nucleus sentence may consist of or contain a finite verb (*sc.* an imperative) (*Stop! — Hurry up!*).

581. In some sentences, such as *The dogs barked furiously*, *My sister married young*, *They saw a light*, it seems as if we have not two nuclei, but three. In the first example, however, *furiously* merely adds something to the idea expressed by *barked*; it may, therefore, be considered as part of the second nucleus. But this is not the case with the other two: *young* is just as essential as *married*, *a light* equally important as *saw*.

Here are a few more examples of the second type of sentence; the third will be dealt with in 584.

a. The party arrived *safe and sound.*
The idea sounds *all right.*
b. We parted *the best of friends.*
He left home *a beggar*; he came back *a millionaire.*

It will be seen that, whereas *furiously* in the above example only refers to *barked*, the adjectives and nouns under *a* and *b* refer to the subject of the sentence as well as to the verbal predicate.[1] They are called respectively PREDICATIVE ADJECTIVES and PREDICATIVE NOUNS.

582. The verb in the second sentence of 581*a* is to be pronounced with fairly strong stress (suggesting: *but still I have my doubts*). The sentence may also be pronounced on a less sceptical tone, in which case the emphasis shifts to the predicative adjective, and we see the three-nucleus type of sentence shifting to the commoner two-nucleus type, with the predicative noun or adjective as the principal part of the second nucleus. This intermediate type is found especially after verbs like *to seem, to become, to get* (= to become), *to keep* (= to remain), *to feel, to lie*, etc.

The situation seemed *hopeless.*
It is getting *dark* (578).
She kept *very quiet.*
The snow lay *thick* upon the ground.
Old Jolyon sat *alone.*
Do you feel *tired*?

Note the same construction with a number of verbs of movement, whose meaning in combination with certain predicative adjectives and nouns is weakened to that of *to become*:

The dog went *mad.*
His brother fell *ill.*
All my misgivings came *true.*
Our provisions ran *short.*
Morris turned *socialist* (cf. 351).

583. The return to the two-nucleus type (with the verbal part of the predicate comparatively insignificant, apart from the expression of person, number, tense and mood) is practically complete when the verb is the copula *to be*, which merely serves as a link between the subject and the nominal part of the predicate. Besides nouns

---

[1] Note the alternative construction illustrated by *All our aircraft returned safely.*

and adjectives, the latter may also consist of an adverb, a pronoun, a numeral, or a noun preceded by a preposition, so long as these express a quality or condition of the subject.

Are you *tired*?
His brother was *a sailor*.
These books are *mine*.
Is Mr. Smith *in*? (or: *at home*?)
So be it.
I shall be *fifty* next Sunday.

The limit to which English can go in this respect is shown by such a sentence as *He a gentleman!* — in which the predicate-nucleus is purely nominal, a type which occurs especially in indignant exclamations and in exclamatory questions (*His father dead?*) uttered in response to a preceding sentence with a finite verb (*Do you know that his father is dead?*). Cf. also the 2nd ex. of 388 (*No one so fallible . . .*).

1. English also uses the copula type of sentence, with a predicative noun preceded by an article, a pronoun or a numeral, to indicate such qualities of the subject as size, colour, age, price, etc.

This hat is exactly the right size.
They are much the same height.
What colour are her eyes?
What age is she?
These melons are sixpence.

2. The transitions discussed in 581, 582 and 583 may be summed up by the following examples: *He awoke very tired — He felt very tired — He was very tired — He tired!*

3. When an adjective or a participle stands to a noun in the relation described here, but without a copula or other connecting verb, we call it 'semi-predicative'. For examples see 81*a*, 111 n., 702, 704.

584. In sentences of the type *They saw a light* the predicate consists of a so-called TRANSITIVE verb, followed by a noun or pronoun denoting a person or thing affected by the action expressed by the verb. This noun or pronoun is called an OBJECT.

A verb that does not take an object is called INTRANSITIVE.

1. Note that some verbs (such as *to arrive, to seem, to lie*) are always intransitive, while others may be used either transitively or intransitively: *He plays the violin — He plays extremely well*; *He left London — He left yesterday*;[1] *He divided his discourse into three parts — The river divides and sub-divides.* Some are always transitive: *to detest, to discover, to outwit.*

[1] Jespersen, *Essentials of English Grammar*, p. 116.

2. What was said in 118 of a number of primarily intransitive verbs also applies to the active voice. Cf.: *The policeman walked the man off*; *The only hope of seeing the birds during the day-time is to shine a torch into every cranny and hole among the boulders* (*London Calling*, May 10, 1951).

3. Note the intransitive use, with non-personal subjects, of such verbs as *to act* (of a play), *to iron, to sell*: *Browning's plays won't act*; *Clothes iron more easily when damp*; *The book sells well.* See also *English Studies*, Aug. 1950, and the quotation from Tillyard in 448.

585. In a sentence like *I gave him his ticket*, which contains two objects, the person denoted by the former (*him*) is affected by the activity expressed by the transitive verb and the other object together; similarly in *He promised my brother a copy*; *He offered her a chair*. We distinguish the former as an INDIRECT OBJECT from the latter as a DIRECT OBJECT.

1. The term 'affected' (if taken in a somewhat wide sense) covers most, though not all relations between a transitive verb and its object(s). Thus in *Will waiting do him any good?* (577) the direct object (*any good*) rather denotes what is 'effected' by the activity of the verb (*do*).

2. The use of 'former' and 'latter' in the above definition is not meant to imply that an indirect object *always* precedes a direct object. See 695, on Word Order. Note that it is possible, e.g. after *to give*, for the indirect object to denote a thing: *They never gave the plan a fair trial.*

3. In passive sentences like *A message was sent him* (596) the indirect object denotes the person affected by the activity expressed by the verb and the SUBJECT together.

4. On the use of 'formal' objects see 384.

5. In cases like *I dreamed a wonderful dream*, *He lived a double life*, where the object repeats the meaning (frequently also the form; but cf. *to run a race*) of the verb, we speak of a COGNATE [ˈkɔgneit] (i.e. 'kindred'] OBJECT. (Cf. Sweet, *New English Grammar*, I, § 253.)

586. The tendency to return to the two-nucleus type (582) is also apparent in some combinations of a transitive verb + object. Compare the following series with that in 583.2: *He took an apple — He took a walk — He took leave*; or: *She had many friends — She had a cold — She had breakfast.*

Other combinations in which the object is more important than the verb are *to give a cry, to give a jump, to give orders*; *to do good, to do harm, to do credit*; *to take place, to take part, to take care; to pay attention, to pay a visit*; *to have a shave, to have a smoke*, etc.

587. In sentences like *He looked at her*, *I never thought of him*, *Father seems to disapprove of the idea*, the verb plus preposition is practically equivalent to a single transitive verb; cf. *He saw her*, *I don't remember him*, *Father does not like the idea*. *Her*, *him*, *the idea* are called PREPOSITIONAL OBJECTS.[1]

588. Any parts of a sentence other than those hitherto discussed are called ADJUNCTS. An adjunct may be defined as an 'amplification of the predicate, subject, &c.' (COD). We distinguish *a.* attributive adjuncts, *b.* predicative adjuncts, *c.* adverbial adjuncts.

589. ATTRIBUTIVE ADJUNCTS qualify nouns. Examples from the preceding paragraphs are: *twenty* people, *my* sister, *some* time, *no* wind, *your* brother, *any* good, *next* Sunday, the *right* size, the *same* height, *what* colour, an *honest* man; to which may be added nouns like: a *brick* wall, a *village* church, the *Liverpool* docks; nouns in the genitive, like: *my mother's* picture, *a summer's* day (285, 286); an *of*-construction like: her *scamp of a* (= *rascally*) husband, a *gem of a* (= very *fine*) poem; and occasional adverbs like: the *above* remark, the *off* side. See 792 ff.

Attributive adjuncts are subordinate to the nouns they qualify. On the difference between such groups as *consumer needs* and *consumer's needs*, see *English Studies*, Febr. 1950.

590. In groups like (*St.*) *John the Baptist*, *William the Conqueror*, the bearer of the proper name is further identified by the following class-noun; the latter is said to be in apposition to the proper name, or simply called an APPOSITION.

In *my brother Charles*, *the Emperor Jones*, *the river Thames*, either noun may be considered to further identify the other. Which of the two is regarded as the apposition depends on the speaker's or writer's intention: *my brother* (*whose name is Charles*) or *Charles* (*who is my brother*).

In the above examples there is no clear subordination of one noun to another. When the apposition precedes the proper name, and is not preceded by a definite article or by an attributive adjunct, its subordination to the proper name is more apparent. This is the case with titles like *King George*, *Lord Halifax*, *Sir John*, etc.; and even more so in *Mr. Smith*, *Mrs. Brown*, *Miss Wylie*, in which the first word is little more than a prefix to the proper name.

---

[1] Though it is really the *verb* rather than the *object* which is 'prepositional'.

In *His father, the* (or: *a*) *renowned physician, died last week*, the apposition shows a tendency to dissociate itself from the sentence and take up a semi-independent position (cf. 594). The difference between this collocation and one like *his brother the explorer* (to distinguish him from other brothers) is similar to that between continuative and restrictive clauses (see the chapter on Relative Pronouns, 462; also section 610 of the present chapter).

591. Attributive adjectives usually denote a quality or condition of the person or thing indicated by the noun they qualify: *blue eyes, an old man, a serious mistake.* In these cases the noun and the adjective may also occur in the subject-predicate relation discussed in 583: *Her eyes were blue*; *The man was old*; *The mistake was a serious one.*

There are many cases, however, where this conversion would be impossible; thus in *an early riser, a small eater, a heavy smoker*; *a perfect stranger.* In the first three examples we have to do with nouns derived from verbs, and the adjectives closely resemble adverbs in their meaning: *I am an early riser = I always rise early.* Similarly in *a perfect stranger*, where the noun is related to an adjective: *He was perfectly strange to me.* One might say that **the riser was early*, **the stranger was perfect* are impossible because the adjectives only apply to these persons *qua* riser or stranger.

Compare also, from this point of view, *conscientious work, conscientious objections*, and *conscientious objectors*; *a married woman* and *their married life*; *a criminal neglect of duty* and *the criminal courts*;[1] *a dramatic scene* and a *dramatic critic*; and such combinations as *a born orator, a born fool*; *a large landowner, a public school-boy* (or *a public-school boy*).

1. Note that adjectives in *-en* denoting materials (*wooden, woollen*, etc.) are only used attributively; in predicative function (*made*) *of* (*wood*, etc.) are used instead: *He had a wooden leg — The leg was* (*made*) *of wood.* When the material meaning is lost sight of, *wooden* may be used predicatively: *His manners were extremely wooden* (= stiff). So also *golden*: *Silence is golden.* Cf. 918 f.

2. Attributive pronouns are dealt with in the chapter on Pronouns; for further information on attributive nouns and adverbs see the chapter on Conversion.

592. PREDICATIVE ADJUNCTS qualify nouns and pronouns without being subordinated to them. The term is usually restricted to

[1] Jespersen, *Essentials of English Grammar*, p. 92.

nouns and adjectives (occasionally adverbs, preposition groups, etc. as in 583; see also 77) accompanying a direct object to which they are related in much the same way as the nominal part of a predicate (583) to its subject. In such sentences, therefore, the two-nucleus pattern occurs twice; we may represent them by the formula S + P (o/s + p), in which S stands for the subject of the sentence, P for the (verbal) predicate, o/s for the object, which at the same time functions as a subject to p (the predicative adjunct).

> Have I made this *clear*?
> I like my coffee *strong*.
> The headache drove me *nearly mad*.
> I consider him *an honest man*.
> They elected him *chairman*.
> They found the place *a prosperous village*, and left it *a ruin*.
> Let's have him *in*.
> I found the room *in an awful mess*.

A predicative adjunct may be preceded by *as* or *for*:

> They chose him *as* (*for*) *their leader*.

The term 'predicative adjunct' is sometimes applied to the nominal parts of the predicates discussed in 581. If this terminology is adopted we may distinguish predicative adjuncts to the subject from predicative adjuncts to the object of the sentence.

593. ADVERBIAL ADJUNCTS qualify verbs, adjectives and adverbs. Examples: The dogs barked *furiously*; I *never* smoke; The letter was *nowhere* to be found; The idea sounds *all* right; She kept *very* quiet; The headache drove me *nearly* mad; He plays *really well*; they arrived *last Wednesday*. They may also accompany numerals and indefinite pronouns: How old is he? — *About* forty; There was *hardly* anybody there.

A classification of adverbs and other adverbial adjuncts according to their meaning will be given in the chapter on Word-Order (717 ff.). On verb-adverb combinations like *carry out* etc. see 698 f.

594. An adverbial adjunct may also refer to a number of words together, either the whole group of words outside the subject (*a*), or the subject and predicate combined (*b*).

> *a.* A bathe *always* makes me sleepy.
> She *quietly* sat down.
> I didn't wake up *till nine o'clock*.

b. After some time they saw a light.
Fortunately I had plenty of food with me.
The trip was quite enjoyable *after all.*

The distinction between *a* and *b* is not always easy to make. In clear cases of *b*, however, there is a tendency for the adverbial adjunct to dissociate itself from the sentence it qualifies, and to take up a semi-independent position (cf. 590). This may be indicated in writing by a comma: *Fortunately, I had plenty of food with me.* See further 610, 718 and 722.

595. Adverbial adjuncts, when single words, are usually adverbs; those of more than one word often consist of a preposition + (pro)noun, and may then be called PREPOSITIONAL ADJUNCTS. These should be distinguished from prepositional objects (587); cf. *They sat on the sofa, The dog lay on the floor*, with *They sent for a doctor, He listened to her.* But passive constructions like *That chair has been sat on, The bed had evidently been slept in*, show that cases may shift from one category to the other.

596. Prepositional adjuncts should also be distinguished from indirect objects accompanied by *to* (cf. 439). Compare *Give your brother this note*, and *Give this note to your brother*; *A message was sent him*, and *A message was sent to him.* In passive sentences there is no appreciable difference between the two constructions, that without *to* being especially common in American English.[1] In active sentences the construction with *to* (in end-position after the direct object) is used to emphasize the indirect object.

1. The alternative construction with *to* is impossible in cases like *Get me a newspaper, I got him a job, Cut that boy a piece of cake, Her mother bought her a new dress.* In a different position in the sentence the person benefited may, however, be denoted by an adjunct with *for*: *For whom did you get that newspaper? — Mother bought it for me, not for you. A piece of cake was specially cut for him.* (In passive sentences *for* is never omitted.) Cf. 453.

2. When *to* clearly expresses *direction*, we have to do with a prepositional adjunct, not an indirect object: *He sent his servant to the doctor* and, *a fortiori, He sent his servant to the station.*

3. On verbs that can take only one object and a prepositional adjunct (not two objects), see Appendix, p. 343 f.

[1] Where we also find *the money due him*; European English: *the money due to him.* Cf. 122.

597. It is sometimes hard to say, especially after a form of *to be*, whether a preposition plus (pro)noun functions as an adverbial or as a predicative (592 n.) adjunct. When the prepositional group is equivalent to an adjective (*He is at liberty — He is free*; *He is in good health — He is healthy*) its predicative character is clear; when it denotes place, we should rather call it adverbial (*He is in London, at Oxford*). Jespersen (*Essentials of English Grammar*, p. 131) says that *at home* may be used in both ways: *He is not at home* (local) — *He feels perfectly at home in France* (predicative). Yet *Is Mr. Smith at home?* often means: *Is he ready to receive visitors?* (cf. Fr.: *Monsieur est-il visible?*), when we should undoubtedly call it predicative.

598. An adverbial adjunct may consist of a single noun, or of a noun preceded by an article or an attributive adjunct: *I have walked* (*six*) *miles*; *centuries old*;[1] *He died last night*.

There is usually little difficulty in distinguishing a noun used as an adverbial adjunct to an intransitive verb from one used as an object to a transitive verb. Cf. *We stayed a week at Bath — We spent a week at Bath*. Also: *the play ran 100 nights* (COD) — *they ran a race* (cf. 585.5).

---

599. As appears from 574–577 sentences may be divided into STATEMENTS (or declarative sentences), QUESTIONS (or interrogative sentences), COMMANDS (or imperative sentences), and EXCLAMATIONS (or exclamatory sentences). Many specimens of the fourth group also belong to the third, and vice versa: cf. *Stop! — Silence! — Away with them!*

600. DECLARATIVE SENTENCES may be either AFFIRMATIVE or NEGATIVE.

Negative sentences are characterized by a negative adverb or another negative word, the commonest being *not*. English differs from other languages in having a special form for the predicate of

---

[1] Onions, *An Advanced English Syntax*, § 11. Kruisinga (*Handbook*[5], § 1932) wrongly says 'a preposition is necessary in *We have walked for miles*'. Cf. the last ex. of 156.

negative sentences, viz. *do not* (*don't*), *does not* (*doesn't*), *did not* (*didn't*) followed by a plain infinitive. On its use see 200, 201.

Note that the presence of *not* does not necessarily make the *sentence* in which it occurs negative: *He decided not to go.* Cf. also: *Do you think we shall be late? — I hope not.* — where *not* is equivalent to a clause (*that we shall not be late*) and does not negative *I hope*.

601. INTERROGATIVE SENTENCES are of two kinds, which may be illustrated by the following examples: *Did you see him?* (*a*) — *What did he say?* (*b*).

Interrogative sentences of type *a* open with a finite verb (usually an auxiliary or a copula) and usually end with a rising intonation. The answer expected is either 'yes' or 'no', or other words expressing various nuances of affirmation or denial (*certainly*, *perhaps*, *hardly*, *not at all*, etc.). They may be called VERBAL QUESTIONS.

Those of type *b* open with an interrogative pronoun or pronominal adverb (*Why*, *When*, *How*, etc.) and usually end with a falling intonation.[1] The answer expected is a piece of information.[2] They may be called PRONOMINAL QUESTIONS.

ALTERNATIVE QUESTIONS (*Is it right or wrong?* — [*Do you want your coffee*] *black or white?*) resemble type *a* in that they open with an auxiliary or copula. They are, however, pronounced with a falling intonation.

602. As in the case of negative sentences, English has a special form for the predicate of questions; on its use see 200, 201.

Verbal and, less often, pronominal questions may at the same time be negative.

Didn't you see him?
Why didn't you ask?

603. A question may take the form of a statement, except (sometimes) for a rising intonation at the end. This is the case (*a*) when an affirmative answer is expected, (*b*) when surprise or incredulity is to be expressed.

---

[1] See C. A. Bodelsen, 'The Two English Intonation Tunes', *English Studies*, October 1943. Also *ibid.*, February 1942, pp. 8–12, or R. W. Zandvoort, *Collected Papers*, pp. 131–136.
[2] Kruisinga and Erades, *An English Grammar*, I, § 29.

a. You live here?[1]
You asked to see his identity card?[2]
b. You are not going yet?[1]
His father dead?[1, 3]

604. The examples of 603*b* partake of the character of exclamations. This is also the case with so-called rhetorical questions, which are 'asked not for information but to produce effect' (COD).

Is this your gratitude?
Who cares?

605. IMPERATIVE SENTENCES usually contain the imperative of a verb. As Jespersen (*Essentials of English Grammar*, p. 294) observes, 'The imperative is used in requests, which according to circumstances may range from brusque commands to humble entreaties, the tone generally serving as a key to the exact meaning.' When a request rather than a command is intended, *please* is often added. (On its relation to the rest of the sentence cf. 594*b*.)

Shut the door!
Have a good time!
Hurry up, please!

1. A pressing request may be expressed by *do* followed by a plain infinitive: *Do take some more.* Cf. 199.

2. On the construction imperative + *and*, see 663.

606. For the sake of emphasis or specification, an imperative may be preceded by *you*, or followed (occasionally preceded) by *somebody*, *everybody*, in the function of a subject. Cf 61, last ex.

a. *You* be quiet.
You mind your own business.
You get out of this room.
b. Come on, everybody!
Get a light, some one!
c. Somebody run back!

As regards *somebody* etc., see the remark on *please* in 605.

In the colloquial phrase *mind you* (= please to observe; also *mark you*), added by way of a tag to another sentence, the subject-pronoun follows the imperative:

But I have no objection, mind you.

---

[1] Rising intonation.
[2] Falling intonation: see Bodelsen, *l.c.*, p. 134.
[3] See Onions, *An Advanced English Syntax*, § 44, 4.

607. PROHIBITIONS, i.e. negative imperative sentences, usually open with *Don't* followed by an infinitive without *to*.

Don't shoot!

This also applies when the infinitive is *be*, a verb that does not otherwise take *to do* in negative sentences (201): *Don't be silly*.

For the sake of emphasis or precision, *Don't* may be followed by *you* in the function of a subject:

Don't you forget it!

A prohibition does not necessarily contain the imperative of a verb: *No smoking* (*allowed*); *No thoroughfare*.

608. To what has already been said on exclamatory sentences, it is only necessary to add something about INTERJECTIONS, i.e. 'natural ejaculation(s) viewed as part(s) of speech[1] (e.g. *ah!*, *whew!*[2])' (COD). Interjections may be divided into regular[3] and occasional interjections. Further examples of regular interjections are *Oh!* — *Ha!* — *Hey!* — *Aha!* — *Oho!* — *Alas!* Examples of occasional interjections are *Damn!* — *Dear me!* — *Dear, dear!* — (*Good*) *Lord!* — (*Good*) *heavens!* — *By Jove!* — *Nonsense!*

Occasional interjections primarily belong to other parts of speech (nouns, adjectives, verbs, etc.); their use as interjections is something secondary. In a few cases, though a word may also occur as another part of speech, its use as an interjection is felt to be the primary one: *Hoity-toity!* (also noun and adj.); *Boo!* (also noun and verb).

Interjections may also be prefixed (occasionally suffixed) to a sentence (cf. 590, 594, 605): *Oh, what a lie!* — *We came too late, alas!*

Note that *eh* is mostly, *oh* sometimes used interrogatively:

You're joking, eh?
He refused to see me. — Oh?

609. It was pointed out in 580 that a one-nucleus sentence may consist of or contain a finite verb, *sc.* an imperative (*Stop!* — *Hurry up!*). As compared with the two-nucleus type, such a

---

[1] On the meaning of 'part of speech' see 770.
[2] On the pronunciation of *whew*, see Jones's *Pronouncing Dictionary*.
[3] 'devoted exclusively or primarily to its nominal function' (COD).

sentence may be said to contain a predicate, but no subject. It is not, however, felt to be defective; on the contrary, the subject, if any (606), is felt to be an addition.

In familiar speech, on the other hand, a pronominal[1] subject of what is essentially a two-nucleus sentence may be omitted if the reference is clear enough without it. The result is also a sentence without a subject, but one which is felt as a shortening of the regular pattern. When the verbal predicate contains an auxiliary this is often omitted as well, except in negative sentences, where it is inseparable from the negative adverb.

a. Better say yes, if they ask you. [= You had better . . .]
Got to do something, you know. [= I've got . . .]
Seems that people who are interested in radio are just as interested in T.V. [= It seems . . .]
b. Don't think I'll be in time. [= I don't . . .]
Haven't the slightest idea. [= I haven't . . .]
c. Coming, John? [= Are you coming?]
Feeling any better to-day?

Examples of the omission of a pronoun of the third person are probably less common; cf. the following from Kruisinga's *Handbook*[5], § 2130: '*Take care*', *said Mrs. G.*, '*he might hear you.*' — '*Do him good,*' *said the squire cheerfully.* [= *It would do . . .*] — Cf. also 67, last ex. but three; and: *Any news?* (= *Is there any news?*).

---

610. Attention has repeatedly been drawn (cf. 590, 594, 605, 608) to words which, while forming part of a sentence, take up a semi-detached position with regard to the rest of the sentence, from which they are separated by a break less marked than that which separates one sentence from another.

It will have been seen from the examples given that the degree of separation from the main body of the sentence varies considerably, from cases where it is hardly noticeable, or even doubtful (*After some time* they saw a light), through such where a word, though distinct from the rest of the sentence, is still closely connected with it (*Fortunately*(,) I had plenty of food with me; Hurry

[1] The phenomenon is really limited to *personal* pronouns.

up, *please!*), to those in which the semi-independent character of a word or group of words is unmistakable (His father, *the renowned physician*, died last week.).

611. Most of the semi-independent words so far dealt with are ADJUNCTS, in the sense defined in 588. When they are separated from the rest of the sentence by a clear break, they are called FREE ADJUNCTS. The construction occurs more frequently in written than in spoken English. Several examples have been given in the chapter on Verbs, 81 ff. Cf. also 27, 28, 57, 67 (3rd ex.), 72 (2nd ex.), 141 (1st ex.), 181 (1st ex.), 194 (1st ex.), 205 (4th ex.).

612. As will be seen, many of these examples contain a non-finite verb (infinitive with *to* or present participle). Here are some examples of free adjuncts without a verbal form; those under *b* open with a conjunction. Cf. also 823, 3rd ex.

> *a*. *An orphan at six,* he was brought up by a distant relative.
> *Always a keen skater,* he made the most of the opportunity to indulge in his favourite sport.
> At five o'clock the following day old Jolyon sat alone, *a cigar between his lips.*
> *b*. (*Though*) *a delicate child,* he was exposed to all the hardships of a rigorous climate.
> *When at home,* he worked at his notes from morning till night.
> He had become worse, *if anything,* since his wife died.

613. If it be asked to define the relation of a free adjunct to the rest of the sentence, the answer is that it usually expresses ATTENDANT CIRCUMSTANCES, i.e. circumstances attending the activity expressed by the main part of the sentence. In many cases this general relation can be further specified as the expression of cause, reason, time, contrariety, etc. This special relation may be merely implied (as in the examples of 612*a*), or it may be made explicit by the use of conjunctions (612*b*). (The same applies, of course, to free adjuncts *with* a verbal form.) In the last example of 612, the free adjunct contains a modification of the statement in the main part of the sentence.

614. For a discussion of RELATED, UNRELATED and ABSOLUTE FREE ADJUNCTS the student is referred to 84 and 86. It only remains to add that absolute adjuncts clearly belong to the two-nucleus type described in 577. When they contain a verbal form their structural pattern is practically identical with that of the usual type of sentence, the difference being that in the latter the verb is always finite, in the former *non-finite*: *The authorities having arrived*, *the ceremony began.*

Note the special type of absolute adjunct introduced by *with*:

DOROTHY: Is this the first time you've worked in St. John's Wood?
VERA: Yes, madam. It's ever so pretty, with all the trees coming out.
Dodie Smith, *Call it a Day*, Act I, sc. I.

There is not always a clear break in pronunciation between the *with*-adjunct and the rest of the sentence:

We can't have a party with a man dead just outside the front gate.
They filed downstairs with the job completed.
See also 660.5.

615. With the type illustrated by the first example of 614 we have reached the utmost limit of what can still be called a SIMPLE SENTENCE, if, indeed, we have not already gone beyond it.

When the 'amplification' (588) takes the form of a two-nucleus group with a subject and a *finite* verb, the amplification is called a CLAUSE, and the sentence, a COMPOUND[1] SENTENCE: *When the authorities had arrived*, *the ceremony began.* By extension, the term CLAUSE may be applied to both (or all) members of a sentence, the leading member being distinguished as the MAIN CLAUSE from the other(s) as SUB-CLAUSE(S).[2]

---

[1] Some grammarians prefer the term COMPLEX sentence, and reserve the name COMPOUND for the type described in 659 ff.

[2] Also called SUBORDINATE CLAUSES or DEPENDENT CLAUSES. Other names for MAIN CLAUSES are HEAD-CLAUSES or PRINCIPAL CLAUSES.

CHAPTER TWO

THE COMPOUND SENTENCE

616. As regards the structure of the members of a compound sentence it is to be observed that a main clause may take any of the structural forms of a simple sentence.

It follows from the definition given in 615 that a sub-clause always contains a subject and a finite verb. Sub-clauses are mostly, though not always, introduced by a conjunction or another connecting word, such as a relative pronoun.

617. Parallel to the division of adjuncts in 588, we may distinguish sub-clauses into ATTRIBUTIVE CLAUSES, PREDICATIVE CLAUSES and ADVERBIAL CLAUSES. It will be seen, however, that this classification is not exhaustive, and that we have to add OBJECT CLAUSES, SUBJECT CLAUSES, and PREDICATE CLAUSES.

618. Like attributive adjuncts, ATTRIBUTIVE CLAUSES qualify nouns, the noun qualified being called the ANTECEDENT of the attributive clause. (The antecedent may also be a pronoun.) For examples the student is referred to the chapter on Relative Pronouns.

619. In section 462 of that chapter attributive clauses were divided into RESTRICTIVE and CONTINUATIVE clauses, although it was hinted (in footnote 6) that the distinction is too absolute to fit all specimens. The point is best discussed in conjunction with the statement in 463 that relative *that* occurs chiefly in restrictive clauses.

620. Sentences like the following, all from modern English authors,[1] seem a little difficult to reconcile with the above-mentioned definitions.

> *a.* In the September sunshine that cut half across the narrow street, vehicles choked the thoroughfare.

[1] From a collection by P. Fijn van Draat, published in *Neophilologus* IV, 47–51.

Mr. Britling ran through a little list of stay-at-homes that began with a Duke.

b. He had been out riding a little pony, that was not so determined as its rider.

And a gloom fell upon the boy, that was quite unmistakable.

The antecedents under *a* do not require 'restricting' in the same way as the specimens referred to in 462; the function of the attributive clauses is rather descriptive, but they agree with the clearly 'restrictive' specimens in being closely connected with their antecedents. The same applies to the examples under *b*, in spite of the fact that the sub-clauses are preceded by a slight pause, which the writer has thought it desirable to indicate by a comma. Like the clearly restrictive specimens, all these attributive clauses are *essential* to their antecedents.

Cf. COD s.v. *that*[1] 3. Rel. pron.: 'used, exc. archaic., rhet., poet., only to introduce defining-clause essential or rhet. viewed as essential to identification'.

621. To accommodate such specimens of attributive clauses as are neither clearly restrictive nor clearly continuative, a third category has sometimes been set up, the semi-adverbial.[1] Now there is no doubt that many attributive clauses imply a causal or other adverbial notion, but this is true of some that are clearly restrictive or continuative as well as of some that are not clearly either one or the other. Cf. *Any man that knows three words of Greek could settle the point*:[2] undoubtedly restrictive, yet also semi-adverbial: such a man could settle the point *because* he knows three words of Greek. And on the other hand: *My uncle, who will be seventy to-morrow, is still a keen sportsman*: undoubtedly continuative, yet also semi-adverbial: my uncle is still a keen sportsman, *although* he will be seventy to-morrow.

Again, here is a non-adverbial specimen of either type: *I wish I knew the man who wrote that book*; *My mother, who is eighty years old, is coming to stay with us next week.*[3]

---

[1] Kruisinga and Erades, *An English Grammar*, I, § 117.

[2] *Ibid.*, § 109.

[3] Vechtman-Veth, *A Syntax of Living English*, § 20. Note also that there is nothing 'semi-adverbial' in the first and third examples in Kruisinga's *Handbook*[5], § 2273*b*.

Lastly, if the authentic examples of 620 are neither clearly restrictive nor continuative, it is at least clear that they are not semi-adverbial either.

622. Attributive clauses may be introduced not only by relative pronouns, but also by what are usually called relative adverbs, though in this function they are really conjunctions: *when, where, why.* This is the case when the antecedent expresses a corresponding meaning, resp. time, place, reason.

I was out of town (on) the day when it happened.
I remember the house where I was born.
We never really understood the reason why he left us.

Though these clauses are best looked upon as attributive, seeing that they qualify a noun in the main clause, there is no doubt that they also contain an adverbial element, which is especially prominent when the clause is continuative: *In the old days, when I was a boy there,* . . . (Kruisinga and Erades, *An English Grammar*, I, p. 129).

623. *That* is similarly used after an antecedent denoting time. In this case it has to be regarded as a conjunction rather than as a relative. Note that the antecedent stands to the clause in the relation of an adverbial adjunct. Cf. 463.

He fell ill the night that we went to France.

624. Clauses introduced by *as*, after an antecedent qualified by *same* or *such*, show the same partly attributive, partly adverbial character.

I want a cake of bath-soap, not scented. — The same as you always have?[1]
We had such grapes as you never saw.[2]

After *same* one also finds *that*, less often *which*: *The same that you always have?*

625. In literary English a noun in a negative sentence may be defined by a clause introduced by *but.*

Not a day went by but brought us news of yet another calamity.

When a *but*-clause has a subject of its own, it is purely adverbial (634):

Not a day went by but some new calamity happened.

[1] See *English Studies* XXV (1943), p. 134.

[2] See also 435.

626. As was explained in 467 and 468, attributive clauses may under certain conditions be joined to their antecedents without a connecting word. This also applies to the type defined in 623: *He fell ill the night we went to France*, and to a case like *I don't like the way she smiles*.

Note also cases like the following:

> He turned pale the moment he saw her.
> It's a disgrace the way he drinks.

A shifting is to be observed here: from being noun-antecedents, *the moment* and *the way* become conjunctions (or conjunctional phrases) introducing the sub-clause.

627. It may be useful to remind the student of what was said in **381** and 468 on compound sentences beginning with *it is* (*was*) and having an attributive clause for their second member. They differ from those hitherto discussed in that the main clause, though it has the form of a two-nucleus sentence, does not always contain a complete utterance, and in that the sub-clause, though attributive in form, does not really qualify the 'antecedent'. In *meaning* such sentences are essentially simple, in spite of their compound structure.

---

628. PREDICATIVE CLAUSES qualify the direct object of the main clause, their function running parallel to that of predicative adjuncts (592).

> He has made the company what it is to-day.[1] (Cf. He made the company famous.)
> Call it what you will. (Cf. What do you call it?)
> I found him as I had left him. (Cf. I found him ill.)

Predicative clauses are introduced by *what* or *as*; the latter are related to adverbial clauses of manner (642*b*).

---

629. ADVERBIAL CLAUSES, like the adverbial adjuncts discussed in 594, usually qualify the main clause as a whole. In accordance with the meaning expressed they can be divided into adverbial clauses

---

[1] Cf. Kruisinga and Erades, *English Grammar*, § 105.

of time, place, cause or reason, purpose, result, condition, concession or contrast, comparison, manner, restriction, and perhaps one or two more. The meaning intended is usually indicated by the introductory conjunction, though it sometimes has to be inferred from the sentence as a whole.

630. Adverbial clauses of TIME may be introduced by *when*, *whenever*, *as*, *while*, *before*, *after*, *until*, *till*, *since*, *now* (*that*), *as long as*, *as soon as*, *the moment* (626), etc.

He turned pale when he saw me.
It struck me as I was speaking.
I have only been ill once since I came to live here.
Now (that) you mention it, I do remember.
I will stay as long as I can.

1. Note the use of *when* in sentences like the following:

I had practically decided not to go, when I received another urgent message.
Hardly (Scarcely) had I sat down when the telephone bell rang again.

In the first example the second member is coordinate (659) rather than subordinate (= 'but just then'); cf. continuative attributive clauses (619).

2. *Now* (*that*) expresses reason as well as time.

631. Adverbial clauses of PLACE may be introduced by *where*, *wherever*, *whence* (spoken English *where . . . from*). They are less usual than attributive clauses of the type discussed in 622.

Stay where you are.
Go back (to) where you came from.[1]

Not all clauses introduced by *when* or *where* are adverbial; cf. 622.

632. Adverbial clauses of CAUSE OR REASON may be introduced by *as*, *because*, *since*, *seeing* (*that*), *in that*, etc.

As you are not ready, we must go on (COD).
Did you go on because he was not ready, or for another reason?
Since there is no help, let us try to bear it as best we may.

The difference between a clause introduced by *as* and one beginning with *because* is that in the former (which usually comes first) the emphasis is on the main clause, in the latter (which usually comes second) on the sub-clause. *Since* agrees with *as* in this respect, but implies at the same time that the cause or reason is an undisputed fact. Cf. 738.

---

[1] Cf. Onions, *An Advanced English Syntax*, § 48.

In that, which is limited to literary English, means primarily: 'consisting in this, that . . . '; this may be either restrictive ('in so far as') or explanatory, or both. The student is advised to study the quotations given by Kruisinga in his *Handbook*[5], § 2307, though he need not accept the interpretation proposed there at the bottom of p. 409.

1. Note the following example of a non-introduced clause (with *so*): *I paid him double, I was so pleased.* The second member contains an explanation (cf. COD s.v. *so*).

2. Cause or reason may also be expressed by a clause beginning with an adjective or participle followed by *as*: *Shut off as they were, the colonists lost step with developments at home.* Cf. 196 and 638; also 465.

3. Note the use of *that* in: *Have you nothing to do, that you are sitting there idle?* This might be called an inverted clause of reason: the person addressed is sitting idle because he has nothing to do. In this construction the main clause is always a question or a negative exclamation. (Cf. *English Studies*, Oct. 1952, p. 237.)

633. Clauses of PURPOSE may be introduced by *that*, *so that*, *in order that*.

If the clause expresses what is to be prevented it may be introduced by the same words, accompanied by *not*, or it may open with *lest* (in literary English only), *for fear* (*that*), *in case*. See also 159 and 175, and, for a comparison with the infinitive of purpose, 28.

Note that *that* in this function is not very common, *so that*, which combines the notions of purpose and result, occurring much oftener.

Stand there, (so) that I may have a good look at you.
He worked himself to death, in order that his wife might live in luxury.
We had to be very careful lest the news should become known too early.
Better chain up the dog in case he bites.

634. Clauses of RESULT may be introduced by *that* or *so that*; in the former case the main clause contains *so* (occasionally *such*). A clause of result may also be non-introduced, but only when *so* occurs in the main clause.

When the main clause is negative, the sub-clause may be introduced by *but* (*that*).

I was so tired (that) I could hardly stand.
All precautions have been taken, so that we may expect to succeed.

Even Scrooge was not so dreadfully cut up by the sad event, but that he was an excellent man of business on the very day of the funeral.
It never rains but it pours.

Inversion of the two members of the first example would yield a sentence of the type illustrated in 632. 1: *I could hardly stand, I was so tired.*

635. Clauses of CONDITION may be introduced by *if*, *supposing*, *suppose* (in questions), *in case*, *so that*, *so long as*. Emphatic condition is expressed by *provided* (*that*) or *on condition* (*that*). Clauses of negative condition may be introduced by *unless*, which is more emphatic than *if . . . not*.

If it is time, we had better go.
I should not mind so much, if I was not so busy.
Suppose your father saw you, what would he say?
Better take an umbrella, in case it rains. (Cf. 633.)
So (that) it is done, it matters not how. (Literary.)
So long as it is done, it does not matter how.
He declared himself willing to try, provided (that) he was given a free hand.
I always walked, unless I could catch a bus.

1. Note that *so that* may express purpose (633), result (634) or condition. In the first case *so* may be omitted, in the third case *that*.

2. *If* may also be equivalent to *whenever*: *If I feel any doubt I inquire* (cf. COD s.v. *if*).

636. Clauses expressing a condition that is not, or is not likely to be, realized (see the second ex. of 635) are called clauses of REJECTED CONDITION; they contain a modal preterite or pluperfect (cf. 137, 144 and 222). Others (like the first ex. of 635) are called clauses of OPEN CONDITION.

637. Clauses of rejected condition, and clauses of open condition expressing uncertainty, may open with the modal preterite of an auxiliary. The construction is mainly literary.

Had I but taken your advice, all this misery might have been avoided.
Should he call, tell him I am not at home. (Cf. 176.)

But compare:

If only I knew his address! (Cf. 139.)

Incidentally, the last sentence provides an instructive example of incongruity of meaning and form: in form it is a conditional clause, in meaning a simple sentence. Similarly with *Had I but taken your advice!*

638. Clauses of CONCESSION OR CONTRAST may be introduced by *though*, *although*; occasionally by *when*, *for all*, *no matter* (*how*, *when*), or *whereas* (= while on the contrary). In emphatic style *though* may be preceded by a plain infinitive (cf. 20), a predicative noun, adjective or participle, or an adverb. In these cases *as* and, after an infinitive, *what* also occur in concessive function. Cf. 632, 689, 690.

I will do my best, although I cannot say I am very keen.
Though I am poor, I am honest.
Poor though (or: as) I am,[1] I am honest.
Much as I admire his courage, I cannot think he acted wisely.
Try as I might, I could not lift the stone.
Say what I would, he refused to go.
He walks when he might ride.
For all he seems to dislike me, I still like him. (COD s.v. *for*.)
He is never satisfied, no matter how hard I work. (Cf. 640.)
He had always imagined his cousin to be a captain, whereas he was only a sergeant.

639. When the idea of concession is tinged with a slight amount of reserve, *if* may be used.

If they are poor, they are at any rate happy.

640. Concessive clauses may also be introduced by compound relative pronouns and adverbs in *-ever*. Cf. 473.

He is always finding fault, whatever I do.
However weak we may be, we shall never surrender.

641. A sub-clause introduced by *granting* (84) or *granted* (115) might be called one of concession, but it does not express contrast:

Granting (granted) that this is true, what is your conclusion?

642. It remains to give a few examples of adverbial clauses of COMPARISON (*a*), MANNER (*b*), and RESTRICTION (*c*).

a. They behaved as well as could be expected.
You are more patient than I should be in your case.
He did as if there were nothing wrong.
b. I will do (just) as you advise.
They don't have long intervals here, like they do at some theatres.
c. The Act is good as far as it goes.[2]
Has Catherine come back yet? — Not that I know of.[2]
The man may be dead, for all we know.

1. The third example might also have been given under *b*.

2. *Like* as a conjunction (5th ex.) is limited to colloquial English.

---

[1] In American English often: *As poor as I am . . .*
[2] Poutsma. *Grammar*², I, Ch. XVII, §§ 147, 149.

643. It will have been observed that several conjunctions may introduce more than one kind of adverbial clause. Thus *as long as* may introduce a clause expressing either time or condition; *since*, time or reason; *when*, time or concession; *so that*, purpose, result or condition; *if*, condition or concession; *for all*, concession or restriction; *that*, purpose, result or restriction (and cf. 632.3); *as*, time, reason, comparison, manner or concession.[1]

The meanings of adverbial clauses often shade off into one another; thus time and condition in clauses introduced by *as long as*; time and concession in clauses introduced by *when*; purpose and result in clauses introduced by *so that*; condition and concession in clauses introduced by *if* (639), etc.

Now (*that*) (630.2) expresses the ideas of time and reason combined.

Clauses of result (634) and clauses of condition (635) are the only adverbial clauses that may occur without a conjunction.

---

644. The sub-clauses hitherto discussed have a function analogous to that of the adjuncts defined in 588.

A sub-clause may also function as the object of a transitive verb; such a clause is called an OBJECT CLAUSE. Object clauses contain either a statement (including the expression of a desire) (*a*), or a question (*b*). The former may be introduced by *that*, or they may be non-introduced; the latter are introduced by the same words as pronominal questions (601), or, in the case of verbal questions, by *if* or *whether*.

a. They say (that) he is better.
Theseus commanded that the prisoners should be taken to Athens.[2]
I would rather you stayed at home. (Cf. 16*d*.)
b. Do you know who lives here?
Show me what you have done.[3]

---

[1] In sentences like the following, *as* may be said to introduce a clause of PROPORTIONATE AGREEMENT (Poutsma, *Grammar*[2], I, Ch. XVII, § 140):
As I grew richer, I grew more ambitious.
You'll pick it up (some knowledge of a foreign language, for instance as you go along.

[2] See also the other examples in 172. [3] Cf. 470.

I wonder if he'll come.
Please let us know whether you agree.

These two kinds of object-clauses may be denoted respectively as DEPENDENT STATEMENTS and DEPENDENT QUESTIONS.

645. Dependent questions (including sub-clauses introduced by relative *what* [470]) may be preceded by a preposition.

It reminded me of how I once caught a magpie.
They were debating about which was the better plan, his or mine. (Cf. 555.3.)
Look at what you've done.

Before applying the term PREPOSITIONAL OBJECT CLAUSES to all these, and similar, examples indiscriminately (as is done by Kruisinga and Erades), it is well to consider what was said in 595 as to the difference (and the occasional difficulty of distinguishing) between prepositional objects and prepositional adjuncts. If the latter are regarded as adverbial, many dependent questions preceded by a preposition will have to be considered adverbial as well; they might be called 'prepositional adjunct clauses', if this was not a contradiction in terms.

646. A number of predicative adjectives expressing a feeling or perception are regularly construed with a preposition (mostly *of*) + (pro)noun: *I am glad of it*; *I am not aware of it*; *Are you sure of it?*; *I am not afraid of him*; *I am anxious for his safety*; *I am surprised at you.* The same construction is found before a *what*-clause (*a*); a dependent statement, however, is joined to the predicative adjective without a preposition (*b*), frequently also without a conjunction.

a. I was surprised at what he said next.
Are you sorry for what you've done?
b. I am almost certain that he saw me.
I am not aware that I have done wrong.
I am *so* glad you've come.
I'm afraid I must trouble you for your subscription.

647. As in some of the examples of 645, the 'object' character of some of these clauses may not be immediately evident. Comparison with an undoubted object clause *I believe* (*that*) *he saw me* will probably make it clear, however, that the sub-clauses of 646*b*, at any rate, may be regarded as object clauses.

1. In some cases they might be regarded as semi-adverbial, *sc.* as sub-clauses of cause or reason: *I was surprised that he agreed*; *I'm sorry you're hurt.*

2. The use of *that* in clauses of type *b* is literary rather than colloquial. When *I'm afraid* is no more than an apologetic formula it is not, as a rule, followed by *that*.

648. The name 'object clauses' is sometimes extended to sub-clauses dependent on a noun related in form and meaning to a transitive verb. It should be noted, however, that unconnected clauses do not occur.

> I politely expressed the hope that he might speedily recover.
> Is there any proof that the pistol was his?

649. It is difficult, however, to separate these clauses from *that*-clauses dependent on nouns not related to verbs.

> The room was in complete darkness, owing to the fact that the electric light had been short-circuited.
> The news that Singapore had fallen struck us like a thunderbolt.

Such clauses have been called apposition clauses (see e.g. Kruisinga, *Handbook*⁵, § 2263); comparison with 590 will show, however, that the two constructions are not on all fours. Something might be said for the term CONTENT CLAUSES to denote those discussed in this and the preceding section: they express the 'contents' of the noun on which they depend, i.e. what the hope, proof, fact, news, etc., consisted in.

The term is borrowed from Jespersen (*Essentials of English Syntax*, § 33), who, however, applies it to all object clauses, as well as to subject clauses and predicate clauses.

650. The sub-clauses hitherto discussed are used in functions that are not among the syntactically indispensable elements of the sentence.[1] There are two types of sub-clauses, however, that function as one of the essential elements of a two-nucleus sentence: SUBJECT CLAUSES and PREDICATE CLAUSES. Neither type is as common as those hitherto discussed.

651. SUBJECT CLAUSES occur only as parts of declarative compound sentences. Like the subject of a simple declarative sentence, therefore, they always have front position.

Like the object clauses treated in 644, a subject clause may contain either a statement (*a*) or a question (*b*). In the former case it is always introduced by *that* (which, in initial position, is necessary

[1] i.e. the sentence in the abstract. Cf. Kruisinga, *Handbook*[5], § 2264.

to mark it as a *sub*-clause); in the latter it is introduced by the same words as interrogative object clauses.

a. That he will refuse is improbable, to say the least of it.
That any one should believe such nonsense seems almost unthinkable.
b. What did you say to him? — What I *said* does not matter.
How he manages to keep going is beyond me.
Whether he will come is another question.

Note that the verbal predicate is nearly always *to be*, or a verb of related meaning.

652. A type of sentence that is commoner than that of 651*a* is one with initial *it*, with the *that*-clause in end-position. This type also occurs in interrogative compound sentences.

It is improbable that he will refuse.
It seems almost unthinkable that any one should believe such nonsense.
Is it possible that he did not recognize me?

The very fact that the sub-clause now has end-position obscures its character as a subject clause. Indeed, we are reminded of the object clauses of 646*b* (*I am almost certain that he saw me*), though it would be going too far to call the specimens of the type discussed here object clauses. See also what was said in 379.

653. Predicate clauses function as the nominal predicate of a compound sentence. They are introduced by the same words as subject clauses; they may also be introduced by *as*.

a. The trouble is that we none of us know anything about chemistry.
What surprised me most was that he did not seem to have any luggage.
b. The question is how we are going to find the money.
Rice is to the Japanese what potatoes are to many Europeans.
c. That is as it should be.

The second sentence is an example of one consisting of a subject clause and a predicate clause linked by a copula. If the order of the two members is inverted they do not only change places, but functions as well, the *that*-clause becoming the subject: *That he did not seem to have any luggage was what surprised me most.*

654. A predicate clause is sometimes non-introduced, especially after a main clause like *The fact is*, *The reason was*, etc. The two members of such a compound sentence are usually divided by a somewhat abrupt break, which may or may not be indicated by a comma.

The fact is, I hardly know how to begin.
The reason was, nobody had expected him so early.

Though formally a predicate clause, the second member of such a sentence is almost felt to be independent.

---

655. What was said in 643 about the meanings of adverbial clauses shading off into one another, also applies to the classification of sub-clauses in general. The student is referred to 645 n. (on 'prepositional object' clauses); 647 ('object' clauses and adverbial clauses); 648 and 649 ('object' clauses and 'apposition' clauses); 652 ('subject' clauses and 'object' clauses). Note that the last example of 653 is something half-way between a predicate clause and an adverbial clause of manner (cf. also 628).

---

656. There is in English a certain type of compound sentence, consisting of a statement followed by an APPENDED QUESTION (or 'tag question') modelled on the main clause. The question serves either to ask the person addressed to confirm the statement made (CONFIRMATIVE QUESTIONS) (*a*), or to express the speaker's reaction to a previous statement by the person addressed which is repeated by the speaker (REACTIVE QUESTIONS) (*b*).

a. You are not ill, are you?
Fine day, isn't it?
She paints, doesn't she?
b. 'Where's the rest of the money?' — 'I'm afraid it's all spent, sir.' — 'Oh, it's all spent, is it?'
You can't catch me. — I can't, can't I? said Philip.[1]

Note that an auxiliary or copula in the first member is repeated in the second; if the first member contains neither, *to do* is used in the second. If the subject of the first member is a personal pronoun, it is repeated; if it is another word, it is referred to by a personal pronoun in the second member. In sentences of type *a* either the first or the second member is negative; in those of type *b* both members are either negative or affirmative.

1. The feelings expressed in appended questions of type *b* may range from friendly interest to irony or sarcasm. Cf. Kruisinga, *Handbook*[5], § 426.

---

[1] Jespersen, MEG V, 25.35.

2. In a sentence like *Let's mix ourselves another drink, shall we?* the tag is added, not to a statement, but to an exhortation, and follows the familiar pattern of *Shall we have another drink?* (Cf. 169 and 657, 1st par.)

3. A case like *We* had *to learn everything for ourselves,* didn't *we?* (Kruisinga and Erades, *An English Grammar*, § 94, 2) is to be explained in accordance with 201.1.

4. On appended questions introduced by *or*, see 660.5.

657. A confirmative question may also be appended to a statement without being formed on the same pattern:

He is a nice man, don't you think?
It's such a bore, don't you know.

In the second example (which really represents 'Mayfair' English) the 'tag' practically ceases to be a question, and there is little to choose between it and an APPENDED STATEMENT:

It's an awful bore, you know.

Here are some more examples of appended statements:

It's raining, I think.
We shall have to go back, I'm afraid.
What's it all about, I wonder?
All right, she said.

By inverting the sequence of the two members, the appended statement becomes the main clause, the other member an object clause: *I think it's raining*. This sounds more matter-of-fact than the other form, which contains a spontaneous utterance, only slightly modified afterwards.

Appended questions and statements are usually pronounced on a lower pitch than the main clause. On the intonation of tag questions see an article by J. D. O'Connor in *English Studies*, June, 1955.

Short sentences like *I think*, *she said*, etc. may also be inserted parenthetically: *This, I think, is his best novel*; '*But then,' she said, 'we are all in the same boat.*'

658. In colloquial English there is another form of appended statement, modelled on the pattern of the main clause. Here are a few examples.

a. He was always very particular, was Mr. Gibbons.
She is a nice woman, is your aunt.
He never cared much for smoking, did your brother.

They're all alike, men are.
b. That's a good one, that is — best joke I ever heard.
I'm proud, I am.

As in the appended questions of 656, the auxiliary or copula is repeated, or a form of *to do* is used. But, whereas the subject of an appended question is always a personal pronoun, here it is the main clause that contains a personal pronoun, the person (or thing) it refers to being specified by a noun in the appendix (*a*). The noun in this case usually has end-position, though it sometimes precedes the copula or auxiliary.

When the two subjects are identical pronouns, as in the examples under *b*, the appended statement, being merely repetitive [ri ˈpetitiv], serves to reinforce the statement in the main clause; it is unstressed, and pronounced on a low pitch.

A similar construction, with an appendix containing nothing but a subject, is found in cases like the following:

She is a nice woman, your aunt.
He knew what he was talking of, that old philosopher.

For more examples see Kruisinga, *Handbook*[5], §§ 2417, 2420.

---

659. All the types of compound sentences so far discussed contain one member that is SUBORDINATE to the other.

The two[1] members may also be COORDINATE; in this case neither member is subordinate to the other.

Coordination, like subordination of members is usually, though not always, indicated by a conjunction. Here are some examples without conjunctions; the phenomenon[2] is limited to non-interrogative sentences.

Father was in the shop, Mother was in the kitchen cooking dinner.
I wouldn't live in a place like London; I hate big cities.
Il ooked at my watch: it was ten o'clock.

As appears from the second and third examples, the relations expressed in

---

[1] There may be more than two members, but this makes no essential difference.

[2] The technical term for it is *asyndeton* [æˈsindətən] (Gr. = unlinked). There is a good example in Galsworthy, *The Man of Property*, Part I, Ch. II, 3rd sentence.

sentences with a subordinate clause (reason, result, etc.) may be *implied* in sentences with two unconnected coordinate members. Note the rising intonation at the end of the first member of the third example.

660. The conjunctions usually connecting two coordinate members of a compound sentence are *and*, *but*, *or*, *nor*; *for* (*a*).

The two members may also be connected by adverbs like *so*, *still*, *yet*, *indeed*, *however*, etc. (*b*). See 661.

Here are a few examples of type *a*.

He took a pen and wrote as follows.
She wanted to make a speech but did not know how to begin.
We can ask him now, or wait till to-morrow.
All that is true, nor must we forget that he warned us repeatedly.
I never found out, for I was too shy to ask.

1. If the two members have the subject (or the subject and part of the predicate) in common, it is (they are) usually expressed in the former only.

2. *Nor* is rather literary in this function; in spoken English the second member of the fourth example would be replaced by: *and we must not forget either. . . .*

3. *And, but, or, nor* can also connect words (*you and I*) or groups of words (*to be or not to be*); *for* connects clauses only.[1] For further details see 679.

4. Note the following use of *or*:

Hurry up, or we shall be late.
She was already engaged, or she might have accepted him.

The second member expresses what will happen (or might have happened) if the action or event mentioned in the first member does not become (or was not) an actual fact.

5. A recent use of *or* is exemplified by the following quotation from *The Times Literary Supplement*, Oct. 3, 1952, p. 642: *With most European countries none too certain of themselves* (614) *eager glances are being cast towards Scandinavia, where it seems life is managed better. Or is it?* The last three words express a feeling of doubt. See *English Studies*, XXV (1943) 41–45, XXXI (1950) 174–179, 217.

661. Here are some examples of coordinate members of a compound sentence connected by adverbs:

There was nobody at the office, so I went home again.
It looks a pretty hopeless job; still, there's no harm in trying.
It looks a pretty hopeless job; indeed, I don't think it's any use trying.
She never returned the book; however, that's another story.

Note that, with the exception of *so*, these adverbs are usually separated from the second member by a clear pause.

---

[1] According to A. S. Hornby, *A Guide to Patterns and Usage in English*, § 121c, coordinating *for* is rarely used in spoken English.

662. Two sub-clauses of the same type may be linked by a coordinating conjunction (except *for*); they are then coordinate with one another.[1]

He said that he wanted a room, and that his luggage was following immediately.

I declined the invitation, not because I did not want to go, but because I had no time.

663. As with unlinked coordinate clauses (659 n.), a relation usually expressed by subordination (esp. condition or result) may be implied in a sentence consisting of two members connected by *and*.

Ask no questions and you'll be told no lies.

Stir, and you are a dead man.

A predicate-object relation (*a*), or one of purpose (*b*), often exists between two imperatives connected by *and*:

a. Mind and bring your violin.
Try and come early.

b. Come and have a cup of tea.
Go and see what they're doing.

1. The same relations may exist between two verbal stems functioning as infinitives: *I'll try and come early*; *I'll go and see*; but in this case we have to do with a simple, not a compound sentence, though the distinction is formal rather than essential here.

2. *But* introducing a clause of result (634) differs too much from coordinating *but* to be regarded as a special use of the latter.

---

[1] Onions, *An Advanced English Syntax*, § 14, 6; cf. also Kruisinga, *Handbook*^{5}, § 2389*b*.

CHAPTER THREE

SENTENCE GROUPS

664. Much of what has been said of Compound Sentences applies to groups of two adjoining sentences uttered by two different speakers in immediate succession, or by the same speaker (or writer).

In the following discussion the same sequence will be observed as in dealing with the Compound Sentence.

665. The second of two sentences may be introduced by relative *who* or *which* referring to a noun in the first sentence. The character of the second sentence is, of course, continuative (462).

So then we waited for the next messenger. — Who, of course, did not turn up. — That's right.

He sent in a bill for a hundred guineas. — Which surely you refused to pay? — Of course.

666. The second sentence may also be introduced by relative *which* referring to the preceding sentence; cf. 459.

The meeting was adjourned, with nothing decided on. — Which, I suppose, was what you wanted?

He threatened to turn her out of doors if she refused to obey him. Which he actually did a year later.

667. The second of two sentences may correspond to almost any of the adverbial clauses treated in 629 ff. A few examples only will be given.

When may we come? — Whenever you like.

Why did you snub him? — Why did I snub him? Because he annoyed me.

Why did you kill him? — So that he should not betray me.

He meant to make you his sole heir. — Though he never told me!

Everything will be all right, I think. — *If* you do as I told you.

Will you take this chair? — As you please.

668. The second of two sentences may function as an object clause (644 ff.).

What did he say? — That you were an ass.
What did he ask you? — Whether I was engaged.

Similarly as a subject clause (651, 652) or a predicate clause (653):

What is improbable? — That he will refuse.
What is the trouble? — That we none of us know anything about chemistry.

Note that second sentences like those hitherto discussed always require a conjunction to begin with.

669. A CONFIRMATIVE QUESTION of the kind discussed in 656 may be pronounced by another speaker when the preceding sentence expresses an opinion. Compare:

She paints well, doesn't she?
She paints well. — Doesn't she?
He is a character, isn't he?
He is a character. — Isn't he?

Observe that when pronounced by another speaker the question becomes half exclamatory; indeed, it might be written *Doesn't she! — Isn't he!*

It is not possible, however, to divide a compound sentence like *She paints, doesn't she?* between two speakers. The reason is that this sentence serves, not to express an opinion, but to state a fact, and that there would be no point in the second speaker asking the first to confirm his own statement. What the second speaker *can* do is to intimate that the information is news to him, or even that he feels slightly doubtful towards it; in this case both sentences are either affirmative or negative.

She paints. — Does she?
I am not a teetotaller. — Aren't you?

In this case the question is, of course, anything but confirmative; it is equivalent to *Really?* or *Indeed?*[1]

From the definition and the examples of reactive questions given in 656*b* it will be clear that a sentence like '*Oh, it's all spent, is it?*' cannot be divided between two speakers.

670. The second sentence (whether uttered by the same, or by another speaker) may also contain a CONFIRMATIVE STATEMENT modelled on the preceding sentence. Positive statements of this

[1] Cf. F. L. Sack, *The Structure of English*, § 147, 2.

kind are often introduced by *so* (cf. 429*a*) (*a*), negative ones by *no more* (*b*).

a. They told me you were ill. — So I was.
You've called me an adventurer. So I am.[1]
Why, we've forgotten to ask after his health. — So we have.
b. I thought you did not like beer? — No more I do.
Everybody says you cannot stand the fellow. — No more I can.

A confirmative statement may also be non-introduced, though with a slight difference of meaning. Thus *I was* and *I don't* in answer to the first sentences of *a* and *b* sound more emphatic than *So I was* and *No more I do*.

671. DENIALS may likewise be modelled on the preceding statement. They may be introduced by *yes* or *no*, never by *so* or *no more*. A denial not introduced by *yes* or *no* is often more emphatic (compare the last paragraph), amounting to a protest; in this sense it may be introduced by *but*.[2]

You're jealous of her. — No, I'm not. (Or: I'm not!)
You cannot guess what I mean. — Yes, I can.
You don't mean that! — But I do!

672. ANSWERS to verbal questions (601) may be modelled on the question asked; they are not introduced by *so* or *no more*. Those introduced by *yes* or *no* usually sound less abrupt (or less formal) than those without.[3]

Are you Mr. Simpson? — (Yes,) I am.
Do you agree with me? — (No,) I don't.

673. We find a similar pattern to that described in 670, only in inverse order, in sentences applying the predicate of the preceding sentence to another subject (cf. 429*b*). In negative sentences of the kind we find not only *no more*, but also *neither* and *nor*.

---

[1] Modelled on the other speaker's: *You are an adventurer*.
[2] Cf. F. L. Sack, *The Structure of English*, § 147, 1, Note 2*b*.
[3] This also applies to *yes* and *no* followed by *I am* or a similar sentence, as compared with *yes* and *no* used by themselves: *Are you Mr. S.? — Yes*. Cf., however, the following entry from Dieth and Orton, *A Questionnaire for a Linguistic Atlas of England*, p. 678:
If I asked you: Have you met that man, you could say: . . . *Yes, No*.
If I said to you: You haven't met that man, have you? and you had, you'd answer: . . . *Yes*, I have.

a. I am very fond of opera. — So am I.
Jackie loathes cod-liver oil. — So do most children.
b. I cannot stand the fellow. — No more can I. (Neither, nor, can I.)
Peter does not seem very pleased. — No more (neither, nor) do you.

674. Sentences of the types described in 670, 671 and 673 may also occur combined in a compound sentence uttered by one speaker or writer. In this case the two members are usually connected by a coordinating conjunction.

(670) You've called me an adventurer, and (so) I am.
You said I didn't know anything about politics, and no more I do (or: and I don't).
(671) He says I'm jealous of him, but I'm not.
(673) John is a conceited puppy, and so are you.
I don't know anything about it, (and)[1] nor do you.

675. The second of two sentences, whether uttered by the same or by another speaker or writer, may be introduced by one of the coordinating conjunctions mentioned in 660. This may be done (in the case of a single speaker or writer) to leave time for the listener (or reader) to digest the first statement; or it may give to the second sentence the character of an afterthought.

He left me to deal with the whole job single-handed. And it was not a very pleasant job either.
He lived here from 1920–1925. But that would be[2] before your time.
He was very fond of me at the time. Or so he said.

In all these examples the two sentences might also be combined into one; but in each case the pause dividing them is intentional and significant.

Here is an example involving two different speakers:

He asked me to lend him fifty pounds. — But surely you refused?

Coordinate sentences of the type described in 659 may easily be turned into sentence groups: *I am not going out to-night. I'm tired.*[3]

676. Compound sentences connected by adverbs (661) may also be divided into two, whether uttered by one speaker or writer, or by two.

There was nobody at the office. — So you went home again? (603).
It looks a pretty hopeless job. Still, there's no harm in trying.

---

[1] Cf. Kruisinga, *Handbook*[5], § 2396.
[2] Cf. 192.
[3] Cf. A. S. Hornby, *op. cit.*, § 121*a*.

677. A sentence of the type illustrated in 662 might be divided between two speakers in the event of the listener taking the words out of the speaker's mouth:

> 'He said that he wanted a room, . . .' — 'And that his luggage was following immediately? That's his usual trick. The fellow is an impostor.'

The student should verify and supplement the above remarks by studying the way sentences (and paragraphs) are connected (or left unconnected) in a few pages of continuous prose.

CHAPTER FOUR

ADDITIONAL REMARKS ON CONJUNCTIONS

678. Many SUBORDINATING CONJUNCTIONS (*that* is a conspicuous exception) may introduce FREE ADJUNCTS (611). One or two examples may be added to those given in 612*b*.

> 'You'll want all day to-morrow, I suppose?' said Scrooge. — 'If quite convenient,[1] sir.'
> Whatever the result, the experiment is worth trying.[2]

679. COORDINATING CONJUNCTIONS (with the exception of *for*) can join any two (or more) parallel parts of a sentence, though *nor* does so only in combination with *neither*, and *but* when expressing contradiction (not when expressing contrast) in combination with *not*. *And* and *or* may occur in combination resp. with *both* (*at once*, *alike*) and *either*. Such groups (*not . . . but*, *not only . . . but also*, *neither . . . nor*, *both . . . and*, *at once . . . and*, *alike . . . and*, *either . . . or*) are called CORRELATIVE.

> *a.* John and Mary have just come home.
> They talked and talked.
> Will he come to-day or to-morrow?
> Little but brave.
> *b.* Both John and Mary have come.
> At once far off and near.
> He will come either to-day or to-morrow.
> *c.* Not John, but Mary has come.
> Letters used to be delivered not only on week-days, but also on Sundays.
> That's neither here nor there.

Of two adjectives connected by *and* the former (usually *nice*) may function as an adverbial adjunct to the latter:

> It's nice and warm here.

---

[1] To what is this an adjunct?
[2] The order of the two members may be inverted, though with a difference of emphasis.

680. Many conjunctions also function as other parts of speech, chiefly as prepositions. Some of those expressing time, indeed, are prepositions in the first place, conjunctions only in the second: *before, after, until, till, since.*

As was pointed out in 361, *as, but* and *than* followed by a personal pronoun parallel with the subject may function either as conjunctions or as prepositions: *She is as tall as I — She is as tall as me.* It is true that the interpretation of the second *as* as a preposition is based exclusively on the fact that it is followed by an oblique pronoun in a context where a nominative would also be possible. If, on the other hand, the obliques are regarded as 'absolute' forms of the personal pronouns (cf. French *aussi grand que* moi), we may continue to regard *as* as a conjunction, an interpretation supported by its correlation with the preceding *as.*

On nouns functioning occasionally as conjunctions, see 626. They are usually preceded by a definite article; sometimes by a preposition and a definite article, a preposition only, a pronoun (*each* or *every*), or *last.*

By the time we reached the house, it was dark.
Have the medicine ready, in case he wakes up.
Every time I opened my eyes I saw him looking at me.
The last time I was in London, I went to a concert in Queen's Hall.
The last I heard from Jane she was enjoying herself.

Perhaps it would be better to say that the prepositions and nouns mentioned above sometimes function as conjunctions (or as regards the nouns, as part of conjunctional phrases).

PART VI

ORDER OF WORDS

681. In any sentence of more than one word there arises the question of WORD-ORDER. Thus, to take some of the examples of 575, one may ask why *awfully* follows *Thanks*, why *Poor* precedes *dog*, why *not* precedes *at all*. In two-nucleus sentences it is necessary to inquire into the relative positions of the subject and the (verbal) predicate, and of the other elements of the sentence (if any), such as objects and adjuncts, relatively to the two nuclei and to each other. Lastly, there is the question of the sequence of the members of compound sentences.

As the rules of word-order in English and other Germanic languages have a good deal in common, we shall deal chiefly with those cases where they differ. It will not be necessary to discuss word-order in sentences of the type illustrated in 575 separately, as they do not differ from two-nucleus sentences in this respect.

As in the chapter on Sentence Structure, we shall deal with Simple Sentences first, (members of) Compound Sentences afterwards.

682. With regard to the relative positions of subject and (verbal) predicate there are, theoretically, two possibilities, which we may denote by S — P and P — S respectively. A study of the examples of 577 will reveal a third possibility: P may be split up into two parts, with S coming between them. As in this case the most important part of the predicate follows the subject, we may denote it by p — S — P.

On the assumption that S — P is the 'normal' order, P — S and p — S — P are sometimes called the 'inverted' order, and the placing of the subject after (part of) the (verbal) predicate is known as 'inversion'.

683. Roughly speaking, S — P is the usual word-order in DECLARATIVE sentences (600), P — S and p — S — P occurring chiefly in INTERROGATIVE sentences. But each of these patterns may also be found in the other type.

684. A sentence beginning with unstressed *there* [ðə] shows the word-order P — S, the verbal predicate consisting of a verb denoting a state or a motion (*a*). The construction is occasionally found with a passive predicate, in which case the word-order is either P — S or p — S — P (*b*).

a. There is [ðəz] a man at the door.
There have been many accidents lately.
Once upon a time there lived a king.
There comes a time when it is useless to struggle.[1]
The door opened, and there entered a shrivelled old woman.
b. Then there was committed the greatest crime of that or any succeeding age.
There was very little work done that morning.

1. The word-order of the first example of *b* is found when the subject is so weighty that it has end-position. For more examples see Kruisinga, *Handbook*[5], § 451. Apart from this case, the subject after *there is* etc. usually has a general meaning, i.e. it consists of a noun preceded by an indefinite article or pronoun (*There was no wind*), or of a plain noun in the plural, or of a similar indefinite word (e.g. *There are those* (= some) *who believe* . . .). But also: *There were five boys in the room.*

2. Note that in appended questions of the kind discussed in 656, *there* is repeated:

There was no wind, was there?

3. The construction with introductory *there* and a passive predicate occurs less frequently than the corresponding construction in Dutch or German. Thus it could not be used in cases like the following:

An amicable settlement has been arrived at.
His warning was taken no notice of.
My brother has been offered a job in Canada.

But also in 'plain' passive constructions front-position of the subject is commoner than the use of introductory *there*:

A prize is offered for the best solution.

685. DECLARATIVE sentences sometimes show the word-order P — S, or p — S — P. This 'inverted' order is restricted[2] to sentences opening with another element, i.e. either an adjunct or an object. The phenomenon occurs chiefly in writing, and even there by no means invariably.

686. Inversion is fairly regular when a NEGATIVE adjunct opens the sentence (see also 690). As was pointed out in 202, a form of *to do*

[1] C. C. Fries, *The Structure of English*, p. 161.
[2] Apart from the construction discussed in 637.

precedes the subject in sentences not containing either another auxiliary or a copula. Here are some more examples.

Not only was he a first-rate mathematician, but he also excelled at chess.
No sooner had she said it than she realized her mistake.
Never did sun more beautifully steep In his first splendour valley, rock or hill.[1]

In a sentence like *Hardly a word was spoken* there is no inversion, because the negative word modifies the subject only, not the whole sentence.

687. When another than a negative adjunct opens the sentence, inversion of subject and predicate (P — S or p — S — P) may also occur.

Sentences WITHOUT AN OBJECT often show the order P — S when the subject is more important than the verbal predicate, on the principle that the weighter element is given end-position.

Before them lay miles and miles of undulating moors.
Lower and lower bent Uncle Charlie's head over his plate.[2]
Out rushed the man and his wife.[3]
There [ˈðɛə] comes the station bus![4]
In the gap were the footprints of the sheep.[5]
Such was the accommodation offered by the White House.[6]

But cf:

Lower and lower he bent.
Out they rushed.

688. Sentences WITH AN OBJECT (or a similar ADJUNCT to the verbal predicate) opening with another than a negative adjunct often show the word-order p — S — P.

Well do I remember the day.
Often did we go for walks together.
Many a time has he given me good advice.

689. When a sentence opens with an object we sometimes find the sequence p — S — P.

Many a rabbit had he snared, without the game-keeper noticing it.

---

[1] Wordsworth, *Composed Upon Westminster Bridge.*
[2] Kruisinga, *Handbook*[5], § 2190.
[3] Jespersen, *Essentials*, § 10.46.
[4] Cf. *There* [ðə] *comes a time* . . . in 684*a*.
[5] Kruisinga and Erades, *English Grammar*, § 56.
[6] This is an example of front-position of the nominal part of the predicate. Cf. *A great cricketer was Hobbs*, which resembles the cases of emphatic front-position discussed in 688–689. Cf. also 465.

The construction is only found, however, after an object preceded by such an emphatic (and emotional) word as *much* or *many*; one would not say or write: **A rabbit had he snared.*

Sometimes emphatic front-position is found without inversion, thus with objects referring to what immediately precedes in the context.

> Dates I could never remember.
> Invalids we have no use for.

Cf. 19.

690. As was pointed out in 202, inversion caused by front-position of an adjunct or object occurs chiefly in emphatic or emotional style. In more matter-of-fact communications the adjunct or object either does not have front-position (*We often went for walks together*; *He had snared many a rabbit*); or if it has, it does not cause inversion (*After some time they saw a light*). In the former case there is an alternative (*Often did we go . . .*); in the latter there is none.

This principle explains why sentences beginning with a negative adjunct (686) usually have the word-order P — S or p — S — P. Compare the following quotations from Kruisinga's *Handbook*[5], § 2182, with the same sentences with a positive adjunct:

At no point of the river have the enemy advanced more than a mile or two.	At one point south of the river the enemy have advanced a mile or two.
In no religion do birth and death play the part which they play in Christianity.	In this religion birth and death play the same part that they do in Christianity.
Only so is communication possible.	In this way communication is possible.

In a sentence like the following the different word-order in the two parallel halves of the sentence may be due to a desire for variety, as much as to the requirements of sentence-rhythm.

> In Ulster alone had the tenant some protection, and in Ulster alone the population was largely British and Protestant.
>
> Trevelyan, *History of England*, p. 423.

On front-position in causal and concessive clauses cf. 20, 632 and 638.

691. As stated in 683, INTERROGATIVE sentences usually have the word-order P — S or p — S — P. PRONOMINAL questions (601) beginning with the subject necessarily form an exception.

Compare:

Who knows you here?
Who(m) do you know here?

The questions discussed in 603 of course have the order S — P.

692. As regards the order of words in IMPERATIVE sentences there is little to add to what has been said in 605–607, except, perhaps, that those without a subject open with the imperative (if any).

693. In EXCLAMATORY (non-imperative) sentences beginning with *how* or *what* there is usually no 'inversion'.

How unreasonable people are!
What a sneak he is!

But cf., with a two-word subject balancing the two-word predicate:

How green was my valley.

---

694. Apart from the case treated in 689, and from pronominal questions beginning with the object (691), OBJECTS follow the verbal predicate to which they belong.

He made a bad mistake.
I have lost my umbrella.
Do you want to see the manager?

On constructions like *I have no money saved*, see 113.

695. When a sentence contains two objects (585), the indirect object precedes the direct object, if, as is usually the case, the latter is the weightier of the two (cf. 687) (*a*). This principle also accounts for the opposite order in cases where a phonetically light direct object pronoun is put before an indirect ditto (*b*).

a. This will save you a lot of trouble.
He promised my brother a copy.
b. I gave it him (COD).
Give it him hot! (*ibid.*).

According to Prof. Kemp Malone (*Modern Language Notes*, Dec. 1949) '*I gave it him* rarely occurs in American English; we say, *I gave it to him.*' Same remark in Partridge and Clark, *British and American English*, p. 327.

696. As was shown in 596, a construction with two non-prepositional objects may alternate with one in which the direct object is followed by an indirect object with *to* (occ. *for*), the latter word-order usually emphasizing the indirect as compared with the direct object (*a*). That a *to*-object is not *always* stronger-stressed than the direct object before it, is clear from some of the examples in COD s.v. *give* (*b*).

a. Give this note to your brother.
If you cannot read the letter yourself, show it to me.
b. He gave his life to it.
(The river) gave its name to the battle.

697. In the first example of 696*b*, owing to the peculiar meaning of *give* (= devote) the construction with a non-prepositional indirect object would not be possible. Similarly in *He devoted his life to it*; *He addressed his complaint to the manager*; *He ascribed his success to his pertinacity*. For a list of such verbs, see Appendix, p. 343 f.

If the *to*-adjunct is not very weighty, it sometimes precedes the direct object:

Can you explain to us the enormous effect this discovery has had on commerce?

A *to*-adjunct that may alternate with a non-prepositional indirect object is also sometimes given front-position:

This gave (to) the problem an entirely different aspect.

698. Regular verb-adverb combinations, like *to carry out*, *to lock up*, *to put on*, *to take off*, *to wind up*, etc., usually take a short pronoun object before, but a noun or a long pronoun object after the adverb.

a. Here's your hat; put it on.
When we catch him, we'll lock him up.
b. Next week is my birthday and we'll get up[1] a party.
Why don't you take off your coat?
I have packed up everything.[2]

699. So long as it does not jar on the speaker's or writer's feeling for rhythm, the alternative order may also occur.

Get your gloves on.
Take your coat off.
We cannot pack up *that*.

---

700. As will appear from the examples in 589 and 591, ATTRIBUTIVE ADJUNCTS usually precede the noun they qualify.

[1] The adverb in such cases is usually weak-stressed: [ˈget ʌp ə ˈpɑːti], not [ˈget ˈʌp ə ˈpɑːti]. But [ˈget it ˈʌp]. Note the rhythm!
[2] Kruisinga, *Handbook*[5], § 2207.

Of two or more adjectives preceding a noun, that referring to inherent qualities such as colour, material, physical state, nationality, etc., usually comes last: *a long, dark road*; *a steep rocky hill*; *a pretty French girl.*[1]

Post-position of attributive adjuncts occurs, (1) with unaccompanied adjectives; (2) with adjectives accompanied by other words.

701. Among the former, we may distinguish non-verbal from verbal adjectives.

Post-position of an unaccompanied non-verbal adjective occurs chiefly in the case of *proper* (= strictly so called), and in traditional combinations, mostly borrowings from French. It is also found with pronouns, and with semi-pronominal nouns like *things*, *matters*.

a. Within the sphere of architecture proper (COD).
China proper.
[But cf.: in the proper (= accurate, correct) sense of the word (COD).]
b. Heir apparent; heir presumptive.
Lords spiritual; Lords temporal.
Solicitor-General.
To give a person the lie direct.

In other combinations these adjectives from French may have front position: *presumptive evidence*; *temporal affairs*; *direct action* (by means of strikes).

c. Something big is about to happen.
He was an expert on things theatrical.[2]

702. Groups like those in 701 should be distinguished from the examples of noun + adjective given by Kruisinga in his *Handbook*[5], § 1978, last three quotations.[3] One of them runs:

Vowels uttered with *the tongue tense* have a clearer, shriller sound, and a higher pitch, than those uttered with *the tongue slack*. Wyld, *Hist.*, p. 44.

Whereas *China proper*, *heir apparent*, form close groups expressing a single idea, *with the tongue tense* (*slack*) contains two distinct ideas expressed by two strong-stressed words (cf. *with his tongue in his cheek*). The relation between the noun and the adjective is semi-predicative (*while the tongue is tense*) rather than attributive.

---

[1] See *Language*, 21, 1, Jan.–March 1945, p. 5.

[2] Slightly literary. In spoken English: *on everything connected with the theatre*.

[3] The first quotation does not belong with the others.

703. Unaccompanied verbal adjectives (i.e. adjectives derived from or connected with verbs) follow their noun when they are distinctly verbal in meaning (i.e. when they express an action or an occurrence, rather than a state or a quality). They include especially participles[1] and adjectives in *-able*, *-ible*. Even when its meaning is not clearly verbal, post-position of an adjective gives it a semi-predicative character (cf. 702), whereas before its noun it is purely attributive. Examples will be given of both positions, if possible. Cf. also 81*a*.

a. He gave us a clear idea of the problems involved.
[His prose is full of such involved constructions.]
The scene described here will be familiar to sportsmen.
The classification adopted has many advantages.
[Mary was an adopted child.]
A penny saved is a penny gained (got, earned).
Things seen are mightier than things heard.
b. All the accommodation available was put at our disposal.
[All the available accommodation . . .]
His car, or what he chose to call a car, was the quaintest contraption[2] conceivable.
[A cyclopedia contains information on all conceivable subjects.]
c. All the women present began to sob.
[Present company excepted, of course.]
I am the happiest man alive.
[A real live elephant.]

704. Often a linked group of adjectives follows the noun qualified, where any *one* of these adjectives would have to precede. We quote the first example of Kruisinga's *Handbook*[5], § 1978:

Before him stretched the long laborious road, dry, empty and white. Hardy, *Return of the Native*, I, Ch. 2, p. 9.

Compare also the same *Handbook*[5], § 1983, p. 217, second and third examples from the top; and the same section, p. 216, bottom: *literary work pure and simple.*

705. An adjective preceded by *so*, *more* or *most* may follow the noun it qualifies.

Ne'er saw I, never felt, a calm so deep.[3]
He could not have chosen a time more favourable.[4]

---

[1] Cf. also the fourth example of 724.
[2] '(Slang). Queer machine, makeshift contrivance' (COD).
[3] Wordsworth, *Composed Upon Westminster Bridge*. — Alternative: *so deep a calm*. Cf. 711.
[4] More literary (and emphatic) than *a more favourable time*.

706. Adjectives (whether verbal or non-verbal) accompanied by nouns denoting measure, or by a prepositional group, usually have post-position.

a. They had to climb a wall six feet high.
b. There was a complete lack of the ceremonies and compliments usual on such occasions.
He had made a thorough study of all the dialects spoken in Scotland.

Adjectives accompanied by nouns denoting measure may also precede their headword: *a six-feet-high wall* (more usually: *a wall s.f.h.*), *a ten-year-old boy* (cf. 256). Cf. also 319.

707. ATTRIBUTIVE NOUNS precede their headwords; see the examples in 254–258.

708. On the place of appositions, see 590.

Personal nouns like *family*, *girl(s)*, *sisters*, *children*, accompanied by a definite article (occasionally by a demonstrative pronoun) usually follow a proper name.

The Baines family.
The Brontë sisters.[1]
That Mansfield girl.[1]

Note also: *Lever* [ˈliːvə] *Brothers.*

The same applies to combinations like *The Angel Inn, The Red Lion Hotel*, which, besides, have even stress on the name and on the class-noun.

709. ATTRIBUTIVE PRONOUNS precede their headwords; they also precede any adjectives that stand before the headword: *this* (*old*) *man*, *my* (*old*) *clothes*.

All and *both* precede possessive and demonstrative pronouns: *all my books*.

1. Note the mainly literary construction exemplified by *both their lives* (= *the lives of both of them*); *It went to all our hearts* (or: *to all of our hearts*). For more examples, see Kruisinga, *Handbook*⁵, §§ 2004 and 2016 (*for all our sakes* = *for the sake of all of us*).

2. Numerals usually follow attributive words like *first, last, front, rear, other*: *the other two sides* (of a triangle), *the rear two carriages* (of a train), *the last three acts* (of a play). (But: *three little pigs*, etc.)

---

[1] Less often: *The sisters Brontë.* In *Call it a Day*, A Comedy in Three Acts, by Dodie Smith (London, 1936), we find on p. 71: *That girl Gwynne*, followed lower down on the same page by *that Gwynne girl* (same speaker).

710. *All* also precedes independent *this* or *that*.

Now then, what's all this? (416.)
All that does not matter.
A man's a man for a' that.[1]

See also the sections on *all* and *both* in the chapter on Pronouns.

711. An INDEFINITE ARTICLE is placed after *half* and *many* (*a*); after adjectives preceded by *so* (cf. 705), *as*, *too*, *how* and *however* (*b*); and after the adverbs *quite* and (less regularly) *rather*.

a. Half a loaf is better than no bread.
Many a little makes a mickle.
b. She was as fine a schooner as you'll ever come across.
You allow too short an interval for lunch.
Travelling on however humble a scale is expensive in Scotland.
c. He seems quite a decent fellow.
The performance was rather a failure.

1. Note the difference between *half a crown*, or *half-a-crown* (a sum of money, viz. 2/6), and *a half crown*, or *a half-crown* (a coin).[2] When the connection between *half* and the accompanying noun is very close, the article precedes: *a half-brother*, *a half-truth*; cf. also *a halfpenny* [ˈheipni].

2. In American English *a half hour*, *a half mile*, *a half dozen horsemen*, etc., is a common construction.

3. When the noun is preceded by an adjective, the article may precede *quite*, *rather* or *too*: *a quite decent fellow*, *a rather surprising remark*, *a too bad mistake*.

712. Similarly, a DEFINITE ARTICLE follows *all*, *both* (*a*); *half*, *double*, *twice*, *treble*, etc. (*b*). Cf. 492 n.

a. She was ill all the time[3] she was abroad. (Cf. 626.)
Both (the) brothers are dead.
b. Half the men were too tired to go.
He sat dozing half the day.
I offered him double (twice) the amount, but he still refused.

As in the case of 711.1, the definite article may precede when the connection between *half* and the accompanying noun is very close: *He waited for the half-hour to strike*.

---

713. The place of PREDICATIVE ADJUNCTS will be sufficiently clear from the examples given in 592.

---

[1] Burns.
[2] Sometimes, though, we find *half-a-crown* when the coin is meant. — The plural is *half-crowns*.
[3] But: *the whole time*.

714. Adverbial adjuncts usually precede adjectives, adverbs, numerals and pronouns (cf. 593).

715. *Enough* always follows adverbs and predicative adjectives; note that it does not always mean *sufficiently*.

> Are you warm enough?[1]
> She sings well enough[2] (= tolerably).
> You know well enough (= quite well) what I mean.
> Oddly enough, he had lost his purse.
> Sure enough, there it was.

As a rule, *enough* also follows attributive adjectives, though it may be separated from the adjective by the noun. (Cf. Kruisinga, *Handbook*[5], § 2213.)

> He is a decent enough clerk.
> He is a decent clerk enough.

As an adjective, *enough* either follows or precedes its noun: *beer enough*, or *enough beer*. It always follows a predicative noun: *I was fool enough to believe him.*

716. *Not* precedes adverbs and adverbial adjuncts negatived by it: *not always, not quite.*

This also applies to a few combinations in which the negative adverb follows in Dutch and German: *not yet, not . . . either, not at all.*

In *Did you kick him? — Certainly not! — certainly* qualifies *not*, which is equivalent to a negative sentence.

717. Adverbial adjuncts qualifying verbs, and those referring to the whole group of words outside the subject, or to the subject and predicate combined (594), may take up various positions, according to their meaning and function, though they are not often found between a verbal predicate and its object.

The particle *to* (13) is sometimes separated from the infinitive by an adverb (*seems to partly correspond*, COD). This construction, known as the 'Split Infinitive', is often frowned upon for stylistic reasons; see, for instance, Fowler's article in MEU.

718. Adjuncts of place and of definite time, and such as denote means, agents or attendant circumstances, follow the whole of the predicate. They may also open the sentence, except in questions.

---

[1] Stress on *warm*. [2] Stress on both *well* and *enough*.

Adjuncts of place usually precede those of definite time.[1] Of two adjuncts of time, the one denoting the smaller unit usually comes first.

Katherine Mansfield was born in New Zealand.
On Saturdays shops were allowed to be open till ten.
Bunyan stayed in prison for more than twelve years.[1]
The exhibition was opened at three o'clock this afternoon.
At six it had been visited by eight hundred persons.
The actors left the stage amid thunderous applause.
Did the Joneses stay all night?

It will usually be found that an adverbial adjunct in initial position links the sentence it opens with that preceding it (see the last example but two).

719. Brief adverbial adjuncts of place or definite time are sometimes put before the (principal part of the) verbal predicate.

I now see that I was wrong.
I will here remark that the responsibility for the undertaking was entirely mine.

720. The same position is usual for adverbs of INDEFINITE TIME and of DEGREE, and for *also*.[2]

a. We soon found out his address.
I have never understood him, and I'm afraid I never shall.
Do you always go to church on Sundays?
b. I almost wished I had not come.
I quite see what you mean.
I've hardly had a minute to myself.
c. Are you also going to town?
They also serve who only stand and wait.[3]

721. *a.* When a verbal predicate contains more than one auxiliary, these adverbs usually follow the first: *He should never have been left alone.* But they are occasionally found after the last: *It has been often observed that . . .* (instead of the more usual *It has often been observed*). And they precede a non-finite first auxiliary: *Never having seen him . . .*

---

[1] But cf.: *People stayed for months in the same house without stirring from it even for a night.* (Viscount Grey, *The Pleasure of Reading*, in *Essays by Modern Writers*, Longmans, p. 81.)
[2] Which may be classed as an adverb of manner (cf. *likewise*).
[3] Milton, *On his Blindness.*

b. These adverbs usually follow the present and preterite of *to be*: *She is never at home*; *John was also there*; *Were they also there?* But they precede a stressed form of this verb (cf. *c*): '*They aren't at home.*' — '*They never are.*'

c. These adverbs may precede a strong-stressed auxiliary (see the second half of the second ex. of 720*a*); or they may take precedence because they are themselves emphasized, as in *You never can tell.* Cf. the following quotation from *The Nine Tailors* by Dorothy Sayers (Albatross ed. p. 19):

Wimsey shook his head, and helped himself to his fourth muffin. 'Grandsire Triples[1] are most venerable', he said solemnly, 'but you can never get the same music. . . .'
'That's what I say', crowed[2] the Rector. 'You never can get the same music when the tenor is rung behind — . . .'

d. For the sake of emphasis, these adverbs are sometimes placed at the beginning or at the end of the sentence. Cf.: *Did you see him very often?* — *We got up early* (thus usually with *early* and *late*).

The second ex. of 688 (*Often did we go for walks together*) is a case in point. Front-position does not entail the use of *to do* in a less rhetorical utterance like the following:

He refuses to see man in isolation: always he views him in relation to other men, in relation to other planes of being.

Duthie, *Shakespeare*, p. 54.

722. Adverbs of MODALITY (i.e. such as express the degree of reality belonging to a statement), such as *possibly*, *probably*, *surely*, *certainly*,[3] *really*, mostly occupy the same position as adverbs of degree, some of which, indeed, closely resemble them in meaning.

You probably remember the night we first discussed the question. (Cf. I hardly remember . . .)
You must really be more careful in future.
Will you send me word as soon as you know something? — I certainly will. (Cf. 721*c*.)

Perhaps may occupy the same position, but oftener occurs at the beginning of a sentence:

It is perhaps safer not to tell him anything.
Perhaps we'd better stop now.

---

[1] A special series of changes on a set of church bells.
[2] Observe the connection between *crowed* and the front-position of *never*.
[3] Difference between *surely* and *certainly*?

With some of the other adverbs of modality, front-position may lead to their being separated from the rest of the sentence by a slight pause (594):

Surely you're not going yet?
Really, I'm surprised at you.

Indeed is chiefly found after a form of *to be*: *He was, indeed, a remarkable man*; *There are indeed exceptions.* As an intensifying adverb it follows an adjective, or a group of adjective + noun: *I shall be very glad indeed*; *This is quick work indeed.* (See also the other exx. in COD.)

723. Adverbs of MANNER (most of which end in *-ly*) either immediately precede the (principal) verb, or follow the predicate and its object (if any). In the latter case they are usually more emphatic than in the former, though a great deal depends on the structure of the whole sentence. Of the following examples, the second and third probably represent the most common construction:

He quietly closed the door behind him.
He closed the door quietly behind him.
The book has been very carefully printed.
The book has been printed very carefully.

1. Note the different position of the adverb in *The book has been carefully printed* and *The book has often been reprinted* (or: *The book has been often reprinted*, 720*a*).

2. For the sake of emphasis an adverb of manner may be given front-position: *Slowly and impressively he rose from his seat.*

3. Adverbial adjuncts of manner, other than adverbs, follow the predicate: *The book has been printed with great care.*

724. Unlike most of the adverbial adjuncts discussed in 718–722, adverbs of manner usually qualify the verbal predicate only. Many of them, however, also occur in a different function: they may express an opinion on the rest of the sentence. Their position may then be the same as with adverbs of indefinite time and degree, except that they precede the whole of a negative predicate.

He wisely held his tongue.
Mrs. Jones has kindly promised to bring her gramophone and a supply of records.
[But cf.: When the poor fellow recovered, she spoke kindly to him and assured him he had nothing to fear. (723.)]
Their leaders unfortunately could not agree on the policy to be adopted. (Cf. 703.)

The same applies to adverbs like *admittedly*, *allegedly* (four syllables!), *presumably*, etc.:

His own share in the undertaking was presumably a modest one.

These adverbs are often equivalent to a sentence (or clause): *wisely* = *which was wise*; *presumably* = *as may be presumed* — which is why they have been called SENTENCE-ADVERBS.

725. Sentence-adverbs may also stand at the beginning, or, less often, at the end of a sentence. In this case they are apt to become semi-independent of the rest of the sentence (cf. 594 and 722, end). The resulting pause (if any) may or may not be indicated by a comma.

Fortunately I had plenty of food with me.
Honestly, I don't think much of your idea.
There was nothing to be done apparently.

726. The adverb *only* is difficult to class in any of the above categories. Its place is very free, consistently, of course, with clarity.

When *only* refers to a single word, it may either precede or follow it: *Only you can guess* or *You only can guess* (i.e. no one else can); *You can only guess* or *You can guess only* (i.e. you can do no more) (COD).

When it refers to the whole sentence, it may have mid- or end-position: *It is right because it is customary only*; *It is right only because it is customary*; *It is only right because it is customary.* See also the other examples in COD.

727. In PREPOSITIONAL ADJUNCTS (595) the preposition usually precedes its (pro)noun; but in pronominal questions and exclamations it is usually placed after the predicate.

What are you doing that for?
What part of the country do you come from?
What an attractive girl your daughter has grown into!

The same applies to prepositional objects:

What are you thinking of?
Who (439) are you speaking to?

In formal speech the preposition generally precedes an interrogative pronoun: *To whom did I give it?* Cf. Palmer, *A Grammar of Spoken English*, § 400.

If end-position would give a preposition too much prominence, it is put first: *At what time did you go? — In what year was that? — In what respect do the two reports differ?*[1]

728. As was stated in 717, adverbial adjuncts are not often found between a verbal predicate and its object. The student may be referred to the examples collected by Kruisinga in *Handbook*[5], § 2241*a*, and by Kruisinga & Erades in *English Grammar*, § 76.

Mid-position of an adverb is apt to entail a brief pause between the adverb and the object; in other words, it has a retarding effect. Cf.: *He discusses admirably the development of the legend* with *He admirably discusses the development of the legend.*

729. The order of two or more adverbial adjuncts in cases not covered by the above remarks is usually determined by the closeness of their connection with the predicate, and, to some extent, by conscious or unconscious considerations of sentence-rhythm. It would hardly be feasible to give examples of all the various possible combinations; the best way to acquire an insight into this matter is for the student to pay attention to it in his reading of modern prose.

The word-order of verse is freer than that of prose, and preserves relics of the word-order of older periods of the language. It is best studied in specimens of poetry familiar to the student.

---

730. The above observations apply both to simple sentences and to the head-clauses of compound sentences.

Sub-clauses generally have the same word-order as the corresponding head-clauses.

> I shall warn you as soon as I see him. (Cf. I see him.)
> If I had known it I should have told you. (Cf. I had known it.)

731. Dependent questions generally have the same word-order as declarative sentences.

> He asked me what I was doing. (Cf. What are you doing?)

Occasionally we find the interrogative word-order, viz. when close reproduction of direct speech is aimed at.

> He asked me, would I go with him as far as Reading? (Cf. 'Will you go with me . . .?')

---

[1] Cf. F. L. Sack, *op. cit.*, § 128.

732. When the subject or object of an attributive clause is qualified by a relative pronoun preceded by a preposition, preposition + pronoun may either precede or follow the subject (object). Cf. 453.

The only consonants of which the notation (or: the notation of which) requires special notice are the following.

733. When the relative pronoun is the object of an infinitive or a gerund, the latter is usually placed at or towards the end of the clause, though it sometimes precedes the relative.

Such was the ingratitude of the man whom he almost lost his life in defending (*less usual*: in defending whom he almost lost his life).
He betrayed the cause (which)[1] he was paid to support (*less usual*: to support which he was paid).

734. End-position of prepositions, optional in the case of direct questions (727), is obligatory in sub-clauses after relative *that* and *what*, and after *as* and *than*; also in unconnected adjective clauses (467; cf. 469).

It's the very word (that) I was thinking of.
It all depends on what you are accustomed to.
Things turned out better than we had dared to hope for.

735. In sentences with *to say* or a verb of similar meaning appended to a direct quotation, the subject may follow the predicate if the latter is the less weighty of the two. Consequently, when the subject is a personal pronoun, it usually comes first.

a. 'What's that? A new stamp? Show me!' said Edward (or: Edward said).
b. 'Stop!' Edward (or: he) exclaimed.

Colloquially, *says* or *said he* &c., *said I*, *says I* [sez ai], are often inserted in reporting a conversation (COD); though 'in America at least, *says I* (though not *says he*) is a vulgarism' (Prof. Kemp Malone). Cf. 133 n.

All right, says he, let's call it a bargain. — No, says I, not so fast, my lad.

736. In a compound sentence containing two sub-clauses (or a sub-clause and a free adjunct), the former introduced by *that*, the latter inserted between *that* and the rest of the (other) clause, *that*

[1] In an unconnected clause the infinitive or gerund *must* have end-position.

is strong-stressed, and an unstressed subject-pronoun follows the intermediate clause or adjunct.

He promised me that, if I was a good boy, I should have a half-holiday.
She confessed that, on further consideration, she did not like the idea at all.

---

737. As a re-reading of the examples of 620–654 will show, sub-clauses either follow or precede their head-clauses in much the same way as in other Germanic languages.

Thus ATTRIBUTIVE CLAUSES always follow the head-clause containing their antecedent (see also the examples in 452–469).

PREDICATIVE CLAUSES also follow their head-clause (628).

ADVERBIAL CLAUSES, like adverbs, are freer in their place. Those that may precede their head-clauses in other Germanic languages may have the same position in English.

Since I came to live here I have only been ill once. (Cf. 630.)
If it is time, we had better go. (Cf. 635.)

Note that front-position of the sub-clause does not entail inversion of subject and finite predicate in English.

738. Whether or not an adverbial clause precedes its head-clause, largely depends on its meaning. Thus an *as*-clause of reason usually precedes, but a more emphatic clause opening with *because* usually follows the head-clause. In the case of the second example of 632 there is, of course, the additional (and, indeed, sufficient) reason that the sentence is interrogative, but if it were declarative, the adverbial clause would still come second: *I went on because he was not ready, and for no other reason.*

739. OBJECT CLAUSES usually follow their head-clause, though if the idea expressed by them is foremost in the speaker's or writer's mind, they may precede them. In that case they must begin with a conjunction or a connective pronoun.

That he is a coward I knew.
What he has once heard he never forgets.

740. SUBJECT CLAUSES (apart from those introduced by 'provisional' *it*, 652) always precede their head-clause; PREDICATE CLAUSES follow it.

741. The order of co-ordinate members of a sentence, and of the members of sentence groups, depends on the sequence of thought: what occurs first to the speaker or writer is expressed first. In this respect, too, English and other Germanic languages do not appreciably differ. Differences of order between them are almost exclusively found within the smaller units, i.e. simple sentences and clauses.

In connection with the last remark, attention may be called to co-ordinate groups of words linked by *and* or *or* (cf. 679), in which the order of the first and the second member is sometimes the opposite of that in other Germanic languages: *bow and arrow(s)*; *night and day*; *supply and demand*; *more or less.* It would be difficult to give a reason for the difference, except that the existing order is more rhythmical than the reverse would be. Note also that the longer word usually comes last: *bed and breakfast, board and lodging, bow and arrow(s), weights and measures*; but cf. *between finger and thumb.*

PART VII

CONCORD

742. By CONCORD is meant formal agreement in person, number, gender or tense (or more than one of these combined) between two or more parts of a sentence.

743. 'Formal' agreement is not to be taken in the sense of outward similarity, but in the sense that of two forms showing concord the use of one necessitates the use of the other.[1] If we call these forms P and Q, two cases may be distinguished:

1. P can only be combined with Q, and vice versa. Thus, in the present tense of *to be*, *I* can only be combined with *am*, and vice versa; this may be called BILATERAL CONCORD.

2. P can only be combined with Q, but Q may also be combined with R (or even, perhaps, S and T). Thus in the present tense of *to be*, *we* can only be combined with *are*; but *are* may also be combined with *you* (sing. & pl.) or *they*. This may be called UNILATERAL CONCORD. Cf. also *I go*, *you do*, etc.

In both these cases, Q represents a selection made from more than one available form (in case 1 from *am*, *are*, *is*; in case 2 from the same, or from *go* — *goes*, *do* — *does*). If there is only one available form (as with *can*, *may*, etc., and with the preterite of verbs[2]), the question of concord does not arise.

744. CONCORD OF PERSON occurs (A) between a subject and its finite verb; (B) between a noun or pronoun and the pronoun(s) referring to it.[3]

It usually occurs in combination with concord of number.

745. (A) BILATERAL concord of person occurs between a subject in the third person singular and the present tense form of a verb in

[1] Or at least, of a form belonging to the same category; see the examples of 745.

[2] With the solitary exception of *to be*; see 745.

[3] Poutsma, *Grammar*, II, Ch. XXVI, § 25.

(*e*)*s*: *he* (*she*, *it*) *goes*, *my brother thinks*, etc. Also in the first and third persons singular of *to be*: *I am*, *he* (*she*, *it*, *my brother*) *is*, and in the third person singular of *to have*: *he* (*she*, etc.) *has*.

UNILATERAL concord of person occurs between a subject in the first or second person singular, or in one of the three persons of the plural, and the stem of a verb that takes (*e*)*s* in the third person singular of the present tense: *I* (*you*, *we*, *they*) *go*, *some say*, *his parents live*, etc. Also in the second person singular and the three persons of the plural of *to be*: *you* (*we*, *they*) *are*; in the preterite of *to be*: *I*, *he* (*she*, etc.) *was*, as against *you* (*we*, *they*, etc.) *were*; and in the first and second persons singular, and in all the persons of the plural, of the present tense of *to have*: *I* (*you*, *we*, *they*, *my parents*, etc.) *have*.

746. (B) Concord of person between a noun or pronoun and the pronoun(s) referring to it is always bilateral. Exx.: *I* could have kicked *myself*; *Rab* and *his* friends; *Birds* were building *their* nests.

747. CONCORD OF NUMBER occurs (A) between a subject and its finite verb; (B) between a noun or pronoun and the pronoun(s) referring to it. In these cases it usually occurs in combination with concord of person. It is bilateral or unilateral in the same cases as concord of person, except that with *was* it is always bilateral.

Concord of number may also occur (C) between a noun and its attributive adjuncts; (D) between a subject and the nominal part of the predicate;[1] (E) between a noun or pronoun denoting persons or animals, and a(nother) noun denoting something belonging to them.

748. (A) In sentences with a pronoun-subject and a nominal predicate concord of number in English sometimes operates differently from its operation in other Germanic languages.

In emphatic and identifying sentences (381, 382, first half) the verb (*to be*) agrees in number with the pronoun-subject.

a. It is they who arrange everything.
b. There was a knock. I opened the door. It was John and Mary.

In descriptive sentences, however (382, second half), and in

[1] Poutsma, *Grammar*, II, Ch. XXVI, § 2.

sentences with a deictic pronoun (413–420), both the subject-pronoun and the verb agree in number with the nominal predicate.

c. They are very nice people.
d. Are those your children?

In colloquial English we sometimes find *there is* [ðəz] with a subject in the plural: *There's worse things than domestic service* (usu.: *there are worse things . . .*); *There's lots of good fish in the sea.* For more examples see Kruisinga, *Handbook*[5], § 2150.

749. As was pointed out in 470.2, relative *what* may be the subject of a plural verb. Observe that the compound sentence given there as an example has a plural noun-subject. In the following example from Kruisinga, *Handbook*[5], § 2146, there is a plural predicative noun: *He is always ready to question what are regarded as established views on the New Testament.*

750. Concord of number implies that a plural subject requires a plural predicative verb, a singular subject a singular predicative verb.

This rule is not observed very strictly in English, where we often find a plural subject with a singular verb, or a singular subject with a plural verb.

751. On plural nouns with a singular predicative verb, see 242 and 243. In such cases the noun, in spite of its plural form, more or less distinctly denotes a singular idea.

To the examples given in the sections referred to may be added:

a. names of games in *-s*: *billiards*, *dominoes*, *draughts*, etc.

Billiards is not exclusively a men's game.
Draughts is entirely a game of mathematical calculation.[1]

But:

Cards were strictly forbidden.

because the idea of the cards ('oblong pieces of pasteboard', COD) used in the game is prominent.

b. names of sciences in *-ics*: *economics*, *ethics*, *mechanics*, *phonetics*, *physics*, etc.

Economics was taught by Professor X.
What is phonetics?

---

[1] OED s.v. *draught* 22.

But a plural verb also occurs, especially with names of practical matters (OED s.v. *-ic*, 2).

Gymnastics are now a regular feature of popular education.
Politics sometimes exert an unhappy influence on character.[1]

c. The United States usually takes a singular verb:

The United States of to-day is nine times as large as the United States of 1800.[2]
Is the United States imperialist? (*Yale Review*, Autumn 1951.)

But *The Netherlands* (usually Holland, sometimes Holland and Belgium) generally takes a plural verb:

The Netherlands are washed by the North Sea.

d. Works (= factory) may take a singular verb:

Price's works was small.[3]

752. As in other Germanic languages, we usually find a singular verb:

a. after titles of books in the plural:

Percy's *Reliques* [ˈreliks] was published in 1765.

b. after a plural noun regarded merely as a word:

The Netherlands always takes a plural verb.

c. after a plural noun denoting time, measure, etc., preceded by a numeral, especially when there is a predicative noun expressing the same idea:

Fifty years is a long time.

In multiplications we find both the singular and the plural of *to be* or *to make*:

Twice twelve is (are; makes/make) twenty-four.

753. Singular nouns denoting a number of individuals take a plural verb when the persons composing the group are thought of individually, a singular verb when the group is thought of collectively. Cf. 461 and 759; also 375.

---

[1] OED s.v. *politic(s)* 3*e*.
[2] Jespersen, *A Modern English Grammar*, II, 5.18.
[3] Quoted by Jespersen and Kruisinga from A. Bennett, *Anna of the Five Towns*, Ch. III. Similarly in Ch. VIII: *Mynors' works was acknowledged to be one of the best, of its size, in the district.*

The crowd were deeply affected.[1]
An immense crowd was assembled.
My family are early risers.[2]
His family was an old one. (His was an old family.)
The majority of the strikers are already resuming work.
The Government majority in the Lower House[3] was perilously small.

754. Sometimes a plural verb is used although the members of the group are not clearly individualized; in such cases a singular verb may also occur.

The Government are determined to resist aggression.
The Government has made a grant of land to the Zoological Society.

Compare the following quotations from *Strong Poison* by Dorothy Sayers:

. . . it is, in the modern slang phrase, 'up to' the Crown[4] to prove guilt, and unless you are quite satisfied that *the Crown has* done this beyond all reasonable doubt, it is your duty to return a verdict of 'Not guilty'.
. . . it simply means that *the Crown has* failed to produce in your minds an undoubted conviction of her guilt. (p. 6)
. . . *The Crown say* he died of arsenical poisoning, and *the defence do* not dispute it . . .
. . . *the Crown have* failed to prove any purchase of arsenic before the meeting in March . . . (p. 15)
. . . And I may remind you here that *the defence have* brought no evidence to show that Philip Boyes ever bought any arsenic, . . . (p. 30)
. . . but the fact remains that *the defence have* not been able to show that the deceased ever had arsenic in his possession. (p. 30)

755. The collective nouns mentioned in the second paragraph of 239 (*cattle*, *clergy*, *police*), besides *people*, *folk* (in combinations like

---

[1] Poutsma, *Grammar* II, Ch. XXVI, § 9*c*.
[2] Jespersen, *A Modern English Grammar*, II, 4.814.
[3] Usually called the House of Commons.
[4] See the COD definition of 'metonymy', and cf. the following quotation from E. Marjoribanks, *The Life of Sir Edward Marshall Hall* (London, 1929, p. 295):
The trial came on at the Old Bailey on March 4th, 1912. In accordance with the custom in poison trials at the Old Bailey, the Attorney-General himself came down to lead for the Crown. The holder of that office was now Marshall's old friend Sir Rufus Isaacs. With him were Muir, Rowlatt (soon to be a judge), and Travers Humphreys, surely as strong a combination as had ever appeared at the Old Bailey. The Crown had indeed brought down their heavy guns against the two wretched people in the dock, and in truth they had not miscalculated.

kinsfolk, men folk), *horse*[1] (=cavalry), *foot*[1] (= infantry), *poultry*, *vermin*, nearly always take a plural verb.

> Cattle were allowed to graze in the cemetery.
> Extra police were drafted into the district.
> People are always so inquisitive.
> The poultry are being fed.[2]
> The vermin that infest race-courses (COD).

1. Note that *cattle, clergy, police, poultry*, and *vermin* never take a plural form; that *horse* and *foot* have no plural form when used collectively; that *people* may take a plural ending (or an indefinite article; in other words may be a class-noun) when its meaning is akin to that of 'nation' (*the peoples of Europe*); and that *folks* exists beside *folk*, though neither is very common in educated English.

2. Unchanged plurals, like *deer, sheep* (240), *trout, salmon*, etc. (259–261) are treated like plurals in *-s*: *Sheep were raised in great numbers*; *Salmon are plentiful.*

756. *Either* and *neither* (495–499) often take a plural verb, especially when accompanied by a plural adjunct. (Cf. the conclusion of the last sentence of 755.1.

> Neither of them know(s). (COD.)
> Have (has) either of them told you?

See also Poutsma, *Grammar*, II, Ch. XXVI, § 18 *a*.

757. (B) Concord of number is usual between a noun or pronoun and the pronoun(s) referring to it. It generally occurs in combination with concord of person. For examples see 746; for special cases, 748 and 749.

758. Plural nouns taking a singular verb (751) may also be referred to by singular pronouns. Thus the first example of 751*a* might be continued by: *It is also played by women.* Cf. also the following example from OED s.v. *-ic*, 2: *Mathematics is the science of quantity; its students are mathematicians.*

That usage wavers in many cases may be seen by comparing the two quotations in Poutsma's *Grammar*, II, Ch. XXV, § 19*g*, in which *metaphysics* is referred to by *it* and *its*, with the second quotation in Kruisinga's *Handbook*[5], § 2159, in which the same word is referred to by *them.*

---

[1] Cf. 264.
[2] Onions, *An Advanced English Syntax*, § 18.

759. The collective nouns discussed in 753, 754, may be referred to by plural pronouns. Cf. the following examples collected by Poutsma, *Grammar*, II, Ch. XXVI, § 9 *c*:

The whole party sprang upon their feet.
The Party had better not count its chickens before they are hatched.

760. It is sometimes possible for a subject to be accompanied by a predicative verb in the singular, and referred to by a pronoun in the plural. Compare the last example in the section from Kruisinga's *Handbook*[5] just mentioned:

As no man of seven could reach the upper shelves, *a pair of steps was* provided for Darius, and up *these* he had to scamper.
Arnold Bennett, *Clayhanger*, I, Ch. 4, § 2.

Here *pair of steps* is conceived as a unit, hence *was*; but the boy had to climb up a number of steps, hence *these*. But such an explanation is not always available. In many cases a plural referring to a collective noun accompanied by a verb in the singular is accounted for by its greater distance from the noun. Compare the following examples:

But as we know now, *the enemy was* exhausted also. *Their* pursuit was a chase by blown horses and puffed men. *They* called a halt and breathed heavily, at the very time when a last gallop and a hard fight would have given *them their* prize — the flower of the British army.
Philip Gibbs, *The Soul of War*.[1]

We've just got word that my wife's *family is*[2] coming to spend Christmas with us. If *they* weren't coming to us, we should have to visit *them*.
Schut and Zandvoort, *Engelse Spraakkunst voor Gymnasia*, II, p. 86.

761. The indefinite pronouns *everybody*, *every one*, *nobody*, *no one*, *anybody*, *any one* take a predicative verb in the singular, but may be referred to by a personal, reflexive or possessive pronoun in the plural. The same thing applies to *a person*.[3]

Everybody was running as fast as they could.
No one had failed in their duty.

---

[1] Quoted in an article on Number by W. Azzalino in *Zeitschrift für neuere Sprachen*, 1944, 1, p. 27.

[2] Cf. COD s.v. *family*: '*set* of parents & children, or *of relations, living together* or not'.

[3] The construction is not always approved of. Thus a British reviewer writes: 'But though the lack of an epicene pronoun in the singular makes this sort of thing tempting and frequent, careful writers avoid it, and foreign students might be told so.' [Epicene = denoting either sex.]

One didn't pay an incompetent person twenty pounds a year and then give them a promiscuous day off in this manner.

The last example (from I. C. Clarke, *Haworth Parsonage*, Penguin ed., p. 65) shows the reason for (or the advantage of) the use of the plural pronoun: it relieves the speaker of the need of specifying the sex of the person referred to (in this case Charlotte Brontë), and enables her to put her sentence in the form of a general statement.

If for some reason the speaker wishes to be more specific, we may get something like the following:

Well, every one will have to decide for himself and herself whether they go or stay. (Rose Macaulay, *Orphan Island*, Tauchnitz ed., p. 145.)

762. (C) As a rule there is concord of number between a noun and its attributive adjuncts, if the latter have distinct number forms: *this man — these men*; *much money — many friends*; (*a*) *little time* — (*a*) *few minutes*.

763. Plural nouns taking a singular verb may also take an attributive adjunct (including an indefinite article) in the singular. Examples are not, however, very common.

What we need is a new metaphysics.[1]
Anna was a little alarmed to find herself the owner of this works.[2]

Cf. also *a gallows*; *a bellows* is a kind of instrument (242, 267, and Poutsma, *Grammar*, II, Ch. XXV, § 19; *the place looked like a shambles*; *a new headquarters*. See also 810, 2nd par. — But, in spite of 751*c*: *These United States* (cf. 416).

Pains, in the sense of *trouble*, *effort*, usually takes a plural verb, but a singular attributive adjunct:

Much pains have been taken to give the most approved spelling.[3]
She took little pains with her French.

764. A plural noun denoting time, measure, etc., preceded by a numeral (752*c*) may take either a singular or a plural attributive adjunct. See 413 and Kruisinga, *Handbook*[5], § 2157.

His purpose in regard to that fifty thousand pounds.
He is a good six days overdue.

---

[1] On the analogy of French and German, a singular *metaphysic* is sometimes used; and similarly *aesthetic*, and one or two others.

[2] A. Bennett, *Anna of the Five Towns*, Ch. III.

[3] Poutsma, *Grammar*, II, Ch. XXV, § 20.

765. The collective nouns discussed in 753 and 754 take an attributive adjunct in the singular: *This family*, *that crowd*, etc.

Those discussed in 755, on the other hand, take an attributive adjunct in the plural; some of them may also be preceded by a numeral. Cf. 260.

Look at these cattle!
Twenty people were killed.

Cattle is usually joined to a numeral by a numerative (268): *twenty head of cattle*.

Note also: *A hundred extra police were drafted into the city*, but *Six policemen were injured*. Similarly *1,725*[1] *Anglican clergy*, but *five clergymen*.

766. (D) Concord of number between the subject and the nominal part of the predicate exists in English when the latter denotes a profession or a religion (cf. 348).

Both her brothers are officers.
Most of her relatives were Catholics.

767. (E) Concord of number is mostly observed in English between a noun or pronoun denoting persons or animals and a(nother) noun denoting something belonging to them. The latter is usually preceded by a possessive pronoun.

The boys took off their caps.
The birds were building their nests under the roof.
We've been used to it all our lives.

The first of the following examples should also be compared with 761:

It is not very difficult to write in a book that in the author's imaginary country the streets are clean, the houses beautiful, the clothes hygienic, *that every one has gardens*, that no one is overworked, and so on.
Chr. Hollis, *Sir Thomas More*, p. 67.

It is not easy for unqualified women to get posts. (Margaret Kennedy, *The Constant Nymph*, Tauchnitz ed., p. 123.)

768. CONCORD OF GENDER occurs between a noun or pronoun and one of the pronouns of the third person singular.

It has been dealt with in the chapter on Pronouns.

---

[1] Note the use of a comma after the figure denoting the thousands.

769. CONCORD OF TENSE usually occurs between the finite verb in the main clause and that in the object clause of a compound sentence reporting a statement or question (what is called INDIRECT STYLE).

He says he knows all about it.
He said he knew all about it.
[I know all about it.]
I asked him if he wasn't afraid.
[Aren't you afraid?]

The adjustments that take place when a statement is converted from direct to indirect style (*I* > *he*, *you* > *he*, etc.) are, on the whole, the same as in other languages. Hence there is no concord of tense when the objectivity of the statement is to be emphasized: *Did not you know that my wife is ill?* — Cf. 186, 187.

1. For an example of what the French call 'style indirect libre', the Germans 'Erlebte Rede', and what may be called in English 'Substitutionary Speech', see Galsworthy, *The Man of Property*, Part I, Ch. VII, 2nd and 3rd paragraphs.

On other varieties of indirect style, see an article by Prof. Bernhard Fehr, 'Substitutionary Narration and Description', in *English Studies*, XX (1938), 97–107.

2. On cases of incomplete concord such as *Japan* has *not and* will *not* make *any such demand*, see an article by Prof. F. Th. Visser in *English Studies*, XXXI (1950) 11–27.

PART VIII

CONVERSION

770. According to their grammatical functions, words fall into a number of classes called PARTS OF SPEECH, viz. nouns, adjectives, pronouns, verbs, adverbs, prepositions, conjunctions, interjections;[1] some would add articles and numerals.

771. Many English words belong to more than one part of speech. Thus *hope*, *love*, *sleep*, etc., may be nouns as well as verbs; *chief*, *general*, *vegetable*, etc., nouns as well as adjectives; *clean*, *dead*, *wide*, etc., adjectives as well as adverbs; *while* may be either a noun, a verb, or a conjunction; *since* may be an adverb, a preposition, or a conjunction; etc.

Owing to their more extensive use of inflexions, examples are much rarer in other languages.

772. The appurtenance of words to more than one part of speech,[2] which is mainly owing to the paucity of inflections, should be distinguished from another feature that is even more typically English, viz. the deliberate transfer of a word from one part of speech to another, technically known as CONVERSION.[3] Examples: I want *a shave* (verb > noun); Don't *sir* me, it's hardly English (noun > verb); He never gave anything to *the poor* (adj. > noun); the train *slowed* down (adj. > verb); etc., etc. A moment's reflection suffices to realize that *shave* is primarily a verb, *sir* a noun, *poor* and *slow* adjectives, and their functioning as other parts of speech is something subsidiary and occasional. On the other hand, *sleep* as a verb, and the same word as a noun, are each felt to exist in their own right, and neither is felt to be really the other transferred to a different part of speech.

---

[1] Cf. COD s.v. *part*.

[2] Jespersen (*Essentials of English Grammar*, p. 73) aptly calls such words 'grammatical homophones'. He does not, however, sufficiently distinguish between cases such as those instanced in 771, and those in 772 ff.

[3] The phenomenon is also called 'functional shift'.

This is not to say that all words that are used as more than one part of speech easily fall into either of these categories. Like metaphors, conversions may become stereotyped and cease to be felt as such. In doubtful cases it is the linguistic sense of native speakers, not the historical dictionary, that forms the ultimate test.

773. We should distinguish cases of COMPLETE CONVERSION from those of PARTIAL CONVERSION. In the former the converted word has to all intents and purposes become another part of speech, taking the adjuncts and endings proper to that part of speech, and has ceased to belong to its original part of speech. Thus, when *slow* is used as a verb, it may take any of the forms and functions of a verb, and can no longer take those of an adjective; and similarly when adverbs like *up* and *down* are converted into nouns (*the ups and downs of life*).

In cases of partial conversion, however, the converted word takes on only some of the characteristics of the other part of speech, so that it really belongs to two parts of speech at the same time. Thus, *the poor*, though plural in meaning, does not take a plural ending: it becomes a noun to some extent only, while remaining to some extent an adjective (cf. *the poorest of the poor*). Similarly, in the *boy king* (noun > adj.), *boy* is a noun and an adjective at the same time; it is used attributively, but it could not, for instance, take *-er* and *-est*, like most monosyllabic adjectives.

In what follows, cases of complete conversion will be treated first.

Complete Conversion

774. Verbs as Nouns. Stems of verbs, especially such as denote actions performed by a person, may be used as nouns, though chiefly in the singular, and preceded by an indefinite article. Like the local genitive (282, 283), they primarily belong to the less formal stratum of the language.[1]

I like a quiet read after supper.
Let's go for a spin.
She was having a good cry.[2]

---

[1] Cf. also the use of the prop-word *one* (513 n.).
[2] But *She gave a cry* is *not* a case of conversion!

In some prepositional phrases the converted verb-stem is preceded by a definite article.

He is always on the go.
A Scotchman on the make ('intent on gain').
The water is on (off) the boil.

In the last example the action is not performed by a person. Cf. also:

A divide (=a water-shed).
A repeat (*radio, theatre*, etc.).
The whole thing was a wash-out.

A bathe (in the sea, a river, or a swimming-bath) should be distinguished from *a bath* (at home).

Cf. also *a few don'ts* (607) (*don't drink, don't smoke*, etc.); *the haves and the have-nots* = *the rich and the poor*; *a visit to the Louvre is a must for every tourist in Paris* (= something not to be missed); and, with adverbs, *a* ˈ*break-down* (= collapse), *a* ˈ*get-away* (= escape).

775. NOUNS AS VERBS. The conversion of nouns into verbs is not subject to such limitations as are mentioned in 774. We may distinguish (*a*) names of things; (*b*) names of animals; (*c*) names of persons.

a. He motored back to town.
He elbowed his way through the crowd.
His work consisted in gumming stamps on forms.
The patient's chest had been X-rayed.
b. He is always aping his superiors.
Misfortune dogged his steps.
Our cat has kittened.
c. Kitty was always mothering her younger brothers and sisters.
He lorded it over the other boys. (Cf. 384*c*.)

1. Use of nouns as verbs is sometimes (practically) limited to the form in *-ing* (cf. 99): *blackberrying, nutting, bird's nesting*, etc.

2. The meanings expressed by these verbs in regard to the nouns from which they are 'converted' are mainly three: *a. to make use of* or *to treat with* (*motor, elbows,*[1] *gum, X-rays*[1]); *b. to act as, to behave like* (*ape, dog, mother, lord*); *c.* (sometimes in the case of animals) *to bring forth* (kittens;[1] similarly with *to cub, to foal, to lamb, to pig, to pup*).

---

[1] As with verbs > nouns (774), it is the STEM of a noun that is converted into a verb, not the form in *-s*. Cf. also *an X-ray photograph* (255).

776. ADJECTIVES AS VERBS. Adjectives may also be converted into verbs.

His hair was beginning to grey.
The train slowed down.
Have you blacked your boots?
Don't idle away all your time.

On verbs derived from adjectives by means of the suffix *-en*, see 945.

777. ADVERBS may be used AS NOUNS (*a*) and AS VERBS (*b*).

a. The ups and downs of life.
b. Twenty thousand colliers have downed tools.

PARTIAL CONVERSION

778. ADJECTIVES AS NOUNS. Adjectives[1] denoting a quality or a state common to a group of persons may be used without an accompanying noun to denote such PERSONS AS A GROUP. In this case the adjective is usually preceded by the definite article; it does not take a plural ending.

More nurses were urgently required to tend the sick and the wounded.
The poor were oppressed by the rich, and no provision was made for the old and infirm.

779. Other languages also use adjectives without nouns (or, what comes to the same thing, adjectives converted into nouns) to denote individuals, whether in the singular or in the plural. In English the adjective in such cases is usually accompanied by a noun.

During the latter part of the nineteenth century, the Sultan of Turkey was often referred to as 'the Sick Man'.
Old people will find a quiet and comfortable home there.

Cf. also *a dead man*; *a drowning man*; *the Evil One* (522).

In appositions to proper names English may use an adjective preceded by a definite article to refer to a single person: *Charles the Bold.*

780. What is said in 778 and 779 also applies to some half-dozen adjectives in *-sh* and *-ch* denoting peoples living round or near

[1] Including participles.

the North Sea: *English*, *Cornish* (cf. 795), *Irish*, *Welsh*, *Scotch*,[1] *Dutch*, *French*. When followed by *man* (*men*), *woman* (*women*), however, they form one word with them, in pronunciation as well as in spelling. *British* is only used as in 778.

a. In former ages the English and the Scotch were often at war.
b. Many Frenchmen cannot understand why women should be allowed to vote.
Amy Johnson was the first Englishwoman to fly to Australia.

781. Adjectives denoting a quality in the abstract, or as manifested in several objects, may be used substantively, preceded by the definite article.

In his descriptions of foreign countries, he shows a marked predilection for the quaint and the picturesque.
You must take the rough with the smooth.

782. Some languages also use adjectives preceded by the neuter article in other cases than these. As in the specimens discussed in 779, English usually adds a noun, especially *thing*.

It's the only thing you can do.
It was the first thing he said.
The best plan (the wisest course) would be to call a meeting as soon as possible.
The curious part of it was that he seemed to have forgotten all about his promise.

But we do find superlatives without nouns:

The worst of it is that he has not got a penny.
We must make the best of a bad job.

Cf. also idiomatic expressions like:

The long and the short of it is that he refuses to come. (Cf. 400.)

783. The rules of 778–780 do not exhaust the number of cases in which adjectives denoting personal qualities may be used substantively.

First of all, as with nouns proper, the definite article is usually dispensed with in enumerations. (Cf. p. 121, n. 2.)

---

[1] The Scotch themselves prefer the form *Scottish* which, however, like *British*, can only be used in the way discussed in 778; or the noun *Scot*, plural *Scots*. — *Scots* is also used as an adjective (see COD and MEU, and a note on *Scotch* and *Scottish* in *English Studies*, Febr. 1956).

Young and old, they all fell a-dancing.
(Cf. Out upon the wharf they came, Knight and burgher, lord and dame.)

Though these quotations are taken from poems, they are no different in this respect from the language of prose. Note that in both the forms without *-s* refer to more than one person.

784. *Poor* differs from the other adjectives mentioned in 778 in that it may be preceded by a possessive or a demonstrative pronoun: *our poor*, *those poor*. The reason may be that 'the poor' are a kind of social institution (cf. Matthew XXVI. 11).

Similarly *young*, denoting the offspring of an animal, may be preceded by a possessive pronoun, though we also find *young ones*: *A rabbit and its young* (*ones*).

785. Especially in the language of women and children, emotional adjectives such as *silly*, *stupid*, *dear*, *innocent*, may be used as vocatives in addressing a single person: *no*, *you silly*; *you stupid*; *poor innocent*; *my dear*.

These same adjectives may also be preceded by an indefinite article, or take a plural ending, in which case their conversion into nouns is complete.

You're such a silly.
Men are great sillies.
Jack's a dear.
Come along, (my) dears.
Poor innocents!

786. Mainly in the language of special trades and professions an adjective denoting a quality of a person (*a*), or even of a thing (*b*), may be completely converted into a noun, taking *-s* in the plural. Such converted adjectives are, indeed, chiefly used in the plural.

a. There was a large percentage of drunks among the commitments. (Cf. OED s.v. *drunk* sb.² 2.)[1]
b. Empties (empty boxes, etc.).
Earlies (early vegetables).

Cf. also *the Reds* (= the Socialists, or the Communists). Some are also found in the singular: *a daily* (*sc.* paper); *an old blue* (one who has represented his university in athletics, etc.); *a still* ('an ordinary

[1] Also COD s.v.: '(from police charge-sheets) case of drunkenness (hence gen.) man charged with drunkenness, drunken man'.

photograph, as distinct from a motion picture', COD); *an undesirable* (*sc.* person).

787. Mainly in professional language, again, the participles *accused* and *deceased* may be used with a definite article to denote a single person. In the language of lawyers these words belong to the same group with nouns like *defendant, plaintiff, prisoner.* Like them, they even occur in the genitive, a point in which they differ from other 'converted' adjectives. Thus in a biography of Sir Edward Marshall Hall, a famous criminal lawyer (*d.* 1927), we find *the deceased's alcoholic disposition* (p. 266) [but: *the deceased woman's gold* (p. 303)]; *the accused's maid* (p. 320); *the accused's condition* (p. 439).

Besides being used in the ordinary way in the sense of 'all who are dead', *the dead* (also *my*, *her*, etc., *dead*) is sometimes found in somewhat solemn speech to refer to a single person. In matter-of-fact English it may be preceded by a numeral: *fourteen dead.*

With the latter may be compared: 2,700 *homeless poor* (Kruisinga, *Handbook*[5], § 1798, last ex. but one); *Certain Irish . . . Certain English* (contrary to the rule of 778!), *ibid.*, § 1807, 3rd ex.

788. Note the substantival use of adjectives to denote languages (*a*) and colours (*b*); the latter sometimes in the plural.

a. He spoke both French and German fluently.
b. Your hair is lovely. I never saw such a brown.[1]
She turned a deadly white.
Browns and greens.

Persons are referred to when we speak of *whites and blacks.*[2] Cf. *Reds* in 786; also *the white of an egg* (*of the eye*).

789. As was pointed out in 324, adverbial superlatives are sometimes preceded by a definite article (*a*). This usage may be looked upon as another case of conversion; the same is true of adverbial superlatives preceded by the preposition *at* (*b*).

These converted superlatives may also be preceded by a possessive pronoun referring to the subject (*c*). (Cf. 568 n.)

---

[1] A. Bennett, *Anna of the Five Towns*, Ch. VII.
[2] But the reference may also be to different colours, though the order would then usually be *blacks and whites*, esp. in figurative use: *It is one of those ideologies that reduce everything to blacks and whites, and that know no greys.*

Lastly, a converted superlative preceded by *at* and a possessive pronoun referring to the subject[1] may be used predicatively (*d*).

a. Those who disliked him (the) most.[2]
b. Man is but a poor creature at best.
c. She stitched her best and her hardest.[3]
d. He is at his happiest in his descriptions of country life.

Note that in the example under ***a*** different persons are compared, whereas those under *b*, *c* and *d* refer to the same person at different times.

790. A (converted) superlative may be followed by *of* + plural noun to express a very high degree of a quality.

He was the most generous of men.
He was not in the best of tempers (humours).

When the noun in the adjunct is more or less abstract in meaning, as in the last example, it is also found in the singular. This is always the case with clearly abstract, material or collective nouns.

They only took the gentlest of exercise.
If we hold this opinion, we are in the best of company.
Primitives or peasants are not always in the rudest of health. (*Times Lit. Suppl.*, June 12, 1935, 376/5.)

Another way of expressing a very high degree is by means of an *of*-adjunct containing a (converted) superlative.

His description was of the vaguest.

791. It is hardly possible to enumerate all the instances of the complete or partial conversion of adjectives into nouns; even Poutsma's lists are not complete. We can only refer in passing to such cases as *Two shorts* (*sc.* short syllables) *are equivalent to one long* (quoted by Poutsma, *Grammar*, II, Ch. XXIX, § 12 *b*); or *to go to the bad*, *out of the common* (*ibid.*, § 21), *to the quick* (*ibid.*, § 22 I), *the dead of night* (*ibid.*, § 22 VI), *in general* (*ibid.*, § 22 VIII), *at large* (*ibid.*), *what's the good?* etc., etc.

It remains to say that English does not, like some other languages, use the genitive of a converted adjective after words denoting a quantity.

---

[1] Occasionally to the object: see the sixth ex. in Kruisinga, *Handbook*[5], § 1816.

[2] *Ibid.*, § 1189, last ex. but two. Note the rhythmical function of the article.—There is no example of adverbial *the most* in the Oxford Dictionary.

[3] A. Bennett, *Anna of the Five Towns*, Ch. VII.

I'll show you something new.[1]
The book contains little that is new.
She has many good points.

News (= tidings) is an ordinary noun:

Is there any news to-day?

792. Nouns as Adjectives. Nouns may be said to function as adjectives when they are used attributively (253 ff.); see, however, 773. On some cases approaching complete conversion see 800.

793. Attributive nouns may occur in any of the four following forms: (*a*) the stem; (*b*) the plural; (*c*) the genitive singular; (*d*) the genitive plural. See the chapter on Nouns.

Note that a genitive shares one more property with an adjective than a stem or a plural; for we can say *this (stamp) is my brother's* (276), as well as *this is my brother's stamp*.

794. There are two groups of attributive nouns that often correspond to adjectives in other Germanic languages, viz. place-names (i.e. geographical proper names, from names of counties [less often names of countries] down to names of rivers, towns and villages), and material nouns. Here are some examples of the former:

He began his career as a Durham miner.
The London season is in full swing now.
Aberdeen fishermen.
The Thames basin.

795. Names of countries usually have adjectives derived from (or connected with) them: *English*, *Welsh*, *German*, *Italian*, etc. By the side of these, we sometimes find the name of the country itself used attributively, often with a slight difference of meaning. Cf. *a Turkey* (or *Turkish*) *carpet* and *the Turkish Government*; *the Australia Eleven* (representing Australia) and *the Australian troops*.

Among names of English counties, those in the four corners (*Cornwall*, *Kent*, *Northumberland* and *Cumberland*) as well as *Lancashire* form adjectives: *Cornish*, *Kentish*, *Northumbrian*, *Cumbrian*, *Lancastrian*. Of these only *Cornish* seems to be in regular use; *Kentish* (e.g. *a Kentish orchard*) often has an emotional value absent in the matter-of-fact attributive *Kent* (e.g. *the Kent County Council*).

---

[1] Thus after pronouns in *-thing*.

A few names of foreign towns have adjectives derived from them: *Parisian*, *Viennese*, *Venetian*, *Roman*, *Neapolitan*; but the names themselves (*Paris*, *Vienna*, *Venice*, *Rome*, *Naples*) are often used attributively. As with names of countries, there may be a slight difference of meaning; cf. *our Rome correspondent* and *the Roman school of painting*, where *Rome* merely denotes place, *Roman* implying close connection with Rome.

Many of the adjectives mentioned in the first and third paragraphs are also used as nouns: *German*, *Italian*, *Parisian*, etc. They are not to be regarded as 'converted' adjectives, however, as they may take an indefinite article, a plural *-s*, etc.

796. Place-names as well as personal names may combine with certain class-nouns (*road*, *square*, *forest*, etc.) to form names of localities: *Hampstead Road*, *Trafalgar Square*, *Windsor Forest*; *Leicester Square*, *Hyde Park*.

With the exception of those with *Street*, the English combinations have even stress.

Another attributive use of personal names is found in cases like *Monk Lewis* (M. G. Lewis, chiefly known for his novel *The Monk* [1796]), '*Ossian*' *Macpherson*, and similar designations of authors whose fame rests mainly on one book.

797. Material nouns are often used attributively. On those forming adjectives in *-en*, see 918.

He was killed by an iron bar falling on his head.
Brick houses far outnumber stone ones in Holland.
All his books were in leather bindings.
His parents were celebrating their silver wedding.

As regards stress, these groups (*iron bar*, etc.) agree with the place-names of 796. When the material noun is not used in the sense of 'made of' (either literally or figuratively) we usually have uneven stress, and the two words practically form a compound: *an* ˈ*ivory dealer* (*a dealer in ivory*), *a* ˈ*wood fire*, ˈ*wool prices*. Cf. 808.

798. In other cases, too, an English attributive noun may correspond to an adjective in other languages. Only a few examples can be given here.

Put this book on the top shelf, there's a good fellow.
His photo is on the front page of the *Daily Mail*. Some publicity!
He never quite succeeded in shaking off his small town habits.

The last example shows a group of adjective + noun used attributively. In *the pocket-handkerchief* (= diminutive) *lawn* (Clemence Dane, *Wild Decembers*, Act I), we have a compound noun used attributively.

799. From an English point of view there is little to choose between the groups instanced in 798 and such as correspond to compounds in other languages; indeed, some of the English combinations are compounds as well in everything except spelling. See the chapter on Composition, esp. 831, and an article on groups like *Twilight Splendor* in *Modern Language Notes*, Nov. 1946.

I should not care to live in a corner house.
Garden cities are an outcome of modern ideas on town planning.

800. The use of nouns as adjectives is mainly limited to the ATTRIBUTIVE function. Occasionally, however, we find nouns used as PREDICATIVE adjectives; in this case there is some justification for looking on them as cases of complete conversion, especially when we find such a predicative noun qualified by an adverb.

Their correspondence was strictly business. (Cf. business correspondence.)
I suppose you're Church of England? *I'm* chapel.
(Cf. chapel people = dissenters.)
The Barfields were county.
(Cf. county family: with ancestral seat in a county.)
A copyright edition — this edition is copyright.

In the above examples the predicative noun may also be used attributively. The following are only used predicatively in the sense here illustrated; note that they are qualified by an adjective, not an adverb.

Skating is great fun.
He can be excellent company.
'It's me' isn't grammar.[1]

'Converted' predicative nouns should be distinguished from 'ordinary' predicative nouns which do not remind us of adjectives. Thus in *Truro was fun when I was a girl* (Kruisinga, *Handbook*[5], § 1894), *fun* is, but *girl* is not, an instance of 'conversion'.

801. When ADVERBS are used as ADJECTIVES we have another case of partial conversion (cf. 777); similarly in compounds of preposition + noun.

---

[1] According to a widespread prejudice. Cf. 360. — Of course, *grammar* may be used attributively, as in *a grammar school*, but not, e.g., in **a grammar expression*.

a. An up train, a down train.
An off chance;[1] the then secretary.
The above statement.
b. Up-country districts; uphill work.

802. In conclusion, it may be observed that a COMPLETE SENTENCE may occasionally be used AS A NOUN (*a*), or AS A VERB (*b*), at least with the verbal suffix *-ing*. Cf. 99.

a. Young What's his name has got into a bad scrape, I hear.
b. All this 'how d'ye doing' is really a bit absurd.

In a word like *forget-me-not* the phenomenon has become stereotyped; cf. 806.

[1] Also spelt *off-chance*.

PART IX

WORD FORMATION

CHAPTER ONE

COMPOSITION

803. English, like other Germanic languages, has a great many examples of vocables[1] which, though felt and used as single words, are made up of two or more elements each of which may also be used as a separate word. Such vocables are called COMPOUNDS.

Compounds occur among all parts of speech, with the exception of articles. One example will be given for each, in the order in which they were enumerated in 770: *goldsmith*, *seasick*, *myself*, *overcome*, *somewhere*, *without*, *although*, *heigh-ho*, *twenty-two*.

Here are some examples of compounds made up of more than two elements: *ˈson-in-law*, *ˈmaid-of-ˈall-work*; *ˌnevertheˈless*; *ˈtwo and ˈtwenty*. They are chiefly nouns, adverbs or numerals.

On so-called String Compounds (type: *dead-letter office*) see 814.

804. COMPOUND NOUNS mostly consist of two elements, the second of which is usually a noun. As a rule the first element has the main stress and qualifies the second. On the formation of the plural and the genitive (if any) see 228–230, 237 and 238.

The first element may be: *a.* a noun (*goldsmith*); *b.* an adjective (*blackboard*); *c.* a pronoun (*he-goat*); *d.* a verb (*drawbridge*); *e.* an adverb (*outpost*).

Of a different type are those mentioned in 229: *ˈlooker-ˈon*, *passer-by*, *runner-up*, *goings-on*, etc., which are formed on the pattern of the corresponding verb + adverb: *look on*, *pass by*, etc.

Compound nouns of more than two elements usually consist of a noun with a prepositional adjunct: *ˈson-in-law*, *part of speech*,

[1] 'Word, esp. w. ref. to form rather than meaning' (COD).

maid-of-all-work, or of a first and a last element connected by *and*: *bread and butter, whisky and soda*;[1] *coach and six*.

A few compound nouns have a verb-stem for their second element: *boot-black, shoeblack, chimney-sweep* (by the side of *c.-sweeper*, cf. 807, 1), *bar-keep* (Am., by the side of *b.-keeper*); *card-sharp* (by the side of *c.-sharper*).

805. A special type of compound noun is formed by those consisting of a classifying genitive + noun: *child's play, lady's maid, bird's nest*. See 286 ff.

Sometimes combinations of genitive + noun and of noun-stem + noun exist side by side: *a large schoolboy hand* and *a great floundering boy's hand* (Jespersen, MEG VI, 8.82). Cf. also *bearskin* '(wrap &c.) of b.'s skin, Guards' tall furry cap' (COD); *bird-nest* (COD), by the side of *bird's nest*; *dog('s)-ear* 'corner of page turned down with use' (COD); E. *barber's shop*, Am. *barber shop* (through the latter is now frequently to be seen on sign-boards in London).

806. The compounds discussed in 804 and 805 should be distinguished from such as owe their origin to the CONVERSION of a syntactic word-group into a noun. Such groups mainly consist of an adjective with its adjunct (*good-for-nothing*), a verb with its adjunct(s) or object (*ˈbreak-down, ˈlook-ˈout, ˈmake-ˈup, ˈgrown-ˈup(s), stay-at-home* (cf. 620, 2nd ex.), *ne'er-do-well* or *ne'er-do-weel, ˈDie-Hard, ˈgo-between, ˈhold-all, forget-me-not*), a preposition plus (pro)noun (*ˈoverall(s), out-of-work*), or a preposition plus numeral (*the under-fives, the over-forties*). Cf. 228 on the formation of the plural.

Note especially combinations of a verb stem plus object denoting persons (*ˈcut-throat, ˈpickpocket, ˈturncoat*, etc.) or things (*ˈbreak-water, ˈhold-all, ˈmakeshift*), and compare the essentially different type represented by *drawbridge* (804*d*).

The case of a compound like *ˈclose-ˈup* is slightly different: it is short for *close-up picture*.

807. Of the various types of compound nouns enumerated in 804, the first, consisting of NOUN + NOUN, is by far the commonest, and new specimens are constantly being formed.

The semantic relations between the two parts of these compounds exhibit great variety; only a few can be pointed out here.[2]

[1] But in the plural: *two whiskies and sodas*.

[2] For further particulars see Jespersen, MEG VI, 8.22 ff., and Koziol, *Handbuch der englischen Wortbildungslehre*, § 87 ff., to which, as well as to the treatment in Kruisinga's *Handbook*[5], Vol. III, and to COD, this chapter and the next owe a good deal.

1. If the second element denotes an action, the first element may denote either the SUBJECT or the OBJECT of the action: *daybreak*, *sunrise*; *sun-worship*, *housekeeping*. In the latter case the second element may also denote an agent: *housekeeper*. Note also *self-command*, and many other compounds with *self*.

2. The first element may denote PLACE or TIME: *headache*, *nightclub*, *night-porter*.

3. The first element may denote PURPOSE: *wineglass*, *dining-room*, *inkstand*.

4. The first element may denote a MEANS or an INSTRUMENT: *handwriting*, *fly-fishing*, *sabre-cut*.

5. The first element may denote RESEMBLANCE: *goldfish*, *silver-fox*.

6. If the second element denotes a person or an animal, the first element may denote the SEX: *man-servant*, *maid-servant*; *billy-goat*, *nanny-goat*; *bull elephant*, *cow elephant*.

Other relations are implied in compounds like *goldsmith*, *newspaper*, *rainbow*, *lawsuit*, *air-raid*, *foot-bridge*, *lily-flower*, *motor-car*, *ironware*, etc., etc.

808. The rule that in compound nouns consisting of two elements the first element has the main stress (804) is not without exceptions. Thus undoubted compounds like *armchair*, *farmyard*, *pea-soup*, are usually pronounced with even stress (see Jones, *An English Pronouncing Dictionary*).[1] This way of stressing compounds seems to be on the increase in English.

Even stress naturally has the tendency of lessening the unity of a compound and emphasizing the individuality of its component parts. Cf. *ˈlady ˈdoctor*, *ˈgentleman ˈfarmer*, *ˈdeputy ˈgovernor*, *ˈfellow-ˈman*, *ˈqueen ˈmother*, *ˈpoet-ˈartist*, etc. Whether such combinations are to be regarded as compounds or as word-groups largely depends on the intention of the speaker or writer, and on the linguistic feeling of the hearer or reader. We shall probably be right in regarding the examples just given as compounds in spite of their even stress. In the same way *ˈHyde ˈPark*, *ˈLeicester ˈSquare*, etc.

[1] Of course such words are subject to the rules of sentence-stress; cf. *a ˈbig armˈchair*, but *an ˈarmchair phiˈlosopher*.

(796) may be looked upon as compounds, because few, if any, people using these names will think of the ancient manor of Hyde or of the Earl of Leicester in connection with them; but with *a Durham miner*, *the London season*, etc. (794), or *an iron bar* (797), the case is different: here we have to do with GROUPS of attributive noun + noun, not with compounds.

ˈ*Boy-child* (= male child) and ˈ*girl-child* (= female child) are to be regarded as compounds (cf. 807, 6); so, probably, are ˈ*boy-*ˈ*husband* (= young husband), ˈ*child* ˈ*wife*, ˈ*girl* ˈ*guides* and similar collocations, in spite of their even stress (cf. the definition of 803: 'felt and used as single words'), though all these cases are at the same time instances of the attributive use of nouns.

809. The second type of compound noun, consisting of ADJECTIVE + NOUN, is also fairly common. Initial stress is found in *blackbird*, *blackboard*, *bluebell*, *common law* (also pronounced with even stress), *commonwealth*, *first-fruits*, ˋ*free-mason*, *green-room* (see COD), *highway*, *hothouse*, *nobleman*, *quicksilver*, *shorthand*, *smallpox*, *strong-box*, *whitewash*, *wildfire*, *wildfowl*; even stress in *common sense*, *dead letter*, *easy-chair* (cf. *armchair* 808), *first night* (Fr. *première*), *free-trade*, *public-house*, *public school*; final stress in *young man*, *young lady*, *old maid*.

In ˈ*greenhouse*, ˈ*mad doctor*, ˈ*madhouse*, ˈ*sick-room*, ˈ*sweet-shop*, etc. the first element is an adjective 'converted' into a noun, so that they form a special case of 804*a*.

810. A special type of adj. + noun compounds is represented by *blackshirt*, *greybeard*, *pale-face*, *red-breast*, *tenderfoot*. They have initial stress, and signify 'person or animal having or wearing (what the adj. and noun indicate)'.

Some of them have a plural noun for their second element: *a lazy-bones*, *a light-skirts*, *a daddy-longlegs* (= crane-fly). (Cf. 763.)

These compounds should be distinguished from similar ones with a noun for their first element: *blockhead* (one having a 'wooden' head), *feather-brain* (one having a light or weak brain). In such forms the first noun is used in a figurative sense. Some of them have two meanings, e.g. *pot-belly*, 1. protuberant belly, 2. person having such a belly; *humpback* or *hunchback*, (person having a) deformed back. (In this last example, by the way, the first noun is *not* used figuratively.)

The second element is a noun in the plural in *butter-fingers* 'person unable to hold things, esp. a catch at cricket' (COD).

811. In compounds of the type *he-goat*, *she-wolf*, the pronoun usually indicates the sex (cf. 807, 6). Note *he-man* (U. S.): 'masterful or virile ['virail] man' (COD).

812. When the first element is a VERB, it may either take the form of the stem, or that of the stem + *ing*. Examples of the former are *drawbridge*, *grindstone*, *playground*, *treadmill* (and cf. 806); of the latter *drawing-room*, *knitting-needle*, *looking-glass*.

1. Sometimes the two forms exist side by side: *flash-point* and *flashing-point* (see COD); *swim-bladder* and *swimming-bladder* (of a fish); *wash-stand* and *washing-stand*; Am. *sailboat*, E. *sailing-boat*; Am. *spark plug*, E. *sparking plug*. Cf. 805 n.

2. *Hearsay* (stressed on the first syllable) is probably the only ex. of a compound noun made up of two verbs: *This is mere hearsay*. Also used attributively: *hearsay evidence*. Cf. 17, 820 (*daresay*) and 826 (*maybe*).

813. Combinations of ADVERB + NOUN are of two types. In the former the noun is not, in the latter it is identical in form with a corresponding verb. Examples: *a. afterthought*, *by-way*, *outpost*, *overcoat*, *underclothes*; *b. downpour*, *offshoot*, *outbreak*, *upkeep*.

Those in *-er* (*bystander* etc.) will be dealt with in the chapter on Derivation.

814. The first element of a compound noun may itself be a compound. Thus arise what Jespersen (MEG VI, 8.91) calls STRING COMPOUNDS.[1] Examples: *dead-letter office*, *dirty-clothes basket*,[2] *high churchman*, *public schoolboy* (cf. 591). Here is one of which the first element is not an adjective: *penny-in-the-slot machine*. *New Year Eve fancy dress ball* (*ibid.*, last example) should, perhaps, rather be interpreted as consisting of two string-compounds (*New Year Eve* and *fancy dress ball*), with the former serving as an attribute to the latter. Cf. also: Lord Luke, Chairman of the *Empire Air Raid Distress Fund Flag Day Committee* (Times Weekly Ed., Sept. 2, 1942).

---

815. COMPOUND ADJECTIVES mostly consist of two elements, the second of which is usually an adjective. (On compound participles, see 822; on formations of the type *narrow-minded*, 917.)

[1] Many of his examples, however, are rather to be interpreted as groups of attrib. compound noun + headword.

[2] Spelled *dirty clothes-basket* in MEG II, 12.322 (cf. 831).

The first element may be: *a.* a noun (*seasick*); *b.* an adjective (*red-hot*); *c.* an adverb (*over-anxious*). Those formed with a noun usually have initial stress, the others mostly even stress.[1]

Combinations of verb + adj. do not seem to exist in English.[2] In ˈ*breakneck* (= dangerous: *a breakneck climb*) we have an adj. consisting of verb + noun, of a type similar to that discussed in 806; in *barefoot* (*a barefoot pilgrimage*), *bareback* (like *barefoot* also used adverbially), *hot-foot* (always adverbial = in hot haste), one of adj. + noun. Note also combinations of ordinal numeral + noun: *first-rate, second-hand.*

816. Combinations of NOUN + ADJECTIVE exhibit various semantic relations. The following list is not exhaustive.

1. In compounds with *-worthy*, the first element denotes what may be called the OBJECT: ˈ*blameworthy*, ˈ*trustworthy* (= who deserves blame, trust, etc.). In *seaworthy* (of ship: in fit state to put to sea) the relation is rather adverbial.

2. The first element may denote CAUSE: *seasick*, *snow-blind*; or PURPOSE: *blood-thirsty* (= eager for bloodshed).

3. The first element may denote RESEMBLANCE: *blood-red*, *nut-brown*, *stone-cold.* When the first element also serves to indicate a high DEGREE, these compounds usually have even stress: ˈ*blood-*ˈ*red*, ˈ*snow-*ˈ*white*, ˈ*stone-*ˈ*cold*; but ˈ*milk-white*, ˈ*nut-brown.* With adjectives not expressing colour, composition of this kind is only possible if the first element expresses a high degree; thus *paper-thin* (= very thin).

4. The first element may devote MEASURE or EXTENT: ˈ*knee-*ˈ*deep*, ˈ*shoulder* ˈ*high*; ˈ*lifelong*, ˈ*world-wide.*[3]

5. The first element may RESTRICT the meaning of the second: ˈ*colour-blind* (blind in regard to colours), ˈ*waterproof* ('impervious to water'). Cf. also *carefree* = free from care.

817. Combinations of TWO ADJECTIVES usually have even stress. Three groups may be distinguished:

1. The compound expresses a combination of two qualities; the two elements are, therefore, coordinate: *bitter-sweet*, (a)

---

[1] With the same reservation as on p. 279, n. 1: ˈ*red-*ˈ*hot*, but *a* ˈ*red-hot* ˈ*poker.*

[2] On *choke-full* see COD s.v. *chock.*

[3] Also with even stress (see Jones): the first element may be meant to express a high degree.

brown-grey (beard), *dead-alive* ('dead while yet alive; . . . spiritless' OED).

2. A special case of this is the combination of two adjectives the former of which ends in *-o*: *serio-comic*, *Franco-German*, *Anglo-Saxon*; and see 3.

3. The first adjective, which is semi-adverbial in character, qualifies the second, and is, therefore, subordinate to it: *dark-blue*, *red-hot*, *reddish-brown*, *Roman-Catholic* (hence also *Anglo-Catholic*, which as regards its form belongs to 2).

In *deaf and dumb* (= *deaf-mute*, see 1) we have a formation analogous to that of *bread and butter* (804).

818. ADVERB + ADJECTIVE. There is one compound with *ever*, viz. ˈ*evergreen* (also used as a noun); an unlimited number with *over* (all of them even-stressed): *over-anxious*, *over-ripe*, *over-sensitive*, etc.; and one or two with *under*: *under-ripe*. Cf. also such combinations as *all-important*, *all-sufficient*.

As in the case of nouns (806), a syntactic word-group may be converted into an adjective: *up-to-date* (information), *well-to-do* (citizens). The same is true of such a non-syntactic group as *happy-go-lucky* (= haphazard).

819. For COMPOUND PRONOUNS (*myself*, *nobody*, etc.) see the chapter on Pronouns.

---

820. COMPOUND VERBS fall into three groups: *a.* those with an adverb for their first element (*overcome*); *b.* those occurring as participles only (*hand-made*, *everlasting*), which might also have been treated as compound adjectives; *c.* those formed by shortening from compound verbal nouns in *-er* or *-ing*, so-called BACK-FORMATIONS (*housekeep*).

Daresay (204) is a verbal compound made up of two verbs. Cf. the adverb *maybe* (826).

821. ADVERB + VERB. The principal adverbs used are:

out: *outbid*, *outdo*, *outlive*, *outwit*, etc.
over: *overcome*, *overlook*, *overtake*, *overdo*, *overwork*, etc.
under: *undermine*, *undersell*, *underestimate*, *understate*, etc.
up: *uphold*, *upset*, etc.

All these adverbs are also used as prepositions.[1] A different kind of adverb is found in *ill-treat*, *ill-use*. Cf. also *dry-clean* (without using water), *dry-cure* (without pickling in liquid).

ˈ*Broadcast* is a case of conversion of the adjective and adverb ˈ*broadcast* (from *broad* + p.p. *cast*) into a verb.

822. COMPOUND PARTICIPLES. The following cases may be distinguished:

1. If the second element is the past participle of a transitive verb, the first element may denote the AGENT or the INSTRUMENT of the action: *hand-made*, *machine-made*, *pock-marked*, *thunderstruck*, *weather-beaten*; *Government-owned*, *British-owned*.

2. If the second element is the present participle of a transitive verb, the first element may denote the OBJECT: *heart-rending*, *self-denying*, *all-seeing*.

3. If the second element is a participle, the first element may denote PLACE, TIME or MANNER: ˈ*home-*ˈ*brewed*, ˈ*town-bred*, ˈ*heart-felt*; ˈ*far-*ˈ*fetched*, *far-seeing*; ˈ*sea-faring*, ˈ*shore-going*; *forth*ˈ*coming*; *ever*ˈ*lasting*, *night-blooming* (flowers); *easy-going*, *good-looking*, *true-born*, *well-meaning* (of person or attempt) = *well meant* (of attempt).

4. Some of the combinations of adverb + verb mentioned in 821 occur only or chiefly as participles: ˈ*outstretched*, ˈ*outlying*; *over*ˈ*joyed*; ˈ*under*ˈ*done*;[2] *up*ˈ*standing*;[3] to which may be added ˈ*downcast* (eyes), ˈ*inborn* (shyness).

823. BACK-FORMATION. As was pointed out in 807, compound nouns of which the second element denotes an agent or an action, may have for their first element a noun denoting the object of the action: *housekeeper*, *housekeeping*. On the analogy of the morphological pattern *keeper/keeping* — *keep*, a verb-stem *housekeep* is sometimes formed by subtraction from *housekeeper/housekeeping*. As a combination like *housekeep* runs counter to the rule of English word-order that an object shall follow, not precede its verb, such

[1] *Out* only in American English (. . . *we invariably hung out the front window on such occasions* . . . Dreiser, *Dawn*, p. 37), and in combination with *from*: *from out the dungeon came a groan* (COD).

[2] But an ˈ*underdone po*ˈ*tato*.

[3] 'Well set up, erect' (COD): *a fine, upstanding young fellow*.

formations are usually felt to have an incongruous effect, and are, therefore, often coined with humorous intention. In course of time, however, if the back-formation 'catches on', the incongruous effect of what was at first a mere nonce-word,[1] may wear off, and the new word may come to be accepted as part of the normal vocabulary. Thus *to partake*, now an 'ordinary' verb, was originally formed by subtraction from *partaker*, i.e. *part-taker*.

Further examples are *caretake*,[2] *fire-watch*, *housebreak*, *house-hunt*, *home-keep*, *lip-read*, *thought-read*, *type-write*, etc.

> A gardener who was not really a gardener, and a game-keeper who did not game-keep.[3] (*Punch*.)
> A lady who housekeeps for all humanity.[4]
> A schoolmaster, he fire-watches one night in eight at the Town Hall. (*Daily Telegraph and Morning Post*, Sept. 23, 1944.)

Type-write from *type-writer* ('a writing-machine having types [= printed characters] for the letters of the alphabet', OED) was probably never meant humorously, but produced after the model of those that were, by the need of a convenient form. In *a typewritten letter* the relation between the two elements of the compound becomes adverbial rather than objective (cf. *hand-written*, 822, 1); see the next paragraph.

824. We have an adverbial relation between the two elements in back-formations like ˈ*sleep-walk*, ˈ*spring-*ˈ*clean*, ˈ*sun-bathe*; perhaps also in *stage-*ˈ*manage* (from *stage-manager*):

> Important plays badly stage-managed.

Back-formation is not limited to compounds; see 956.

825. It is, perhaps, worth pointing out that formations like *to hamstring*, *to waterproof*, etc. are not cases of verbal composition, but of CONVERSION, resp. of a compound noun and a compound adjective.

To cold-shoulder, *to wet-blanket*, on the other hand, are cases of

---

[1] 'coined for one occasion' (COD).
[2] From *care-taker*, 'person hired to take charge, esp. of house in owner's absence'. Note the difference between *to caretake* and *to take care*!
[3] From an article on Backformations by A. E. H. Swaen in *The Student's Monthly*, Febr. and March 1917.
[4] Jespersen, MEG VI, p. 168. — 'Back-formed' compound verbs occur chiefly as stems; other than stem forms are infrequent, except with a matter-of-fact word like *type-write* (though I have never come across a form like *she type-wrote for him*). Cf. Krusinga, *Handbook*[5], § 1910.

the conversion of syntactic groups (of adj. + noun) analogous to those discussed in 806.

826. Other compound parts of speech call for little comment. In so far as they are felt as units, ADVERBIAL groups like *at once* (= directly), *of late* (= lately) etc. may be regarded as compounds; the same holds good of PREPOSITIONAL groups like *on to* (also spelt *onto*; cf. *into*), *out of*, *up to*; and of CONJUNCTIONAL groups like *as* ˈ*if*, ˈ*so that* (cf. 634).

Compound numerals containing *twenty* (less often those containing *thirty* or beyond) have the alternative forms *twenty-one* — *one and twenty*, *thirty-five* — *five and thirty*, etc. Their elements (like those of *bread and butter* [804], *deaf-mute*, *deaf and dumb* [817]), are coordinate.

ˈ*Maybe* (= perhaps) is an instance of the conversion of a syntactic word-group into an adverb (806 and 820). ˈ*Would-be* (see COD) may be either an adjective or an adverb.

Repetition Compounds

827. No mention has yet been made of a type of compound which consists in the repetition of the word constituting its first element: *goody-goody*, *pretty-pretty*, *fifty-fifty* (half and half), *bye-bye* (=goodbye), *pooh-pooh* (interjection, and, by conversion, verb), *so so*, etc. Most of them are affective in meaning: *goody-goody* and *pretty-pretty* express disapproval, *pooh-pooh* contempt, *so so* depreciation, *bye-bye* intimacy, etc. They are especially common in familiar speech.

828. A good many of these repetition compounds are onomatopoeic [ˈɔnomətoˈpi:ik], i.e. they imitate or suggest (repeated) sounds.[1] *Pooh-pooh* is one of them;[2] others are *chug-chug* (of engine), *clank-clank* (of chain), *drip-drip* (of rain; also fig., e.g. of propaganda), *hush-hush* (secret), *tap-tap*, *thump-thump* (of a crutch), etc. They are mostly used as nouns (*the drip-drip of the rain*); in this function they may also take the verbal *ing*-suffix (*the clank-clanking of chains*, cf. 99); occasionally they take other verbal endings (*he snip-snipped with his scissors*). They are also used

[1] A word may be onomatopoeic without being a compound; cf. *ping*, n., & v.i., 'abrupt ringing sound as of rifle bullet flying through air' (COD).
[2] COD *pooh*: 'imit. f. sound of blowing a thing away'.

attributively: *a hush-hush policy* — policy of keeping everything secret.

829. By the side of these repetition compounds there exists another type in which the first element is repeated with a different medial or final vowel. The alternative most frequently found is [i] — [æ]: *dilly-dally* (vacillate; loiter), *fiddle-faddle* (nonsense), *flim-flam*[1] (ditto), the *jim jams* (panic; slang), *(k)nick-(k)nacks* (trinkets), *riff-raff* (rabble), *shilly-shally* (vacillate), *tick-tack, tittle-tattle* (gossip), *wishy-washy* (with [ɔ] for [æ] after [w]), *zig-zag.*

The alternation [i] — [ɔ] also occurs: *criss-cross, ping-pong, sing-song, tip-top.* Other vowel-alternations are rarer: cf. *heigh-ho* (interj. expr. boredom, disappointment, etc.), *see-saw.*

Many of these formations do not fully agree with the definition of a compound given in 803, because their elements are not used as separate words (*flim-flam*), or because only one of them is (*fiddle-faddle*).

Some of these compounds are onomatopoeic (*tick-tack, ping-pong*). Most of them are used as nouns (*riff-raff*, etc.); some may also be converted into adjectives (*a zig-zag course*) or verbs (*a road zig-zagging up the mountain*); *dilly-dally* is exclusively a verb.

830. Thirdly, the first element (which often begins with an *h*) may be repeated with a different initial consonant, usually a stop: *harum-scarum* (reckless), *helter-skelter* ([in] disordered haste), *higgledy-piggledy* ([in] utter confusion), *hob-nob* (drink together), *hocus-pocus, hotch-potch* ('heterogeneous mixture'), *hurly-burly* (commotion); *Mumbo Jumbo* (see COD), *namby-pamby* (sentimental), *razzle-dazzle* (spree), *roly-poly* (pudding). A recent acquisition is *walkie-talkie* (portable wireless transmitter).

Many of them are nursery words, and often nonce-words as well: *Georgy-Porgy, piggie-wiggie, tootsy-wootsies* (feet), etc.; note the affective *-y, -ie* ending (888).

Only one verb (*hob-nob*) seems to belong to this group; what was said of the definition of a compound in 829 applies here as well.

---

[1] 'One of the many onomatopoeic reduplications expressive of contempt' OED).

831. The reader of the last and other sections of this handbook cannot fail to have been struck by a lack of consistency in the use of HYPHENS in the writing of compounds. This lack of consistency is entirely in keeping with English practice, on which the late H. W. Fowler in his *Dictionary of Modern English Usage* (a book to be used with care) expresses himself thus: 'The chaos prevailing among writers or printers or both regarding the use of hyphens is discreditable to English education.' Logic would, of course, prescribe that undoubted compounds, like *goldsmith*, should be spelt as single words; that a hyphen should be used when the two elements are only occasionally combined, and, therefore, to some extent preserve their individuality in combination (*she-wolf*); and that the two words should be written apart when they form a group of adjective + noun, or attrib. noun + noun, etc., not a compound (*the London streets*). The very logic of this division, however, makes it difficult to apply in many cases, with the result that it is often ignored in cases of less difficulty. The best advice to be given in this matter is: When in doubt, consult the Concise Oxford Dictionary.

CHAPTER TWO

DERIVATION

832. As was stated or implied in 803, we understand by COMPOSITION the formation of a word by the close combination of two or more elements each of which is also used as a separate word: *goldsmith.*

If only one of the elements can be used as a separate word, we speak of DERIVATION.[1] The other element, if the first, is called a PREFIX, if the last, a SUFFIX: *unkind, kindness.*

833. As derivation is distinguished from composition on the one hand, so it is to be distinguished from INFLEXION on the other. Both make use of suffixes; but whereas derivation results in the formation of a different word (*kind* — *kindness*, *sleep* — *sleepy*), inflexion merely modifies a word (noun or verb) in the ways described in the chapters on those parts of speech (*book* — *book's* — *books*, *hope* — *hopes* — *hoped* — *hoping*). Hence we distinguish DERIVATIONAL[2] from INFLEXIONAL suffixes. Prefixes are always derivational in English (not, for instance, in Latin and Greek: *cado* — *cecidi*; cf. also Dutch *gelopen*, German *gelaufen*).

834. There are a few border-line cases between composition and derivation. Let us take words in *-ful(l)*. *Brim-full*, 'full to the brim', is evidently a compound. The word is also spelt *brimful*, and as OED observes: 'properly pronounced [ˈbrim ˈful]; cf. *half full*, *quite full*, and the like;[3] erroneously [ˈbrimful], by association with adjs. like *mindful*.' This, of course, mainly goes to show that *brim-full* (which was, acc. to OED, originally written as two words), has

[1] See also 836 n.

[2] Not 'derivative', which is passive in meaning: 'derived from a source' (COD). *A derivative* = a derived word.

[3] Also ˈ*chock*-ˈ*full* (see Jones, *Pronouncing Dictionary*, which gives *brimful* with even as well as with initial stress) and ˈ*cram*-ˈ*full*.

become a closer unit in pronunciation as well as in spelling. It is equally clear, however, that *mindful* can hardly be called a compound: it does not mean 'full of mind', and the second syllable is only faintly associated in the linguistic sense with the adjective *full*; consequently, it is a derivative. This is borne out by its transcriptions in Jones's *Pronouncing Dictionary*, where the italicized *u* indicates that the word is pronounced [ˈmaindfl] as well as [ˈmaindful]. And though words like *beautiful*, *cheerful*, etc. may be analysed as 'full of beauty', 'full of cheer', it is doubtful ('full of doubt'?) whether that is how we actually apprehend them.[1]

By the same criterion, nouns like *handful*, *mouthful*, *spoonful*, will have to be regarded as compounds, though their status as such is none too assured; for though Jones does not italicize the [u] in *handful* and *mouthful*, he does in *spoonful*. (Cf. 924 and 936.)

835. A similar problem arises in regard to word-formation with prefixes like *counter-* and *extra-*: *counter-attack*, *extra-mural* (= outside the walls; cf. COD). Are such words compounds or derivatives? *Counter* and *extra* do exist as separate words: *He acted counter to his instructions*; *extra charges*. As appears from COD, however, *counter* (adj. & adv.) is derived by subtraction from words like *counter-attack*, not *vice versa*; and though from a modern English point of view it is, perhaps, irrelevant that *extra* = *additional* is probably shortened from *extraordinary*, it is clear that in *extra-mural* its meaning is different from that in *extra charges*. It seems, therefore, that we shall have to regard *counter-* and *extra-* as prefixes, and the words formed with them as derivatives. (Cf. also 842 and 852.)

836. Prefixes and suffixes fall into two groups, according as they can or cannot be used to form new words. In the former case they are called LIVING OF PRODUCTIVE, in the latter DEAD OF UNPRODUCTIVE. All the prefixes and suffixes hitherto mentioned in this chapter are productive.[2] Examples of unproductive prefixes and

[1] The analysis is impossible in derivatives from verbs, such as *forgetful*, *mournful*, *resentful*.

[2] As a study of the following lists will show, not all living prefixes and suffixes are *equally* productive.

suffixes are *for-*, as in *forget, forgive*; *with-*, as in *withdraw, withhold*;[1] *-ant* or *-ent*, as in *servant, different*; *-le*, as in *handle*; *-t*, as in *gift* (cf. *to give*). The latter group are of mainly historical interest; the former are of paramount importance for the structure of present-day English, and will be briefly discussed here. For information on other prefixes and suffixes see COD.

Words beginning or ending with one of the prefixes or suffixes listed below, but whose remaining part does not exist as a separate word (e.g. *de|prive, dis|cuss*; *speci|al, dubi|ous*) are not derivatives from a modern English point of view. Only such instances will be discussed as are closely related, in form and meaning, to real derivatives (cf. *biograph|ee* 875, *dent|ist* 882, etc.).

Prefixes

837. Contrary to what we find in other Germanic languages, all English prefixes are inseparable. They will be listed here in alphabetical order.

With the exception of *a-* (838), *be-*, *fore-*, *mis-* and *un-*, all living English prefixes are of non-Germanic origin; apart from negative *a-*, *auto-*, *hyper-* and *mal-*, however, they can be combined with Germanic as well as non-Germanic words. Many of them are international.[2]

838. *a-* [ə] may be prefixed to the stem of monosyllabic intransitive verbs, and of disyllabic intransitive verbs ending in unstressed *-le*, *-er*, or *-en*, to form predicative adjectives denoting a state: *adrift*, *asleep*, *awash*; *a-flicker*, *a-quiver*, *atremble*. Many of them are literary rather than colloquial. (Jespersen, MEG VI, 7.5.)

> Rocks which are awash[3] at low tide (OED).
> She was all atremble.

This is the only instance of adjectives being derived from another part of speech by means of a prefix; and they cannot even be used attributively.

---

[1] On the question: derivative or compound? cf. what was said on *extra-mural* in 835.

[2] By some authorities (Kruisinga; COD; Jones, *An English Pronouncing Dictionary*) forms with prefixes are usually regarded as compounds. Koziol (*Handbuch* § 618) speaks of 'die Zusammensetzung mit Vorsilben und die Ableitung durch Nachsilben'.

[3] 'On a level or flush with the surface of the water, so that it just washes over' (OED).

839. *a-* [ei], [æ] is a negative prefix, denoting the mere absence of a quality (cf. *in-/un-*, *non-*): *a-moral*[1] [ei ˈmɔrəl], *asexual*, *asexuality*.

840. *ante-* (= before) is used in nouns, like ˈ*antechapel*, ˈ*anteroom* (= room leading to another), but chiefly to form adjectives or attributive nouns referring to time: ˈ*antediˈluvian*,[2] ˈ*ante-reformation* (times). An example with a verb is *to* ˈ*anteˈdate* (a letter). It competes with *pre-*, which is, indeed, more frequently found: *pre-reformation* (less often *prediluvian*).

841. *anti-* (= against)[3] is combined with nouns, the prefix having the meaning 'rival, enemy of': ˈ*antichrist*, ˈ*antipope*. It also combines with nouns to form attributive nouns: ˈ*anti-*ˈ*aircraft* (gun), and with adjectives: ˈ*anti-Se*ˈ*mitic* (movement). Thirdly, it combines with nouns with a suffix, with the sense: 'person opposed to' or 'movement opposed to': ˈ*anti-*ˈ*militarist*, ˈ*anti-*ˈ*Darwinism*.

842. *arch-* [ɑːtʃ] is only combined with nouns. It is used either with favourable or with unfavourable meaning. In the former case it means 'chief, pre-eminent': ˈ*arch*ˈ*bishop*, ˈ*arch*ˈ*prophet* (COD); in the latter, 'chief, worst': ˈ*arch-*ˈ*enemy*, ˈ*arch-*ˈ*liar*. In instances of the latter type, *arch* is sometimes felt as an independent adjective, and written accordingly: *arch liar*, *arch impostor*. (Cf. what was said on *counter* in 835.) [This, by the way, is the origin of the adj. *arch* = cunning, clever, innocently roguish (COD).] — Note *archangel* [ˈɑːkˌeindʒəl].

843. *auto-* (= self) is combined with nouns, and with adjectives derived from them: ˌ*autobi*ˈ*ography*, ˈ*auto*ˌ*bio*ˈ*graphic*(*al*), ˈ*auto-su*ˈ*ggestion*.

844. *be-* differs from most other prefixes in having (like *a-* [ə]) no independent meaning and being, consequently, unstressed. It is

[1] Also written without a hyphen. The first syllable of this and the next word is also pronounced [æ].

[2] Also with medium stress on the first syllable.

[3] 'Numerous compounds [see note to 837] may be formed by prefixing *anti-* to other words. Those not entered below have double stress.' (Jones, *Pronouncing Dictionary*.) Jones's list should be carefully studied. Note expecially ˈ*anti-*ˈ*climax* with even stress, though grouped by COD with ˈ*antipope*.

used to form transitive verbs from *a*. nouns, *b*. adjectives, *c*. verbs. Examples of *a* are especially common as past participles, and often somewhat contemptuous in meaning: *be-medalled, bespectacled.*[1] An example formed from an adjective is *to belittle* (usu. = to depreciate); but this group is small and unproductive. Examples from verbs are *to bemoan*, *to bemock*, *to besmear*, *to bespatter*. The prefix has a somewhat intensive meaning here, as is also the case with those of group *a*, though there is no implication of contempt.

845. *bi-* is prefixed (usually with a hyphen) to *weekly* and *monthly* (adj. & n.) in the sense of (periodical) 'appearing every two (weeks, months)', sometimes in that of 'appearing twice in a (week, month)'. In scientific adjectives it often means 'having two . . .', e.g. *bisexual* (even stress, or main stress on the second syllable).

846. *co-* (= together) is prefixed to nouns, adjectives and verbs: *ˈco-ˌeduˈcation*, *ˈco-ˈheir*; *co-eˈternal*;[2] *to ˈco-eˈxist*, *to co-ˈoperate.*[2] 'In unfamiliar words, a hyphen or diaeresis is used to indicate pronunciation, and the three methods (cooperate, co-operate, coöperate) are employed arbitrarily.' (COD.) (But *coöperate* is more usual in America than in England.)

847. *counter-* (= against) can be prefixed to nouns and verbs: *ˈcounter-attack* (also vb.), *ˈcounter-revolution*; *to counterˈact*, *to counterˈbalance*. The nouns are usually stressed on the first element, the verbs on the second (but *to ˈcounter-attack*, which may be a case of conversion from noun to verb).

Forms with *counter-* differ from those with *anti-* in that the former usually express an activity, the latter a state of mind.

848. *de-* is a living prefix when it means: 'to remove, to undo (what is indicated by the second element)'. It forms verbs from nouns: *to ˈdeˈcode* (= to decipher code telegram etc.), *to ˈdeˈtrain* (= to discharge troops etc. from train); and from other verbs: *to ˈde-ˈhumanize* (= to divest of human characteristics), *to ˈdeˈmobilize*[3]

[1] But cf. *to befriend* = to help. Those in *-ed* are perhaps rather to be looked upon as cases of 917.

[2] As the stressing shows, the feeling for the meaning of the prefix is weakened in these words; *co-operate* (or *cooperate*) is not really felt as a derivative from *operate*.

[3] Also without full stress on the first syllable (why?).

(troops), *to 'de'nationalize* (= to deprive a person of the membership of his nation; to restore [a nationalized industry] to private ownership). The prefix is pronounced [di:], with strong or medium stress.

De- is not a living prefix and, consequently, unstressed in such words as *defend, depart(ure)*.

849. *dis-* negatives the noun, adjective or verb to which it is prefixed: *dishonour, distrust*; *disobedient, dis'reputable*; *to disagree, to disbelieve.* It may also express deprivation: *to disarm, to disbranch, to discourage*; or the reversal of an action: *to disconnect, to disown* (cf. 869). It occurs mainly in verbs and words with some inherent verbal idea.[1] When it emphatically negatives the second element it may have strong stress: *'disbe'lief, to 'disbe'lieve.* Otherwise it has weak stress before a stressed syllable (*to dis'arm*), medium stress before an unstressed syllable (*ˌdiso'bedient*).

In a few cases there is an alternative pronunciation [diz] besides the regular pronunciation [dis]: [dis'ɑ:m] or [di'zɑ:m], [dis'ɔnist] or [di'zɔnist]; see Jones. In some words always pronounced with [diz], the prefix has lost its clearly negative meaning: *disaster* [di'zɑ:stə], *disease* [di'zi:z] (which is not the opposite of *ease*!).

850. *en-*, *em-* (only before *b* and *p*) forms verbs from nouns, adjectives and verbs. The meaning is chiefly 'to put into': *to embed, to endanger*; or 'to make (into)': *to enslave, to embitter.* With verbs it often has intensive force: *to enkindle, to enwrap.* It is always unstressed.

851. *ex-* (= former, sometime) may be prefixed to personal nouns denoting office or occupation: *ex-chancellor, ex-Prime-Minister, ex-service man*; cf. COD, and *English Studies* XXVII (1946), 21–24, 75–77). In *ex-schoolroom* (Priestley, *English Journey*, Tauchnitz ed., p. 291) it is prefixed to a non-personal noun.

852. On *extra-* (= outside) see 835. Here are some more examples, all of them adjectives or attributive nouns: *ex(tra)-territorial, extra-tropical*, his *extra-cathedral* life.[2] The prefix is strong-stressed; in *extraordinary* [iks'trɔ:dnri] it is hardly felt as such.

---

[1] Jespersen, MEG VI, 26.53.

[2] Kruisinga, *Handbook*^{5}, § 1604.

853. *fore-* might be thought to form compounds rather than derivatives; but as COD shows, *fore* as an independent word is 'developed from compounds with *fore-*', so that the case is the same as that of *counter-* and *extra-*. It is used with nouns as well as verbs, and may refer to place or to time: ˈ*foreground, foreword* (see COD), ˈ*foretaste*; *to fore*ˈ*see*. In ˈ*forearm* it denotes 'the front part of'; *forehead* [ˈfɔrid] is hardly felt to consist of two elements.[1]

854. *hyper-* (= excessively) is used to form adjectives and nouns derived from them: *hyper-critical, hyper-sensitive(ness)*.

855. *in-*: see *un-*.

856. *inter-* (= among, between) is used to form nouns, adjectives and verbs: *intermarriage, international, to interlock*. Note also its combination with attributive nouns: *interschool* (matches), the *inter-war* (period); cf. 840, 841, 851, 852. It has strong or medium stress.

857. *mal-* (= bad[ly]) is a pejorative prefix added chiefly to nouns of action, occasionally to adjectives, rarely to verbs. The second element is always a word of foreign origin.[2] Exx.: ˈ*mala*ˈ*djustment*, ˈ*mal*ˈ*practice*; ˈ*ma*ˈ*lodorous*; *to mal*ˈ*treat*.

858. *mis-* (= bad[ly], wrong[ly]) is more widely used than *mal-*. It is not confined to nouns of action, but freely added to verbs as well. Exx.: ˈ*mis*ˈ*conduct*, ˈ*misde*ˈ*meanor*; *to* ˈ*mis*ˈ*manage, to* ˈ*mis*ˈ*read*. The force, and, consequently, the stress of the prefix is less in words like *mis*ˈ*fortune, to mis*ˈ*lead*.

859. *non-* expresses the same idea as negative *a-*, but is much more widely used. It is prefixed to nouns of action,[3] sometimes in attributive function: ˈ*non-*ˈ*payment*, ˈ*non-a*ˈ*ggression* (pact); to adjectives: ˈ*non-*ˈ*combatant* (also noun), ˈ*non-e*ˈ*xistent*; and occasionally to a verb-stem: ˈ*non-*ˈ*stop* (train, flight, revue, etc.).

ˈ*Noncon*ˈ*formist* is usually written without a hyphen, in spite of even stress; for though *con*ˈ*formist* exists, *Nonconformist* is in far commoner use, and is hardly felt as a derivative from the shorter word.

860. *post-* (opp.: *ante-, pre-*) refers to time or order (rarely to place: *post-genitive*). It is chiefly used to form adjectives and attributive

---

[1] In spite of this, the spelling-pronunciation [ˈfɔːhed] is gaining ground.

[2] The same applies to derivatives with negative *a-*, *auto-* and *hyper-*.

[3] Occasionally to other nouns: *non-member(ship)* (with even or initial stress).

nouns: *ˈpost-diˈluvian* (= after the Flood), *ˈpost-reforˈmation* (times), *ˈpost-ˈwar* (literature). An example with a verb is *to ˈpost-ˈdate* (a letter).

861. *pre-* (= before) is used either in the sense of 'beforehand': (*to*) *ˈpre-aˈrrange*(*ment*); or in that of 'existing before the time of': *ˈpre-Shakeˈspearian* (drama), *ˈpre-Reforˈmation* (times), *ˈpre-ˈwar* (England). In the former sense it forms verbs and verbal nouns; in the latter, adjectives and attributive nouns. It is the opposite of *post-* in the latter sense only.

Verbs like *precede, prepare, prescribe* and their derivatives do not belong here, as their second syllables do not exist separately (at least not in this sense); note also that their first syllables have weak stress. Nor does an adjective like *premature* [ˌpreməˈtjuə], which, of course, does not mean 'mature beforehand'. — Even the standing of a word like *premeditate* is somewhat doubtful, although COD explains it as 'think out beforehand': its first syllable has weak stress, according to Jones: [pri(:)ˈmediteit]. Nor does *prepossess* [ˌpri:pəˈzes] mean 'possess beforehand'.

862. *pro-* (opposite: *anti-*) is used to form adjectives and adjectival nouns: *pro-Boer, pro-German.*

Words like *proceed, propel,* etc. do not belong here, for reasons explained in connection with *pre-* in 861.

863. *re-* (= again) is prefixed to verbs, and to nouns and adjectives connected with them: *to ˈreˈbuild, to ˈreconˈsider, to ˈreˈfuel* (aeroplane during flight); *ˈreˈbirth, ˈreconsˈtruction*; *ˈre-ˈeligible.* Pron. [ri:].

For reasons similar to those given in 861, words like *to reˈmain, to reˈmember, reˈmote* etc., with weak-stressed [ri], or *to ˌrecoˈllect* (= to remember), *ˌrecomˈpense* etc., with medium-stressed [re], do not belong here. Note, however, *to ˈre-coˈllect* (= to collect again), *to ˈre-ˈcover* (an umbrella), by the side of *to reˈcover* [riˈkʌvə] (to regain), and similar pairs. — The case of a word like *to recall* [riˈkɔ:l] is similar to that of *to premeditate* (861).

864. *semi-* (= half) is chiefly prefixed to nouns of foreign origin: *ˈsemiˈcircle, ˈsemiˈvowel*;[1] occasionally to adjectives: *ˈsemi-oˈfficial, ˈsemi-cenˈtennial* (occurring every fifty years); or to participles: *ˈsemi-ˈcivilized, ˈsemi-deˈtached* ('of house: joined to another by party-wall on one side only', COD).

865. *sub-* (= under) usually forms nouns: *ˈsubmarine* (orig. and also adjective), *ˈsubway* (in England: covered, usually underground

[1] Also with medium stress on the third syllable (Jones).

way; in U.S.: underground railway); occasionally adjectives: ˈ*sub*ˈ*conscious* (= not quite conscious); rarely verbs: *to sub*ˈ*let* (of tenant letting part of house to another). It expresses subordination in ˈ*sub-com*ˌ*mittee*, ˈ*sub-*ˈ*editor*, from which by back-formation (823) *to* ˈ*sub-*ˈ*edit*.

866. *super-* (= above) forms nouns and verbs. Exx.: ˈ*super*ˈ*structure*; *to* ˈ*super*ˈ*scribe*. In adjectives it usually means 'beyond': ˈ*super-*ˈ*natural*, or 'excessively': ˈ*super-*ˈ*subtle*. ˈ*Superman* is Bernard Shaw's translation of Nietzsche's *Übermensch*.

867. *trans-*[1] (= across) is used in geographical terms like *transatlantic* (steamer: crossing the Atlantic), in which, however, it may also mean 'beyond' (= American), *transalpine*. It often means: 'from one (place, etc.) to another': *to transplant*, *to trans(s)hip*.

Words like *translation*, *transport* etc., are not derivatives from an English point of view. Cf. 848, 849, 861, 862, 863.

868. *ultra-* (= beyond) is used in a local sense in ˈ*ultra-*ˈ*violet* (rays). Usually, however, it means 'excessively', and receives strong stress: ˈ*ultra-con*ˈ*servative*, ˈ*ultra-*ˈ*fashionable*. From such adjectives nouns may be derived, like ˈ*ultra-con*ˈ*servatism*.

869. *un-* is the commonest negative prefix. It is used with native English words (chiefly adjectives and adverbs) and, to a less extent, with words of foreign (Latin or French) origin. It is hardly necessary to give examples: *un*ˈ*happy*, *un*ˈ*kind*; ˈ*unim*ˈ*portant*; with nouns (less numerous): ˈ*un*ˈ*rest*, ˈ*unem*ˈ*ployment*.

When prefixed to verbs, it denotes an 'action contrary to or annulling that of the simple verb' (COD). Exx.: *to* ˈ*un*ˈ*bend*, *to* ˈ*un*ˈ*button*, *to* ˈ*un*ˈ*dress*, etc. Similar formations from nouns are *to* ˈ*un*ˈ*earth*, *to* ˈ*un*ˈ*horse*; cf. COD *un-*[1] (3). See 849. (Note: *unloose* v. = *loose* v.)

870. In words of Latin or French origin the negative prefix is usually *in-*, assimilated to *im-* before a labial, to *il-* before *l*, and to *ir-* before *r*: *inaudible*, *impolite*, *illegible*, *irreligious*. Though clearly negative in meaning, *in-* (*im-* etc.) is a far less productive prefix

[1] [trænz] or [trɑːnz] in geographical terms, and in a few other words before a voiced sound (see Jones); otherwise [træns], resp. [trɑːns].

than *un-*, which is more firmly rooted in the linguistic consciousness of English people.

'It should also be noted that while most of the *in*-words are settled once for all, and have to be learned by children as wholes, there is always a possibility of forming new words on the spur of the moment with the prefix *un-*.' (Jespersen, MEG VI. 26.16.)

871. In some cases, *un-* is used before an adjective, *in-* before the corresponding noun, which is probably less usual than the adjective:[1] *unable* — *inability*; *unjust* — *injustice*; *unequal* — *inequality*.

872. In a few cases an adjective with the prefix *un-* expresses a neutral meaning, the same adjective with *in-* an unfavourable meaning: *unartistic* — *inartistic*; *unmoral* (also *a-moral*, *non-moral*) — *immoral*.

'The purely neutral sense thus ascribed to *un-* is not that found in many of the most familiar adjectives (*unbeautiful*, *unfair*, *ungraceful*, etc.)' (COD). *Untrue* means 'culpably inconsistent with truth' (*ibid.*).

873. Negative participles may allow of either of two interpretations, depending on the context. Thus *unbending* may be apprehended either as *un-bending*, i.e. 'not bending', or as *unbend-ing*, i.e. 'changing from bent position, relaxing'. Similarly *unmasked*, either *un-masked*, i.e. 'not masked', or *unmask-ed*, i.e. 'deprived of his mask'. When speaking emphatically, the prefix in the former of each pair may receive extra stress.

SUFFIXES

874. An important difference between prefixes and suffixes (apart from their position) is that whereas the former, though not used as separate words, mostly have a distinct meaning of their own (for exceptions see 838 and 844), the latter rarely have, but as a rule only serve to modify the meaning of the main element (*red* — *reddish*), or to convert it into another part of speech (*kind* — *kindness*).

The proportion of Germanic elements is larger among the suffixes than among the prefixes.

The suffixes will be classified according to the parts of speech they help to form: nouns, adjectives, verbs, adverbs.

[1] Kruisinga, *Handbook*[5], § 1621.

Nouns

Personal and Concrete Non-Personal Nouns

875. *-ee* is added to verb stems to denote the person affected by the action: *addressee, employee, payee* ('person to whom bill or cheque is made payable', OED), *testee, trainee.* Words of this kind are stressed on the last syllable. They are often associated with agent-nouns in *-er*: *employer*; occasionally with an agent-noun not derived from an English verb: *biographer — biographee.* In *evacuee* the suffix is added to a truncated verb stem (*to evacuate*).[1] It is further used in forming nonce-words, some of them (half-)humorous: *boree, murderee*;[2] *townee* (see COD). Cf. also *standee* (Am.), 'one who stands, as at a theatrical performance'.

In some law terms the first element is not an English word at all: *lessee* 'person to whom a property is let'; *vendee* 'person to whom a sale is made'.[3] The corresponding agent-nouns end in *-or*: *lessor* [ˈlesɔː], *vendor* [ˈvendɔː].

The passive meaning is less prominent in words like *referee, trustee,* which have no agent-nouns in *-er* or *-or* corresponding to them.

876. *-eer* is added to names of things to form agent-nouns denoting the 'person concerned with' (COD): *auctioneer, mountaineer.* They are stressed on the last syllable. Some have a contemptuous meaning: *pamphleteer, profiteer, racketeer*[4] (orig. Am.: one who practices *racketeering*, i.e. 'organized blackmail of traders by intimidation and violence' [COD]).

As appears from the last word italicized, a derivative in *-eer* may give rise to a noun of action in *-eering*. Another example of this is *privateering* from *privateer*, which is unique in being formed from an adjective, and denoting, not a person, but a vessel (see the definition in COD).

Words like *pioneer, volunteer,* have the same termination, but are not derived from English words.

The suffix is spelt *-ier* in *gondolier* from *gondola*, and a few other words.

877. *-er*[5] is freely used to form agent-nouns from verbs: *baker, hunter, painter, writer,* etc. Most of these denote persons following a regular trade or profession; they often form compounds with

---

[1] It may have been modelled on the French *évacué*.

[2] Jespersen, MEG VI, 13.62.

[3] Kruisinga, *Handbook*[5], § 1655.

[4] They all happen to end in *-teer* (Jespersen, MEG VI, 15.52).

[5] Where nothing is said as to accentuation, the suffix is unstressed.

words denoting the object of the action: *bookseller*, *bricklayer* (807, 1).

Agent-nouns in *-er* may also denote persons doing something either regularly or occasionally, but not by way of trade or profession: a steady *drinker*, a poor *plodder*; *onlooker*, *passer-by* (804), the *writer* of the letter, the *reader* of this book, etc.[1]

878. In some cases *-er* is added to a noun, to denote a person engaged in a trade or profession: *banker*, *glover*, *hatter*. Such formations cannot refer to occasional actions.

On the other hand, *-er* may be added to a verb to denote a tool or an instrument: *duster*, *poker*, *lawn-mower*, *paper-cutter*; or an occurrence: *eye-opener* 'enlightening or surprising circumstance' (COD). A *header* is a 'plunge head first' (COD).[2]

879. In some formations in *-er* the verbal idea is absent. Thus a ˈ*two-*ˈ*seater* is a car with two seats;[3] a *fiver* is a five-pound (or five-dollar) note; a *teen-ager* (Am.) a young person whose age ends in *-teen*; a *lifer* (slang) 'one sentenced to, sentence of, penal servitude for life' (COD); a *three-master*, a vessel with three masts; an *old stager*, an 'experienced person, old hand' (COD).

Non-verbal *-er* is also found in personal nouns derived from geographical nouns or adjectives: *Londoner*, *Hollander*, *foreigner*, *southerner* [ˈsʌðənə].

Note the (school and university) slang use of *-er* to replace another ending: *Rugger* (= Rugby football), *Soccer* [ˈsɔkə] (= Association football), *footer*, *brekker* (= breakfast).

880. It is often said that words like *inspector*, *possessor*, *sailor*, *beggar*, *liar*, are formed with the same suffix, only spelt differently; but though all these nouns have verb stems by the side of them (*to inspect*, etc.), it is doubtful whether they are felt to be *derived* from these verbs in the same way as *writer* is felt to be derived from *to write*. It is probably better not to regard *-or* and *-ar* as English suffixes, but to look upon the specimens mentioned as simple words.

---

[1] This disproves Kruisinga's statement in his *Handbook*[5], § 1661: 'All the names of agents in *-er* denote a permanent occupation or regular action.'

[2] Cf. also COD s.vv. *fruiter* and *fruiterer*.

[3] Cf. p. 267, n. 1; also 806.

881. *-ess* is used to denote female persons as distinct from male persons in similar positions: *countess, hostess, stewardess.* In these cases the first element can denote only a man.

Occasionally *-ess* is added to names of persons that may denote either sex: *authoress, poetess. Murderer* and *adventurer* are shortened by one syllable in this case: *murderess, adventuress.*

We find similar shortenings in some feminine words where the corresponding masculine word can only denote a man: *actor-actress*; *emperor-empress, waiter-waitress*; *warder-wardress. Proprietor-proprietress* and *protector-protectress* belong with the same group phonetically, but with that of the preceding paragraph semantically.

The suffix occurs in three names of animals: *leopardess, lioness, tigress.* (Cf. Bradley, *The Making of English*, p. 58.)

The following pairs show the same suffix in the feminine noun, which, however, can hardly be regarded as a *derivative* from the masculine: *abbot — abbess*; *duke — duchess*; *marquis — marchioness*; *master — mistress*; *negro — negress.*

882. *-ist* can be said to be *added* to only a limited number of nouns: *Calvinist, novelist, violinist*, etc.; an even smaller number of verbs: *copyist*, etc., and to adjectives in *-al*: *loyalist,*[1] *royalist, socialist*, etc. It is difficult, however, to separate these from the numerous words in *-ist* whose first elements are not used as separate words: *atheist, dentist, egoist,*[2] etc.

883. Nouns in *-ist* may be divided into those denoting:

a. persons practising a science or art: *archaeologist, dramatist, novelist, philologist, violinist*;

b. persons exercising a trade or profession: *balloonist, copyist, dentist, tobacconist*;

c. adherents of a system or principle denoted by a noun in *-ism*: *atheist, Calvinist, loyalist, pacifist, Platonist, royalist, socialist*, etc.

d. other persons: *antagonist, colonist, egoist, faddist, sadist* [ˈsædist], etc.

---

[1] Supporter of government (e.g. in Spanish civil war).
[2] *Ego* is not an ordinary English word.

There is also a word *egotist* (see COD), whose *-t-* may be compared with that of *dramatist* (though COD suggests a different explanation). The idea that the *n* of *tobacconist* may be due to the example of *Platonist* (*ibid.*) seems a little fanciful. One might as well compare words like *botanist*, *organist*, etc.

884. *-ite* [ait] may be added to proper names denoting places or persons, in the sense of 'person belonging to or connected with'. On the analogy of *Sybarite*, 'inhabitant of Sybaris; luxurious and effeminate person', the suffix is sometimes added to English place-names: *Claphamite*, *Durhamite*; like *Sybarite*, such names are mostly used contemptuously. A similarly pejorative sense attaches to derivatives from names of persons: *Browningite*, *Ibsenite*, *Wagnerite*. *Pre-Raphaelite* as a term in literary and art history is neutral in meaning.

-ite is also used in scientific words to denote minerals, fossils, explosives, etc.: *anthracite*, *ammonite*, *dynamite*; but what remains of such forms if we remove the suffix is not used as a separate word.

885. *-ster* is another pejorative suffix: *gamester*, *gangster*, *punster*, *trickster*, etc. It is added to non-personal nouns, and expresses: 'person given to the practice of (gaming, etc.), or belonging to (a gang)'.

No pejorative meaning is implied in *roadster*, *songster*, *speedster*, *youngster*, and one or two other words.

Spinster, 'unmarried elderly woman', has ceased to be felt as a derivative.

Diminutives

886. English differs from such languages as Dutch and German by its far more restricted use of diminutives, i.e. 'word(s) describing small specimen of the thing denoted by corresponding primitive word' (COD); and as a rule even those that are usually called diminutive are often rather, or at the same time, AFFECTIVE, i.e. they express the *feeling* with which the person or thing described is regarded. Mere smallness not inducing any kind of feeling is usually denoted by the adjective *small*: *a small glass of milk*, or left unexpressed: *to make a fire*, or implied: *a cottage*.

Smallness may also be denoted by *little*, which, however, is usually affective as well: *a little child*.

887. *-ette* forms pure diminutives denoting things, in modern words like *kitchenette* ('miniature kitchen in modern flat', COD), *leaderette* ('short editorial paragraph in same type as leading article'), *sermonette*. They are stressed on the last syllable.

In those denoting persons the suffix expresses femininity: hence *undergraduette* ('female undergraduate', what is called a 'co-ed' in America; the word is now obsolete), *usherette* ('girl usher at a cinema', Jespersen). These forms are usually facetious as well. The older word *suffragette* (pre-1914) is unique in meaning 'woman who agitated for woman suffrage' (COD); in its origin it was also facetious.

In commercial use, the meaning is 'sham', 'substitute': *flannelette*, *leatherette*.

Cellaret ('cabinet for wine-bottles') is stressed in the same way, in spite of its different spelling. *Owlet* ('young owl'), however, *cablet* (COD) and *islet* stress the first syllable (cf. *-let*). Other words in *-et* (*pocket*, *singlet*, etc.) are no longer derivatives, but simple words.

888. *-ie*/*-y* is used to form pet names of persons or animals from monosyllabic proper names and class-nouns: *Johnny*, *Annie*; *piggy*, *doggie*; occasionally from adjectives: *darky* (= nigger), *deary* or *dearie* (usu. voc.), *fatty*. The suffix implies affection or familiarity (COD).

-ie is originally a Scottish spelling, also adopted in some of the English words.

On forms like *hanky*, *nighty*, etc., see 958.

1. *-ie*/*y* is often added to shortened (and sometimes altered) proper names: *Bobby* (from *Robert*), *Charley* (or *Charlie*), *Kitty* (from *Catherine*), etc.

2. The technical term for attributive 'pet' is 'hypocoristic' (adj. and noun).

889. *-kin* occurs as a diminutive suffix in such words as *catkin* (of willow or birch), *lambkin*, *pilchkin* (see COD s.v. *pilch*).

890. *-let* is more frequently added to names of things than to names of persons. Examples of the former: *booklet*, *eyelet* (see COD), *flatlet*, *leaflet* (COD), *ringlet* (hair!), *streamlet*; a special use (not properly diminutive) is to denote articles of dress or ornaments: *anklet*, *armlet*, *necklet*. Words in *-let* denoting persons usually have a depreciatory meaning: *kinglet*, *princelet*; though less strongly so than those formed with the next suffix.

891. *-ling* has diminutive force[1] in some names of young animals: *catling*, *duckling*, *fledgeling* (see COD), *gosling*; and of young plants: *sapling*, *seedling*. In this sense, however, it is unproductive. The same applies to some words in *-ling* denoting persons: *nurs(e)ling*, *suckling*. The suffix is productive only when expressing contempt: *lordling*, *princeling*; *hireling* (from noun); *weakling* (from adj.); *underling* (from prep./adv.). Words in *-ling* denoting persons of royal or noble rank suggest insignificance (in the speaker's or writer's eyes at least), and may, therefore, to some extent be regarded as diminutives (cf. *-let*).

Abstract and Collective Nouns

892. *-age* forms nouns expressing:

a. an aggregate or collectivity: *acreage* [ˈeikəridʒ] (surface in acres), *cellarage* ('cellar space'), *peerage* (the peers; also, list of peers), etc.;

b. function or condition: *bondage* (slavery), *orphanage* (orphanhood), *peerage* (rank of peer), *shortage*;

c. action: *breakage*, *drainage*, *stoppage* (of wages, etc.);

d. fee or charge: *cartage* ('cost of carting'), *cellarage* ('charge made for storage (*c*) in a cellar', Jespersen), *postage*, etc.; cf. also *percentage*;

e. abode or residence:[2] *hermitage*, *orphanage*, *vicarage*. As will be seen, several nouns in *-age* belong to more than one of these groups.

With the exception of those denoting action, practically all these words are derived from nouns; *shortage* and *roughage* (see COD) are from adjectives.

893. *-al* forms nouns of action from verbs, mostly of French origin: *approval*, *denial*, *recital*, *refusal*, *revival*, *trial*, etc.; *bestowal*, *betrothal*, *renewal*, *withdrawal*.

894. *-ana* [ɑːnə], [einə] is appended to names of persons (sometimes to names of places or other nouns) to denote: 'notable sayings of, [more usually] anecdotes about, publications bearing on':

[1] Though it is *youth* rather than *smallness* that is expressed.

[2] In this sense the nouns are, of course, concrete.

Walpoliana, *Shakespeariana*; *Tunbrigiana* (anecdotes about life at Tunbridge Wells); *Golfiana*.[1]

Though it is always preceded by *i*, the suffix is apprehended as *ana*, as appears from its use as a noun: '(With pl. *anas*) collection of person's memorable sayings; (collect. pl.) anecdotes, literary gossip, about a person' (COD).

895. *-ance*. In 836 *-ant* and *-ent* were mentioned as examples of unproductive suffixes; the same applies to the corresponding nominal terminations *-ance*, *-ence*, *-ancy*, *-ency* (*distance*, *difference*, *constancy*, *consistency*). Yet it seems desirable to point out that *-ance* has been added to a number of native verbs to form nouns of action: *forbearance*, *hindrance*, (good) *riddance*, *utterance*.

896. *-ation*, which in most of the words in which it occurs (*operation*, *stagnation*, etc.) is not combined with an English word, has been analogically added to a few native verbs: *botheration*, *flirtation*, *flo(a)tation* (COD), *starvation*, and to one adverb: *backwardation* (see COD).

897. *-cy* has been abstracted from nouns like *accuracy*, *constancy*, (*lieu*)*tenancy*, etc. corresponding to adjectives like *accurate*, *constant*, etc., or to nouns like (*lieu*)*tenant*, etc., and added to nouns in *-n*, as in *captaincy*, *chaplaincy*, and by analogy to *colonelcy* (in these *-cy* is practically equivalent to *-ship*); to an adjective in *-t* in *bankruptcy* [ˈbæŋk-rəp*t*si]; and to one in *-l* in *normalcy* (= normal conditions; coined by President Harding some time before his election in 1920, and since in common use in U.S.).

898. *-dom* [dəm] is added to (usu. personal) nouns to form nouns expressing:

a. rank or condition: *dukedom*, *earldom*, *martyrdom*, *savagedom*. *Boredom* is from the verb *bore* (cf. COD); *freedom* from the adjective *free*; *wisdom* corresponds to the adjective *wise*.

b. domain or realm:[2] *Christendom* [ˈkrisndəm] (= Christian countries), *heathendom*, *kingdom*, *savagedom*; (in former times also) *dukedom*, *earldom*.

c. a group of persons collectively, 'or = the ways of' (COD):

---

[1] Title of a book about golf; see Kruisinga, *Handbook*[5], § 1635.

[2] Not really abstract; though *Christendom*, *heathendom*, and *savagedom* are, perhaps, collective in this sense.

Christendom (= Christians), *heathendom*; *parsondom*, *schoolmasterdom*; *officialdom* (= officials and their ways; bureaucracy). The last three have an unfavourable meaning; so has *villadom* 'suburban society', which, like *filmdom* (the film world; not necessarily unfavourable), is derived from a non-personal noun.

899. *-ful.* On the question whether nouns in *-ful* (*handful*, etc.) are to be regarded as derivatives or as compounds, see 834.

Note that the plural is *handfuls*, not **handsful*.

900. *-hood* [hud] is added to names of persons, especially such as express family relations, to indicate condition or age: *fatherhood*, *motherhood*, *childhood*, *boyhood*, *girlhood*, *womanhood*, *bachelorhood*, *widowhood*.

A few may have a collective meaning: *brotherhood*, *neighbourhood*, *priesthood*, though they may also express condition; cf. 892 and 898. (On *neighbourhood* cf. COD.)

Falsehood, *hardihood* and *likelihood* are derived from adjectives.

Two derivatives take *-head* as well as *-hood*, with a difference of meaning: *godhead* (= deity) — *godhood* (rarer: state of being a god); *maidenhead* (= virginity) — *maidenhood* (= maiden age).

901. *-ing* as an inflexional suffix (forming gerunds and present participles) has been dealt with in the chapter on Verbs.

When it has neither verbal function nor clearly verbal meaning, it is ad erivational suffix. Examples of derivatives in *-ing* from verbs have been given in 62. Some are derived from nouns; they are either collective in meaning: *bedding*, *matting*, *shipping*, *stabling* (cf. the COD definition of *mews*); or denote 'material for': *sacking*, *shirting*. Cf. COD s.v. *-ing*[1].

902. *-ism* is added to nouns and adjectives to form nouns expressing:

a. typical conduct or condition: *despotism*, *patriotism*, *quixotism*, (cf. COD); *parallelism*.

Heroism [ˈherouizm] from *hero* [ˈhiərou] alters its stressed vowel; *barbarism* corresponds to *barbarous*.

b. a system or principle: *Calvinism*, *Platonism*, *imperialism*, *socialism*, etc. They are often derived from the name of the founder or from adjectives in *-al*; but cf. also *Toryism*, *Whiggism*, *jingoism* (see COD), *classicism* (*classic*[*al*]). Some of them correspond to personal names in *-ist* (883*c*). This also applies to some that do not have an English word for their principal element: *atheism*, *pacifism*, etc. Cf. further *conservatism* (*conservative*).

Note the shifting of stress in *Ca'tholicism* from *'catholic*.

c. a peculiarity of language: *Americanism*, *Anglicism* (and, by analogy, *Briticism*, U.S.), *modernism*, *provincialism*. Not derived from an English word: *archaism* (cf. *archaic*); with shortening of the original word: *euphuism* (rhetorical style of John Lyly's *Euphues* ['ju:fju(:)i:z], 1578).

The suffix is added to syntactic word groups (cf. 806 and 879) in such formations as *sour-grapeism*, *spread-eagleism* (noisy patriotism). It is also used as a noun (chiefly in the plural; cf. *ana*), meaning: 'any distinctive doctrine or practice' (COD) (*He is very fond of isms*).

903. *-itis*, which occurs in names of inflammatory diseases (*appendicitis*, *bronchitis*) is sometimes added to nouns or proper names to express a craze or mania: *allotmentitis* (the craze for allotment-gardens during the war), *Kiplingitis*, *pageantitis* (a craze for pageants, see COD); or a disease (by way of speaking), as in *consulitis*, *Puritanitis* (see the examples in Kruisinga's *Handbook*[5], § 1644).

904. *-ity* in most of the words in which it occurs (*identity*, *voracity*, etc.) is not added to an English word. It is used, however, to derive nouns from some adjectives in *-able* or *-ible*, *-al* and *-ic*(*al*): *readable* — *readability*, *visible* — *visibility*; *sentimental* — *sentimentality*; *historic* — *historicity*; *comical* — *comicality*. Note the modification of the adjective-suffix, and the shifting of the stress.

An isolated example is *oddity* from *odd*. — In words like *certainty*, *cruelty*, *loyalty*, *safety* ['seifti], the suffix takes the shorter form *-ty*. Note *nicety* (['naisiti] or ['naisəti]) from *nice*.

905. *-ment* [mənt] is added to verbs to form nouns expressing action: *acknowledgement*, *argument*, *fulfilment*, *treatment*. Many of these words are formed with the prefix *em-*/*en-*: *embankment*, *embodiment*, *employment*, *endowment*, *enlightenment*, etc. Some of them denote the concrete result of the action: *embankment*, *pavement*, *settlement*. Words like *bewilderment*, *fulfilment*, *refreshment* are really passive in meaning: being bewildered, fulfilled, etc.[1]

Three nouns in *-ment* are formed on adjectives: *oddments* (= odds and ends), *merriment*,[2] and the less common *funniment*. *Oddments* is, of course, a concrete noun (like *embankment*, etc.).

906. *-ness* [nis] may be added to almost any adjective to form nouns expressing state or condition: *goodness*, *kindness*, *harshness*, *sweetness*, *wickedness*, etc. Words of Romance [rəˈmæns] origin often prefer a different formation: *able* — *ability*; *cruel* — *cruelty*; *possible* — *possibility*; *simple* — *simplicity*; *vain* — *vanity*. By the side of these and similar Romance derivatives English derivatives in *-ness* do exist, but are rarely used. Occasionally a derivative in *-ness* is preferred because it is more expressive than the common Romance form, or because the latter might be taken in a concrete sense: *courteousness* — *courtesy*, *divineness* — *divinity*.[3]

907. Present, and especially past participles may also take the suffix: *knowingness*, *lovingness*; *fixedness*, *preparedness*, *unexpectedness*. The participial ending in these latter words is pronounced [id] after [d] or [t], and in participles of one syllable (*fixedness*) or with the stress on the last syllable (*preparedness*), but [d] or [t] in participles of more than one syllable with the last syllable unstressed: *determinedness*.[4]

908. The suffix may also be added to compound adjectives and occasionally to syntactic word-groups: *kind-heartedness*, *self-consciousness*; *matter-of-factness*, *up-to-dateness*, etc.

909. *-ry*/*-ery*. The latter suffix is added to words (chiefly nouns) of one syllable, the former to words of more than one syllable. The meaning expressed may be:

a. action or condition: *pedantry*, *rivalry*; *drudgery*, (*tom*)-*foolery*,[5] *slavery*.

---

[1] Jespersen, MEG VI, 21.83.

[2] When COD says that *merriment* is 'really' from obs. vb *merry*, it means 'historically'. In Modern English, however, *merriment* can only be associated with the adjective *merry*.

[3] Cf. Kruisinga, *Handbook*[5], § 1648.

[4] Less common than *determination*.

[5] In compounds the number of syllables of the second element decides.

b. science, occupation, trade, etc.: *chemistry*, *dentistry*; *cookery*.

c. abode of one or more persons; colony of animals: *deanery*, *nunnery*, *nursery*; *gullery*, *rookery*, *swannery*; cf. also *pinery* 'place in which pineapples are grown; plantation of pines' (COD), *shrubbery*, and the curious word *snuggery* 'snug place, esp. person's private room or den' (COD).

d. collectivity of persons: *Irishry*, *peasantry*, *yeomanry*; or of things: *crockery*. Cf. also some of the words under *c*.

e. A special group is formed by words like *bakery*, *brewery*, *fishery*,[1] *pottery*,[1] which are connected with the agent-nouns *baker*, *brewer*, *fisher*,[2] *potter*, as well as with the verbs or nouns *bake*, *brew*, *fish*, *pot*. They denote a baker's, brewer's, etc. place of work, the place where fish is caught or pots are made.

1. *Beggary* (*a*), from *beggar* (880) rather than from *to beg*; *soldiery* (*d*), from *soldier*; and *rectory* (*c*) from *rector*, are formed with a suffix *-y* rather than *-ery*.

2. Note that some of these derivatives may belong to more than one group; thus *deanery* may also mean 'group of parishes presided over by rural dean' (COD). Cf. 892.

910. *-ship* may be added to nouns (chiefly names of persons) to form abstract nouns expressing state or condition: *authorship*, *friendship*, *membership*, *scholarship*. In *hardship* (see COD) the suffix is added to an adjective.

Lordship, *ladyship*, and the similarly formed *worship* are used with a possessive pronoun of the second or third person 'in speaking deferentially to or of a lord' (COD), lady or magistrate.

Words like *fellowship* and *scholarship* may also denote the emoluments pertaining to the position of a 'fellow' or 'scholar' in the special sense which these terms have at English universities (and, as regards the latter, public schools).

Township (see COD) is concrete in meaning.

Adjectives

911. *-able* [əbl] is chiefly added to transitive verbs to form adjectives meaning 'that can or deserves to be *-ed*' (in which *-ed* stands

[1] *Fishery* and *pottery* may also belong to *b*.
[2] Now usu. *fisherman*.

for any past participle of a transitive verb): *breakable*, *eatable*, *exchangeable*, *pitiable*, *readable*, *reliable*,[1] *understandable*, etc. It is often used in combination with the negative prefix *un-*: *unforgettable*, *unknowable*, *unspeakable*, *unthinkable*.

A number of such derivatives have an active sense: *agreeable*, *comfortable*, *suitable*.

912. A few adjectives in *-able* are derived from nouns: *impressionable*, *knowledgeable* (= well-informed), (*un*)*objectionable*,[1] (*un*)-*sal*(*e*)*able*, *treasonable* (= guilty of treason).

913. In words of Latin origin the suffix is often spelt *-ible* [əbl]: *convertible*, *discernible*, *inexpressible* (but cf. *delectable*, *detectable*, and others). Most of these, however, are not derived from English words: *audible*, *incorrigible*, *intelligible*, (*il*)*legible*, *negligible*, *responsible*, (*in*)*visible*.

The following words, though spelt with *-able*, are not *derived*[2] from modern English words either, as is shown by the difference of stress and, consequently, of vowel-sounds: *ˈadmirable — to adˈmire*; *ˈcomparable — to comˈpare*; *ˈpreferable — to preˈfer*; (*ir*)*ˈrevocable — to reˈvoke*. See also Jones's *Pronouncing Dictionary*.

914. Some derivatives in *-able* are often used as nouns, especially in the plural: *drinkables*, *eatables*, *valuables*; and similarly *combustibles*, *comestibles*. Cf. 786.

915. *-al* is added to nouns to form adjectives meaning 'of the nature of', 'belonging to':[3] *brutal*, *cultural*, *educational*, *fictional*, *occasional*, *provisional*. Only a few are derived from native words: *coastal*,[4] *tidal*.

Note the change of vowel-sound in words like *nation* [ˈneiʃən] — *national* [ˈnæʃnl], *nature* [ˈneitʃə] — *natural* [ˈnætʃrəl].

---

[1] Meaning: 'that can be relied *on*'. Similarly *available* 'that one can avail *oneself of*'; *indispensable* 'that cannot be dispensed *with*'; *unobjectionable* (912) 'that cannot be objected *to*'. (The italics do not, of course, mean that these prepositions are to be stressed.)

[2] They are, of course, *associated* with them.

[3] Jespersen, MEG VI, 22.14.

[4] *Coast* may not be a native word in origin, but is at any rate felt as a native word.

Words like *continual*, *corporal*, *individual*, *papal*, *royal*, etc. are not derived from English words. *Colossal* is from a shortening of *colossus*.

On adjectives in *-ical* see 928.

916. *-an* is used to derive adjectives (also used as nouns) from geographical names in *-a*, the vowel being dropped before the suffix: *African*, *American*, *Indian*, *Russian*, etc.[1] That the suffix is apprehended as *-an*, not as *-n*, appears from such a form as *Chi'cagoan*.[2]

The suffix may also be added to personal names: *Lutheran*, *Mohammedan*, *Thackerayan* ['θækəriən], *Victorian*; note also *republican*. Such derivatives are used either as adjectives or as nouns, meaning either '(person) following the doctrines or style of'[1] or: 'belonging to the period of'. *Elizabethan* [iˌlizə'bi:θən] from *Elizabeth* is chiefly used to denote the period (1558–1603).

Note the change of spelling and pronunciation in *Bodleian* [bɔd'li(:)ən] (founded by Sir Thomas *Bodley*), *Rugbeian* (= of *Rugby*) [rʌg'bi(:)ən], due to the learned character of these words; but *Bodleian* is also stressed on the first syllable. — The stress is also shifted in *suburban* [sə'bə:bən] (adj. only) from *suburb* ['sʌbə:b].

917. *-ed* is added to nouns to form adjectives meaning 'having', 'provided with': *booted and spurred*, *cultured*, *landed*[3] (property), *moneyed*, *talented*, *wooded*. Cf. also 844*a*; and, as regards pronunciation, 1*d*.

It is especially common in compounds consisting of adj. (or numeral) + noun + *ed*: *'blue-'eyed*, *'fair-'haired*, *'high-'spirited*, *'old-'fashioned*, *'broad-'leaved* (cf. 233), *'good-'natured*, *'quick-'witted*[4]; *one-eyed*, *double-barrelled*, *three-cornered*.

The first element may also be an attributive noun: *ash-coloured*, *'gold-'laced*, *'horn-'rimmed*.

Of a different, though outwardly similar type are combinations of an adverb + derivative in *-ed*: *'well-'mannered*, *'moderately-'sized*

[1] Jespersen, MEG VI, 21.11.
[2] The vowel of the second syllable is [ɑ:] in England, often [ɔ:] in America, never [ei].
[3] In *landed property* the adjective means 'consisting of —'; in *the landed nobility* it has the usual sense of 'provided with —'.
[4] But, of course, *a 'quick-witted 'lad* etc. The same with *half-witted*.

(beside ˈ*moderate-*ˈ*sized*). Such groups are not always hyphened: ˈ*cheerfully* ˈ*minded*, ˈ*highly* ˈ*priced*.

Adjectives in *-ed* may also be preceded by *un-*: *unskilled* (cf. 911). OED gives as one of the meanings of *area*: 'the *unseated* part of a church'.

Derivatives in *-ed* from nouns should be distinguished from the past participles of regular verbs; thus *wooded* is from the noun *wood*, but *weeded* from the verb *to weed*.

918. *-en* is used as a suffix in a few adjectives derived from names of materials: *wooden*, *woollen*, *leaden*, *earthen*, *flaxen*, *wheaten*, etc.

The *-en* forms have to compete with the material nouns used attributively (797), and are steadily losing ground. Compounds with *-wood*, e.g., do not take *-en*: *a sandalwood box* (see Kruisinga, *Handbook*[5], § 1868). We find *lead pipes* as well as *a leaden roof*. *Earthen* alone seems to be successfully resisting the encroachment of the attributive noun: *earthen pots* (never *earth pots*). Usually *woollen stockings* and *wheaten bread*; *flax* (also *flaxen*) thread.

In the cases of *silver* and *beech* adjectives in *-(e)n* are now hardly ever used; in those of *copper*, *glass*, *iron*, *steel*, and a few others, such adjectives do not even exist.

919. Some adjectives in *-en* are only or chiefly used in a figurative sense ('resembling', not 'made of'). Such are *golden* (*a golden opportunity*, *the Golden Age*, *the Golden Fleece*), *silken* (*her silken hair*), *brazen* (cf. *brass*) (*a brazen hussy*); *flaxen hair* (cf. 918).

When *leaden* and *wooden* are used figuratively (in the sense of 'heavy', resp. 'stiff'), they do not have to compete with the nouns: *a leaden atmosphere*, *wooden manners*. Cf. 591.1.[1]

In literary (biblical) English we find *the Golden Calf* and *the Brazen Serpent*; in Greek mythology *the golden apples* (of the Hesperides).

920. *-ern* [ən][2] is added to the names of the points of the compass, not, however, without phonetic modifications in the case of two of them: *eastern* (*the Eastern Empire*), *western* (*the western hemisphere*), *northern* (ˈnɔːðən], *southern* [ˈsʌðən].

Especially in reference to wind, forms in *-erly* also occur: *a northerly* [ˈnɔːðəli] *wind*.

---

[1] See also the article on *-En Adjectives* in Fowler's MEU.

[2] Continental students are warned against a tendency to pronounce a consonantal [r] in this ending, and in such a word as *modern*.

921. *-ese* is used to form adjectives from some names of foreign countries and towns, an unstressed final syllable being dropped (cf. 916): *Chinese, Japanese, Maltese, Portuguese*; *Genoese, Milanese, Pekinese, Viennese.*

These adjectives are also used as nouns in the way explained in 778, to describe the whole population or a representative group (e.g. the army) as distinct from individuals (*the Chinese* v. *some Chinamen*).[1] In addition to this they may be used to denote one or more individuals: *a Japanese, many Portuguese.* They are not, however, used in the genitive.

922. Adjectives in *-ese* are further used to denote the language in question: *Chinese* etc. In this function they are also used as nouns. The suffix may be added in a derogatory sense to names of authors and some other nouns to denote a mannered diction or style: *Johnsonese, Carlylese* ('as though a non-English language', COD); *journalese, translationese.* These words are almost exclusively used as nouns.

923. *-esque* [ˈ*esk*] is added to names of artists to express 'after the manner of': *Danˈtesque, Rembrandtesque, Turneresque*; in 1936 a newspaper coined the word *Garboesque.*[2] Unlike *-ese* (in *Johnsonese* etc.), this suffix is not derogatory.

Cf. also *picaresque* (novel; from Sp. *pícaro*), *picturesque.*

924. *-fold* is added to cardinal numerals higher than one with the sense of 'multiplied by': *twofold, tenfold, a thousandfold.* Also to *many* [ˈmeni]: *manifold* [ˈmænifold]. These words are chiefly literary (which also explains the phonetic dissociation of *manifold* from *many*).

They are also used adverbially: *repaid tenfold* (COD).

The occasional use of the hyphen shows that we have here another borderline case between composition and derivation; see 834 f.

925. *-ful* has been dealt with in 834 (mark note 1 on *forgetful*, etc.).

926. *-ian* [iən] is added to surnames and to the Christian names of kings and queens: *Dickensian, Gladstonian, Pickwickian, Shakespearian*; *Arthurian*; *Edwardian, Georgian.* The latter, like *Eliza-*

---

[1] Jespersen, MEG VI, 19.82.
[2] Jespersen, MEG VI, 19.66.

bethan and *Victorian* (916), chiefly express 'belonging to the period of' (*Georgian poetry*, etc.). *Arthurian* is used in much the same way as, e.g., *Shakespearian*: *Arthurian romance*, etc.; cf. *Shakespearian tragedy*.

The mainly literary character of these adjectives also appears from the shifting of the stress to the syllable immediately before the ending, and the consequent change of vowel-sound: [ˈglædstən] — [glædsˈtouniən].[1] Cf. also *Shavian* [ʃeiviən] from (George Bernard) *Shaw* [ʃɔ:].

The suffix is also added to geographical names: *Bostonian*, *Canadian*, *Corinthian*, *Parisian*, *Venetian*; in the case of English towns chiefly to their Latinized stems: *Oxonian*, *Mancunian*.[2]

Like derivatives in *-ese*, forms in *-ian* are freely used as nouns; but unlike them, they take *-s* in the plural.

927. *-ic*. Most adjectives in *-ic* are not of English formation: *energetic* (cf. *energy*), *emphatic* (cf. *emphasis*), *systematic* (cf. *system*), etc.; and, *a fortiori*,[3] such words as *comic*, *domestic*, *laconic*, *phonetic*, *tragic*.

We have English derivatives in some adjectives from surnames (*Byronic*, *Miltonic*, *quixotic*) or from names of countries (*Icelandic*); also in such a semi-ironical form as *aldermanic* (gown, etc.). These show the same shifting of stress as those in *-ian*: [ˈɔ:ldəmən] — [ˌɔ:ldəˈmænik].

928. *-ical*. Many (not all) adjectives in *-ic* that are not felt as English derivatives may take the living suffix *-al* (915): *classical*, *economical*, *historical*, *political*, *tragical*. It is in accordance with the different status of *-ic* and *-ical* from a modern English point of view that adjectives in *-ic* usually have a more scientific, those in *-ical* a more popular signification[4], as *economic subjects* (= that have to do with the science of economics), but *we shall have to be more economical* (= less wasteful). This is not in disagreement with the statement of COD that '*-ical* indicates a vaguer connection with the

[1] Except after [r], the [i] sounds almost like [j]; see the transcriptions in Jones's *Pronouncing Dictionary*.

[2] An *Old Mancunian* is an old pupil of the Manchester Grammar School.

[3] For pronunciation(s), see Jones.

[4] Cf. Kruisinga, *Handbook*[5], § 1696.

original noun[1] than *-ic* (*comic* paper, *comical story*)'. Cf. also *a historic spot* (= noted in history), and *a historical novel* (= dealing with history); *a great philosophic advance* (= advance in philosophy), and *Don't be so philosophical* (if one were poking fun at someone's metaphysical talk or air).[2]

929. Some adjectives in *-ical* are derived from *nouns* in *-ic*: *critical, logical, musical, stoical.* Cf. 915.

Words like *practical* and *technical* can hardly be called derivatives, for the former is not from *practice*, and *technic*, whether as a noun or as an adjective, is little used.

An example of an adjective in *-ical* formed by adding this termination to a word not ending in *-ic*, is *non'sensical* (imitated in the nonce-word *'common-'sensical*).

930. *-ing.* It was pointed out in 63 that a form in *-ing* derived from a verb may have the function and meaning of an adjective: *an amusing story*; *My experience was trifling and amateurish compared with his* (Priestley, *English Journey*, Ch. X). The adjectival character of such forms also appears from their being qualified by the adverb *very*, which is not used with verbal forms: *a very amusing story* (cf. *a story that amused me very* much; *he was* much *amused by it*).

Adjectives in *-ing* may also be used predicatively: *They were too (un)enterprising* (note the possibility of prefixing *un-*). For further examples see Kruisinga, *Handbook*[5], § 1698.

931. *-ish* occurs in adjectives denoting nationalities or languages, some of them derived from the name of the country (or county, cf. 795) or the race (*Kentish*; *Danish, Jewish, Polish, Swedish, Turkish*), others only associated with them (*British, Cornish, English, Flemish, Irish, Spanish*). To these may be added *out'landish* (= foreign looking or sounding), and, perhaps, *heathenish* (= like a heathen).

932. The last two words lead on to the addition of *-ish* to other personal nouns: *boyish, girlish* (= proper to the nature of), and to a few non-personal nouns (*feverish*). When added to a noun denoting

---

[1] Though one wonders what the 'orig. n.' is in the case of *comic(al)*; surely not *comedy*?

[2] Jespersen, MEG VI, 22.37.

something objectionable, the derivative naturally has an unfavourable meaning: *brutish* (cf. *brutal*, 915), *devilish*, *foolish*, *hellish*, *slavish*, *snobbish*, *wolfish*; from a verb: *snappish*. This is also the case in some derivatives from personal nouns in themselves neutral in sense: *childish* (as against *childlike*, 937), *amateurish*, *mannish* (as against *manly*, 937), *womanish* (as against *womanly*), *popish* (as against *papal*), *selfish*; from a non-personal noun: *bookish*; from an adverb: *uppish*; and from a syntactic group of verb + adverb: *stand-offish*.

-ish may form various nonce-words from names of persons or things: *John Bullish*, *old-maidish*, *honey-moonish*, *will-o'-wispish*, etc. See Jespersen, MEG VI, 19.64.

933. The suffix may be added to adjectives of one or (less often) two syllables, especially those denoting colour, in the sense of 'rather': *bluish*, *greenish*, *reddish*; *earlyish*, *heavyish*, *longish*, *oldish*, *stiffish*, *youngish*.

In recent colloquial use *-ish* may be added to numerals in approximate designations of time:

> Eightish then, next Tuesday, eh?[1]
> How old is she? — Thirtyish.

934. *-less* [lis] (= without) may be freely added to nouns: *endless*, *fearless*, *lifeless*, *penniless*, *restless*, etc. *Doubtless* is used only as an adverb.

On the analogy of derivatives in which the noun is identical in form with a verb (*countless*, *restless*), the suffix has come to be added to some verbs, with the sense of 'not to be — ed': *dauntless*, *tameless* (poetical), *tireless*; and, with intransitive meaning, *fadeless*, *relentless*.

935. *-less* is the negative counterpart of *-ful*;[2] hence such pairs as *faithless* — *unfaithful*, *merciless* — *unmerciful*. There is considerable difference in meaning between *lawless* and *unlawful*; see COD.

In other cases *-less* competes with *un-*/*in-* . . . *-able*: *countless* — *uncountable*; *numberless* — *innumerable*.

936. *-like* forms adjectives from nouns: *childlike*, *godlike*, *ladylike*,

[1] OED Supplement, *-ish*.
[2] Jespersen, MEG VI, 23.33.

owl-like. Such words are again on the border-line between derivatives and compounds; cf. *-fold* and *-ful*.

937. *-ly* is added to personal nouns to form adjectives meaning 'having the qualities of': *cowardly*, *gentlemanly*, *kingly*, *manly*, *masterly*,[1] *scholarly*; and to non-personal nouns: *earthly*, *heavenly*, *leisurely*, *lively* (< *life*), *lovely* (= beautiful).

When there is also a derivative in *-ish* (932) with an unfavourable meaning (*a mannish woman*), the adjective in *-ly* has a laudatory sense: *manly*, *womanly*, that in *-like* a neutral one: *manlike* = 'having good or bad qualities of a man' (COD). Cf. also *gentlemanly* (of inner qualities) and *gentlemanlike* (of appearance, dress, etc.);[2] but only: *ladylike*.

In derivatives from *hour*, *day*, *night*, *week*, *fortnight*, *month*, *quarter*, *year*, the adjective in *-ly* denotes periodic recurrence. Cf. also *bi-weekly*, *bi-monthly* (845).

On forms like *northerly* see 920.

938. There are a few derivatives in *-ly* from adjectives: *kind* — *kindly*, *low* — *lowly*, *sick* — *sickly*. *Cleanly* [ˈklenli] is phonetically different from *clean* [kliːn].

939. *-ous* [əs] in words like *conscious*, *dubious*, *tremendous*, is not an English derivational suffix. It would be hard to deny it this status, however, in words like *dangerous*, *mountainous*, *nervous*, etc., where the adjective consists of the corresponding noun + *-ous*. And we have undoubted derivatives in cases like *murderous*, *slumb(e)rous*, *thunderous*, where the noun-element is a native word.

Note also the addition of -(*i*)*ous* in *flirtatious* (cf. *flirtation*, 896), *burglarious*, *uproarious* (the two latter with shifting of stress).

940. *-some* [səm] forms adjectives from nouns, with the sense 'productive of': *burdensome*, *fearsome* (usu. jocular), *quarrelsome*, *troublesome*. It is also added to some verbs, in the sense of 'apt to': *tiresome*, *wearisome*.

Words like *handsome* and *wholesome* are not felt as derivatives.

We have a different suffix in *foursome* 'game of golf between two pairs' and *twosome* '(game, dance, etc.) for two persons' (COD).

[1] To be distinguished from *masterful* = 'self-willed, imperious' (COD).

[2] Jespersen, MEG VI, 22.72. The distinction is not an absolute one; cf. COD.

941. *-th* is added to most cardinal numerals to form the corresponding ordinals: *fourth*, *ninth*, *thirteenth*, *twenty-sixth*, *hundredth*, *thousandth*; and, with phonetic changes, *fifth* and *twelfth*. Note the spelling *eighth* [eitθ].

Cardinals in *-ty* take [iθ] or [əθ][1]: *twentieth* [ˈtwentiiθ], [ˈtwentiəθ], *sixtieth*, etc.

Cf. also *the* n^{th} [enθ] *power*, *for the* n^{th} *time*.

942. *-ward* is added to local adverbs and to certain nouns denoting place to form adjectives expressing direction: *backward*, *downward*, *forward* (< *fore*), *onward*, *upward*; *eastward*, *heavenward*, *homeward*, *landward*.

As adverbs these words often take *-s*: *backwards*, etc. The forms without *s* are commoner in Am.

943. *-y* is freely added to nouns to form adjectives meaning 'full of, composed of, having the character of' (COD): *bony*, *catty* ('sly and spiteful'), *earthy*, *fiery* [ˈfaiəri] (< *fire* [faiə]), *horsy* [ˈhɔːsi] (= having to do with horses; cf. COD), *noisy* [ˈnɔizi], *panicky*, *slangy*, *stony*, etc. As OED points out, 'New derivatives tend in a large measure to be colloquial, undignified or trivial' — cf. *fishy* (COD), *nervy* (COD), *headachy*, *second-classy*, etc.[2]

Adjectives in *-y* are occasionally derived from adjectives: *paly* (poet.: 'somewhat pale', COD), *stilly* (poet., = still, quiet), *whity-brown* (i.e. brown inclining to white); and from verbs: *catchy* (= attractive), *choos(e)y* (= fastidious), *sticky*, etc.

Some adjectives in *-y* are not derived from existing E. words: *empty heavy*, *merry*.

944. In a form like *woodsy* (Am.), *-y* is added to the plural *woods* used in a collective sense (cf. 249). Similar forms are *sudsy* (water) (from [*soap*]-*suds*) (Am.), and *folksy* 'sociable' (OED and Supplement). From these we may pass on to *tricksy* 'playful', as distinct from *tricky* 'crafty', and to *cocksy*, by the side of *cocky*, both meaning 'conceited'. From the latter one might abstract a suffix *-sy* [zi/si]; but whether the presence of such a suffix is to be

[1] See Jespersen, MEG VI, 24.42.
[2] Jespersen, MEG VI, 13.32.

assumed in *tipsy* (COD) seems rather doubtful. Cf. also OED s.vv. *Flimsy* and *Pudsy*.

The nonce-word *weepsy*, quoted by Jespersen in MEG VI, 13.39, is probably formed on the analogy of *tipsy*.

Verbs

945. *-en* [ən] is added to adjectives to form verbs, most of which may be transitive as well as intransitive: *to blacken* 'to make, or to become black', *to darken, to deepen, to fasten, to harden, to moisten, to shorten, to widen*, etc.[1]

The suffix is never added to adjectives ending in a vowel or vowel-like; these are either converted into verbs without any suffix: *to free, to narrow, to clean, to pale*, or give rise to different formations: *to renew, to impoverish* (= to make poor), etc. Sometimes both a converted adjective and a derivative in *-en* exist: *to black, to blacken; to loose, to loosen; to rough, to roughen*; on the difference see COD.

A few derivatives show a prefix as well as a suffix *en*: *to enlighten, to enliven, to embolden*. The identity of the first and last syllables, however, is merely a matter of spelling; in sound the two are quite different: [inˈlaitn).

946. In *to lessen* and *to worsen* the suffix is added to a comparative; in *to frighten, to heighten* [ˈhaitn], *to lengthen* and *to strengthen* it is added to nouns, all but the first associated with adjectives.

947. *-fy* [fai] in verbs like *to certify, to satisfy, to signify*, etc., is not added to English words. Derivatives in *-fy* formed from English words are often jocular or colloquial; their meaning is 'to make' (what the main element expresses or suggests). The suffix is added in the first place to nouns and adjectives in [i]: *cockneyfied, countrified, dandified, ladified; to prettify*, etc. Those given in the *ed*-form occur chiefly as past participles. In some the original spelling of the noun may be preserved: *countryfied*, etc. Nouns and adjectives not ending in [i] take *-ify*: *to speechify; to Frenchify*.

There is no jocular or colloquial suggestion about derivatives like *to beautify, to glorify, to intensify*. The latter word was coined by Coleridge in 1817 (see OED s.v. *intensify*).

[1] Note that all these adjectives are monosyllabic, and (with one exception) of native origin. — The student is recommended to read the article on *-En Verbs from Adjectives* in Fowler's MEU.

948. *-ize* occurs in many verbs adopted from Greek, Latin or French: *to scandalize, to civilize, to organize.* As a derivational suffix it has been added to many English nouns (esp. proper names) and adjectives: *to Bowdlerize, to circularize, to macadamize, to mesmerize; to Americanize, to familiarize, to legalize, to nationalize, to soberize.* Note *to patronize* (with [æ]) from *patron* (with [ei]).

The meaning is chiefly 'to make', 'to treat in the way of'. Most of these verbs are transitive; *to materialize* (cf. COD) may also be intransitive. *To apologize, to botanize, to sympathize,* etc., are always intransitive; note that the form minus the suffix is not an English word.

By the side of *-ize,* we also find the spelling *-ise*; the latter is the rule in words *not* from Greek (*advertise, despise,* etc.; but cf. *recognize*).

Adverbs

949. *-ly* forms adverbs (chiefly of manner) from adjectives (including participles and ordinal numerals): *greatly, roughly, sweetly; first(ly), secondly, thirdly, lastly; mostly; lovingly, smilingly; decidedly, hurriedly.* A few are derived from nouns: *instantly, namely, partly, purposely.*

Adjectives ending in consonant + syllabic [l] have adverbs in consonant + [li]: *noble — nobly, possible — possibly.*

Participles in *-ed* followed by the suffix *-ly* are pronounced according to the rule of 907: *fixedly* [ˈfiksidli], *determinedly* [diˈtəːmindli], etc.

950. Adjectives in *-ic* (927) do not have adverbs in *-icly,* except *politicly* (= prudently) and *publicly.* The adverbial suffix is freely added to adjectives in *-ical* (928): *historically,* etc. Hence *-ally* is transferred to those that only end in *-ic*: *emphatically, systematically,* etc.

951. Adjectives in *-ly* (937) rarely take the adverbial suffix *-ly*: *friendlily, jollily, livelily.* As a rule the adverbial idea is expressed by a phrase, as *in a friendly way, in a lively manner,* etc. Cf. also *with difficulty* instead of the rare form *difficultly*; *with perfect ease* by the side of *perfectly easily* (Jespersen, MEG II, 12.25).

Likely is sometimes used as an adverb, chiefly when preceded by *most* or *very*: *You may be very likely*[1] *right in that* (COD). (Cf. *a likely story*; *it is not likely to happen.*) Cf. also the not uncommon use of *masterly* as an adverb: *It is masterly done* (E. M. W. Tillyard, *Shakespeare's Problem Plays*, p. 27).

The adjectives in *-ly* mentioned in the last paragraph of 937 (*hourly*, etc.) are also used as adverbs: *I am expecting him hourly.*

952. The negative of *possibly* as an adverb of modality is *not possibly*:

> Possibly they are related.
> I cannot possibly come.

Impossibly is not used as an adverb of modality, but *not impossibly* is:

> Not impossibly they are related.

Impossibly is used as an adverb of degree:

> He came at an impossibly early hour.

953. As was pointed out in 771, some words may function as adverbs as well as adjectives: *clean* (= completely) (*gone*), *dead* (*tired*), *wide* (*awake*). These are used as adverbs of degree. Other examples are: *bitter* (*cold*), *clear* (*-cut*) (= well defined), *pretty* (*good*). Some of these combinations occur so frequently that they come to be regarded as compounds. This is sometimes indicated by the spelling with a hyphen (cf. also *wide-spread*, and the noun *wide-awake* 'soft wide-brimmed felt hat' [COD]; *his new-found prosperity*).

Occasionally the adverb in these combinations has an alternative form in *-ly*: *deadly tired*, *bitterly cold.*

954. Adverbs without *-ly* may also be used as adjuncts of manner. Exx.: *He ran as hard as he could*; *Don't talk so loud!* (But: *talking loudly all the time.*) *Come quick*(*ly*)! *Look sharp!*[2] In case there is an alternative (*loud* — *loudly*, *quick* — *quickly*) colloquial English usually prefers the shorter form. Note *close behind*, but *closely guarded.*

There is an adverb of manner *hardly* (*He had been hardly* [=

---

[1] This is, of course, an adverb of modality, not of manner.

[2] Cf. also *easy-going*, *true-born* (822), *dry-clean* (821).

harshly] *treated*), but as a rule *hardly* is an adverb of degree equivalent to *scarcely*: *It is hardly fair.*[1] — *Fast* never takes *-ly*. — After *more than*, *usual* only takes *-ly* before an adjective: *more than usually bitter*, but *He spoke more than usual*;[2] also: *as much as usual.*

On *quicker* and *quickest* etc. as adverbs see 556.

955. *-ways*, *-wise* is used in a group of adverbs derived from nouns, pronouns or (occasionally) adjectives. Some occur with either ending: *lengthways, lengthwise*; *noways, nowise* ('in no manner, not at all'); *sideways, sidewise*. *Always* (not felt as a derivative; see also the pronunciations registered by Jones) has no alternative. Many others only take *-wise*: *clockwise, likewise, otherwise, sunwise.* It is, in fact, the only productive suffix of the two: *Use it clubwise or pokerwise, Go crabwise or frogwise*, etc. (Fowler, MEU).

Forms in *-ways* occasionally occur without *s*: *noway.*

On the character of these forms (whether derivatives or compounds) cf. 834 f.; cf. also such evident compounds as *to walk crab-fashion* (COD).

---

[1] Often as an understatement for *it is unfair.*

[2] Jespersen, MEG VI, 22.98. Cf.: We *usually* went to church on Sunday mornings.

CHAPTER THREE

ADDITIONAL REMARKS ON WORD FORMATION

956. Attention was drawn in 823–824 to the phenomenon called BACK-FORMATION: *housekeeper* > *to housekeep* (usually: *to keep house*); *sleep-walking* > *to sleep-walk* (usually: *to walk in one's sleep*).

The phenomenon is not limited to compounds, but also occurs with simple words ending in a syllable that may be mistaken for a suffix. The resulting new word is usually a verb, the original one a noun or adjective: *burglar* > *to burgle*; *butcher* > *to butch*; *(sub-)editor* > *to (sub-)edit* (865); *legislator* > *to legislate*; *enthusiasm* > *to enthuse*; *reminiscence* > *to reminisce*; *resurrection* > *to resurrect*; — *frivolous* > *to frivol*; *lazy* > *to laze*; *peevish* > *to peeve.* Most of these formations are slightly humorous; *to (sub-)edit* (in the sense of 'to be (sub-)editor of a newspaper or periodical') and *to legislate* are technical, like *to televise* (< *television*) and *to typewrite* (823).

957. Back-formation, which results in a new word usually belonging to a different part of speech from the original word,[1] should be distinguished from mere SHORTENING, which does not affect the identity of the word.

In shortening it is usually the unstressed syllables that are lost: *dig(ging)s*, *lab(oratory)*,[2] *photo(graph)*, *vet(erinary surgeon)*,[3] etc. Also in Christian names: *Ben(jamin)*, *Em(ily)*, *Fred(erick)*, etc.

---

[1] *To sleep-walk* (or rather a finite form like *the heroine sleep-walks* [Jespersen, MEG VI, 9.71; not in OED]) < *sleep-walking* is no exception, for the latter is a verbal noun.

[2] Acc. to Jones, [ləˈbɔrətəri] is now more usual in England than [ˈlæbərətəri].

[3] Hence, by conversion, *to vet*: 1. to treat an animal medically; 2. (orig. humorous) to treat a person medically; 3. to test or examine (a person, apparatus).

Sometimes a stressed syllable gets lost as well: *exam(ination)*,[1] *prep(aration)* (at school), *Prom(enade concert)*, *a good spec(ulation)*; *maths* < *mathematics*. In these cases the medium-stressed syllable takes over the word-stress. Shortenings like *pro(fessional)*, *Zoo(logical Gardens)* must have been made through the eye rather than through the ear; but compare *Vic(toria)*.

958. A shortened name like *Vic* < *Victoria* may have the 'hypocoristic' ending *-y* affixed to it: *Vicky*, *Freddy*, etc. (cf. 888).

Similar formations, but without an actually existing intermediate stage, occur in words like *handkerchief* > *hanky*, *nightgown* > *nighty*, *pinafore* > *pinny*, *underwear* > *undies*. Most of them are nursery words. Cf. also *comfortable* > *comfy*, the only adjective of this type.

959. Sometimes a new word is deliberately coined by blending the sounds and combining the meanings of two others: *mingy* = mean and stingy (COD); *slithy* = lithe and slimy;[2] *squarson* '(facet.) Squire and parson in one' (COD). Such words are mostly humorous, and rarely become very common.

Of a somewhat different type are formations like *Americanadian*, *Eurasian*, *Bakerloo* (= Baker Street and Waterloo Underground Railway). The interpenetration of the two elements is less complete, and they are made for practical convenience, not for humorous effect.

Compare also such recent formations as *smog* (*sm*oke and f*og*), and the trade name *spam* (COD: *sp*iced h*am*).

960. In conclusion, attention may be called to words composed of the initials of other words, such as SHAEF [ʃeif] (*S*upreme *H*eadquarters *A*llied *E*xpeditionary *F*orce), UNRRA [ˈʌnrɑː] *U*nited *N*ations *R*elief and *R*ehabilitation *A*dministration), *Waaf* [wæf][3] ([Member of the] *W*omen's *A*uxiliary *A*ir *F*orce), etc., etc. Many of them arose during or after the last war; others, such as *cif* (*c*ost, *i*nsurance, *f*reight) and *fob* (*f*ree *o*n *b*oard), have long been in

[1] Continental students are apt to forget that in words like *examination*, *pronunciation*, etc., it is the *second*, not the first syllable that has medium stress.

[2] See COD s.v. *portmanteau-word*.

[3] Now W.R.A.F. [ræf] (Women's Royal Air Force).

technical use. They can only be pronounced as words if the sequence of initials does not run counter to the principles of syllable construction in English; in other cases (B.B.C., D.D.T., etc.) the initials are given their alphabetic values. The latter also happens with abbreviations like P.O.W., Y.M.C.A., and others, even though it would be possible to syllabize them.

APPENDIX

IRREGULAR VERBS

R denotes that the regular form also occurs
* An asterisk indicates an archaic or poetical form

STEM	PAST TENSE	PAST PART.
Abide	abode	abode
Arise	arose	arisen
Awake	awoke, R	R, awoke(n)
Be	was	been [bi(:)n]
Bear [bɛə]	bore	borne[1]
Beat	beat	beaten[2]
Become	became	become
Befall	befell	befallen
Begin	began	begun
Behold	beheld	beheld
Bend	bent	bent[3]
Bereave	bereft, R	bereft, R[4]
Beseech	besought	besought
Bet	bet, R	bet, R
*Bid (=command)	*bade [bæd, beid], *bid	*bidden[5]
Bid (at auction)	bid	bid
Bind	bound	bound
Bite	bit	bitten[6]
Bleed	bled	bled

[1] *to be born*: to come into the world by birth (COD).
[2] *beat* in *dead-beat,* colloquial for 'exhausted by fatigue'; and cf. 113.
[3] R in *bended knees.*
[4] *Bereaved* is mostly used in reference to the loss of relatives.
[5] But *do as you are bid.*
[6] occasionally *bit,* e.g. *the biter bit.*

STEM	PAST TENSE	PAST PART.
Blend	R, *blent	R, *blent
Blow	blew	blown[1]
Break [breik]	broke	broken
Breed	bred	bred
Bring	brought	brought
Build	built	built
Burn	burnt, R*	burnt, R*
Burst	burst	burst
Buy	bought	bought[2]
Cast	cast	cast
Catch	caught	caught
Chide	chid, R	chid(den), R
Choose	chose	chosen
Cleave	cleft, clove	cleft, cloven[3]
*Cleave	*clave, R	*cleaved
Cling	clung	clung
Come	came	come
Cost	cost	cost
Creep	crept	crept
Crow	R, *crew[4]	crowed
Cut	cut	cut
Dare	R, durst	dared
Deal	dealt [delt]	dealt
Dig	dug	dug
Do	did	done
Draw	drew	drawn
Dream	dreamt [dremt], R	dreamt, R[5]
Drink	drank	drunk
Drive	drove	driven
Dwell	dwelt	dwelt

[1] Note sl. *I'll be blowed* = cursed, hanged.

[2] Note attributive *boughten* (Am.), 'purchased at a shop' (COD): *his first boughten haircut*.

[3] He had cleft the trunk; in a cleft stick; the cloven hoof.

[4] The cock *crew*, in reference to the gospel narrative (St. Matthew, 26: 74); otherwise usually *crowed* (cf. 721 *c*).

[5] The form *dreamed* [dri:md] is preferred in poetry and elevated style.

STEM	PAST TENSE	PAST PART.
Eat	ate [et, eit]	eaten
Fall	fell	fallen
Feed	fed	fed
Feel	felt	felt
Fight	fought	fought
Find	found	found
{*Flee Fly	fled	fled
Fling	flung	flung
Fly (with wings)	flew	flown
Forbid	forbade [fəˈbæd, fəˈbeid]	forbidden
Forget	forgot	forgotten
Forgive	forgave	forgiven
Forsake	forsook	forsaken
Freeze	froze	frozen
Get	got	got[1]
Gild	gilded	R, gilt[2]
Gird	R, girt	R, girt
Give	gave	given
Go	went	gone
Grind	ground	ground
Grow	grew	grown
Hang	hung, R[3]	hung, R[3]
Have	had	had
Hear [hiə]	heard [hə:d]	heard [hə:d]
Heave	R, hove	R, hove
Hew	hewed	R, hewn
Hide	hid	hid(den)
Hit	hit	hit
Hold	held	held
Hurt	hurt	hurt

[1] Often *gotten* in American English.
[2] The form *gilt* is chiefly used as an adjective.
[3] *Hanged* means 'killed by hanging'; even in this sense, however, *hung* is common (cf. Jespersen, MEG VI, 5.17).

STEM	PAST TENSE	PAST PART.
Keep	kept	kept
Kneel	knelt, R	knelt, R
Knit	R, knit[1]	R, knit[1]
Know	knew	known
*Lade	*laded	laden
Lay	laid[2]	laid[2]
Lead	led	led
Lean	R, leant	R, leant
Leap	leapt, R	leapt, R
Learn	learnt, R	learnt, R
Leave	left	left
Lend	lent	lent
Let	let	let
Lie[3]	lay	lain
Light	lit, R	lit, R[4]
Lose [lu:z]	lost	lost
Make	made	made
Mean	meant	meant
Meet	met	met
Mow	mowed	mown, R[5]
Overcome	overcame	overcome
Pay	paid[2]	paid[2]
Put	put	put
Quit	R, quit[6]	R, quit[6]
Read [ri:d]	read [red]	read [red]
Reeve (naut.)	rove, R	rove, R
Rend	rent	rent
Rid	R, rid	rid[7]
Ride	rode	ridden
Ring	rang	rung

[1] The short form is now usual in the sense of 'making with knitting-needles'.
[2] Irregular in spelling only!
[3] *To lie* in the meaning of 'to speak falsely' is regular.
[4] As an attributive adjective *lighted* is used.
[5] As an attributive adjective only *mown*: *mown grass*.
[6] The irregular forms are chiefly American.
[7] Chiefly used in the expressions *to be* (or *get*) *rid of*.

STEM	PAST TENSE	PAST PART.
Rise	rose	risen
*Rive	*rived	*riven, R
Run	ran	run
Saw	sawed	sawn, R
Say[1]	said [sed]	said [sed]
See	saw	seen
Seek	sought	sought
Seethe	R, *sod	R, *sodden
Sell	sold	sold
Send	sent	sent
Set	set	set
Sew [sou]	sewed [soud]	sewn [soun], R
Shake	shook	shaken
Shave	shaved	R, shaven[2]
Shear [ʃiə]	R, *shore	shorn, R
Shed	shed	shed
Shine	shone [ʃɔn]	shone[3]
Shoe [ʃu:]	shod	shod
Shoot	shot	shot[4]
Show[5]	showed	shown, R
Shred	R, *shred	R, *shred
Shrink	shrank	shrunk
*Shrive	*shrove, R[6]	*shriven, R[6]
Shut	shut	shut
Sing	sang, *sung	sung
Sink	sank, *sunk	sunk
Sit	sat	sat
*Slay	*slew	*slain
Sleep	slept	slept
Slide	slid	slid

[1] Third person sg. present indicative [sez].
[2] *Shaven* is used as an adjective; *clean-shaven* occurs by the side of *clean-shaved*.
[3] But: *I've shined your boots*.
[4] *Shotten fish*: f. that has spawned.
[5] Sometimes written *shew* [ʃou].
[6] The regular forms are Am.

STEM	PAST TENSE	PAST PART.
Sling	slung	slung
Slink	slunk	slunk
Slit	slit	slit
Smell	smelt, R	smelt, R
Smite	smote, *smit	smitten, *smit
Sow	sowed	sown, R[1]
Speak	spoke	spoken
Speed	sped[2]	sped[2]
Spell	spelt, spelled [spelt]	spelt, spelled [spelt]
Spend	spent	spent
Spill	spilt, R	spilt, R
Spin	spun, span	spun
Spit	spat, *spit	spat, *spit
Split	split	split
Spoil	spoilt, R	spoilt, R
Spread [spred]	spread [spred]	spread [spred]
Spring	sprang	sprung
Stand	stood	stood
Steal	stole	stolen
Stick	stuck	stuck
Sting	stung	stung
Stink	stank, stunk	stunk
Strew	strewed	strewn, R
Stride	strode	stridden, strid
Strike	struck	struck
String	strung	strung
Strive	strove	striven
Swear	swore	sworn
Sweat [swet]	R, sweat[3]	R, sweat[3]
Sweep	swept	swept
Swell	swelled	swollen, R
Swim	swam	swum

[1] The p.p. *sown* is four times as frequent, in the OED 19th–20th-century quotations, as *sowed* (MEU).
[2] On regular forms see COD.
[3] The irregular forms are Am.

STEM	PAST TENSE	PAST PART.
Swing	swung	swung
Take	took	taken
Teach	taught	taught
Tear [tɛə]	tore	torn
Tell	told	told
Think	thought	thought
Thrive	throve, R[1]	thriven, R[1]
Throw	threw	thrown
Thrust	thrust	thrust
Tread [tred]	trod	trodden
Understood	understood	understood
Wake	woke, R	R, woken, woke
Wear [wɛə]	wore	worn
Weave	wove	woven, wove[2]
Weep	wept	wept
Wet	R, wet[3]	R, wet[3]
Win	won	won
Wind [waind][4]	wound [waund]	wound [waund]
Withdraw	withdrew	withdrawn
Withhold	withheld	withheld
Withstand	withstood	withstood
Work	*wrought	*wrought[5]
Wring	wrung	wrung
Write	wrote	written

[1] The regular forms are chiefly Am.

[2] *Wove* is chiefly used in commercial terms as *wove paper*. When used of aircraft ('dodge, take evasive action'), ships, etc., the p.t. and p.p. are regular.

[3] The irregular forms are Am.

[4] *To wind* (i.e. to sound) *a horn* is regular, although *wound* also occurs.

[5] Still current in *wrought iron* (i.e. forged iron). Apart from this, *to work* is usually regular.

The following verbs show similarity of formation within each group:

a. Bleed —bled —bled
Breed —bred —bred
Feed —fed —fed
Meet —met —met
Speed —sped —sped

b. Creep —crept —crept
Deal —dealt —dealt
Feel —felt —felt
Keep —kept —kept
Kneel —knelt —knelt
Mean —meant —meant
Sleep —slept —slept
Sweep —swept —swept
Weep —wept —wept

c. Bend —bent —bent
Lend —lent —lent
Rend —rent —rent
Send —sent —sent
Spend —spent —spent

d. Sell —sold —sold
Tell —told —told

e. Beseech —besought —besought
Bring —brought —brought
Buy —bought —bought
Fight —fought —fought
Seek —sought —sought
Think —thought —thought
Catch —caught —caught
Teach —taught —taught

f. Burst —burst —burst
Cast —cast —cast
Cost —cost —cost
Cut —cut —cut
Hit —hit —hit
Hurt —hurt —hurt
Knit —knit —knit
Put —put —put
Quit —quit (*Am.*) —quit (*Am.*)
Rid —rid —rid
Set —set —set
Shed —shed —shed
Shut —shut —shut
Slit —slit —slit
Split —split —split
Spread —spread —spread
Sweat —sweat (*Am.*) —sweat (*Am.*)
Thrust —thrust —thrust
Wet —wet (*Am.*) —wet (*Am.*)

g. Forsake —forsook —forsaken
Shake —shook —shaken
Take —took —taken

h. Break —broke —broken
Freeze —froze —frozen
Steal —stole —stolen
Speak —spoke —spoken
Weave —wove —woven
Bear —bore —borne
Swear —swore —sworn
Tear —tore —torn
Wear —wore —worn

i. Drive —drove —driven
Ride —rode —ridden

	Rise	—rose	—risen
	Smite	—smote	—smitten
	Stride	—strode	—stridden
	Strive	—strove	—striven
	Thrive	—throve	—thriven
	Write	—wrote	—written
j.	Blow	—blew	—blown
	Grow	—grew	—grown
	Know	—knew	—known
	Throw	—threw	—thrown
k.	Get	—got	—got(ten)
	Forget	—forgot	—forgotten
l.	Sit	—sat	—sat
	Spit	—spat	—spat
m.	Dig	—dug	—dug
	Spin	—spun	—spun
	Stick	—stuck	—stuck
	(Strike	—struck	—struck)
n.	Cling	—clung	—clung
	Fling	—flung	—flung
	Sling	—slung	—slung
	Slink	—slunk	—slunk
	Sting	—stung	—stung
	String	—strung	—strung
	Swing	—swung	—swung
	Wring	—wrung	—wrung
o.	Begin	—began	—begun
	Drink	—drank	—drunk
	Ring	—rang	—rung
	Sing	—sang	—sung
	Sink	—sank	—sunk
	Spring	—sprang	—sprung
	Swim	—swam	—swum
p.	Bind	—bound	—bound
	Find	—found	—found
	Grind	—ground	—ground
	Wind	—wound	—wound

NOTE ON PARTICIPIAL AND ALLIED FORMS. Discriminate between attributive and predicative forms in the following cases:

A *drunken* man — The man *is drunk*.
Sunken eyes — The ship has *sunk*.
Roast meat — The meat has been *roasted*.
Molten (or *melted*) lead — The lead is being *melted*.
A *lighted* candle — The candle was *lighted* (or: *lit*).
Mown grass — The grass is being *mowed* (or: *mown*).
A *shaven* head — His head has been *shaved*.
The *stricken* deer — The deer was *struck* down.

Sometimes one form of the participle is used figuratively:

He is *bereft* of all hope (not: *bereaved*). — Well-*stricken* in years;

conscience-*stricken*; poverty-*stricken*; but: thunder-*struck*. — A *swollen* river (but *swelled head* [beside *swollen head*] = conceit); *sodden* (= soaked) clothes; a *sodden* (= bloated) face.

Occasionally one participial form has come to be appropriated to certain expressions, e.g.: He is dead *beat*; He went down on his *bended* knees; It is my *bounden* duty.

To Have

To have drops its final consonant before [z] and [d]: *he has, I* (*you*, etc.) *had, I have had.* The dropping of final *e* before *ing* (*having*) is only a matter of spelling.

The weak forms [əv], [v]; [əz], [z], [s]; [d], often spelt *'ve, 's* and *'d*, are mainly used when *to have* is an auxiliary of tense: *I've told him everything*; *He's made a lot of money*; *I'd forgotten all about it.* When enclitic[1] *not* [nt] follows, however, the full forms are used: *I have not* [hævnt] *told him*;[2] *Hasn't* [hæznt] *he come?*

The full forms are also used in verbal questions (601): *Has he told you?*, and when *to have* is not an auxiliary of tense: *He has a lot of money*; *I had to pay the money back.*[3]

To Be

What is called 'the verb *to be*' is a combination of different verbal forms with fundamentally identical meanings. The stem *be* functions as infinitive, imperative and (present) subjunctive; to it are added the suffixes *ing* (*being*) for the gerund and present participle, and *n* (*been* [bi:n] or [bin]) for the past participle. The forms *am, is, are* serve resp. for the first person singular, the third person singular, and the other persons of the present tense; the form *was* for the first and third persons singular of the past tense; the form

---

[1] '(Word) so unemphatic as to be pronounced as part of preceding word' (COD).
[2] But *I've* not [aiv nɔt] *told him*, when contradicting a preceding statement.
[3] Cf. Kruisinga, *Grammar and Idiom*, § 81.

were ([wə:], [wɛə], [wə]) for the other persons of the past tense (cf. *are*), and for the past subjunctive.

The present tense has weak forms [m]; [z], [s]; [ə], when enclitic: *I'm* [aim]; *he's* [hi:z], *it's* [its]; *we're* [wiə], *you're* [juə],[1] *they're* [ðeə].[2] When enclitic *not* follows, the full forms are used, except for the first person singular: *you aren't*[3] (*aren't you?*) [ɑ:nt], *it isn't* (*isn't it?*) [iznt]; but always *I'm not* [aim nɔt], interrogative *Am I not?* [æm ai nɔt], instead of which familiar English uses *Aren't I?* [ɑ:nt ai].

As with *to have*, the full forms are used in verbal questions: *Are you satisfied?*

The enclitic forms are more widely used than those of *to have*; the reason is that *to be* rarely has a clear meaning of its own. Cf. *God's in his heaven*;[4] *You're to go at once.*

The same rules apply to the stressed and the unstressed forms of *was* and *were*: *It wasn't* [wɔznt] *easy*; *It was* not [wəz nɔt] *a success.*

Note: *What's* [wɔts] *that?*, but *What is* [wɔt iz] *it?*

Verbal Forms with *thou*

With *thou* for a subject (355), [ist] (*est*) is added to the verb stem in the present tense: *thou playest*, *callest*, *waitest*, *passest.*[5]

The verbs of 6 have the following forms: *thou canst*, *mayst*, *must*, *shalt*, *wilt*. Those of 7: *thou darest* [dɛəst], *needest* [ˈni:dist]. Those of 8: *thou art* [ɑ:t], *dost* [dʌst] (but *doest* [ˈdu:ist] as a verb of full meaning, 194), *hast* [hæst].

Regular verbs usually add [idst] (*edst*) to the stem in the past tense: *thou playedst*, *calledst*, *waitedst*, *passedst*. Irregular verbs add

---

[1] For alternative pronunciations, see Jones.

[2] Note the change of vowel. — The enclitic pronunciation is not necessarily reflected in the spelling: *I am* may very well stand for [aim], just as *he has* may stand for [hi(:)əz] or [hi:z].

[3] Cf. *You're* not [juə nɔt], when contradicting a preceding statement (cf. p. 335, n. 2).

[4] There is a whole series of such forms in a song in Browning's *Pippa Passes*, Part I.

[5] The corresponding forms of *to say* are *thou sayest* [ˈseiist] or *sayst* [seist].

[ist] (*est*) or [st] (*st*) to the form for the past tense: *thou brought(e)st* ([ˈbrɔ:tist] or [brɔ:tst]), *saw(e)st* ([ˈsɔ:ist] or [sɔ:st]).[1] The shorter forms are sometimes spelt with an apostrophe: *brought'st*, *saw'st*.

The verbs of 6–8 have the following forms: *thou could(e)st* ([ˈkudist] or [kudst]), *might(e)st* ([ˈmaitist] or [maitst]), etc.; *thou daredst* ([ˈdɛəridst] or [dɛədst]), *neededst* [ˈni:didst]; *thou wert* [wə:t] or *wast* [wɔst], *didst*, *hadst*.

Third Person Singular in (*e*)*th*

A suffix [iθ] (*eth*) occurs in the 3rd p. sing. of the present tense in the same style as the forms used with *thou*: *he playeth* [ˈpleiiθ], *calleth*, *waiteth*, *passeth*.[2] No such forms exist of the verbs of 6, nor of *to be*. *To dare* and *to need* regularly have *he dareth* [ˈdɛəriθ], *needeth*. *To do* has *he doth* [dʌθ] as an auxiliary, but *he doeth* [ˈdu:iθ] as a verb of full meaning; *to have* forms *he hath* [hæθ].

There are no special forms for the past tense.

Spelling of Inflected and Derived Forms

Final e

As observed in the introductory sections of the chapters on Verbs and Nouns, the inflexional suffixes [iz] and [id] are written *s*, *'s*, and *d* after words ending in *-e*: *change* — *changes*; *George* — *George's*; *fade* — *faded*.

The rule may also be stated thus, that words in silent *e* drop it before endings beginning with a vowel-symbol. In this form it also applies not only to such instances as *fine* — *finer* — *finest* (which might be covered by an addition to the formula of the first paragraph), but also to *change* — *changing*, *adore* — *adorable* (but *changeable*, to indicate that the symbol *g* stands for [dʒ]; similarly *singeing* [ˈsindʒiŋ], *swingeing* [ˈswindʒiŋ], to distinguish them from *singing*, *swinging*); *blue* — *bluish*.

---

[1] The corresponding forms of *to say* are *thou saidest* [ˈsedist] or *saidst* [sedst]. — [2] The corresponding form of *to say* is *he saith* [seθ].

Silent *e* is also dropped in *due* — *duly*, *true* — *truly*, *whole* — *wholly* ([ˈhoulli] or [ˈhouli]); not in *sole* — *solely* [ˈsoulli].

It should further be observed that *canoe* [kəˈnu:], *dye*, *eye*, *hoe* [hou], *shoe* [ʃu:] and *rue* retain their *e* before *ing*: *canoeing*, *dyeing* (cf. *die* — *dying*), etc.; and that words in *-ee* never take a third *e*: *free* — *freer* [ˈfri:ə] — *freest* [ˈfri:ist]; *seer* [si:ə] (= prophet); *agree* — *agreed* [əˈgri:d].

Final o

Inflexional [z] is spelt *es* in many familiar words in *-o* preceded by a consonant: *he does* [dʌz], *he goes* [gouz]; *buffaloes*, *cargoes*, *heroes*, *negroes*, *potatoes*.

In other, especially less familiar, words the normal spelling *s* is used: *cantos*, *photos*, *pianos*, *solos*, *violoncellos*.

In some words both spellings are found; when in doubt, consult COD.

Words in *-oo* take either spelling: *coo(e)s*, *woo(e)s*.

Final y

Words in a consonant-symbol + *y* change *y* into *ie* before *s* (not before *'s*) and *(e)d*: *cry* — *cries* — *cried*; also *soliloquy* — *soliloquies*.

Before other endings *y* after a consonant symbol is either changed into *i*, or retained. It is changed before the endings of the comparative and superlative (*dry* — *drier* — *driest*); before the adverbial ending *-ly* in adjectives of more than one syllable (*merry* — *merrily*); before the ending of ordinals in *-eth* (*twenty* — *twentieth*); in agent-nouns in *-er* (*carry* — *carrier*); and in derivatives in *-ness* from adjectives of more than one syllable (*holy* — *holiness*).

-y after a consonant symbol is retained in derivatives in *-ness* from monosyllabic adjectives (*shy* — *shyness*); in derivatives in *-ist*, *-like*, *-ship*, *-ward(s)* (*copyist*, *lady-like*, *ladyship*, *citywards*); sometimes in those in *-fied* (*countrified* or *countryfied*).

In adverbs from monosyllabic words in *-y* both *y* and *i* are found in *dryly* (*drily*) and *slyly* (*slily*); the others occur only with *y* (e.g. *coyly*, *shyly*), but *daily* is always and *gaily* is usually spelt with *i*.[1]

On the other hand, *-ie* changes into *-y* before *-ing*: *die* — *dying*, *lie* — *lying*.

Final consonant

A final consonant-symbol is doubled before an unstressed ending beginning with a vowel-symbol if the consonant-symbol is immediately preceded by a single vowel-symbol representing:[2]

a. a stressed vowel-sound: *admit* — *admitted* — *admitting*;[3] *control* — *controller*; *drug* — *druggist*; *hot* — *hotter* — *hottest*; *stop* — *stoppage*; etc. Exceptions: *bus* — *buses*; *gas* — *gases*; *violin* — *violinist*.

b. a vowel with marked medium stress: *humbug* — *humbugged*; *kidnap* — *kidnapped* — *kidnapping*; etc.

In some words the final consonant-symbol is doubled in an unstressed syllable; thus in *worship* — *worshipped* — *worshipping*. Occasionally both spellings occur: *bias(s)ed*, *focus(s)ed*; Am. E. usually spells *kidnaped*, *worshiped*. Words in *-ic* spell *-ck* before an ending beginning with a vowel to indicate that the symbol *c* stands for [k]: *frolic* — *frolicked* — *frolicking*; *panic* — *panicky*. Contrary to the rule, E. spells *woollen* (Am. *woolen*).

Final l

Words in single unstressed vowel-symbol + *l* double the *l* in British, but not in American English before an ending beginning with a vowel: *travel* — *traveller* — *travelled* — *travelling* (U.S.: *traveler*, etc.); *cruel* — *crueller* — *cruellest*; *marvel* — *marvellous* (U.S.: *marvelous*). (Cf. *kidnaped*, *worshiped*, in the preceding section.)

---

[1] This is the rule as formulated by W. A. van Dongen Sr. in *English Studies* I (1919), p. 77. — Cf. also *gaiety* [ˈgeiəti].

[2] Kruisinga, *English Sounds*[4], § 581.

[3] Cf. *prefer* — *preferred* [priˈfə:d], and *offer* — *offered* [ˈɔfəd]; *r* is equally silent, whether it is written single or double. In the same way, it is in both cases pronounced [r] before *-ing*: *preferring* [priˈfə:riŋ], *offering* [ˈɔfəriŋ].

Full and *fill* are apt to lose one *l* in compounds and derivatives: *brim-full* or *brimful* (cf. 834), *mindful, handful*; *to fulfil, fulfilment* (U.S. often *to fulfill, fulfillment*). Note *ˈalmost, ˈalso, alˈthough, ˈalways*, etc., though these are hardly felt to be connected with *all*; also *altoˈgether*, in which the semantic connection with *all* is often quite clear. Double *l* in *all right*; *alright* is disapproved of (cf. Fowler, MEU).

Note *till*, but *until*; *to install*, but *instalment* (a very different word!).

Pluralia Tantum (241)

For a full account of this subject, which is only partly a matter of grammar, the student is referred to Kruisinga, *Grammar and Idiom*, §§ 1 ff. Only one or two points can here be touched upon.

Nouns *never* used without a plural suffix are not very numerous, for most of the *pluralia tantum* in Kruisinga's lists may also occur without *-s*,[1] if usually in another sense: *compasses* 'instrument for describing circles', but *compass* 'instrument showing magnetic meridian' (for other meanings see COD); *colours* 'flag', but *colour* 'hue'; *dominoes* (game), but *domino* 'loose cloak with half mask' (COD); *metaphysics*, but also, in the same sense, *metaphysic* (cf. p. 262, n. 1).

On the agreement (or disagreement) in number between such plural nouns and their adjuncts or predicates (if any), see 241–243, and the chapter on Concord. It may here be added that most names of things consisting of two equal parts (cf. 267) are construed as plurals; but cf. *bellows* and *gallows*[2] (242, 243).

---

[1] This is often, but not always, indicated in Kr.'s lists, which should be checked by COD and the student's own observation.

[2] That a *gallows* consists of two equal parts is clear from the definition of COD; cf. *gibbet*.

Classical and other Foreign Plurals (245)

On the plurals of classical and other foreign nouns the student should consult his dictionary. The following may be added to those mentioned in 245: *magus* [ˈmeigəs] — *magi* [ˈmeidʒai] (*the three Magi*, the 'wise men' from the East); *radius* — *radii* [ˈreidiai]; *genus* [ˈdʒi:nəs] — *genera* [ˈdʒenərə]; *minutiae* [maiˈnju:ʃii:] ('precise or trivial details'; the singular *minutia* is hardly ever used); *nebula* [ˈnebjulə] — *nebulae* [ˈnebjuli:]; *axis* [ˈæksis] — *axes* [ˈæksi:z]; *basis*[1] [ˈbeisis] — *bases* [ˈbeisi:z]; *hypothesis* [haiˈpɔθisis] — *hypotheses* [haiˈpɔθisi:z]; *oasis* [ouˈeisis] — *oases* [ouˈeisi:z]; *criterion* [kraiˈtiəriən] — *criteria* [kraiˈtiəriə].

The following, like *cactus* etc., have an English as well as a classical plural: *focus* — *foci* [ˈfousai]/*focuses*; *fungus* [ˈfʌngəs] — *fungi* [ˈfʌndʒai]/*funguses*; *genius* — *genii* [ˈdʒi:niai]/*geniuses* (this form always in the sense of 'man of genius'); *terminus* — *termini* [ˈtə:minai]/*terminuses*; *formula* — *formulae* [ˈfɔ:mjuli:]/*formulas*; *lacuna* — *lacunae* [ləˈkju:ni:]/*lacunas*; *appendix* — *appendices* [əˈpendisi:z]/*appendixes*.

The following are the chief foreign plurals of non-classical origin: *beau* — *beaux* [bouz] ('fop; lady's man, lover'); *bandit* — *banditti* [bænˈditi(:)]/*bandits*; *dilettante* [diliˈtænti] — *dilettanti* (same pron.)/*dilettantes*; *virtuoso* — *virtuosi* [və:tjuˈouzi:]/*virtuosos*; *cherub* [ˈtʃerəb] — *cherubim*/*cherubs* (the latter form, naturally, in the sense of 'beautiful or innocent child'); *seraph* [ˈserəf] — *seraphim*/*seraphs*.

Names of native races and other words of little-known languages usually remain unchanged:[2] *a good number of Swahili*; *these Esquimo* (but also *Eskimo[es]*, *Esquimau[x]*, see COD).

Traditional Genitives (273)

Poutsma (*Grammar*, II, Ch. XXIV, § 16 *d*) gives a list, with illustrative quotations, of names of things used in the genitive in certain

[1] The synonym *base* (cf. COD) has a regular plural *bases* [ˈbeisiz].
[2] Kruisinga, *Handbook*[5], § 783.

combinations. The following may be noted in addition to those mentioned in 273: *at* ˈ*death's* ˈ*door* (= soon to die, COD); *a* ˈ*hair's breadth* (also ˈ*hairbreadth* = very narrow) *escape*; *out of* ˈ*harm's* ˈ*way* (= in safety); *to one's* ˈ*heart's con*ˈ*tent* (= as much as one wants); *their* ˈ*journey's* ˈ*end* (cf. *Journey's End*, well-known war play and novel); *in my* ˈ*mind's* ˈ*eye* (= mental view); *at one's* ˈ*wit's* (or ˈ*wits'*) *end* (= utterly at a loss). We have a genitive plural in *to have a subject at one's* ˈ*fingers' ends* (or *at one's finger-ends*) (= to know it familiarly).

Another type of traditional genitive is found in the combination *for . . . sake*. At least[1] we have a genitive proper only in the case of personal names in a sibilant: *for George's sake*, *for Phyllis's sake*; but not in *for Jesus' sake* [fə ˈdʒi:zə ˈseik]. Other personal names take *'s*, though no ending is audible owing to the *s* of *sake*: *for God's sake*, *for the children's sake*. Names of things, like *art*, *heaven*, *name*, *opinion*, etc., are treated like the preceding group: *art for art's sake*, *for heaven's sake*, *for his name's sake*, *for goodness' sake*, *for peace' sake*. — As Poutsma observes, outside more or less traditional combinations, an *of*-adjunct is used instead: He married her *for the sake of her money*.

Weak Forms of Pronouns

Of the Personal Pronouns (354 ff.), *I* [ai] and *it* [it] are the only ones with only one phonetic form for stressed as well as unstressed positions.

He, *she*, *we* and *me* have [i:] in stressed, [i] in unstressed position; *he*, *him*, and *her* frequently drop their [h] in unstressed position; *her* [hə:] and *you* [ju:] may shorten their vowels to [ə] and [u] when unstressed; *them* [ðem], when unstressed, is usually pronounced [ðəm].

Before a vowel, *they* [ðei], if unstressed, may lose its diphthongal character; in *they're* (= *they are*), the first element of the half

[1] = *or rather*; a sense not recorded in most dictionaries, though it is already found in Dickens.

diphthong [ei] combines with the weak form of *are*, i.e. [ə], into a murmur-diphthong: [ðeə]. Similarly, *we're* [wiə], *you're* [juə]. On the weak form of *us*, see p. 129, n. 2.

As regards the Possessive Pronouns, what was said of the personal *h-* forms applies to the possessive *h-* forms (*his*, *her*) as well. *Your* is [jɔː], [jɔə], [joə] or [juə], with occasional weak forms [jo] or [jə]; *their* [ðɛə] is occasionally [ðər] when a vowel follows; *our* [auə], like *its* [its], only has the one form, while some people use weak-stressed [mi] for *my*, by the side of normal (strong or weak) [mai].

The Independent Possessives have full forms only.

The Compound Personal Pronouns may weaken their first elements in the same way as the simple Personal and Possessive Pronouns.

The Demonstrative Pronouns have full forms only.

Relative *that* is usually [ðət]; acc. to Jones (*Pronouncing Dictionary*) the strong form [ðæt] is hardly ever used, except when mentioning the word in isolation.

On the forms of Interrogative and Relative *who*, see 454.

Of the Indefinite Pronouns, *some* [sʌm] has the weak forms [səm] and [sm].

It should be observed that in most of these cases the weak forms are those normally used, the fully stressed forms being exceptional in normal speech. Cf. Kruisinga, *Handbook*[5], § 997.

Objects and Prepositional Adjuncts

Kruisinga's *Grammar and Idiom*, §§ 415 ff., contains a list of verbs that are regularly used with two non-prepositional objects, or with a direct object and an indirect object with *to*. A fuller treatment of this point will be found in Poutsma's *Grammar*[2], I, Ch. III, §§ 44 ff.; and this again has been supplemented by G. Kirchner in a series of articles in *English Studies* XVIII (1936) and XIX (1937) with an abundance of modern (also American) material not available to Poutsma.

Grammar and Idiom, § 418, gives a list of verbs that can only take an object and an adjunct with *to*, not two objects. Here are some that can take two objects in Dutch and German:

He announced his engagement to us.
She administered the medicine to the patient.
He communicated the news to his wife.
Can I confide the secret to you?
The name conveyed nothing to me.
He described the situation to us.
He entrusted the document to his brother.
The teacher explained the difficulty to his pupils.
May I introduce my friend to you?
The doctor prescribed a long rest to (for) him.
I propose to you to drop the matter.
I shall prove to him that he is wrong.
You can say to him exactly what you think.
(But: Tell me everything.)
I swear to you that it is true.

Mood — Modal — Modality

The student who has read the statement in 214 ff. of the uses of the subjunctive in present-day English, American as well as British, may test the validity of the following definitions. (*Non-fact* is not used in the sense of 'contrary to fact' but in that of 'what is not a fact'.)

Mood is a verbal category represented in English by the opposition (*he*) *play* — (*he*) *plays*, of which the former (subjunctive) denotes non-fact, the latter (indicative) either fact or non-fact.

The difference between the subjunctive and the indicative denoting non-fact is one of style.

Modal (from *mode* = *mood*), as commonly used, refers to grammatical expedients, such as the preterite of modality, to express non-fact, or at least a modification of fact.

Modality, as a substantive, expresses the same notion as the adjective *modal*.

American English

The following peculiarities of American, as distinct from British English have been touched upon:

Syntax:

The use of the plain infinitive after *to help* (17), and after *to listen to* and *to look at* (18.2).
For + acc. with inf. (59).
Begin + *to* + infinitive (69).
The accusative with past participle after *to order* (112.2).
Indirect object without *to* in passive sentences (122, 596).
Will in all persons of the future tense (185.1).
Use of *to do* with *to have* not denoting habitual action (201.1).
The subjunctive after verbs of will and wish (p. 87, n. 1, 221).
Nights, *summers* (252).
All of = *all* (488. 2).
As poor as I am (p. 219, n. 1).
I gave it to him (695).
A half hour, etc. (711.2).
Says I, a vulgarism (735).
Out, prep. (p. 284, n. 1).

Morphology:

Bar-keep (804), *barber shop* (805), *sailboat*, *spark plug* (812).
Woodsy, *sudsy* (944).
Gotten (p. 328); *shrived* (p. 330), *thrived* (p. 332); *quit*, past t. (p. 329), *sweat*, past t. (p. 331), *wet*, past t. (p. 332).

Orthography:

Can not (p. 65, n. 2); *kidnaped*, *worshiped*, *traveler* (p. 339); *fulfillment* (p. 340); diaeresis (846).

Semantics:

Alumni (p. 96, n. 1).

It is probably unnecessary to say that, even apart from semantic peculiarities, the list is not exhaustive.

INDEX

(REFERENCES ARE TO SECTIONS
EXCEPT WHEN PRECEDED BY p.)